Seventy

Years Of

Buick

By George H. Dammann

Revised Edition

Crestline Publishing

Box 48, Glen Ellyn, Illinois 60137

CRESTLINE AUTO BOOKS:

    ILLUSTRATED HISTORY OF FORD
       (1,400 Illustrations)

    60 YEARS OF CHEVROLET
       (1,650 Illustrations)

    70 YEARS OF BUICK
       (1,800 Illustrations)

    AMERICAN FUNERAL CARS & AMBULANCES
                SINCE 1900
       (1,900 Illustrations)

    70 YEARS OF CHRYSLER
       (2,000 Illustrations)

    THE DODGE STORY
       (1,600 Illustrations)

70 YEARS OF BUICK

Copyright © By George H. Dammann, 1973

Library of Congress Catalog Card Number 72-94176

ISBN Number 0-912612-04-5

Typesetting by George Munson, Naperville, Ill.

Cover Design by Bob Williams, Arlington Heights, Ill.

Published by Crestline Publishing Company
           Box 48 Glen Ellyn
           Illinois U.S.A. 60137

Printed in U.S.A. by Wallace Press, Hillside, Ill.
Binding by The Engdahl Co., Elmhurst, Ill.

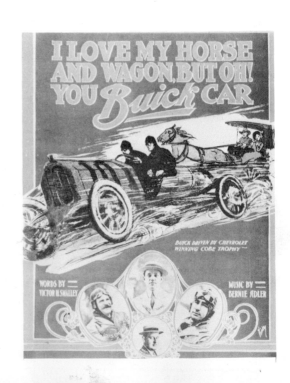

Many Thanks

Obviously a book of this magnitude could not have been compiled or revised without the help of many people. Special thanks are in order to the following persons who contributed freely of their time and knowledge, who opened their own collections of photographs and automobile lore, and who in general assisted tremendously in an effort to make this book the finest and most complete history ever published on the Buick car. They are . .

J. M. Sharp III of Baltimore, Md.

David Chambers of West LaFayette, Ind.

Nicola Bulgari of New York City and Rome, Italy

Roger Van Boldt, Director of the Sloan Museum of Transportation

Merele Perry of Sloan Museum of Transportation, Flint, Mich.

David G. Gosler, formerly of Buick's Public Relations staff.

Samuel Y. Yalda of Flint, Mich., Supervisor of Buick Photographics.

Larry Gustin of Flint, Mich., author of *Billy Durant*.

James J. Bradley, Head of the Automotive History Dept., Detroit Public Library.

James A. Wren of Detroit.

Thomas McPherson of Kitchener, Ontario, author of *The Dodge Story* and *American Funeral Cars & Ambulances Since 1900.*

Terry B. Dunham of Fresno, Cal., Historian of the Buick Club of America.

Eddie Ford of Newstead, Victoria, Australia, Editor of *The Custom Rodder* and *Restored Cars.*

Also deserving of thanks in many varying degrees are James Petrik of Madeira, Ohio; Bart H. Venderveen of Reigate, Surry, England; G. N. Georgano of London, England; James Moloney of Santa Barbara, Cal.; Robert Polli of Rochester, N. Y.; James E. Olsen of Minneapolis, Minn.; Mike Lamm of Stockton, Cal.; David W. Brownell of Iola, Wis.; Editor of *Old Cars,* and Mary Jacobs and Ralph Davis of Buick Photographics, Flint, Mich.

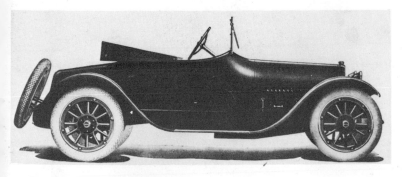

Photo Credits

The major portion of photographs and illustrations used in this book were photographed either on the scene or were taken from original photos by George H. Dammann, Automotive Director of Crestline Publishing. The original photos were derived from the private collection of Crestline Publishing Co. and were obtained from the following sources:

The Photographic Department of Buick Motor Division, Flint, Mich.

The Public Relations Department of Buick Motor Divsion, Flint, Mich.

The Archives of the Sloan Museum of Transportation, Flint, Mich.

The Automotive History Collection of the Detroit Public Library.

The Public Relations Department of Motor Vehicle Manufacturers Assn.

The private collection of Thomas McPherson of Kitchener, Ontario.

The private collection of James Petrik of Madeira, Ohio.

The private collection of Eddie Ford of Newstead, Victoria, Australia.

The private collection of Bart H. Vanderveen of Reigate, Surrey, England.

The private collection of G.N. Georgano of London, England.

The private collection of *Old Cars, Car Classics,* and *Special Interest Autos*

Also, from collections of those who prefer to remain anonymous - - the latter being located in New York, Ontario, Wisconsin, Michigan, Indiana, Ohio, Pennsylvania, Florida, Iowa, Missouri, Minnesota, California, and Nevada. To all of these persons who so willingly opened their collections to Crestline's cameras and research - - Many Thanks.

FOREWORD

From the very first days of its inception when names like David Dunbar Buick, W.C. Durant, and Louis Chevrolet were talked about freely by those familiar with an infant but growing automobile industry; through intervening years filled with interesting and fascinating events to the present day, the proud past of a great automobile manufacturer remains to command the attention and respect of the automobile enthusiast and historian around the world.

In 1900 Detroit inventor David Buick found fascination with the internal combustion gasoline engine and began experimenting with them. Selling his plumbing fixture business for just under $100,000 he formed the Buick Auto Vim and Power Company to develop marine and stationary engines. It soon became apparent that Buick was more of an inventor than a businessman and his profits from the plumbing business were quickly eroded away.

David Dunbar Buick

William Crapo Durant

Locating additional finances Buick formed a new organization, The Buick Manufacturing Company, and continued his experiments. Again he ran out of money. This time Buick approached the Briscoe brothers, Benjamin and Frank, owners of a successful Detroit sheet metal fabricating business, and from whom he had borrowed earlier. He persuaded them to invest again but in order to protect themselves the Briscoes saw to it that another company was formed, The Buick Motor Car Company, and placed themselves in charge. The Briscoes had a total of $99,700 invested with Buick and they wanted to protect it.

Finally, after realizing no profits and watching additional money disappear through more experimenting, the Briscoes decided to sell out in 1903.

At this point in time several of Flint, Michigan's more progressive carriage makers realized that the days of the horse drawn vehicle were numbered and had begun to cast envious eyes at the budding auto makers as well as experimenting on their own "horseless carriages." James H. Whiting, owner of the Flint Wagon Works, was one of these. The Briscoes approached him and eventually closed the deal. In order to bind the sale, $10,000 was loaned by a Flint bank but not until Whiting could persuade a number of prominent local citizens to personally guarantee the note. This was merely the start of a long and rewarding association between Flint's people and the automobile manufacturer which has continued through to this day.

And so it was that the Buick car left Detroit and came to Flint. However, Buick's personal lack of business ability again reared its ugly head, capital again disappeared at an alarming rate, and Whiting was finally forced to approach Billy Durant, then living in New York, about coming with the firm. In 1904 Durant agreed, invested personal monies, and took absolute control. Durant's organizational ability proved to be exactly what the company needed and it prospered from that point forward. Durant later, using Buick as a base, formed the General Motors Corporation.

It is unfortunate to note that discrepancies exist concerning the exact number of cars built in 1903 when Buick first moved from Detroit to Flint. Figures from zero to sixteen have been put forth. In 1923, Buick's 20th anniversary year, newspaper advertisements were placed stating that sixteen cars had been built in 1903. In 1945, Harlow Curtice, writing in a confidential report to the directors of General Motors, mentioned that "sixteen cars were built in the year 1903". With this new information it appears that the question may be put to rest. A car engine is known to exist today which was made by The Buick Motor Car Company in Detroit in 1902.

Of growing interest to many students of Buick history is the period from 1931 to 1953, "the Straight Eight Era". During this time Buick greats such as Harlow Curtice, William F. Hufstader, Charley Chayne, and a host of others rose to fame within Buick and General Motors. It was also during this period that Buick nameplates like Special, Super, Century, Roadmaster, and Limited made their appearance. The excellence of design and engineering were so outstanding that collectors today are finding these Buicks from the mid 1930s and early 1940s in great demand. Buick actually had the audacity, under Curtice, to challenge Cadillac for the luxury and prestige market during the 1940, 1941, and 1942 model years, much to the consternation of Cadillac and others within the Corporation. Recently some of these automobiles were declared as "classic" by one of the clubs involved with this distinction, an honor that we hope will be expanded in the future.

Buick's great retail success in the 1920s, '30s and '40s was typified and climaxed in the most exciting and critical spot in the world, the movie industry of Hollywood. Representing Buick here was the Hollywood branch of The Howard Automobile Company, Under the sales management and guidance of Phil Hall, one of the

greatest Buick salesmen ever born, Buick became the byword of star and studio alike, THE car to own. Hall counted among his personal friends and customers some of the greatest stars to come out of Hollywood and was responsible for the delivery of virtual fleets of Buicks to two studios, Warner Brothers and Paramount.

Though always a heavy road car, the Buicks of the 1936-1941 gender were capable of amazing acceleration, a fact known to many stock class drag racers of several years back. Buick's racing record stretched back to the early days of Durant and remains a proud and important part of the company heritage.

The "Straight Eight Era" was also responsible for such advances as the 1938 self-shifting transmission, the 1940 Estate Wagon (Buick's first production station wagon) and Adolph Braun's compound carburetion of 1941 and 1942. This was later developed by the same engineer into the first production four-barrel carburetor. The custom-built Brunn bodies of 1940 and 1941, the Super Sonomatic short-wave radio of 1941, the Dynaflow transmission of 1948, and the first hardtop styling of 1949 were also Buick products from this same period.

The material George Dammann has gathered together in this Buick reference book has been assembled at no little cost and personal time. We sincerely hope that after finishing it you will agree as we do with what has become one of the greatest advertising slogans of all time: "When better automobiles are built, Buick will build them". Right On!!

Terry B. Dunham
1439 W. Paul
Fresno, California 93705
Historian
The Buick Club of America

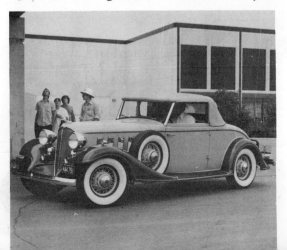

As could be expected, the Buick story began long before the 1903 incorporation date of the Buick company. In a sense the story began in 1854, with the birth of David Dunbar Buick, whose name today graces millions of fine automobiles.

A lifelong inventor and dabbler in mechanics, Buick had become interested in the relatively new indoor plumbing industry in the late 1870s. Sometime during the 1880s, he formed a partnership in Detroit known as Buick & Sherwood, and the firm manufactured plumbing and bathroom fixtures, many of which were Buick's own design. In the 1890s he patented a method of applying porcelain to cast iron bathtubs and sinks. Thus, Buick can be considered the inventor of what today is the modern and world-accepted bathtub.

By 1900, the now 46-year-old Buick had tired of the lucrative but limited plumbing business, and had become fascinated with the gasoline engine. It might be noted here that Buick was an inventor of far above average talent, but as a businessman he was a complete flop.

In 1901, he sold his interests in the flourishing plumbing company and founded the Buick Auto-Vim & Power Company of Detroit, for the production of a 2-cylinder L-head engine primarily for marine use. The company enjoyed some success, but Buick by this time had lost interest in marine engines and become fascinated with the automobile.

Probably Buick saw a much broader field for his inventing and tinkering in the new concept of the horseless carriage than he did in the marine engine business. Certainly he was more concerned with his ability to continue his experiments than he was with his ability to keep his company on a financially sound basis.

During this period, Buick became friends with Walter Marr, an inventor, engineer, and bicycle racer of some note. Marr had been operating his own successful bicycle factory in Detroit since 1896, and had also been dabbling in gasoline engines and had porduced several experimental models. It is believed that Marr worked for Buick Auto-Vim for a very short while, possibly as a consultant, but the relationship didn't last, and after a short stint at Oldsmobile, Marr moved on to Illinois where he designed and built the Marr Autocar.

However, Marr and Buick remained on fairly cordial terms, and in 1901, after Buick completed his first car, he offered to sell it to Marr for $300, to be used as a proto-type for the Marr company. Whether or not the sale was ever completed is not known, nor is there any record of whatever happened to this car. The photo exists of what is believed to be this first experimental Buick, but even here there is a certain degree of doubt concerning the vehicle.

By 1902, the Buick Auto-Vim Company was failing badly, primarily due to erratic production and non-delivery of orders. Buick found new financing and founded Buick Manufacturing Company of Detroit, which then absorbed the bankrupt Auto-Vim firm. The Buick Manufacturing Company immediately began to manufacture a totally new engine called the Buick Valve-In-Head. Dispute arises over who actually designed this engine, with Buick, Marr and Eugene Richard all being given credit by various historians. Richard was an engineer who had been with Olds Motor Works before its disastrous fire, and he joined Buick Auto-Vim in 1901.

By the end of 1902, Buick Manufacturing was in financial trouble, again primarily because of erratic delivery of orders. Now a pair of successful Detroit

Much confusion concerns this car. It is fairly well agreed by most experts that the car can be called an early Buick, via the fact that it was either built by David Buick or Walter Marr, or by both. It is assumed the vehicle was assembled somewhere between 1902 and 1903 in the shops of Buick Mfg. Co. of Detroit. It may very well be the vehicle that was delivered to the Briscoe brothers, though there is no record to substantiate this assumption.

Believed to be David D. Buick's first auto engine, this early photo shows an opposed cylinder block of L-head design. The engines were produced on a rather erratic schedule by Buick's first auto company, the Buick Auto-Vim & Power Co., which operated from 1901 until its takeover in 1902 by the Buick Mfg. Co. of Detroit. All of the early Buick engines were designed primarily for marine use.

1903

sheetmetal manufacturers came onto the scene. These were the Briscoe brothers, who later would build a car under their own name. But at this point, they were content to refinance Buick Manufacturing with the promise that the first car out of the shop would be delivered to them. The car was completed and delivered in early 1903, but by this time the company was again bankrupt.

Buick's third company, the Buick Motor Co. of Detroit, was formed in 1903, once again to manufacture engines only. Its most popular product was this one-cylinder water-cooled model. It had a bore and stroke of 5 x 6 inches, and developed 6.6 horsepower at 580 RPM. It was advertised as being practical for marine, automotive, or stationary use. Again, production was erratic, even though orders were substantial.

Again the Briscoes came to the rescue, but this time they demanded full financial control. Buick agreed, and on May 19, 1903, the Buick Motor Company was incorporated as a Detroit company. But within a short time the Briscoes lost patience with Buick, and again the firm was about to go under. Jonathan D. Maxwell, who in 1904 would help form the Maxwell-Briscoe Company (the basic start of today's Chrysler Corporation) made a passing move at Buick, but then pulled back. Another person, by the name of James H. Whiting, was impressed. Whiting was manager of the Flint Wagon Works of Flint, Michigan, one of the largest wagon makers in a city that had already earned a reputation and nickname of "Vehicle City." Whiting saw the auto manufacturing business as a somewhat logical companion to the wagon manufacturing business, though at this point he saw more of a future in manufacturing automotive components for other auto builders than in building the complete cars himself.

Whiting agreed to buy the Buick Company from the Briscoes, and on September 11, the Flint *Journal* printed an announcement that the Buick Company was moving to Flint and that ground had been broken for factory expansion. The company was again reorganized as the Buick Motor Company of Flint. It was the initial intention that the company at first manufacture only stationary, marine, and automotive engines, transmissions and engine components.

Shortly after the move, Marr rejoined the company. His own auto company had been somewhat of a success, but a

Meanwhile, Walter Marr had left Buick and started his own auto company, with headquarters in Detroit, but production and warehouse facilities in Elgin, Ill. His one and only model was this Touring Runabout, priced at $800. Known as the Marr Auto-Car, the little vehicle incorporated many of the ideas found in the Model B Buick. Orders on the car were coming in at a fairly rapid pace, but a disastrous fire at Elgin burned up the complete stock of cars and parts and manufacturing facilities. Unable to rebuild, Marr closed his business and returned to Buick as chief engineer.

Following the move of the Buick company to Flint, Buick began to experiment with building complete automoblies. This model is believed to be one of the several experimental models which reportedly were built during 1903. Despite claims that up to 16 cars were built by Buick in 1903, there are no records to substantiate that any were built in that year. However, rumors persist of experimental vehicles, such as the one seen here, having been produced and then mysteriously disappearing.

disastrous fire had wiped out his entire stock of cars and parts. To rebuild at this point would have been financially impossible for Marr, and so he returned to his former friend and associate to work as chief engineer.

At this point, vast confusion exists over the exact number of Buick cars actually produced between September, 1903, and January 1, 1904. The Buick company today claims that sixteen vehicles were produced and all were experimental models. Yet there are no records whatever to substantiate this claim. It is known that Whiting was primarily interested in building engines, and that he encouraged Marr to devote all of his time and energy toward improving and experimenting with the valve-in-head one and two cylinder blocks that were being produced. Buick himself was engrossed in chassis and transmission experiments, and possibly some experimental chassis were built. But again, no definite record exists to substantiate this thought.

In fact, there is no record of any production of any sort at Flint until December, 1903, when it is known for sure that twenty-five workers were employed by the company and that several sizes of small engines, up to 13 horsepower, were being built. The most popular of these was a 2-cylinder model with opposed cylinders. It had a bore and strode of 4.5 x 5 inches, displaced 159 cubic inches, and developed 16.2 horsepower.

Late in 1903 it became obvious that the Buick Company was again in financial difficulty. By the start of the year the condition was chaotic, and it became necessary to reorganize again. New papers were filed on January 19, with the new company being the Buick Motor Company of Flint, capitalized at $75,000. The major stockholders were James H. Whiting and other members of his Flint Wagon Works. Officers of the new company were the same as those of the wagon works except that David Dunbar was secretary.

Virtually all of the spring was spent in building the novel valve-in-head engines. The first of these designed strictly for automotive use was completed on May 27. However, both Buick and Marr continued to plead with Whiting to consider the manufacture of complete cars, not just engines. Whiting finally agreed, and by July what can be considered the first production Buick was putting around Flint. But Whiting was still not convinced, and thus the renowned trip from Flint to Detroit and back was conceived. The trip, which followed a rather wandering route, covered 230 miles. The Flint to Detroit portion was made on July 9 while the return was made on July 12. Walter Marr and Tom Buick (David's son) made the run and shared the driving, which gained much publicity for the new company. Whiting was convinced, and production began in earnest — or, at least it began.

The first Buick sold — some feel that it used the same chassis and engine that Marr had used on the Detroit trip — was formally delivered to Dr. H.H. Hills of Flint on August 13. Actually, though, Dr. Hills had had the car at his disposal for test runs since July 27.

In addition to the 2-cylinder engine that Buick used in its own cars and produced for others, the company also made this extremely simple 1-cylinder engine for sale to other auto builders. The engine developed 7 horsepower at 600 RPM. Its cylinder and head were cast in one unit which bolted directly to the semi-open crankcase.

automotive landscape. His name was William C. Durant, already a self-made millionaire at the age of forty, owner of the Durant-Dort Carriage Works of Flint, which was one of America's largest wagon works and a man credited by his contemporaries as being a sheer genius in the business world. But Durant at this time had little use for the small, noisy contraption called an automobile.

Finally, Whiting and other Flint businessmen persuaded the energetic Durant to return home from New York and at least look at the faltering Buick company. Durant took his first ride in a Buick on September 4, and to his surprise, found the car was not nearly as bad as he had imagined. For the remainder of the month, Durant drove a test Buick around Flint, and by early October, he had convinced himself that the car held good promise.

On November 1, an agreement was reached whereby Durant-Dort Carriage Company would refinance the ailing

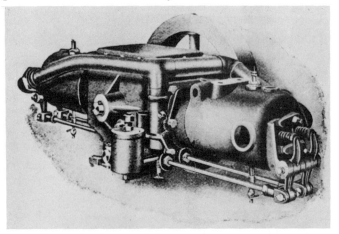

Although Buick was definitely in the car business, its main income still came from the production of automotive and marine engines and of planetary and sliding gear transmissions. This was Buick's 12 horsepower model, an opposed two-cylinder machine using the now-famous valve-in-head design perfected by Marr and Buick.

However, from a financial standpoint, things were not going well. The $75,000 capitalization that the company started with was now gone, and neither cars nor engines could be produced fast enough to keep up with orders or to show a profit. Buick was again in great financial trouble, and Whiting and his backers stood to lose a small fortune.

At this point enters one of the most interesting and controversial giants ever to stride across the American

Buick's first production car was the Model B, a 4-passenger touring car finished in indigo blue with bright yellow wheels and running gear. The car weighed 1,850 pounds and cost $950. This original photo appears to have been taken along side of the Flint Wagon Works factory, where the bodies were built. Though orders were coming in for the car, Buick managed to produce only 37 vehicles this year.

THE FIRST BUICKS — Shown above is the car often credited with being the first Buick. It is the vehicle used by Walter Marr, shown behind the wheel, and Thomas Buick (David's son) to make the historic trip from Flint to Detroit and back. The 2-day, 230-mile run was made to convince apprehensive backers that the car actually was a substantial and functional vehicle worthy of manufacture. Below is the first Buick ever sold. It was delivered to Dr. H.H. Hills of Flint on Aug. 13, 1904, though Dr. Hills actually had the car at his disposal since July 27 for practice runs. There is fairly wide belief that the engine and chassis of Dr. Hills' car were the same as were used in the Flint to Detroit trip by Marr and Buick.

The first "Race To The Clouds," up Mt. Washington in New Hampshire, was staged in 1904, and a privately owned Buick won its class. The car was driven by a Mr. Chase, who had removed all body parts and installed a simple metal driver's seat. Note the perilous perch of the riding mechanic – no wonder he looks so unhappy. As far as can be ascertained, this is the first Buick racing activity on record. It is not known if the car was one of the 37 listed as production models for the year, or if it was a special model turned out specifically for Chase's racing plans.

Although the company produced only 37 cars this year, it was still proud of its product. Here a group of early Model B's lines up on the corner of Saginaw and First Streets in downtown Flint. Note that the two cars on the far right are not yet completed. The photo is dated Nov. 7, 1904.

Buick Company via the purchase of majority stock. A condition of this transaction was that Durant would be in full charge of management, production, promotion and sales. As a sidelight, the agreement stated that Buick production was to be moved from Flint to an idle Durant-Dort factory at Jackson, Michigan.

And so the year closed. Buick had manufactured a total twenty-eight cars in Flint. Some Buick records show cars built in 1904, but the generally accepted figure is twenty-eight cars. These were all Model B styles, of which none are known to exist today. They were 2-cylinder vehicles with 4-passenger bodies built by Flint Wagon Works. It is possible that a few "experimental" racing type models were also turned out for promotional purposes, and these might account for some of the discrepancy in the production figures.

The engines used in these cars were the 159-cubic-inch models that Buick had been producing on a commercial basis. The engine used a bore and stroke of 4.5 x 5 inches and developed 16.2 horsepower at 1200 RPM. However, some reports rate the car at 21 horsepower at 1230 RPM, or 14.5 horsepower at 800 RPM. Actually, since Buick was building several sizes of Marr-designed engines, it is possible that not all of the cars used the advertised 16.2 horsepower block.

All models used right-hand drive, planetary transmissions, and 30 x 3.5 inch tires. The chassis, transmission and body were primarily of David Buick's own design, as was the suspension. This unit used ¾-elliptical springs both front and rear, a design that would be carried through the 1906 models.

With Durant at the helm, the Buick story this year was a far cry from what it had been in the previous year. By the end of 1905, a total of 750 Buicks would roll from the Jackson plant, thus making Buick the ninth largest car producer in the U.S. and far exceeding Durant's initial production of a car a day. Note: Some records claim that only 627 cars were built this year, but the generally accepted figure is 750.

Actually, to say the cars were built in Jackson is misleading. True, at the start of the year, Buick's general offices and assembly operations were moved to the old Imperial Wheel Company plant in Jackson. The Imperial Wheel was a Durant-Dort subsidiary that had been moved to Flint a few years earlier.

However, the production of engines and transmissions remained at the former Buick plant in Flint, and the bodies continued to be made by Flint Wagon Works. The moving of parts from one city to another for assembly was started at first to give Buick a larger home in a currently unused factory. But as the year wore on, it became more and more apparent that a consolidation of the units should be made. It was just too costly and inconvenient to keep shuffling parts and manpower between the two cities. Besides, many Flint residents were unhappy that the move had been made to Jackson. A group of several key men in Flint eventually undertook a project to have the company return to their city, and thus, the groundwork was started for Buick's move back to Flint.

All of the Jackson produced cars were considered the Model C, but in reality these were simply copies of the Model B. The car continued to use right-hand drive and a 2-speed planetary transmission, with the engine now fairly standardized at 159 cubic inches and developing 22 horsepower at 1200 RPM. Its two opposed cylinders still used a bore and strode of 4.5 x 5 inches. A Cape Cart Top, sold as an accessory, and a foot-operated service brake were about the only real changes of the year.

In a sense, Buick's remarkable racing program had its start this year. The program would culminate in the fantastic Buick racing team of the 1908-1910 seasons, but would then die after Durant was forced out of General Motors' control.

But this year, Bob Burman, a Buick test driver, was sent to Grosse Pointe, Michigan to enter a Buick in a local race. The idea was first taken as a lark because the little Buick was far overshadowed by the huge, big name, full-race machinery on the track. But Burman surprised everyone by winning the race. He was then sent to Grand Rapids and St. Louis, where his performance was the same.

Meanwhile, a non-factory sponsored Buick set the world's five-mile speed record for 2-cylinder cars by covering a course at Boston in 6 minutes 13 seconds; another non-factory car set one, three, and six-mile records during a series of races at Newark, N.J., and still another, driven by H.J. Koehler, won an important hill climb at Wilkes-Barre, Pa. Suddenly, Durant and his management team realized the publicity potential that could be gained if Buick cars continued to win races. Thus, the foundation for factory supported racing activities was set.

Buick's only car this year was the Model C, which really was a virtual carbon copy of the Model B. The 5-passenger car was now finished in royal blue with ivory wheels and running gear. Its price was raised to $1,200. During the later part of the year, a detachable tonneau model was available for $1,250. The car still weighed 1,850 pounds, had an 89-inch wheelbase and a 56-inch tread. Front springs were elliptic, while rear springs were semi-elliptic.

New for the year was an accessory Cape Cart Top, which provided some degree of weather protection. The top could be fitted with side curtains and celluloid windshield. This year the name "Buick" was embossed in large letters on the pressed steel running boards.

The Model C chassis was basically the same as the Model B. It used an angle iron frame, center mounted engine, chain drive, and pinion and sector steering. The service brake, activating on the transmission, was now foot operated.

Buick's 750 cars this year all used this standardized double opposed 2-cylinder engine with overhead valves. It used a bore and stroke of 4.5 x 5 inches and developed 22 horsepower at 1200 RPM.

Shown at the Jackson plant is a Buick in the process of assembly. Both engine and body had been made in Flint and shipped to Jackson for final assembly. Here the partially completed all-wood body and the engine have been fitted to the chassis, but all front end components and trim items have yet to be installed.

It had been a long time – in 1955, Buick management located Dr. Hills, the first person to purchase a Buick, and gave him a chance to once again try his hand at his first car. However, since no Model B's are known to survive, Dr. Hills had to settle for a ride in this well restored Model C.

Much to the chagrin of Buick's many Flint backers, the company's first catalog prominently listed the company as being located at Jackson. However, though assembly was done at Jackson, engines, transmissions, bodies, and many other components were still made at Flint.

This was Buick's last official year in Jackson, but for Buick it was a banner time. Production from January until the plant's shut-down in November totalled 1,400 cars, thus moving Buick up to eighth place in U.S. ranking. Actually, the Jackson plant was not closed down entirely, and some assembly work was still being done there as late as 1912. It is known for sure that 200 cars were built at Jackson in July, 1908, and it is believed that most of the Buick trucks were assembled at the Jackson factory, and not at Flint. This would indicate that the Jackson plant did not stop assembly at least until the truck line was dropped in 1912.

Of the 1906 production, approximately 1,200 units were the new 2-cylinder Model F Touring Cars, while an additional 200 were the new 2-cylinder Model G Roadsters. The 4-cylinder Model D's were introduced in May, but for practical purposes, this book considers them all 1907 models, as that is what the factory termed them.

The Model F, with serial numbers running from 1 to 1207, was basically unchanged from the 1905 Model B. It used the same 159-cubic-inch engine, but with a slightly improved crankcase. It was still equipped with chain drive and a 2-speed planetary transmission, and had a large side lever for neutral and high-speed engagement.

One of the most noticeable changes on this year's cars was the doing away with the old radiator, and the installation of a full-length radiator running from the top of the hood to the front axle line. The new radiator allowed all water to be carried in a recirculating cooling system, and thus did away with the large water storage tanks so often found on cars of this era. The 16-gallon gas tank continued to live under the hood, and the engine continued to be under the front seat. The wheelbase remained 87 inches. A Cape Cart top was available for the Model F for an extra $100. Acetylene headlights and oil side and taillights were now included in the price, and for the first time in a high production car, Buick included a storage battery and vibrator horn as standard equipment.

Buick's famous facing endeavors went into high gear this year. Walter Marr took a Model F to Eagle Rock, New Jersey, scene of a then-famous hill climb, and cut the previous record almost in half. He then went to Mt. Washington and bettered Chase's 1904 victory on that high climb. Meanwhile, H.J. Koehler won a 100-mile race at Yonkers, New York, with an average speed of 47.8 MPH.

Not only was Buick's racing program gaining publicity for the company, it was also serving as a test ground for the engineering department. Under Durant's direction, any factory sponsored racing car was to be driven until the wheels literally fell off. Then the car was to be shipped back to Flint so that the engineers could disassemble the entire machine, see where wear and tear had occurred, and try to find ways to build a more improved version of the worn parts.

New for the year was the Model G Runabout or Roadster, of which 193 were built. The 1,800 pound car cost $1,150. It used the same running gear as the Model C. Later in the year, its price was dropped to $1,000. No, the car does not have two steering wheels — the double exposure was made to show how the steering wheel could be moved forward for easy entrance to the driver's seat.

Replacing the Model C was the new Model F, with its completely changed front end and radiator. The car sold for $1,250 and weighed 1,850 pounds. Production totaled 1,207. Both the Model G and Model F were painted in purple lake, with ivory wheels and running gear.

With the exception of the gas tank and radiator, the chassis of the Model F and Model G cars resembled that of the Model C. The double-opposed engine still had a bore and stroke of 4.5 x 5 inches and was rated at 22 horsepower. Buick was especially proud of its extra quiet muffler and its hot-riveted steel frame.

1906

As could be expected, no sooner was the Model F put on the market, than the accessory manufacturers got busy with ideas of their own. This model is shown sporting such accessories as a Cape Cart Top, two-piece plate glass windshield, a front bumper and oversized kerosene lamps. The car is shown in 1930 with its owner, B.L. Meeden of Yuma, Ariz.

The snowmobiling sport may be big now, but it's not new. As early as 1906, a man by the name of Virgil D. White produced this prototype "Motor Sleigh" using a Model G Buick as its base. The vehicle was probably scheduled for limited production, but nothing more ever appears regarding this company. Note that the standard rear wheels have been moved forward and mounted on a dead axle, while heavy-spoke wheels have been fitted to the standard rear axle. The front runners apparently mounted with a single bolt.

Buick's Jackson plant covered 17.5 acres, and supposedly was equipped with the latest machinery. However, since engines, transmissions, and bodies were still built in Flint, it seems unlikely that the entire plant was used to assemble Buick trucks.

1907

During the early part of the year, most of Buick's production activity returned to Flint, and that city would, from this point on, be Buick's only home. Almost as a way of celebrating the move, production was stoked to a fevered pitch, and new innovations were pouring from the engineering and design studios at a flash-flood rate. Buick produced a total of 4,641 cars, which ranked the company as the second largest car producer in the country, topped only by Ford.

The Model F and Model G remained, but were given a new wheelbase of 89 inches. The 2-cylinder engine continued unchanged with its 4.5 x 5 inch bore and stroke and its 22 horsepower. The two-speed planetary transmission, with its side lever for engaging high gear, also remained unchanged, but both the engine and transmission were now hidden by a bellypan which made its appearance on the late 1906 models. The fuel tank remained under the hood, but its capacity was reduced to 15 gallons.

Brand new for the model year was Buick's first 4-cylinder engine. This had a T-head design, bore and stroke of 4.25 x 4.5 inches, displaced 255 cubic inches, and was rated at 28.9 horsepower. Serial numbers ran 101 to 523.

Along with the new engine were four new models in which to use the plant. They were the Model D Touring and the Model S Roadster, both of which would be continued for two years, and the Model K Roadster and the Model H Touring, both of which would appear for one year only. The Models D and S used a brand new 3-speed sliding gear transmission, while the Models H and K used the 2-speed planetary transmissions. All had right-hand drive.

Tires on all 4-cylinder models were 32 x 4 inches while the 2-cylinder models continued to use 30 x 3.5 inch tires.

During this period, David D. Buick was shuffled from one post to another, each high paying, each with less and less responsibility. Apparently his puttering and procrastinating ways had no place in a high-powered organization such as Durant ran, and though Durant management had no desire to put the car's founder out on the street, they also could not stand to have his bumbling interfere with their fast-paced schedules.

New for the year was Buick's 4-cylinder line, of which the Model D was the most popular, with 543 being built. The 2,250 pound car sold for $2,000 (some price lists show it at $1,850). It was finished in a royal blue body with ivory wheels and running gear. The car had a 102.5-inch wheelbase, used a progressive sliding gear transmission of 3 forward speeds and reverse, and had a multiple disc steel plate clutch running in an oil bath. The upper and lower crankcases, clutch and transmission housings were of cast aluminum.

A sporty looking car was the Model S Roadster, using the new 4-cylinder engine. The car was priced from $2,000 to $2,500 (depending on which price list is used) but did not attract any widespread customer enthusiasm. Only 69 were built. The 2,000 pound vehicle had a 106.5-inch wheelbase. Drive was by bevel gear and torque tube, while the transmission was the same 3-speed progressive sliding gear unit as used on the Model D. It was finished in French gray with green striping.

Produced this year only was the 5-passenger Model H Touring. At $1,750 it was a good bargain, yet only 36 were built. The model shown here is equipped with accessory top and windshield. The car weighed 2,250 pounds, and was finished in royal blue with ivory running gear.

Companion to the Model S Roadster was the Model K Roadster, of which only 13 were built. The car was identical to the Model S except that it used a 2-speed planetary transmission instead of the sliding gear type. At $2,500, it was Buick's most expensive and least popular car. It, too, was finished in French gray with green pin stripes.

Buick's most popular car continued to be the Model F, virtually unchanged from 1906. The 1,850 pound vehicle sold for $1,250. Production reached an amazing 3,465. Its wheelbase remained 89 inches, while its tread was 59 inches. Ignition was by jump spark, with current supplied by a storage battery and a set of dry cells in reserve.

Companion car to the 2-cylinder Model F was the Model G, a 2-passenger turtle back roadster. The car enjoyed nowhere near the the popularity of the Model F, and only 535 were built. It cost $1,150 and weighed 1,800 pounds. Both the Model G and Model F were finished in purple bodies with ivory wheels and running gear. The turtle deck could be used for storage of tools and small packages. A top was $70 extra.

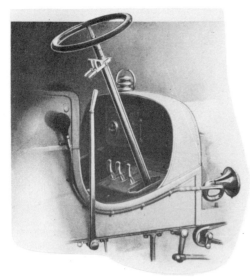

Simplicity of control was one of the main features of the Model F and Model G 2-cylinder cars. Shown here is the Model F cockpit with its three foot pedals controlling low speed forward, reverse, and brakes, from left to right. The lever operated the high speed gear, while the spark and throttle were located on the steering column.

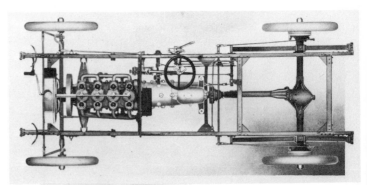

The Model D chassis looks fragile by today's standards, but was about as strong as any comparable make of car of that time. Note the short distance between the end of the transmission and the differential. Buick pioneered the torque tube drive this year, and kept the concept until the 1961 models. All frame rails were of pressed steel.

The concept of hot-rodding is often thought of as having been spawned by the car-hungry years following World War II. Probably the concept received its greatest impetus during that era, but almost from the time the first cars left the factory, there were those who were ready to strip them down, hop them up, and turn them into far faster and sportier vehicles than they had been originally. Here two middle-aged gentlemen have turned their Model H Tourer into a sporty looking speedster, via the removal of body and fenders, and the installation of a rakish speedster seat, gas tank and spare tire carrier.

Buick's new 4-cylinder engine and sliding gear transmission was a beautifully designed piece of machinery, featuring all of the current innovations in automotive engineering. Inlet and exhaust ports were on opposite sides of the cylinder in T-head fashion. Crankshafts were provided with bearings between each cylinder plus extra-length main bearings at each end. Shown here is the easy access to the multiple disc clutch and the transmission.

Despite an economic recession in the latter part of 1907, production continued at its fevered pitch and a total of 8,820 Buicks were produced. Buick now called itself the largest auto producer in the world, having the world's largest auto factory, and producing more cars this year than any other manufacturer. This claim may or may not be true, depending on which production list is used for Ford's annual total. One commonly accepted list shows Ford's 1908 model-year production as being 6,181 cars, and if this list is used, then Buick must rank first in the world. However, another widely accepted list places Ford's 1908 model-year production at 10,202, and if this list is used, then Buick ranked second place. But either way, the production is impressive.

Buick now had four different engines in use, ranging from the basically unchanged 22 horsepower 2-cylinder model used in the Models F and G to the brand new 336-cubic-inch 4-cylinder T-head block used in the new Model 5. This engine developed 34 or 40 horsepower, depending on which figures are used, and ran a bore and stroke of 4-5/8 x 5 inches.

Between these two blocks was a newly designed 4-cylinder engine of 165 cubic inches that developed 22.5 horsepower. It used a square bore and stroke of 3.75 inches and it powered the highly popular Model 10 introduced this year. Also in use was the year-old 225-cubic-inch T-head block of 28.9 horsepower that continued to be used in the unchanged Models D and S.

Though the mechanics of the Models F and G changed very little, the cars had a completely new appearance, due in large part to the wheelbase being extended to 92 inches, and the additions of totally new radiators, hoods, fenders, and cowls that gave the cars completely new lines.

The big news on the scene was the brand new Model 10, which is the car often credited with putting Buick in business for good. The car enjoyed fantastic acceptance by the public, partly because of its ease of control and later because of its racing successes across the country. The ease of control came through its smooth running little 4-cylinder engine, coupled to a 2-speed planetary transmission with Buick's traditional high-speed lever on the side. The car used an 88-inch wheelbase and 30 x 3 inch tires, but its design was such that it looked cute and even dignified despite its short length. Finished only in Buick Gray, it was available only as a three-passenger touring with a detachable tonneau. Its $900 price included acetylene headlights, oil side and taillights, and bulb horn, but a top was $50 extra.

The Model K Roadster, with its very weak planetary transmission, was dropped, as was the Model H Touring. The Model K was not replaced, but a new luxury touring car, the Model 5, filled the spot left by the Model K. This car used a 108-inch wheelbase, 43 x 4 tires, and cost $2,500. It used a 3-speed selective transmission and leather-faced cone clutch. The Models D and S also

The Model 5 engine, seen here on the exhaust side, was Buick's most powerful engine to date. Based on the T-head design, it ran a bore and stroke of 4-5/8 x 5, displaced 336 cubic inches and developed 40 horsepower in stock form. Note that the cylinders were cast in pairs. The crankcase was aluminum.

The car that made Buick — that is how the new Model 10 is often described. And, in a sense, the description is true, as the fantastically successful little 4-cylinder car enjoyed a production run of 4,002 in its first year, with bigger things to follow. Priced at $900, and running on an 88-inch wheelbase, the little white cars provided everything that the market needed — price within reach of the lower middle income person, performance sufficient to tackle most situations of the day, looks on par with anything else in their class, and reliability equal to the best. Here Dave Gosler, a Buick public relations man, prepares to drive a beautifully restored Model 10 from Buick's executive parking garage. Yes, the radiator leaks.

Cute as a bug and twice as quick — that was one of the descriptions used regarding the Model 10. The car was finished in Buick gray, which was an off-white; and the cars were often referred to as the little white Buicks. Here Dave Gosler, Buick public relations man, takes Gloria and Eric Dammann, the author's wife and son, for a tour of the Buick plant at Flint. Plenty of brass meant plenty of weekend polishing on this car.

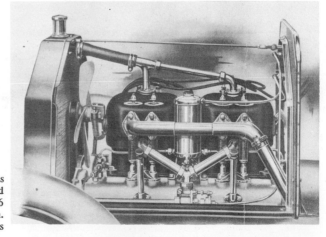

1908

The staff of the Gillespie & VanWagoner Real Estate Office of Flint pose with the firm's first company car. It is the new Model F Touring. The redesigned car now sported a new louvered hood and rounded cowl, even though the engine was still located under the front seat. The 1,850 pound car was still priced at $1,250. Production slipped slightly, and only 3,281 were built. The cars were now finished in a wine body with red wheels and running gear. Top and windshield were still accessories. The car still used chain drive, a planetary 2-speed transmission, and pinion and sector steering. The gas headlights, horn, and tool kit cost $90 extra, but the three kerosene lamps were standard equipment.

Buick's lowest production car this year was the 2-cylinder Model G Roadster, of which only 219 were built. The 1,800 pound car was still priced at $1,150. As did the Model F, it used a Schebler carburetor, Herz timer, storage battery, Splitdorf coil, and Rajah or Champion spark plugs. The service brakes were external contracting on the differential, while the parking brake was internal expanding on the rear drums. It, too, was painted in wine and red. Spark and throttle controls were now located on the steering wheels.

Appearing for the last time this year was the Model D Touring, of which 543 were built. The car sold for $1,750 and weighed 2,250 pounds. Buyers had their choice of solid red or blue body with ivory wheels and gear. The car continued to use its 255-cubic-inch T-head engine with Schebler carburetor. The kerosene lamps were standard but the gas lamps were an accessory, as were a top and windshield.

continued to use a 3-speed selective transmission, but with a multiple-disc clutch.

The Model S went through a body transformation, and dropped $750 in price. It was still available with a turtleback or with a single rumble seat, or, for $50 extra, could be ordered in four-passenger tourabout style. The Model D changed very little, but its price dropped $100 and lights were now standard equipment.

During the year, Durant became ever more fascinated with the vast publicity potential in auto racing, and so he personally set up Buick's renowned racing team. Among its top drivers were Bob Burman, Louis and Arthur Chevrolet, and Lewis Strang. Between 1908 and the close of 1910, this Buick racing team would win more than 500 trophies across the country.

But the biggest occurrence, in retrospect, occurred during the late spring of the year. Durant met with Ford, Briscoe, Olds and the Morgan banking interests to discuss a merger or the formation of a holding company for the primary auto manufacturers of the time. But no agreement could be reached, and after several months of thought and work, Durant decided to make the move alone. His plan was to use Buick as the cornerstone for a new automotive combine to be called General Motors. On September 16, General Motors was incorporated in New Jersey, and on December 28, it was announced that both Buick and Oldsmobile had agreed to a merger under the General Motors heading.

All of this was far too much for David Dunbar Buick. The tempo of the Buick home office under Durant, the decision to stop selling Buick engines to other car makers, and the inability of his ideas to gain the acceptance of other Buick engineers finally wore on him to the point of breakdown. Durant had personally given David Buick $100,000 to invest as he chose, and Buick still had a large block of Buick Company stock (still not paid for) which he kept; so at this point, David Dunbar Buick was far from a poor man. Yet, through an unwise and failure-prone series of investments, Buick was destined to go from riches to rags, and finally finish his life in very obscure poverty.

Buick's most expensive and largest car of the year was the Model 5 Touring, which appeared this year only. The 3,700 pound vehicle ran on a 108-inch wheelbase. It cost $2,500. There were 402 made, but continuity of styling was not maintained throughout the run, as various illustrations show the car with straight and upturned rear fenders and several diffenent treatments of the tonneau doors. Buyers had a choice of colors, either all red or blue with ivory wheels and gear. The engine was 336 cubic inches.

Buick's life story bears a striking parallel to that of Louis Chevrolet, who also gave his name to a great car — and one that became great only under Durant's leadership. Both men made millionaires of many other men, their names still ride on millions of fine cars and trucks worldwide, and yet they themselves slowly slipped from the highest pinnacles of success into the depths of poverty, and as men, were forgotten by the world even though their names have become household words.

But the difference is that Chevrolet was a temperamental and hot-headed genius who continued to have one run-in after another with Durant, whereas Buick was a quiet and methodical experimenter who wanted nothing more than to be left alone in a workshop where he could design and test new innovations.

After leaving Durant, Buick moved to the West Coast where he invested the major portion of his fortune in a newly organized oil company. It began to fail, and the Buick management had to strongly insist that David Buick and the Buick Company were not associated in any way whatsoever.

He returned to Michigan, and with his son Thomas, attempted to form a small carburetor manufacturing company. The company again had the backing of the Briscoe money, but as in earlier associations with the Briscoes, Buick couldn't get production off the ground. He then went to the highly unlikely hill-country village of Walden, New York, where he tried to organize a car company. No luck. Back to Michigan, and in 1922 he took over control of the failing Lorraine Motors Corporation of Grand Rapids. For the company and for the rather attractive Lorraine car, Buick's arrival was the death knell. Eying the Florida real estate boom of the era, he moved down there in the mid-1920s with ideas of becoming a land baron. He returned to Detroit a complete pauper, and in 1927, took a job as instructor-clerk with the Detroit School of Trades. He died in 1929, at the age of 74, his death going virtually unnoticed by the world.

Meanwhile, other activities were taking place up in Canada. There, the famous McLaughlin Carriage Company had decided to enter the auto business. But just as production was to start, the chief engineer became very ill. McLaughlin rushed to Durant, and a fifteen-year agreement was signed with the conditions very favorable to McLaughlin. Under the agreement, Buick would supply engines, running gear, and many body parts, and the cars would be marketed in Canada under the name McLaughlin. The initial McLaughlins carried completely different and more elaborate bodies than did the U.S. Buicks, but as the years wore on, the designs became more and more similar to the U.S. versions, until World War II, when the name McLaughlin was dropped altogether and the cars were simply Canadian-produced carbon copies of the U.S. Buicks.

Appearing for the last time this year was the Model S, which was now available either as a turtle back roadster or with a single rumble seat as shown. A total of 373 were built. The car cost $1,750 and weighed 2,000 pounds. It was finished in French gray with green pin stripes.

Up in Canada, the McLaughlin was produced using Buick running parts exclusively, but with its own independent bodywork. This is the Model F McLaughlin, equipped with accessory spare, top, and large wood-framed windshield.

One of the notable hill climbs of this era was that at Delaware Water Gap, Pennsylvania. Here an unidentified entrant pushes his Model 10 up the dusty course. History did not record the name of the driver nor what place the Buick took.

1908

Bob Burman in action takes a fast curve during the road race at Lowell, Mass. In this type of racing, large gas tanks, tool kits, and at least two spares were required because any repairs made on the car during the race had to be completed with materials carried on the vehicle.

For the very important road races at Savannah, Ga., Bob Burman had a different mount. This was a full-race machine, based on the Model 5, but using an interesting underslung chassis and greatly lowered profile.

Bob Burman, one of Buick's great drivers, takes his racer on a warm-up run through the streets of Lowell, Mass., prior to his winning an important race in that city. The car is based on the Model D chassis.

Buick was on the race tracks this year and in full force. Among the victories were the defeat of all other American cars in an international light car road race, the winning of 11 out of 14 events in two days of racing at Montreal, and the winning of the light car championship in the Vanderbilt Cup Course. Here C.E. Easter pilots the Vandrebilt Cup racer through a dusty turn. The car was based on the Model 10 chassis and engine.

C.E. Easter and his riding mechanic check in with officials prior to one of several light car races entered by Buick this year. The car is a slightly modified Model 10.

With model year production totaling 14,606, Buick still held the title of the second largest auto manufacturer in the country.

As before, both 2-cylinder and 4-cylinder engines were used, and again, there were three different 4-cylinder blocks. Two of these were the 336-cubic-inch model, used in this year's Model 6 Roadster, which replaced the Model 5 Touring as Buick's prestige vehicle, and the 165.6-cubic-inch block used in the popular Model 10.

However, the 255-cubic-inch engine used on the now discontinued Models D and S was dropped along with those cars. In its place was a newly designed 4-cylinder engine of 318 cubic inches that used a bore and stroke of 4.5 x 5 inches and developed 32.4 horsepower. This was used in the newly introduced Model 16 Roadster and the Model 17 Touring. Serial numbers on these chassis ran from 01 to 2500, while engine numbers ran from 01 to 2517. The Model 16 Roadster had a wheelbase of 112 inches, while the Model 17 Touring used a wheelbase of 112.5 inches. All used a 3-speed selective transmission and a cone clutch, and 34 x 4 inch tires. Combined production of these two models was 2,500.

Buick's prestige car, and one of its rarest models, was the Model 6 Roadster, of which only six were produced. This car used the 336-cubic-inch engine of 34.2 horsepower that had been used in the Model 5, but it had very rakish lines due to its extended 113-inch wheelbase. It too used a 3-speed selective transmission and a leather-faced cone clutch.

Buick's most popular car this year was the sporty Model 10 of which 8,149 were built. Despite the continuation of the Model 10 designation, the car took on a much better appearance through the use of a 92-inch wheelbase, which was four inches longer than that used in 1908. The engine continued to be the 165-cubic-inch 4-cylinder block of 22.5 horsepower, hooked to a 2-speed planetary transmission. Stripped, the car sold for $900; with its single rumble seat it cost $1,000, and with a tourabout seat and box or with the surrey seat and box it cost $1,050. All prices included oil lamps, taillights, generator, gas head lights, horn, and repair unit.

Still enjoying good sales were the 2-cylinder Models F and G, now joined by a production delivery car style.

Mamma, grandma, and baby pose for their picture in this quaint photo of the popular Model 10, very possibly this family's first car. This year the Model 10 was available with single rumble, as shown, or with a tourabout seat, surrey seat, or toy tonneau body. Total production of these models reached an unheard-of 8,100. With its single rumble seat the car sold for $1,000, with the price including all of the equipment shown here.

New for the year was the Model 10 with a surrey seat or tourabout seat body. Both models sold for $1,050, with the main difference being that the surrey model had a straight back rear seat that could possibly fit three people while the tourabout model had bucket-type seats both front and rear. The top and windshield shown on this beautifully restored model were accessories.

A totally new style for the year, and one that did not appear until late in the season, was the Model 10 Toy Tonneau style. This differed greatly from the surrey and tourabout models in that the entire body was constructed as one unit, and the tonneau was not detachable. In addition, this car had full rear doors, whereas the other models had only door cut-outs. This beautifully restored version is owned by Les Dunkle of Dayton, Ohio. The top, windshield, spare tires, and tool box were all accessories.

The Model 10 Tourabout followed the same lines of the surrey, but used four individual bucket seats rather than two buckets in front and a bench seat in the tonneau. Because of the relative ease of detaching the tonneau, many Model 10's ended their life as light trucks.

The Model G with its detachable single-seat tonneau sold for $1,250 and weighed 1,850 pounds. The price included kerosene cowl and tail lights, gas headlights and gas generator, bulb horn, and tool kit. Both the Model G and Model F cars were painted in wine with red gear.

Still holding its own in popularity was the Model F Touring, with its 2-cylinder engine still living under the front seat. Production this year reached 3,856. The car retained its $1,250 price tag at the start of the year, but was dropped to $1,000 at mid-season. This price included kerosene cowl and tail lights, gas headlights and gas generator, horn and tool kit. The car weighed 1,850 pounds. It was finished in wine with red wheels and running gear and black leather upholstery.

Appearing for the last year was the Model G Runabout, available with either a turtle back, as shown here, or with a detachable rumble seat. The car was priced at $1,150, but could not attract buyers, and only 144 were produced. In turtle back form, it weighed 1,800 pounds.

The little Model 10 engine, displacing 165 cubic inches, followed Buick's style of casting its cylinders in pairs, without removable heads. The valve gears lived in their own removable cages, and thus a complete engine teardown was not necessary for valve adjustment or replacement.

Buick was a performer in just about every motorized activity right from the start. This Model 17 put in many years as a rural mail carrier and inter-city livery between Carlsbad and Staked Plains, New Mexico. Interestingly, Staked Plains does not appear on modern maps. Note the tow rope on the running board, a necessity in the desert roads of the day.

Powering the Models 16 and 17 was this newly designed 318-cubic-inch engine of T-head design. This view, from the intake side, shows the unusual looking Schebler carburetor. As before, the cylinders continued to be cast in pairs, without separate heads. Push rods and valve gear ran open as shown. The spring device behind the fan assured correct belt tension at all times. Both upper and lower halves of the crankcase were aluminum.

Total Model F and G production was 3,950. The car continued to use its 159-cubic-inch engine of 16.2 horsepower. Its wheelbase remained 92 inches, and it continued to use chain drive and a 2-speed planetary transmission.

Appearing in some late Buick catalogs was the Model 7 Touring, which was a companion car to the Model 6 Roadster. It used a 4-cylinder engine with a square 5-inch bore and stroke, and developed 34.2 horsepower. The car used a 122-inch wheelbase and was priced at $2,750. However, production records indicate that none were built as 1909 models, but that all were sold as 1910 vehicles, even though the car does not appear in 1910 catalogs. Still, a total of only eighty-five of these models were built, and the number is so insignificant that it is almost academic to argue whether they are 1909 or 1910 models. For purposes of model-year continuation, this book treats the Model 6 as a 1909 car and the Model 7 as 1910 vehicle.

Although things appeared to be going great guns at Buick, the General Motors idea was causing trouble. The concept behind the GM plan was the rapid expansion and acquisition of other companies. This was being accomplished, but at a tremendous drain on resources. And Buick would feel the pinch beginning in 1910.

On the positive side, this was the year that manufacture of the Bedford Buicks was begun in England. The chassis were U.S. models, produced in Flint and shipped to England where they were equipped with British Bedford bodywork.

Somewhere in Maine an old gent and his daughter posed proudly in their new Model 17 Touring. The car, new for the year, enjoyed a production run of 2,003. It cost $1,750 and weighed 2,790 pounds. Its specifications were the same as the Model 16, and it, too, was available either in solid red or in blue with white running gear. The car had a pressed steel frame, semi-irreversible steering, and used a T-head engine of 4.5 x 5 inch bore and stroke. Rear drive was by bevel gear and torque tube.

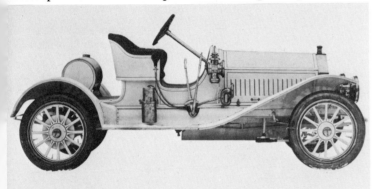

New for the year was the Model 16 Roadster. Priced at $1,750, the car had a production run of 497, divided between roadster and tourabout styles. The car weighed 2,620 pounds, had a 112-inch wheelbase, and used a 318-cubic-inch engine and selective sliding 3-speed gearbox. It was available in solid red or blue with white running gear. As did the Model 10, the Model 16 used semi-elliptic springs in front and full elliptic springs in the rear.

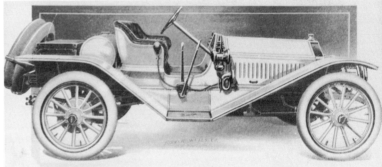

Buick's most expensive and least popular car was the very sporty Model 6 Roadster, of which only six were built. Its price of $2,750 included the trunk, twin tire rack, extra-large gas tank, and full lighting equipment. The 3,700 pound car used the 336-cubic-inch engine of 34 horsepower, and ran on a 113-inch wheelbase.

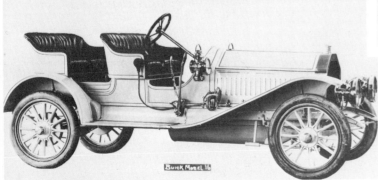

Companion car to the Model 16 Roadster was the Model 16 Tourabout, priced at $1,750. This and the roadster style were the only Buicks this year to use rounded rear fenders.

 New for the year was the Model F Delivery Car, priced at $1,150. Since production of this model was combined with that of the Model F Touring, there is no way to tell how many of these interesting little trucks were built. All specifications of this truck were identical to the Model F. The Delivery Car did not reappear, but was succeeded in 1910 by the Model 2.

Members of Buick's racing team pose with the team's three top drivers. Bob Burman is behind the wheel; Louis Chevrolet is in the mechanic's seat; and Lewis Strang perches on the frame. The car is a modified version of the Model 16, similar to the racer that Burman piloted to victory at Lowell, Mass. The Buick plant is seen in the background.

Bob Burman gets set for the start of a major event at Indianapolis. This was on the old Indianapolis Speedway, which predated today's Classic 500 race and speedway. Buick had three cars in this event. all modified Model 17's, and set American car records in both the class events and in a 10-mile speedway championship.

Louis Chevrolet prepares his Buick entry for the Indianapolis race. In these days of dirt track racing, as is still the case today, a radiator guard was a practical way of keeping flying debris out of the cores. Following this race, Chevrolet went on to win the 393-mile Cobe Trophy Stock Car Road Race at Crown Point, Indiana, and later broke three more American stock car records during a road race at Riverhead, New York.

At Lowell, Mass., Bob Burman again swept the field. His mount was this highly modified racer, which appears to be based primarily on Model 16 parts. The car uses shaft drive, and is equipped with an extra oil tank, oversize gas tank, and radiator shield.

Another Buick at Indianapolis this year was No. 47, driven by a team relief driver identified only as "Ryall." Note that all of these models used standard chassis and suspensions and torque tube drive, and carried large oil reserve tanks behind the gas tanks.

In the early years, Atlanta, Ga., was one of the racing capitals of the country. Here Louis Chevrolet and an unidentified riding mechanic prepare to wipe the field in their modified Model 16 racer. The car may be the same one shown with the entire Buick racing team. The event was the $5,000 Coca-Cola Stock Car Trophy, held on Nov. 19. Chevrolet set an American track record in the 200-mile race with an average speed of 72 MPH.

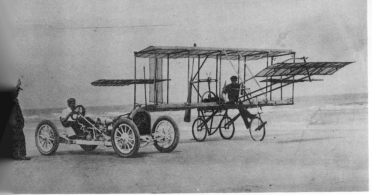

In an unusual race at Daytona Beach, Fla., Bob Burman in a highly modified Buick prepares to race Carl Bates in his bi-plane. Burman won. The event was part of a week-long speed festival held at the popular resort city.

Arthur Chevrolet, whom fate destined to stand in the shadow of his more illustrious brother, is shown here is his modified Buick getting set for a major track race at Lowell, Mass. The car is a slightly modified version of the Model 16 or 17.

Shown close up is the racer that Bob Burman used during this year's speed week at Daytona Beach. The car is an underslung version of the 1908 Model 5, stripped down to bare essentials. Since all races were of the sprint type, the small, bullet-shaped gas tank was sufficient. Note how the chassis has been strengthened forward of the transmission.

Not only did Buick race its own cars, but others bought Buicks for their own racing activities. These unidentified racers, on an unidentified track, have greatly modified a Model 16 or 17. Among the changes are an underslung frame, racing tanks and seats, and braced engine supports. The riding mechanic has a foot pedal to the brakes — either to operate the parking-emergency brakes, or possibly to operate only the left rear brake for faster cornering.

Not all of Buick's racing activities were in the hands of its factory team. Here an unidentified owner prepares to compete in the 1909 Giant's Despair Mountain hill climb at Wilkes-Barre, Pa. History records the fact that the Model 10 Buick won the Light Car Championship, but does not record the name of the owner-driver.

Another privately built Buick racer this year was this converted Model 10, known only as "The Grennor Buick." The scene is the track at Lowell, Mass. Note the unusual exhaust collector on this car, and also the amount of smoke blown by these early racers. The car was undoubtedly entered in a class for light cars. In addition to setting records all across the U.S., Buick this year also set records at two hill climbs at Munich, Germany.

Buick must have built one of its better cars in this Model 16 Tourabout. The car, owned by the E.E. Slason Buick Agency of Plainville, Kan., is shown in the late teens, being inspected by interested onlookers after it had recorded 262,000 miles on its odometer. The car is equipped with accessory hood straps, rakish windshield, and side mounted spare.

Buick production is very open to question this year. Official company statements and records show that production reached an unheard-of figure of 30,525, placing Buick in the number one spot in the world. However, Buick sales literature for 1911 and 1912 claim the company's production for 1910 was an even higher 40,100. But, when series or model production figures are added, the total is only 27,335 vehicles. So, the choice is up to the individual. But, viewed from any side, for the year 1910, Buick produced a tremendous number of cars and was definitely either the largest or the second largest producer of cars in the country, with only Ford coming close to or exceeding its total.

Much of this production confusion resulted from the confused financial conditions within General Motors. The new corporation had vastly over-extended, and since Buick was its cornerstone, the company found itself being drained of reserve capital in order to feed other hungry GM acquisitions. Production was maintained at a high pitch, but not a steady one. Massive layoffs occurred, not because the cars weren't selling, but simply because there were times when there just wasn' t enough cash flow to maintain production.

Finally, in a move to save his beloved General Motors

Buick's least popular car was the pretentious Model 41 Limousine, of which only 40 were built. The car weighed 3,400 pounds and cost $2,750. The 5-passenger rear compartment could be furnished with two disappearing folding seats or two removable chair seats in addition to the 3-passenger bench seat. The body was made of aluminum over wood. The car used thd 318-cubic-inch engine, 3-speed selective sliding gear transmission, and cone clutch.

and Buick, Durant agreed to a $15-million loan from a New York banking syndicate, the terms of which are still considered to have been outrageously costly to the company. Among the terms were that Durant would step out of control and a committee of bankers would step in to "save" the corporation. For the time being, Durant had nothing to say about how Buick, General Motors or any other company within the combine would be run.

Series production on a serial number sequence only, shows 3,950 2-cylinder cars, 10,998 Model 10's, a combined total of 8,253 for the Models 16 and 17, only 84 Model 7 Tourings, and only 39 Model 41 Limousines.

The Models F and G continued to use the 159-cubic-inch 2-cylinder engine and planetary transmissions of two forward speeds. Both models used their proven 92-inch wheelbases and conventional body styles.

Using the same 92-inch wheelbase was the Model 10 Series, which continued to be powered by the proven 165-cubic-inch engine of 22.5 horsepower, hooked to a 2-speed planetary transmission.

The Models 16, 17 and 41 used the year-old 318-cubic-inch engine of 32.4 horsepower, and a selective 3-speed transmission with a leather-faced cone clutch. The Model 16 used a 112-inch wheelbase, while the Models 17 and 41 used a 112.5-inch wheelbase chassis. All used 34 x 4 tires.

The brass-laden Model 7 used the proven 336-cubic-inch engine, 3-speed selective gearbox, cone clutch, and exclusive 122-inch wheelbase chassis, and 36 x 4 inch tires. This car sported a brass-framed windshield, and top and side curtains were available as accessories.

The Model 19 Touring used a revised edition of the former 255-cubic-inch engine of 4.25 x 4.5 bore and stroke, running 28.9 horsepower. This car had its own 105-inch wheelbase, used a 3-speed selective transmission, cone clutch, and 32 x 4 inch tires.

The Model 41 Limousine, which enjoyed only little

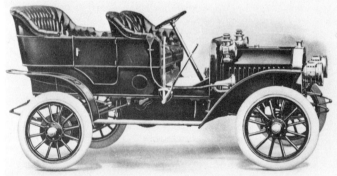

After five straight years of production, Buick began to refer to its 2-cylinder Model F as "Old Faithful," and with good reason. However, despite its continued popularity and the fact that 4,000 were built this year, the car was destined to be dropped at the end of the season. The car now weighed 2,300 pounds and sold for $1,000. It was available only in solid red.

Destined to disappear at the end of the year was the Model 17 Touring, which this year had a production run of 6,002. It cost $1,750 and weighed 2,790 pounds. The spare tire and top were still accessories. The Model 17 was basically a touring version of the Model 16, and all of its specifications were the same as that of the Model 16. It, too, was available either in solid red or with a blue body and white wheels and running gear.

1910

opularity, was Buick's first closed body style. Even the river's compartment could be somewhat protected from he weather via storm curtains, while the rear ompartment was totally enclosed. The car came complete vith speaking tube, imported goatskin upholstery and bulb orn. The car could be ordered with extra disappearing olding seats or removable chair seats.

Appearing late in the year was a highly unusual vehicle. This was the Model 14 Roadster or "Buggyabout" which Buick claimed was in response to the public's demand for a ow cost car with "Buick's known qualities." Actually, the ittle vehicle came out so late in the year that it is often lassed as a 1911 vehicle. However, records indicate that ts sales were carried through the latter part of the 1910 elling season and the early part of the 1911 season before eing dropped. Therefore, for practical purposes, this book onsiders the Model 14 to be both a 1910 and 1911 model, even though its total life span was equal to about one model year.

The little car used a highly unusual 79-inch wheelbase, 2-speed selective transmission and a disc clutch. It had its own unique 2-cylinder engine of 14.2 horsepower, displacing 127 cubic inches from a bore and stroke of 4.5 x 4 inches. This was the smallest engine that Buick had ever made or would ever make. It used 30 x 3 inch tires and carried a price tag of $550.

The Model 16 line, introduced in 1909, was greatly expanded this year, with styles including the roadster shown here, a surrey, and a toy tonneau. Combined production of the three styles totaled 2,252. The 2,620 pound car was finished either in red or in blue with white wheels and running gear. The Roadster, designed primarily for the sporty set, carried an oversize gas tank similar to that used on racing cars of the day.

Though the financial troubles were tremendous and production erratic, there was one area where Buick was an unequaled success. That was on the racetracks of America, where the famed Buick racing team of Burman, Strang and the Chevrolets were capturing almost every race worthy of note. And, on July 1, Burman drove the Buick Bug at 105 MPH, the fastest time ever recorded by an American-built, gasoline-powered vehicle.

The Model 16 is shown here sporting its surrey body. Actually, the rear seats are divided in what was normally considered tourabout style, but Buick apparently wanted to drop the "tourabout" name from its list of styles. The Model 16 used a 112-inch wheelbase. All Model 16 cars, regardless of style, were priced at $1,750, which included both kerosene and gas lights, horn, and repair kit. Upholstery was in black leather.

Not all Buicks were trouble free. This Illinois gent apparently is having timer troubles with his Model 14 Roadster. The car also went under the name of "Buggyabout." Its 127-cubic-inch 2-cylinder engine was the smallest power unit that Buick ever built.

Wearing its Toy Tonneau body is this Model 16. All Model 16 body styles were based on the roadster body, and were fairly easy to remove if the owner decided he would rather have a roadster than a 4-passenger car. The Model 16's used a selective sliding gear 3-speed transmission and cone clutch. The engine displaced 318 cubic inches. The style did not reappear in 1911, although the engine was continued.

One of Buick's strangest cars was the little Model 14 Roadster. Built strictly for the economy market, the 2-cylinder vehicle used a 79-inch wheelbase, weighed 1,425 pounds, and cost $550. Buick built 2,048 this year. Unlike previous 2-cylinder Buicks, this car had its engine under the hood. The car used an odd 2-speed selective sliding gear transmission and disc clutch, but returned to chains for its final drive.

Buick's popularity leader was still the Model 10, available in four different styles, with a choice of colors of Buick gray or blue with white wheels and running gear. A total of almost 11,000 Model 10 cars left the factory this year. a definite record for Buick, and a possible record for the industry. The most expensive of the Model 10's was this Toy Tonnueau, which cost $1,150 and weighed 1,730 pounds. The Toy Tonneau was the only model to use a flat, varnished dashboard. All other Model 10's used a rounded cowl. This example sports accessory windshield and top and wicker picnic basket on the rear fender.

Buick's heaviest and most expensive car was the Model 7 Touring, a 7-passenger car weighing 3,700 pounds and costing $2,750. Only 85 were built and the style was dropped before the season ended. It had a 122-inch wheelbase, and used a 336-cubic-inch engine running through a 3-speed selective sliding gear transmission and leather faced cone clutch.

The little Model 10 Runabout was still a cute car and drew its own fair share of orders. Priced at $1,000, it featured a detachable rumble seat under which was a fairly large storage box. Despite its popularity and high production totals, the Model 10 was destined to be dropped at the end of the 1910 season.

In addition to the surrey style, Buick also continued the Model 10 Tourabout style. This was also priced at $1,050, but drew far less orders than the more practical surrey model. It appears that this style was discontinued at mid-season. Standard equipment included kerosene cowl and taillights, gas headlights and generator, horn, and a repair kit.

A beauty of yesteryear poses in her new Model 19 Touring, which appeared this year only. The 2,500 pound car had a production run of 4,000. It cost $1,400. The car was painted in the new Buick green, with ivory wheels and running gear. It had a 105-inch wheelbase, semi-irreversible steering, and used semi-elliptic front springs and full elliptic rear springs.

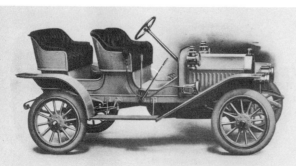

The Model 10 Surrey continued to be priced at $1,050. The Model 10 used a 92-inch wheelbase and 56-inch tread. Its 165-cubic-inch engine developed 22.5 horsepower and was hooked to a 2-speed planetary transmission with high speed activated by the side lever. Ignition was by Remy magnetic and coil and Vesta storage batteries.

Bob Burman christened his Bug the "Space Eater," but from the start the bright red cars were known as the Buick Bugs. It is believed that Burman's car is the one surviving today. On its initial run at Indianapolis, Burman's car ran an astounding lap of 105.8 MPH. In two seasons racing by Burman and Chevrolet, the Bugs are credited with winning half of all of the American road races that they entered, plus setting several American car records.

Among the most famous of the early year racers were the two Buick Bugs. Buick built one each for Louis Chevrolet and Bob Burman, and for two years had these formidable machines storming racetracks around the country. This is Chevrolet's model. Each car weighed 2,600 pounds and carried a tremendous 4-cylinder engine of 622 cubic inches. Although the cars were very similar, they were not identical. One survives today in restored condition in the Sloan Panorama of Transportation in Flint. The fate of the other is unknown.

Even today, from any angle, the Buick Bug is a formidable looking car. The cars used a standard 3-speed selective sliding gear transmission and heavy duty clutch. One weak point was the brakes, which at best were poor, and often were non-existent. Very short springs contributed to a rather harsh ride. The tubes over the cowl actually are the radiator. At the time, the Bugs were officially declared the fastest car ever made in an American shop by American workmen.

At Lowell, Mass., Bob Burman again was victorious in the annual road race in that city. Note the complete lack of spectator protection, plus the fact that spectators could crowd right up to the track edge. Also note the tremendous amount of dust and smoke produced by the car. Pity the driver following behind. During this year's three-day meet at Lowell, Buick won seven of the 10 National Stock Chassis events and also took the Vesper Trophy for cars between 301- and 450-cubic-inch engines.

At this time, the Savannah, Ga., Grand National was considered the world's greatest road race. Here Bob Burman is seen defeating all American cars in the competition with his specially built Buick-Marquette racer. Burman averaged 67.7 MPH for the 415 miles.

Not only were the big Buicks a success on the race tracks — the Model 10 could well hold its own in its class. Here, an independently owned Model 10 is seen leading the pack in a ½-mile dirt track race. The owner removed fenders, hood, and lights, but the running boards and horn were left on. A Buick 10 also won a perfect score in the 386-mile Boston-Bretton Woods 24-hour endurance contest, and also won its class in the New York Trade Assn. efficiency contest, averaging 28.2 miles to a gallon.

New for the year was the Model 2 Truck, Buick's first real venture in to the commercial car field. The truck used the same 2-cylinder double opposed engine as was used in the Model F. This was located under the driver's seat. Drive was through a 2-speed planetary transmission and chain drive to the rear wheels. The wheelbase was 92 inches. This well restored model is owned by the Sloan Panorama of Transportation. It is shown here on loan in the Buick home office lobby.

The *Saturday Evening Post* was one of the larger purchasers of Buick trucks, having a whole fleet operating in New York City. In bisac form, with pick up type body, the truck sold for $950. However, covered bodies such as this had to be specially ordered. Note the large gas-powered spotlight mounted above the radiator.

Built on the Model 2 Truck chassis was this "paddy wagon" type of vehicle owned by the New York Society for the Prevention of Cruelty to Children. Windows in the caged rear section could be raised. Driver protection was by roll-up curtains.

An early example of inter-city public transportation is this Lebanon-Norwich Stage, mounted on a Model 2 truck chassis. The vehicle had seating space for five passengers and the driver, plus a huge luggage bin behind the rear seat. Weather protection was solely by roll-up curtains. Bodies such as this were custom built, often by local carpenter shops.

One of the strangest creatures ever turned out by Buick was its Old English Motor Bus, based on the Model 2 truck chassis. This version was used as a courtesy car by the Plaza Hotel of New York City. The body was 11 feet overall, with 76 inches of usable space behind the driver. Seats faced the center aisle. The car sold for $2,750.

Another version of the Old English Motor Bus was this unit, used as a courtesy car by the Marott Department Store. All windows except those directly behind the driver could be lowered. Passenger entrance was via the rear, with the forward doors being for driver and footman. Electric equipment included two dome lights and a buzzer system, but the headlights were gas.

Shortly after the Model 2 truck had proven itself, Buick came out with a larger model. This was the Model 2 with an 11-inch wheelbase. It cost $1,065 with either the express body shown here or with a stake body. Standard equipment included the small kerosene cowl lamps and taillight, and a horn, but no headlights.

Though the Model 2 used the same engine and transmission as did the Model F, there was no similarity in chassis or drive train. The truck had the engine positioned further forward, and used rather lengthy chains for each rear wheel, rather than one center chain as did the Model F. All engine and transmission components were protected by a large belly pan.

In Nome, Alaska, Jack McQuire produced this ice sled conversion from his Model 10. Runners are used both front and rear, while traction is provided by spikes on the standard rear wheels. It is believed that this conversion went into limited production. The vehicle was designed to travel over ice only, such as frozen rivers and lakes, but was not meant to be used in snow.

The Model 2 110-inch wheelbase truck with a stake body was a hefty looking vehicle of about 1-ton capacity. The large box beneath the passenger's seat was for tools. Pneumatic tires were standard, but solid rubber tires could be ordered.

Buick Motor Company's New York division used this interesting panel version of the Model 2 for local delivery within the city. The highly polished body was probably built by a N.Y.C. wagon maker after the chassis had been shipped to his shop.

They had car races, why not truck races? That's what the *Chicago Evening American* thought, and so it sponsored a race around downtown Chicago for commercial vehicles only. Entering the light truck division was this Buick Model 2. History does not record what place it finished. Later in the year, a Buick truck won the commercial class in the famous Fort Lee, N.J., hill climb.

After four glorious years in the sun, Buick took a tremendous tumble, and only 13,389 cars were produced. This dropped Buick from second place, which it had held since 1907, to fifth place, with its production being beaten by Studebaker, Willys-Overland, and Maxwell, the latter car, ironically, having its foundation in Briscoe money.

Two reasons accounted for this drop in volume. The first was that production got a very late start, due primarily to the chaotic financial circumstances which resulted in General Motors landing in the street. The other factor was the new management's misguided decision to drop the very popular little Model 10, of which production had exceeded 10,000 in 1910, and concentrate instead on heavier and more expensive cars.

Another factor, but one which lies more in speculation than fact, was the growing acceptance by the public of the chattering, brass-nosed inexpensive and well-built little car emanating from a new factory at Highland Park, Michigan. Durant had often watched the activities of Henry Ford, who since 1906 had been America's largest producer of cars. In fact, Durant and Ford had twice negotiated for the sale of the Ford plant to Durant. At this time, Ford wished to concentrate on manufacturing agricultural tractors and implements. But each time the deal fell through, and Ford continued in the car business.

Still, this year 69,762 Model T's were produced and all manufacturers, including Buick, Reo, Studebaker, Maxwell Hudson, and others, were feeling the pinch. To Durant, Ford's Model T concept of rather plain, inexpensive, mass-produced cars for the public held much merit. Ironically, Buick's new management felt that the public should buy a Ford first, then step up to a Buick when they were ready for something better.

Buick's unusual little Model 14 entered its second and final year virtually unchanged except for the design of the rear fenders. Admiring their new car are Mr. and Mrs. E.F. Blackmer of Crown Point, N.Y. The car was still priced at $550, and still weighed 1,500 pounds. Only 1,252 were built before the model was dropped. Mr. Blackmer's car has been fitted with a box-type trunk on the rear deck, probably a homemade affair.

When Durant left, the factory continued to produce 2- and 4-cylinder cars, but it was obvious that the new management had no love for the 2-cylinder variety. Except for the Model 2 Delivery Truck, all production on the 159-cubic-inch engines was stopped fairly early in the year, and the old Model F was discarded, as had been the Model G earlier in the 1910 season. The Model 14 Roadster was reluctantly continued for another half-year, but it was little changed from the initial model introduced late in 1910. It continued to use the 14 horsepower, 127-cubic-inch engine, disc clutch, and unusual 2-speed selective transmission with chain drive.

The story was different in the 4-cylinder line. Here things were all astir, with five different engines being offered this year.

The new Model 32 Roadster and Model 33 Touring used the proven 165-cubic-inch engine of square 3.75 inch bore and stroke. This was the same 22.5 horsepower engine that had been used in the former Model 10. However, the Model 32 Roadster used an 89-inch wheelbase, while the Model 33 Touring used a 100-inch wheelbase. Both used a 2-speed planetary transmission and 30 x 3.5 tires.

The new Model 26 Roadster and Model 27 Touring used

Buick's most expensive and least popular car was the pretentious Model 41 Limousine, of which only 27 were built. The 3,400 pound car was offered at prices ranging from $2,750 to $3,000. It was built on its own 112.5 inch-wheelbase, and used its own exclusive 338-cubic-inch engine, which was the largest production engine that Buick had yet built.

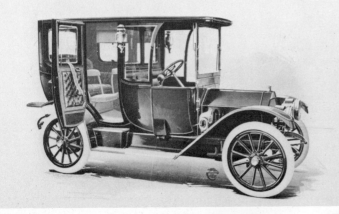

The Model 41 Limousine is shown with its rear door open. This model is equipped with folding center seats, but removable chair-type seats could also be ordered. Buick had the bodies built by a New England coach builder, but it cannot be ascertained which coach builder did the work. The bodies were of aluminum panels over a wood frame. Upholstery was in imported goatskin or gray whipcord, with silk curtains and shades and wool carpets.

1911

brand new 201-cubic-inch engine with a square bore and stroke of 4 inches, and a horsepower rating of 25.6. The Model 26 used a 100-inch wheelbase, though different than the one used on the Model 33, while the Model 27 used its own exclusive 106-inch wheelbase. Tires on both cars were 32 x 3.5 inches.

The Models 21 Touring and Roadster made exclusive use of the old 255-cubic-inch block with a bore and stroke of 4.25 x 4.5 inches, rated at 28.9 horsepower. The car also made exclusive use of a 109-inch wheelbase chassis, and was the only model to use the cone clutch this year. All other models except Models 32 and 33 used a multiple-disc clutch and 3-speed selective transmission.

The 318-cubic-inch engine of 32.4 horsepower, with a bore and stroke of 4 x 4.5 inches, was continued and used in the new Model 38 Roadster and Model 39 Touring. Both of these cars shared the same 116-inch wheelbase and used 36 x 4 inch tires.

Appearing for the first time was the largest engine that Buick had yet built. It was the 388-cubic-inch model of 4.5 x 5 bore and stroke and rated at 32.4 horsepower. It was used only in the carry-over Model 41 Limousine. This car continued to use its 112.5-inch wheelbase, but its tire

Appearing this year only was the popular Model 21 Touring, finished in solid Buick green, with cream wheels being optional. It was available in this touring style, or with a close-coupled touring body with detachable tonneau, or with a single seat rumble seat. Either touring style cost $1,500, while the single rumble seat style cost $1,550. Buick produced 3,000 total, but made no further breakdown as to how many of which style were made. In all forms, the car weighed 2,610 pounds. This beautifully restored full touring is owned by Paul Bell of Latrobe, Pa. All equipment shown here except the top and windshield was included in the price.

The Model 26 Roadster was a cute and sporty looking little car, priced at $1,050. Buick built 1,000 of the cars, all finished in solid battleship gray. It weighed 2,100 pounds. It used a 100-inch wheelbase and 56-inch tread, though a 60-inch Southern tread was available. Its 201-cubic-inch engine was of totally new design. The car used a 3-speed selective sliding gear transmission and multiple disc steel plate clutch running in an oil bath.

An expensive car of only limited appeal was the Model 38 Roadster. The 2,650-pound car was priced at $1,850, but only 153 were built. All were finished in dark blue with gray wheels. The car used a 116-inch wheelbase, 318-cubic-inch engine, and 3-speed selective transmission. The oversize gas tank held 27 gallons, and a small trunk was provided for luggage.

The Model 27 Touring made use of the same new 201-cubic-inch engine as did the Model 26. Other specifications were the same as the Model 26, except that the touring used its own 106-inch wheelbase. The car sold for $1,150 and weighed 2,280 pounds. Buick built 3,000, all finished in dark blue with white wheels. This restored version is owned by Robert Wilgelm of Grand Blanc, Mich. Front doors on this model were a $50 accessory.

Buick's prestige touring was the Model 39, which cost $1,850. It weighed 3,225 pounds. Buick built 905, all finished in dark blue with gray wheels. This was Buick's first car to use front doors, and it was at times referred to as a Fore-Door Touring, which often was misleadingly changed to Four-Door Touring. Actually, only three of the doors were functional, as the one on the driver's side was simply a dummy design. Windshields and tops were still considered accessories. The car used a 116-inch wheelbase and 318-cubic-inch engine.

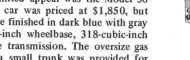

1911

Buick's economy model in the 4-cylinder line was this new Model 32 Roadster, which sold for $800. The 1,695 pound car used the 165-cubic-inch engine that had been used in the Model 10. The car had a 90-inch wheelbase and used a 2-speed planetary transmission and cone clutch. Buick produced 1,150, all finished in solid red with black leather upholstery.

The Model 33 Touring, in a sense, could be considered the successor to the Model 10. It used the same 165-cubic-inch engine and 2-speed planetary transmission that had powered the Model 10. However, its wheelbase was 100 inches and it weighed 1,855 pounds. Priced at $2,000, it had a production run of 2,000. All models were finished in dark blue with ivory wheels and black upholstery. The tonneau was detachable.

Completely different than anything built by Buick was the McLaughlin Model 7 Torpedo Touring. The elegant 7-passenger car cost $4,100 in its standard gray color, or could be ordered in any special finish that the buyer desired. It used its own 122.5-inch wheelbase and was powered by a bored-out version of Buick's standard 338-cubic-inch engine. The McLaughlin version used a square bore and stroke of 5 inches and developed 50 brake horsepower. Standard equipment included mohair top, windshield, combination oil and electric coach and taillights, Prest-O-Lite headlights, horn, complete tool kit, and front bumper. The upper part of the body was completely encircled in wood and wicker trim. Rims were Universal demountable.

size was increased slightly to 36 x 4.5 inches. Both the car and the huge engine were discontinued about mid-way in the model year.

For all models, this was the end of the true open car era. Beginning in 1912, there would be no more open-front touring cars, nor any more virtually doorless roadsters.

When Durant left Buick, he took with him Bill Little, Buick's former general manager. Little was to start work on the newly proposed Little car, which Durant would produce in Flint, and which, in many ways, would provide the groundwork for the yet-to-be-conceived Chevrolet. This left Buick in need of a president, and at Durant's suggestion, Charles W. Nash was hired away from the Durant-Dort Carriage Company. Nash was the same person who would later produce the very successful Nash car. Meanwhile, at Buick he would do so well that by 1913 he would become president of General Motors — quite an impressive record for a man who didn't even have a grade school education.

Also coming into the Buick plant this year was another man who would turn out to be one of America's great automotive giants. This man was Walter P. Chrysler, who in 1911 had just succeeded in putting the Pittsburgh plant of American Locomotive Company on a paying basis. Chrysler was hired as general manager, and he and Nash soon developed a firm friendship. The Nash-Chrsyler team became one of the finest two-man management teams ever to appear in American business, and they provided a good bit of the energy which was to bring Buick up from the depths of its then depressed financial state.

One of the first things that the bankers did after Durant lost the reins was to severely curtail Buick's famous racing activities. This had been a Durant passion, and the move was partly ecomomical and, in retrospect, partly spiteful. But with factory financing gone from the project, the Buick team had little choice but to dissolve and run as best it could wherever it could, without formal backing.

Oddly, though it had set many a mark at Indianapolis, Buick was conspicuously absent from the first 500-mile Memorial Day Classic. Bob Burman was there, but he was

In Canada, the McLaughlin Company was building McLaughlin Buicks with body work quite different from that found in the U.S. The McLaughlin Model 27 is such an example, with its different rear fender treatment and standard front door on the left and dummy door on the right. The car was finished in either dark blue with gray wheels or in complete cherry red. It cost $1,500, but on special order could be bought without the front doors at $1,475. The top and windshield were accessories. The car used the same engine and chassis as used in the U.S. Model 27.

1911

driving a Benz; Lewis Strang was there, but he was driving
a Case; and Louis Chevrolet was not there. Burman ran the
entire race and placed nineteenth after starting in thirty
ninth spot in a field of forty starters. But Strang ran only
109 laps before a broken steering linkage forced his Case
out of competition.

Buick entered two cars, but none of its top drivers were
in command. One was piloted by Arthur Chevrolet, a very
good race driver but without the flair shown by his brother
Louis. The other was in the hands of Charles Basle, again a
good but not an outstanding race driver. Chevrolet and
Basle both qualified highly enough to rank in fourteenth
and fifteenth starting places respectively, but that was
about the best that could be said for the race. Basle ran
forty-six laps before mechanical troubles forced him out,
while Chevrolet managed to complete only thirty laps
before he was forced out by mechanical breakdown.

The little 2-cylinder delivery truck was continued, but this
year it was called the Model 2-A. It was available with either
express body or with a stake body as shown here for $950, or
could be purchased as a bare chassis. Buick built 902, and it
is believed that all were produced at Jackson, rather than at
the Flint factory. This milk hauler is carrying 48 cans of milk
which would weigh approximately 4,800 pounds — quite a
load for a truck rated for ½-ton capacity.

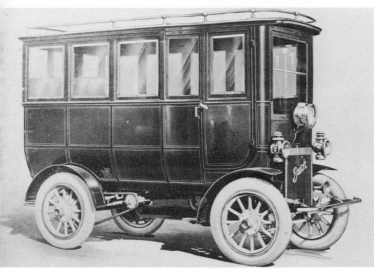

Appearing again this year was the quaint Old English Motor
Bus. There are no production records on this vehicle, as
Buick only built the chassis and contracted for the body
work. The bus used the Model 2-A Delivery Truck chassis,
and was fitted with kerosene coach lights, a single gas
headlight, and electric lights inside. The bumper, Klaxon
horn, and rooftop luggage rack apparently were options.
Passengers entered through the rear, while the driver used his
own right hand front door.

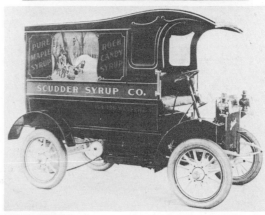

Several different body shops produced "pie wagon" type
delivery bodies for the Model 2-A. As can be seen in these
photos, these trucks proved practical for a wide variety of
businesses needing light delivery trucks.

The Standard express body is shown here with a custom roof
and roll-up side curtains. Visibility through the celluloid
windshield must have been something less than good.

It was obvious that the Nash-Chrysler team was working. It was working so well, in fact, that by November, Nash would be named president of General Motors, and by December, Chrysler would be elected president of Buick.

Production moved back up to 19,812, which enabled Buick to nose out Maxwell and move up to fourth place. Part of this accomplishment was due to Chrysler's trimming of the "fat" out of production, while a good part was also due to Nash's decision to reduce both the number of models and engines available. The 2-cylinder line had been dropped, though the 2-cylinder truck was continued for this year only on a very limited scale. It continued to use the unchanged 159-cubic-inch engine.

Gone also were the Model 14 and the pretentious Model 41 Limousine, together with their exclusive engines. Confusion exists on the Model 41, because this car was carried in the 1912 catalogs. However, none were produced in 1912, and if any were sold in that year, they were 1911 production models. Gone, too, was the Model 21 Touring and its variations and its 225-cubic-inch engine. The Model 38 Roadster also disappeared, though the Model 39 Touring now became the Model 43 in effect.

All vehicles continued to be right-hand drive, but a 3-speed sliding gear transmission and cone clutch were now used on all models. All models also sported completely changed body styling, with new modern lines and forward doors — ending forever the era of the open-front cars.

The year-old 165-cubic-inch engine of square 3.75 inch bore and stroke and 22.5 horsepower was used in the new Model 34 and 36 Roadsters and the Model 35 Touring. The Model 34 Roadster used a 90.75-inch wheelbase and 30 x 3.5 inch tires, while the Models 35 and 36 shared a 101.75-inch wheelbase chassis and used 32 x 3.5 inch tires.

The year-old 201-cubic-inch engine of square 4-inch bore and stroke and 25.5 horsepower was used in the new Model 28 Roadster and Model 29 Touring. Both of these cars used a new 108-inch wheelbase chassis and 34 x 3.5 inch tires.

With the dropping of the Model 41 Limousine, Buick's prestige car became the Model 43 Touring, which except for a new cowl, was not too different from the previous Model 39. It continued to use the proven 318-cubic-inch engine of 32.4 horsepower, and the old 116-inch wheelbase and 36 x 4 inch tires.

On this year's racing scene, Buick was conspicuously absent except for some privately owned cars that were entered by individual racing teams. At this year's Indianapolis 500, only one Buick appeared under private ownership. It was a Marquette chassis, which was a General Motors subsidiary but no close relative of the later Marquette produced by Buick. In this chassis was a Buick engine, and a driver named Billy Liesaw managed to run the hybrid through seventy-two laps before a carburetor fire finished its race. Of the old Buick team, only Bob Burman appeared at this year's 500. He drove a Cutting through 157 laps before a spinout caused a wreck that put the car out of business.

Buick's most popular car this year was the new Model 35 Touring, which weighed 2,100 pounds and cost $1,000. Production totaled 6,050. Normally the car was finished in dark blue with gray wheels, but the owner of this restored model has finished his car in gray with black fenders. The car had three functional doors, with a dummy door on the driver's side holding the parking brake and shift levers. It used the 165-cubic-inch block and a 101.7-inch wheelbase. Gas headlights and kerosene cowl and taillights were standard.

Two Buick salesmen prove the hill climbing ability of the new Model 34 Roadster to a group of onlookers in New York City. Despite such promotion, the little $900 car was Buick's least popular model and only 1,400 were built. The 1,875-pound car had a gray body and wheels and a blue hood and fenders. It used the 165-cubic-inch engine and a 90.7-inch wheelbase.

A hard-working Model 35 Touring was this vehicle, owned by Dr. J.F. Stanford of Fayetteville, Ark. At the time this picture was taken, the car had registered over 50,000 trouble-free miles over the rough mountain roads in the vicinity of Fayetteville.

1912

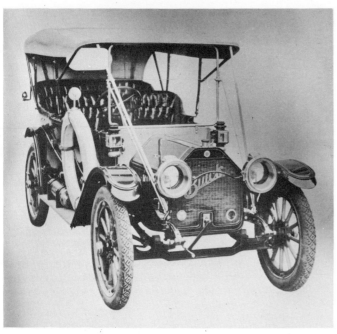

Competing for sales with the Model 34 Roadster was this Model 36 Roadster, also priced at $900. The 1,950-pound car had a production run of 1,600. It used a 102-inch wheelbase and the 165-cubic-inch engine. This restored model sports the accessory windshield and top, but has the wrong paint job. All cars were finished in blue and gray bodies, with Buick gray wheels and blue-black hood, tank and fenders. As an option, buyers could order the car in Buick brown, with blue-black fenders. Buick still used Schebler carburetors on many of its engines.

The Model 29 Touring was Buick's second most popular car, with an even 6,000 being produced. Buyers had a choice of two color combinations, either a gray body or a wine body, with blue-black hood, fenders and wheels being standard regardless of body color. The 2,600-pound car sold for $1,180 without top or windshield. It used a 108-inch wheelbase chassis.

The Model 29, in demi-tonneau form was a more sporty looking car, due to the lower cut of its body line. In order to achieve this style, the front seat had to be moved further back and the controls lowered somewhat. Windshields and tops were still considered accessories.

The Model 28 Roadster was a sporty and relatively popular car using a 108-inch wheelbase and a 201-cubic-inch engine. It cost $1,025 without the accessory top, and weighed 2,375 pounds. Buick built 2,500. Normally, the car was finished in a wine and black body and wheels, with blue-black fenders, hood and tank; but it could be ordered in a Buick gray and black body, gray wheels, and blue-black fenders, hood and tank. It was upholstered in black leather.

Buick's heaviest and most expensive car was the Model 43 Touring, which weighed 3,360 pounds and cost $1,725. Buick built 1,501. The car used a 116-inch wheelbase chassis and the 318-cubic-inch engine, running through a leather faced aluminum cone clutch. The body was of wood construction with metal doors. Fenders, wheels, and chassis parts were blue-black or gray for the body and hood.

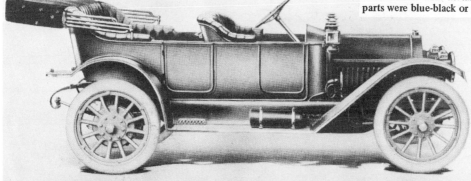

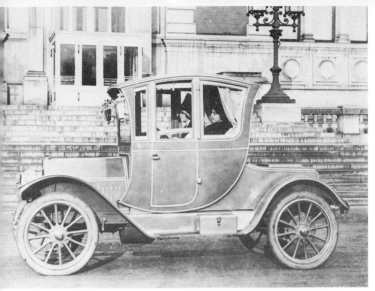

In this era, custom coach builders were not paying too much attention to Buick. Yet, one unidentified custom house turned out this interesting "tulip-type" coupe on what appears to be a Model 35 chassis. The builders not only constructed a completely unique body, but also went so far as to re-form the fenders. This car would have had only one door, the one on the right being made useless by the controls which prevented entry from the driver's side.

Buick's largest engine was the proven 318-cubic-inch model that was used in the Model 43. It is shown here with the heavy bronze flywheel exposed. The engine was rated at 48 brake horsepower or 32.4 SAE horsepower. Its bore and stroke was 4.5 x 5 inches. As with other Buick engines, the valve gear was exposed, with the rocker arms capped by oil cups. Buick still cast its cylinders in pairs, and did not use removable cylinder heads. The two-piece crankcase was cast aluminum.

The 201-cubic-inch engine was used in the Models 28 and 29. It used a square bore and stroke of 4 inches and developed 25.6 horsepower. Its transmission was 3-speed selective sliding gear, coupled to the engine via a leather faced aluminum cone clutch. The open valve gear was standard, as were the oil cups on top of each rocker arm.

Up in Canada, the McLaughlin Company was busy producing their own version of the Buick. This is the McLaughlin Model 35, with completely different body work from that found on the American Buick Model 35. Note that the body features a small cowl extending back from the varnished dash board, and completely different door and lower panel styling. This beautifully restored model, perfect in virtually every detail, is owned by Earl Herbst of Southbury, Conn.

Buick came up with one of its first experimental vehicles this year. It was this nice looking touring, powered by a very unusual V-6 engine. Apparently the problems inherent in a V-6 design were more than Buick engineers of the era could cope with, and the car never went beyond the experimental stage. The body was specially made for the vehicle.

A new innovation this year was Buick's new enclosed control panel. Basically, it was still the same two levers, but these now lived inside their own pod which was bolted to the dummy door on the driver's side of all models. The outside lever was the parking-emergency brake, while the inside one was the gear shift. The pedals were for brake and clutch, while throttle and spark were controlled by the levers on the steering wheel.

Entirely Enclosed

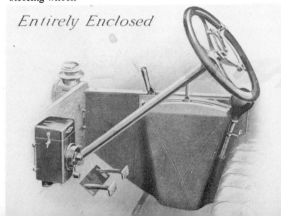

Buick produced a wide spectrum of factory installed bodies for its Model 2-A delivery truck this year, but production of the little vehicle dropped to 761. With the standard open express body, the truck sold for $1,000. It was now rated for a maximum load capacity of one ton. Its standard color was dark green, but it could be ordered in any color that the buyer desired.

An accessory item for the Model 2-A's express body was this canopy top with roll-up weather curtains. The top was covered in oiled duck, and the curtains around the driver's compartment had celluloid windows. The factory installed top was listed as Body No. A-20.

Seen with body removed, the Model A-2 truck is a simple yet sturdy looking little commercial vehicle. Buick also used the designations Model A-92 for its 92-inch wheelbase models, and A-110 for the 110-inch wheelbase design. Standard tires were 32 x 4 inch pneumatic or solid, but 34 x 4 solid tires could be ordered as an option. Brakes were internal expanding on the rear wheel hubs. Normal capacity was 1,500 pounds, with maximum capacity rated at 2,000 pounds. As shown, the stripped chassis weighed 2,190 pounds for the A-92, and 2,230 pounds for the A-110. The transmission was still 2-speed planetary with cone clutch.

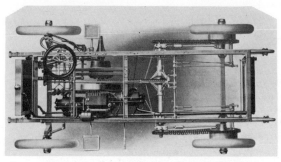

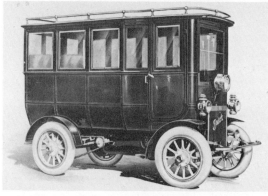

Buick again offered its Special Old English Motor Bus, but it is unknown if any were actually built this year. The catalog this year shows the bus with gas headlight, bumper, and roof rack, formerly accessory items, now listed as standard items included in the $2,750 price. This was the last year that the snub-nosed 2-cylinder truck would appear.

Another variation of the standard express was this combination wagonette and express unit. Basically, it was the canopy express body with removable center-facing seats for 10 passengers. The style was listed as Buick Body No. A-22.

This police patrol wagon utilized the standard express body of the Model 2-A for its lower portion, with the upper body simply added to the existing panels. In this case, the prisoners received better weather protection than the police, because there are curtains for the rear portion, but none for the driver's section.

A top view of the Model-A truck chassis, with body removed, shows the positioning of the components. Buick built most of its own truck bodies, and even advertised that it would build special bodies to order. Yet, it also would sell stripped chassis to other body builders for buyers who wanted locally constructed vehicles. The stripped chassis cost $965 in 92-inch wheelbase form or $980 in 110-inch wheelbase style.

Using a completely different body from the standard express was the screen-side express, listed as Buick Body No.A-24. This style came complete with plate glass windshield and a cage type body screened on all four sides. Coach lights were considered standard equipment, but headlights were an accessory.

Buick's fanciest truck style was the Standard Panel, Body No. A-23. The perky little truck enjoyed limited popularity with small retailers who offered door-step delivery service. It could not be ascertained who made these bodies.

Buick's most popular large truck was Standard Long Body Commercial Car, Model A-4. With the standard express body, it sold for $1,055; but with the stake express body, shown here, it sold for $1,065. It used a 110-inch wheelbase, while its cargo body was 108 inches long by 43 inches wide. Overall, the truck measured 14 feet. The body included a 12-inch drop-type tailgate, and hooks on the stakes for carrying ladders, long pipes, etc. Mechanically, the truck was the same as the Model 2-A.

The Standard Platform, Model A-3, could be ordered with or without the stake sides. Without the stakes, it cost $1,026, but the stakes cost an additional $9. The truck's overall length was 12½ feet, while its cargo space was 88 inches long by 62 inches wide. The platform was 40 inches above the ground. It used the 92-inch Model 2-A wheelbase.

The Model A-23 Standard Panel Truck offered fairly good load capacity for its size, but absolutely no driver protection unless the accessory roll-up curtains were purchased. Note the louvered ventilator over the rear doors.

Using the 110-inch wheelbase truck chassis was Buick's Standard Furniture Car, Model A-5. The truck measured 14½ feet overall, while its cargo body was 114 inches long by 60 inches wide. A 24-inch high drop-type tailgate would add another 2 feet of cargo space when lowered to a horizontal position. Complete as shown, the truck cost $1,160.

Buick bodies were still built almost entirely of wood, as can be seen in this photo of an unfinished Model 29 Touring. At this stage, neither the sheet metal fenders and hood nor the all-wood body have been given their primer coats. Apparently the lights and horn were installed strictly for this photograph, because in actual production, these items would not have been attached until after the final coat of lacquer was rubbed down.

Although Buick's racing activities were over, the cars still ran on. This interesting photo, identified only by the date July, 1912, shows one of the Buick Bugs leading the field on some dirt oval. Sadly, no information could be found regarding this old photo.

For a change, things seemed to be running smoothly in Flint. Production reached 26,666, and Buick held its fourth place position in the industry. In the truck line, a switch was made to left-hand drive, and in the engineering department, a new 6-cylinder engine was well under development. All cars this year used 3-speed selective sliding gear transmissions and cone clutches, hooked to 4-cylinder engines.

The Models 30 and 31 used the proven 201-cubic-inch engine of square 4-inch bore and stroke developing 25.6 horsepower. Both models used the 108-inch wheelbase chassis of the former Models 28 and 29, but the Model 30 Roadster used 34 x 3.5 inch tires while the Model 31 Touring used 34 x 4 inch tires.

The Model 40 Touring used its own brand new 115-inch wheelbase chassis, 36 x 4 inch tires, and sported a reworked version of the proven 255-cubic-inch engine of 4.25 x 4.5 inch bore and stroke. Although Buick claimed 40 horsepower for this engine, SAE ratings listed it at 28.9 horsepower.

The Model 24 Roadster and Model 25 Touring shared a new 105-inch wheelbase chassis and ran on 32 x 3.5 inch tires. Both models were powered by the proven 165-cubic-inch engine of 22.5 horsepower, which used a square bore and stroke of 3.75 inches.

The interesting new truck line used a brand new engine of 141-cubic-inches with a bore and stroke of 3 x 5 inches that developed 14.4 horsepower. The Model 3 truck used a 100-inch wheelbase and ran on 32 x 4 inch tires, while the Model 4 truck used a 122-inch wheelbase and ran on 34 x 4.5 inch tires. The Model 3 was rated at one half ton capacity, while the Model 4 was rated at three-fourths ton. Both used a 3-speed sliding gear transmission.

During this year, Buick engineers took a long and hard look at the Dayton Delco electric system and self starter, which had been used successfully on Cadillac cars for the past year. Both companies collaborated on an extensive engineering program, and by 1914, an entirely new electric and starting system would be available on all Buick cars.

Across the ocean, an agreement was signed with the Abadal Company of Barcelona, Spain, whereby that company was to build a series of customized bodies on Buick chassis for European consumption. The agreement was in effect until 1922, and a small series of these customized Buicks were turned out, but no designs of any great impact ever resulted.

At the Indianapolis 500, Billy Liesaw again was the driver of a Buick-powered machine, though the highly modified car was running under the name of Anel, not Buick. Liesaw ran 148 laps before loose connecting rods forced him from the race. Bob Burman also appeared, this time driving a Keeton, which he ran through the entire 200 laps and placed eleventh after starting in twenty-first place. Liesaw's appearance marked the last time that a Buick would run in th Memorial Day Classic until 1930.

Buick's most popular car this year was the new Model 31 Touring, of which 10,000 were produced. It cost $1,285 and weighed 2,750 pounds. It could be ordered either in all blue-black, or in Buick gray with blue-black fenders and trim. The car used a 108-inch wheelbase, the 201-cubic-inch engine, and a 3-speed selective sliding gear transmission and cone clutch.

Old Buicks never seem to die — that was true even in the early years. In 1922, this Model 31 Touring carried a family from New York to California with no trouble. Note that the sign calls the car a 1912 model, either because the dealer based its age on its original date of sale or because he simply wanted to make the car appear one year older.

Buick's heaviest, most expensive, and least popular car this year was the large Model 40 Touring, of which 1,506 were built. The car was also the first to offer Buick's latest accessory, electric head, tail and side lights, with current supplied by a Dayton Delco generator. The car used a 115-inch wheelbase and the 255-cubic-inch engine of 4.25 x 4.5 inch bore and stroke. It was finished either in Buick blue or Buick gray with blue-black chassis and wheels. All trim was nickel plated.

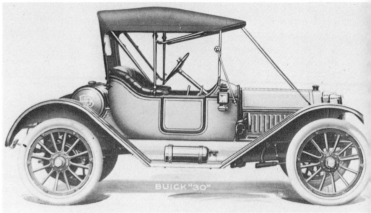

New for the year was the Model 30 Roadster, a cute little car weighing 2,480 pounds and priced at $1,125. Buick produced 3,500. The car used a 108-inch wheelbase and was powered by the 201-cubic-inch engine of 4-inch square bore and stroke. It used 34 x 3.5 inch tires and Baker demountable rims. Buyers had a choice of finishes, either all blue-black or gray body with blue-black wheels. Its clutch was a leather faced aluminum cone.

Shown with its accessory top and windshield raised is the new Model 30. Although it appears to sport a right hand door, this was simply dummy trim. The shift and parking brake controls were located in a closed panel where the right front door normally would have been located. The seat was of the bench-type.

The new Model 25 Touring used the same 105-inch wheelbase and 165-cubic-inch engine as did the Model 24. It weighed 2,335 pounds and sold for $1,050. Production reached 8,150. Its colors were either maroon or Buick gray with blue-black chassis and wheels. The engine used a reinforced aluminum crankcase. Ignition was by Remy magneto and a set of dry cells. Steering was semi-irreversible.

Walter Marr, Buick's chief engineer, came up with one of his few unsuccessful ideas this year. The idea was this Marr Cyclecar, an attempt to cash in on the mini-car craze that was sweeping Europe and having some minor impact on the American automotive scene. Only this one model was built, and it still survives in the Sloan Panorama of Transportation in Flint. The 2-passenger car used many Buick parts. Tandem seating was used, and full weather protection was offered.

Buick's lightest and least expensive car was the Model 24 Roadster, which weighed 2,130 pounds and sold for $950. A total of 2,850 were built. The car was finished either in maroon or gray, with blue-black wheels and chassis. It used a 105-inch wheelbase and the 165-cubic-inch engine of square 3.75 bore and stroke. Its right door was strictly a dummy.

A front view of the experimental Marr Cyclecar shows how narrow the little vehicle really was. Cyclecars became popular in Europe, primarily England, during this era, due mainly to the high tax laws on larger cars, but in the U.S. there really never was a need for such cars.

One of Buick's most popular engines was the 165-cubic-inch-model used this year in both the Model 24 and Model 25. The engine continued to have its cylinders cast in pairs, with no removable cylinder heads, but using valve cages for removal of the valves. The engine used a reinforced aluminum crankcase, integral with the clutch housing, and an aluminum transmission case. The fan was pressed steel. All valve mechanism operated in the open as shown. The Remy magneto can be seen on this side. A Schebler carburetor was still used.

The first car ever to climb Pike's Peak entirely on its own power, without the aid of horses, was this modified 1910 Buick Model 10. The run was made July 17, 1913, by W.W. Brown. Not content with simply scaling the mountain, Mr. Brown then proceeded to drive the car as far up the stairs of the Summit House as he possibly could.

Buick's most popular engine was the well proven unit of 201 cubic inches, running a square bore and stroke of four inches. As was the case with all Buick engines, the cylinders were cast in pairs with no removable heads. A Remy magneto was used on the ignition side, while the carburetor was a Schebler. Note the huge size of the flywheel and the open valve gear.

Although it wouldn't be introduced until 1914, Buick's new 6-cylinder engine was under very thorough and top secret testing this year. Here the unit is seen mounted in the 1914 chassis and using an experimental 1914-type radiator. It was being given a series of test runs around the Buick track at Flint.

Another view of W.W. Brown's successful drive up Pike's Peak shows the type of terrain that the car had to cover. Brown had named his modified Model 10 the Bear Cat, and had used it successfully in local Colorado road races before attempting to climb the mountain.

Buick came up with two entirely new truck chassis this year, replacing the obsolete 2-cylinder vehicle with a new 4-cylinder model of 141 cubic inches. The larger trucks were the Model 4, available in four basic bodies or as stripped chassis. All used a 122-inch wheelbase and were rated at ¾-ton capacity. Of the Model 4 trucks, only 461 were produced. This is the Model 4 with the standard express body and stakes, which sold for $1,300. Without the stakes, the truck sold for $1,250. The bodies were dark green or bright red, with black fenders and hood.

The second basic body in the Model 4 truck line was the canopy express, which sold for $1,325, complete with side curtains all around. It was also available as a screen-side delivery for $1,350. Wheels and chassis were painted gray on all trucks.

Buick TRUCKS

Buick's light truck line was the Model 3. These vehicles used a 100-inch wheelbase and were rated at ½-ton capacity. Only 199 were built. The Model 3 line consisted of five basic bodies plus a stripped chassis. Most expensive of the lot was the panel delivery, shown here, which sold for $1,250. Its body could be ordered either in dark green or, as shown here, in light green and dark red combination. The passenger's seat would fold up to allow access to the rear from inside the truck. Side curtains were an accessory, but the coach lamps were standard.

The Model 3 screen side express used only four posts to hold the top, as compared with the Model 4, which used six posts. The screen side model sold for $1,200, while the plain canopy express sold for $1,175. Side curtains were not included in this price.

Buick's lowest priced truck was the Model 3 open express, which sold for $1,100. The wing boards were standard, but stake sides would cost an additional $50. Neither top, windshield, nor spare tire was included in the price, but the spare tire rack was standard equipment.

Production reached a record 32,889 this year, cementing for still another year Buick's fourth place in the industry.

Buick's big news of the year was the introduction of its completely new 6-cylinder engine, which had been rumored for over a year. But though the new engine was of prime importance, its introduction overshadowed two other highly significant changes — the switch from right-hand drive and right-hand control to left-hand drive and center control; and the discontinuance of Presto-Lite lighting, via the adoption of a Delco electric system and self starter.

The Delco starting, lighting, generating and ignition system was an approach that few other auto makers took in this era. Most makers, except those of prestige cars, preferred to continue with the lower cost magneto ignition and oil or gas lamps, and charge the customers extra for the "luxury" electric systems.

The new Buick Six followed Buick's consistent philosophy of valve-in-head design, with the cylinders cast in pairs. It had a bore and stroke of 3.75 x 5 inches and displaced 331 cubic inches, with a rating of 48 brake horsepower or 33.75 SAE horsepower. The new engine was used only in the Model B 55 Touring car, a five-passenger vehicle using a 130-inch wheelbase and 36 x 4.5 inch tires. Standard features of this model included an electric horn, spare tire rack (but not the tire), mohair top, speedometer, and a complete set of tools.

In the 4-cylinder range, only two engines were used in the car line. They were the well-proven 165-cubic-inch model, and a brand new engine of 221 cubic inches. This had a bore and stroke of 3.75 x 5 and SAE horsepower rating of 22.5. In effect, it was simply a 4-cylinder version of the new 6-cylinder block. The trucks continued to use their own heavy lugging 141-cubic-inch engine.

The 165-cubic-inch engine, with its square bore and stroke of 3.75 inches, was used in Buick's most popular cars, the B-24 Roadster and the B-25 Touring. All used a 105-inch wheelbase and 32 x 3.5 inch tires.

The new 221-cubic-inch engine was used in the B-36 Roadster, the B-37 Touring, and the B-36 Coupe, which was really Buick's first mass production closed car. All of these models used the same 112-inch wheelbase chassis and 34 x 4 inch tires.

Also used on all Buicks this year was the cone clutch and 3-speed sliding gear selective transmission. All models continued to use external rear wheel brakes for service, and internal expanding rear wheel brakes for emergency and parking.

This year, a Buick Model 28, built in 1912, became the first car ever to cross South America. Piloted by Johnson Martin, a Buick dealer in Buenos Aires, the car was driven from that city across the Andes to Santiago, Chile.

The least popular car of the year was the Model B-38 Coupe, of which only 50 were built. The car cost $1,800 on the east coast, $1,950 on the west. It used the same 4-cylinder, 220-cubic-inch engine and 112-inch wheelbase chassis as did the B-36 and B-37. The car weighed 2,930 pounds.

Something new was added to all Buick engines this year. It was the new Delco self-starter, shown here mounted on the ignition side of the engine. The starter gripped the gear teeth cut into the forward edge of the huge flywheel.

Buick's newest design, and also its most expensive and heaviest car was the B-55 Touring, a 3,664 pound machine using the brand new 6-cylinder engine of 331-cubic-inches and a 130-inch wheelbase chassis. The car cost $1,985 on the east coast, $2,135 in the west. Buick built 2,045. Color options were blue with black wheels and fenders or all black.

Buick's brand new 6-cylinder engine was a nice-looking power plant, basically looking like the 4-cylinder block with two more of the paired cylinders tacked on. Cylinder heads were still not removable, but the overhead valves lived in removable cages.

Buick's most popular car this year was the Model B-25 Touring, of which a record 13,446 were built for domestic sales and 1,544 were built for export. The 2,400 pound car cost $1,050 on the east coast, or $1,185 on the west coast. It was finished either in all blue-black, or gray body and blue-black wheels. This restored model is owned by Maurice McIntosh of Flushing, Mich. The car used the same engine and 105-inch wheelbase as did the Model B-24.

A proud couple by the name of Mr. and Mrs. W.E. Gerry, are shown with their new Model B-37 Touring, which they used on a round-trip transcontinental tour. Note the primitive camping trailer. The Model B-37 was Buick's heaviest 4-cylinder model, weighing 2,930 pounds. It cost from $1,335 to $1,485 depending on location of the sale. Buick built 9,050. The car was finished in all blue-black, or gray body and blue-black fenders and wheels.

A New York City Buick dealer is shown here driving the new Model 24 Roadster up a steep bank at 188th street in N.Y.C. The dealer claimed that no other motor car had ever climbed this bank. The car used a 165-cubic-inch engine with a square bore and stroke of 3.75 inches.

The Model B-36 Roadster was reintroduced this year, but it was a substantially different car from what had appeared in 1912. Priced from $1,235 to $1,375, the car attracted 2,550 buyers. It weighed 2,726 pounds. Buyers had a choice of colors, either all blue-black, or gray body with blue-black wheels and fenders. The rear portion was an integral part of the body, not detachable. The car used a 112-inch wheelbase and was powered by a 220-cubic-inch engine of 35 brake horsepower. It used a Marvel carburetor. This model was restored by B.D. Wood of Grand Island, Neb.

This New York City lass poses proudly in her new Model 24 Roadster. It was Buick's least expensive car, selling for $950 on the east coast or $1,060 on the west coast. It weighed 2,200 pounds. It was finished in a gray or maroon body with blue-black wheels and fenders. Buick built 3,126 for domestic sales and 239 for export sales. For the first time, the top and windshield were considered standard equipment, as were the electric headlights and horn.

A New York City dealer drives the new Model 36 Roadster up a steep bank at 188th street, claiming that no other cars except Buicks could run up this grade under their own power. Standard equipment on this car included the top and windshield, kerosene and electric lights.

Buick's little 100-inch wheelbase trucks appeared for the last time this year. In fact, they barely appeared, as only 101 were built. The trucks were built with a basic express body, which could then be fitted with wing boards or, as shown, stake sides. In basic form, the truck cost $1,075. They continued to use the 141-cubic-inch 4-cylinder engine.

Buick's popular truck was the Model 4 which used a 122-inch wheelbase. A total of 738 were built this year. It was available as a basic chassis at $1,225, or with this standard express body with wing boards. It was rated for 1,500 pound load capacity, with the cargo space being 98 inches long by 43 inches wide. Pneumatic tires were standard, but solid tires could be ordered when the load capacity was expected to exceed 1-ton.

Robert Annand and Clark Merritt of Duluth, Minn., apparently figured they could make better use of their Model B-55 Touring, and so they created this early example of today's popular camper. The car, known as a "prairie schooner," was used by the pair for long distance tours around the country. The rear portion was fitted with bunks, cooking gear, and storage.

The chassis of the Model 3, 100-inch wheelbase truck was a rugged piece of engineering, with a surprisingly large number of open running parts. The 141-cubic-inch engine was small in displacement, but strong in lugging power, which was of prime inportance in trucks of the era.

Buyers who wanted to add their own bodies could order the Model 4 truck in stripped form, as shown here. Cowl, hood, and fenders were included, but lights were not. The truck frame was 4.5 inches deep and 4 inches wide at its greatest width, and was constructed of hot riveted pressed steel. Hyatt bearings were used on all wheels and axles.

Not all of the new B-55 models were used as touring cars. This one was bought by the Leach-Johnson Co. of Bedford, Ohio, and rebuilt into an ambulance and invalid car. Although there may have been earlier Buick ambulance conversions made, this is first that the author was able to find.

Across the ocean, the British were offering Bedford Buicks to their customers. These were primarily B-25 chassis, fitted with either the standard B-25 body or with a British coachwork body. Buick shipped 1,544 of these chassis overseas. Now that Buick had switched to left-hand drive, export chassis such as these had to be made specially.

Bob Burman wasn't racing for Buick any longer, but he still preferred Buick cars. Here he is seen in front of the Indiana Democratic Club in Indianapolis in his new Model C-55 Touring, Buick's most expensive and heaviest car this year. The large 6-cylinder touring weighed 3,680 pounds and cost $1,650. Buick built 3,449, all finished in all black or in blue-black body and hood with black wheels. Companion car to the C-55 was the new C-54 Roadster, of which only 352 were built. It weighed 3,400 pounds and cost $1,635. Both models used a huge 130-inch wheelbase chassis and were powered by the 331-cubic-inch 6-cylinder engine of 55 horsepower.

These views of the rear compartment of the Model C-55 Touring car show how the auxiliary jump seats would fold out of the way when not in use. Each rear door was equipped with a fairly large storage pouch, while the front doors held small storage compartments. The dust cover for the top also covered the entire back of the rear seat, and tucked down between the seat back and cushion. The entire interior was finished in black leather.

Production set another record this year, climbing up to 43,946. However, Maxwell also experienced a record-breaking year, and produced 44,000 cars. This temporarily knocked Buick down from fourth place to fifth place in the industry.

In both Buick and General Motors history, 1915 was not noted for its automotive advances as much as it was for its corporate changeover. Durant, having had phenomenonal success with Chevrolet, had used his influence, his Chevrolet Company, and his wide range of friends, including the fabulously wealthy DuPont family of Wilmington, to have Chevrolet Company buy the majority stock in General Motors. On September 16, he announced to the stunned banking syndicate that the $20-million Chevrolet Company owned controlling interest of the $100-million General Motors complex.

In the automotive line, the major changes revolved around the new 6-cylinder engine, which Buick now rated at 55 brake horsepower, though SAE stuck to its 33.75 rating. The engine and running gear was unchanged, but the 130-inch wheelbase car in which it lived now sported a new and much more modern seven-passenger body designated the Model C -55. In addition to the new styling, the car had its price lowered to $1,650, thus making it one of the better buys of the year in comparison with other similar styles.

In the 4-cylinder world, the two light cars continued to use the 165-cubic-inch engine. These cars were now designated the C-24 Roadster and the C-25 Touring. Both models used a new 106-inch wheelbase and totally new bodies. The tires remained 32 x 3.5 inches.

The larger 4-cylinder engine of 221 cubic inches was used in the C-36 Roadster and the C-37 Touring. These cars continued to use the former 112-inch wheelbase chassis and 34 x 4 inch tires of the previous "B" models, but the body styles were greatly improved. In addition, the B-38 coupe was dropped and not replaced.

Late in the year, a 6-cylinder Roadster, Model C-54, was introduced as a companion to the C-55 Touring. This car used the C-55's huge 130-inch wheelbase chassis, and except for body styling, was identical to the touring. Standard equipment on all cars this year included electric lighting and starter, demountable rims, spare tire holder, and a standard speedometer on all but the 106-inch wheelbase models.

A reduction was made in the truck line, with the Model 3 of 100-inch wheelbase and one half ton capacity being dropped. Continued was the Model 14 truck, now called the C-4. It continued to use a 122-inch wheelbase and be rated at three-fourths ton capacity. However, the truck now used the passenger line's 221-cubic-inch engine, and the former exclusive 141-cubic-inch truck engine was discontinued.

This rear view of the 130-inch wheelbase Model C-55 Touring gives some idea of its huge length. The tires were 36 x 4.5, and when new the car used smooth tread on the front and non-skid tread on the rear. This was Buick's only 7-passenger model.

1915

Buick's most popular car continued to be the Model C-25 Touring, priced at $950. It was a companion car to the Model C-24, and shared the same 106-inch wheelbase chassis and 165-cubic-inch 4-cylinder engine. It weighed 2,334 pounds and was finished in blue-black hood and body with black fenders, chassis and wheels. Buick built a record 19,080 for domestic use and an additional 931 for export sales. A Marvel carburetor was used.

Appearing for the last time this year was the Model C-37 Touring, which enjoyed a tremendous production run of 12,450. The 2,980 pound car cost $1,235. It was available in all black, or blue-black hood and body and black fenders and wheels. As did the Model C-36, it used a 112-inch wheelbase chassis, and the 220-cubic-inch 4-cylinder engine of 37 horsepower.

The Model CX-25 Touring was built for export only, primarily to England. The car was quite similar to the U.S. Model C-25, but used left hand steering, and had a large tool box mounted on the running board. It weighed 2,350 pounds. Buick built 931.

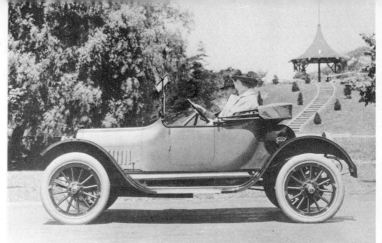

Appearing for the last time was Buick's lightest and lowest price car, the Model C-24 Roadster. The 2,200 pound vehicle still used an exterior gas tank mounted directly behind the body. When the top was lowered, such as here, this tank was almost impossible to fill. The car sold for $900, and was finished in a maroon body with red striping, and black wheels, chassis, and tank. However, this model is painted in what appears to be a gray body, and it is not known if this was an option, or a special order model. Buick built 3,256 for domestic sales and 186 for export sales, primarily to England. Note that kerosene coach lamps were not used.

Shown after 60,000 miles of hard use is this Model C-36 Roadster, which was owned by Richard J. Strobel of Mankato, Minn. The photo was taken in 1921, when the car was six years old. It features an accessory bumper and spotlight, the latter with a broken lense. The C-36 appeared for the last time this year. It cost $1,185 and weighed 2,795 pounds. Production was 2,849, all finished in dark blue. This was Buick's first model to carry an enclosed spare tire. In fact, it had space for two spares in the enclosed rear compartment. It used a 112-inch wheelbase chassis and 220-cubic-inch engine.

Buick turned out 186 of the Model CX-24 Roadsters with right hand steering for export to England. The cars weighed 2,222 pounds, or 22 pounds more than the American versions. On the export models, the large fender-mounted tool box was a standard item.

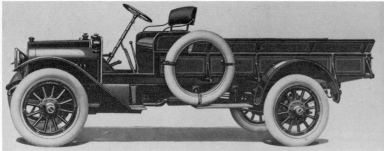

Buick's only truck this year was the Model C-4, available only as an open express for $1,225, as shown here, or as a stripped chassis. With the express body, it weighed 3,200 pounds. Buick built only 645 for domestic use. The truck now used the 221-cubic-inch 4-cylinder engine.

The Cargill-Peninsular Co., a Detroit printing firm used this Model C-4 for its city deliveries. The truck was bought as a stripped chassis, with the body supplied by an outside firm. The C-4 continued to use its 122-inch wheelbase chassis and was still rated at ¾-ton capacity.

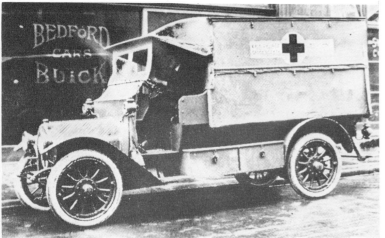

Not surprisingly, with Europe engaged in the start of World War I, Buick produced more trucks for export than it did for domestic use. Designated the Model C-4-X, the export model had a production run of 748. Many were converted into war ambulances, such as the one seen here. The conversions were made by the London Branch of the Red Cross Society after an extensive series of tests were made on various chassis by British army engineers.

A fine example of the beautiful coachwork done on funeral cars of this era is this carved panel hearse based on the C-4 truck chassis. The bodywork was done by A. Geissel & Sons of Philadelphia, a small but significant factor in the early years of motorized hearse and ambulance building. Note that even the cowl, roof rail and door frames are of carved walnut, as are the draperies on the body proper. The door windows could not be lowered, but were removable.

P.J. Oesterling, a flour, feed and potato dealer in Butler, Pa., used this Model C-4 truck as his only delivery vehicle for years, hauling loads far in excess of the 1,500 pound limit recommended for the truck. The vehicle was bought as a stripped chassis, and Mr. Oesterling designed his own canopy body, which was built in a local carpenter shop. The truck is seen here loaded with approximately three tons of potatoes.

Not all Buick trucks began their life as trucks. This attractive service car, owned by the Covert Auto Co. of Austin, Texas, began its life as a C-55 Touring. After several years of use as a private passenger car it was converted into a rather attractive pickup truck.

After 200,000 miles of use in four years, this Model C-25 Touring was purchased from its original owner and converted into a pickup truck by F.J. Weigand of Barberton, Ohio. Mr. Weigand, an appliance dealer in Barberton, then proceeded to use the truck for several more years in this capacity. At the time the photo was taken (1919) Mr. Weigand was operating a fleet of five similarly converted Buick touring cars.

No, it's not a World War I armored car. It's the service car of the Coldwater Telephone Co. of Coldwater, Kansas, wearing about 1-ton of Kansas sod over every conceivable part of its body. This gives some indication of the type of roads faced by drivers in the mid-teens. The car is a Model C-37 Touring, fitted with a special home-made utility body. At the time the photo was taken (1917), the car had covered 25,000 miles, under the most severe operating conditions.

Obviously not all Buick trucks began their lives as trucks. The Columbus Buick Co. of Columbus, Ohio, converted this Model C-24 Roadster into what was described as a "modern" service truck.

The Buick dashboard this year was identical on all models. It was functional to a Spartan degree, and the speedometer mounted on the far right seems difficult to read. Both the brake and clutch pedals had small spurs on the outer edges to keep the operator's feet from slipping.

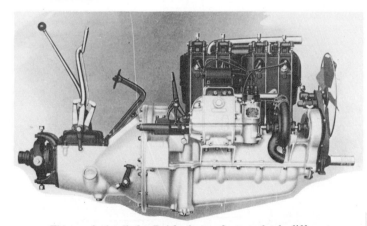

This year's 4-cylinder Buicks featured a completely different style self starter. The Delco unit incorporated into one central body the starting, generating, and ignition functions. Note too that the cylinders were still cast in pairs and the same open valve gear was still in use. The two-peice crankcase continued to be made of reinforced aluminum.

Buick's big 6-cylinder engine was basically an extended version of its 4-cylinder block. It too used the unusual Delco starter-generator-ignition combination. The ignition wiring was protected by chromed tubes, but the valve gear remained in the open. This engine ran a bore and stroke of 3.75 x 5 inches, and developed 55 brake horsepower from its 331 cubic inches.

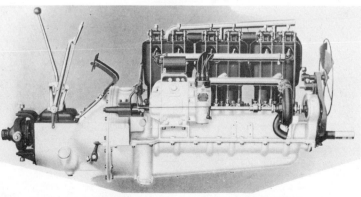

Under Durant's leadership, Buick production soared this year, reaching an unheard-of 124,834, which was not only an all-time record for the company, but a figure which was destined to remain a record until 1923. The move shot Buick up to third place in total production, passing both Dodge and Maxwell, and being exceeded only by Ford and Willys-Overland.

But even though the Buick Company was enjoying phenomenal success (as was the Chevrolet Company) things were far from calm in management's ivory towers. Through consistent trading of his stock, Durant was able to personally acquire controlling interest of General Motors. In May of the year, he announced to the bankers that he alone, not the Chevrolet Company, was solidly in control of General Motors.

The move had one very adverse side. Charles Nash, who had been a friend and a former close associate of Durant,

felt that he simply couldn't manage the corporation unde Durant's ceaseless demands. In June he resigned a president of General Motors and purchased the Jeffery Company of Kenosha, Wisconsin, which subsequently became the famous Nash Motor Company, now a part o American Motors. Meanwhile, Durant took over as pres ident of General Motors, a post he would hold only unti another financial tumble in 1920 would remove him fron the company once and for all.

Although production was way up, the models available were down, with only three engines and three wheelbase sizes being offered. The engines were the now-proven 331-cubic-inch Six of 3.75 x 5 inches bore and stroke available in two 130-inch wheelbase models; a brand new 224-cubic-inch Light Six, with a bore and stroke of 3.25 x 4.5 inches and SAE rating of 25.35 horsepower, available in two basic models using a new 115-inch wheelbase chassis; and a brand new Four of 170 cubic inches, using a bore and stroke of 3-3/8 x 4.75 and having an SAE rating of 18.23 horsepower. This engine was also available in two basic models, both using the old 106-inch wheelbase chassis. Also continued was the 221-cubic-inch Four of

Buick's first sedan appeared this year in the form of the Model D-47. It was Buick's most expensive, heaviest, and least popular car, costing $1,800, weighing 3,130 pounds, and having a production run of only 881. The design was of the center-door style, which meant that all passengers had to enter into the rear compartment, then slide between the two separated front seats to reach the front compartment. For some still unexplained reason, this awkward and seemingly purposeless style became very popular with all car builders during the late teens and early 1920s.

Buick's most popular car was the Model D-45 Touring, of which a record 73,827 were built for domestic sales and another 4,741 were built for export. Finished in Buick green of blue-black with black fenders, the 2,760-pound car sold for $1,020. It used the new 224-cubic-inch Six. This model, from Spokane, Wash., is shown following its trip to Galveston, Texas. The car has been fitted with accessory front bumper and cowl spotlights. Note the luggage piled in the rear compartment.

Buick's first true convertible was the Model D-46 Coupe, which featured plate glass windows that could be lowered, plus a folding top that formed a weather-tight compartment when raised. The car was priced at $1,425 and weighed 2,900 pounds. Buick built only 1,443.

A rather sleek looking car was the new D-44 Roadster, priced at $985. The 2,660-pound car was finished in Delft blue body and hood and black wheels and fenders, with cream wheels being optional. Buick built 12,978 for domestic sales and 541 for export. The car used a 115-inch wheelbase chassis and 224-cubic-inch 6-cylinder engine fo tatally new design. Tires were 34 x 4 inches, plain in the front and non-skid tread in the rear.

1916

2.5 SAE horsepower, but this was used only in the Model D-4 three-quarter ton truck.

Introduced late enough in the year almost to qualify as 1917 models were two closed cars in the D-4 Series. These were the D-46 Coupe and the D-47 Sedan. This gave Buick two medium-price closed cars to go along with its open cars, which in price reached well down into the low-price class and were also well-entrenched in the middle-price class.

At the close of what would have been the 1916 model year, the giant D-55 Touring and D-54 Roadster were dropped, along with their big 331-cubic-inch engine. The move was now in the direction of smaller, lighter, and faster cars, and fewer individual power plants. The era of having a different engine for each series, or even for each model, was closing, and wouldn't reappear again for another forty years.

Before the D-55 was dropped, it came equipped with a notable improvement, via the inclusion of a one-man top. Although this top seldom could be easily put in place by one man, it was still a big improvement over the old top. The new unit used wing nuts to clamp it to the windshield, doing away with the leather strapping used on former models. Also for the first time, the old cup-and-strap arrangement for the spare tire carrier was gone, and the tire was now carried on a circular steel band device made by Detroit Carrier Company.

Appearing for the last time was Buick's huge 6-cylinder roadster, this year designated the Model D-54. The 3,400 pound car was basically unchanged from the Model C-54 of 1915. It cost $1,450, and normally would be finished in royal green. Buick produced 1,194. This version was part of the Flint, Mich., Fire Dept., and was the chief's car.

James A. Bell, a 60-year-old resident of California, is shown with his Model D-55 Touring after having made his seventh coast to coast tour. Travelling was a hobby of the elderly gent, and by 1920, when this picture was taken, he had logged 47,600 miles on his car, mainly driving between the Atlantic and Pacific coasts. The D-55 weighed 3,670 pounds, and cost $1,485. This year Buick built 9,866, all finished in royal green, with black fenders.

Looking very un-Buick-like was the new Model D-34 Roadster, which was Buick's lightest and lowest priced car. Designed to compete for buyers who wanted something better than a Ford, but who could not afford much better, the little 4-cylinder car sold for $660 and weighed 1,900 pounds. Buick built 1,768 for domestic sales and another 163 for export. All 4-cylinder cars used semi-elliptic springs on the rear, a practice that would be continued through the 1924 models.

No, not all Model D-54 Roadsters went to fire departments, but they were popular as the chief's car. This one was assigned to the chief of the Jackson, Miss., Fire Department. Shown in the car are Chief L.R. McDonald and driver H.V. Rice. Note the siren on the running board and the bell on the front. The roadster used a one-piece windshield while the companion D-55 Touring used a two-piece windshield.

Companion car to the Model D-34 was the Model D-35 Touring, which weighed 2,100 pounds and sold for $675. Buick built 13,969 for domestic sales and 944 for export. The cars used the old 106-inch wheelbase chassis, but sported a brand new 4-cylinder of 170 cubic inches, running a bore and stroke of 3-3/8 x 4.75 inches. Both front and rear tires were identical on this model.

One of the oldest undertaking firms in Kentucky, the Mattil, Efinger & Roth Co. of Paducah, motorized with Buick equipment exclusively. Shown here is their private ambulance and their carved panel hearse, both mounted on D-55 chassis.

Appearing for the last time this year was the D-4 truck, shown here with its standard express body and accessory top and front curtain. The truck still used its 122-inch wheelbase chassis, and the outdated 221-cubic-inch 4-cylinder engine. Buick built 1,152 for domestic sales and 1,347 for export. Many of the domestic and most of the export models were sold as stripped chassis rather than with the express body.

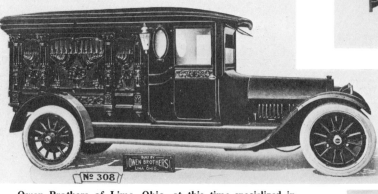

The Hoover Wagon Co. of York, Pa., produced this heavily carved hearse on a Model D-55 chassis. The D-55 fitted the funeral trade well on two counts — its long wheelbase, and its ability to travel long distances at very slow speed without boiling or stalling.

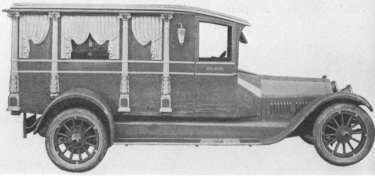

William Pfeiffer Auto & Carriage Works of Omaha, designed this Style No. 31-R Hearse for use on the Buick D-55 chassis. This particular model was built for David D. Reavis of Falls City, Neb. and featured a two-tone paint job of dark and light gray. The drapes were carved from oak.

Owen Brothers of Lima, Ohio, at this time specialized in converting the old elaborately carved horse-drawn hearses into motor vehicles. Here is one example of their work, mounted on a D-55 chassis. The original horse-drawn vehicle extended rearward from the trailing edge of the front doors, while the cab portion was constructed to blend the old vehicle with the new chassis.

Cutting a blazing trail through the Illinois dirt track circuit was this Model D-45 owned by Barney Wetzell, of Sterling, Ill., shown at the wheel. The car had been driven 52,000 miles in its first year as a touring car. In early 1917 Mr. Wetzell converted it to a racer, and it subsaquently won most of the important Illinois races that year, including a 100 mile event at Kewanee. The car had a top speed of 77 miles per hour.

A. Geissel & Sons of Philadelphia, designed this heavily carved hearse body for use on the D-4 truck chassis. Complete as shown, it cost $2,395. Note that even the front roof overhang carried elaborate carving work. The body was finished in ebony black lacquer with gold trim.

1917

Because of war restrictions, lack of materials, and a certain amount of over-production in 1916, this year's calendar year production slid to 115,267. Still, other manufacturers had similar problems, and so Buick retained third place in the industry.

At the start of the year, both the Four and the Six were continued, but the Four was destined to be dropped at mid-year. Actually, in this era of Buick production, a dilemma exists for automotive historians. Buick for years had maintained an August introductory date for its new models, in order to be able to show them at county and state fairs, which traditionally occur in the fall. On the other hand, many auto manufacturers held to a January introductory date, in order to show surprise offerings at the major auto shows in the large metropolitan areas. Buick also wanted to bring out new models at these shows, and hence there were a great many mid-year models introduced.

The result is that 1916 models of August introduction would be carried over into 1917, but then the 1917

Rather nice rear quarter lines graced the new Model D-44 Roadster, which used a 115-inch wheelbase. The 2,660-pound car sold for $985. Buick built 4,366 for domestic sales and 100 for export. This restored version is owned by Donna Ross of Battle Creek, Mich.

Buick's heaviest, most expensive and least popular car continued to be the Model D-47 Sedan. The center-door style car cost $1,800 and weighed 3,130 pounds. Only 132 were built. The spare tire cover shown here was an accessory. Coach handles were still used on the trailing edges of the doors. Roll-up shades were provided for all windows except the windshield and the two front quarter side windows.

Not making any great impact in automotive sales was Buick's pretty Model D-46 Coupe, a true convertible that really was too advanced for its time. The 2,900 pound car sold for $1,425, but sales totaled only 485. This model shows a very tiny window in the quarter panel, while other models were shown with a larger triangular window. Apparently at least two different top designs were used this year.

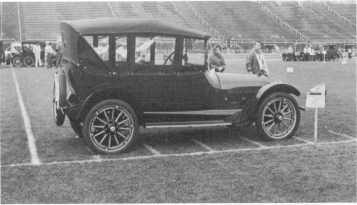

Buick's most popular car was the D-45 Touring, of which 25,371 were built for domestic sales and another 1,371 were built for export. It was finished in Buick special green with black fenders. This restored model is buttoned up for bad weather, with all side curtains in place.

Shown in its original state is this Model D-45, with its proud owner, Carl H. Kreidler of LaPorte, Indiana. Buicks still used a leather faced cone clutch in all cars.

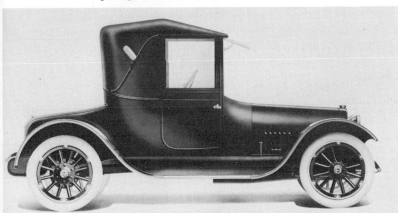

1917

Buick's lowest priced and lightest car was the 4-cylinder Model D-34, built on a 106-inch wheelbase chassis. The car cost $660 and weighed 1,900 pounds. Buick built 2,292 for domestic sales and another 238 for export. This model, shown after registering 60,000 miles in four years, was owned by G.W. Strumm, editor of the Painesville, Ohio, *Lake County Herald*.

Shown with its top down and front windows open is the Model D-34 Touring. This car was owned by the city of Ottumwa, Iowa, and was assigned to the water department. In the car is Horace A. Brown, then superintendent of the water works.

An unusual accessory for the Model D-34 Roadster was this "California" padded solid top, which could be removed. The top was well equipped with roll-up side curtains, and gave somewhat better weather protection than the plain roadster top. Shown here after he had logged 50,000 miles on the car is its owner, Dr. S.B. McGuire of Dover, Ohio.

models introduced in January would be carried over into the 1918 models again introduced in August. This sometimes would cause a condition where new 1916, 1917, and 1918 models would all be on the showroom floor at the same time. Since it is almost impossible to separate the annual models from the carry-overs, two choices appear for the automotive researcher — forget about model-years and concentrate strictly on series, or follow the annual model basis, such as is the format of this book, but listing the cars that were actually considered the model of a given year.

This book takes the latter route, using as its guide Buick's own model-year production sheets, and treating within each year only those models designated as being of that year, regardless of series or date of production. Therefore, the "D" Series, which was begun in 1916, is shown in this chapter because its production continued into 1917, and because the car is regarded by Buick as being its 1917 model. Then, the Series "E" is shown as a 1918 series, even though the major part of its production occurred in 1917. This system continues until the 1921 model year, when Buick changed over to the now traditional one annual model system.

Under this system, new for the year was a two-model line of 106-inch wheelbase cars, which were introduced in August. These were the 4-cylinder Model D-34 Roadster and D-35 Touring, powered by the year-old 170-cubic-inch engine that developed 18.2 SAE horsepower. Tires on these cars were 31 x 4 inches.

The D Series of Light Six cars used the 115-inch wheelbase instituted in 1916, and continued to run the year-old 224-cubic-inch engine of 3.25 x 4.5 bore and stroke. These cars used 34 x 4 inch tires.

Using the 4-cylinder engine of 170 cubic inches and a 106-inch wheelbase was the Model D-35 Touring, which was priced at $675. The car weighed 2,100 pounds. Buick built 20,126 for domestic sales and 1,097 for export. This model was owned by G.L. Schneider of Chicago. It is shown following a trip to California, just after the car had logged 28,000 miles.

The D-45 Touring car took on a completely different appearance when wearing a "Detroit Weatherproof" top, which was a $125 accessory offered by some Buick dealers. The removable "California style" top gave fairly good weather protection when fully sealed. The door openings were covered by rather interesting pull-down panels, that disappeared between the top and the headliner when not in use. However, these panels had to be slid up out of the way whenever anyone wanted to enter or leave the car.

The DuPont Co., which had been a definite factor in the development of Buick, bought a large fleet of Model D-44 Roadsters and converted them into these "salesmen's cars." The large box fitted to the rear was for carrying samples of DuPont merchandise. The spare tire was carried on top of the box, out of the way, but was rather difficult to remove when needed.

Unlike some of the lower priced cars, or the very expensive cars, the middle of the road Buick did not attract many custom body builders in the early years. However, the Bela Body Co. of Framinghan, Mass., did offer this 3-passenger cloverleaf custom body for use on the 115-inch wheelbase chassis. The body was constructed from seamless sheet aluminum, and followed the basic lines of the Model D-46 Coupe body.

Somewhere in England, women volunteers of the British Ambulance Corps tend to the maintenance of their vehicles. Note that these ambulances had completely different bodies from those used on the French ambulances. The chassis appear to be Model D-4 Truck chassis, built for export in 1916, but not actually put into service until 1917. Each ambulance in this line was presented to the Red Cross by some British civic organization.

Somewhere in France, this fleet of Buick ambulances, operated by the American Ambulance Corps, moved into the action. The vehicles were 1916 Model D-4-X trucks, built for export, but not put into actual service until 1917.

The E.M. Miller Co. of Quincy, Ill., was one of the major factors in the production of hearse and bus bodies in the early years. Among their designs this year was this beautiful, carved panel hearse on the 115-inch wheelbase, 6-cylinder chassis.

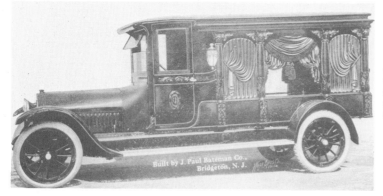

Another builder of fine hearses was the J. Paul Bateman Co. of Bridgeton, N.J. This firm produced this interesting glass and carved panel hearse for installation on the 6-cylinder chassis. The interior was lined with built-up wood, highly varnished and stained.

The Model D-45 chassis was used as a base for this combination ambulance-hearse produced by the August Schubert Wagon Co. of Oneida, N.Y. The body is shown here in hearse style. For ambulance work, the carved center panels on each side were removed, and replaced with plain glass panels, bearing a large red cross and the inscription "Private Ambulance." The Schubert Co. offered buyers a wide range of color options on these vehicles.

Houghton Motor Car Co. of Marion, Ohio, produced this interesting hearse-ambulance body using the Model D-45 chassis for its base. The style is shown here in hearse form, but minor changes on the exterior, and different interior furnishings were all that was required to outfit the vehicle as an ambulance. Coach lamps continued to be very popular on this type of vehicle.

World War I was taking its toll, and calendar year production was down to 77,691. This resulted in Buick dropping from third to fourth place as, for the first time, Chevrolet passed Buick in sales.

Considered in this book as the official model range for 1918 was the Series E, which was continued in both the 4- and 6-cylinder models. However, the Four appeared only at the start of the year. It disappeared in August with the introduction of the H Series, considered here to be the 1919 model range. The big engineering change on the Series E was the introduction of a new multiple disc clutch which replaced the old style cone clutch used for years by Buick.

The 4-cylinder line continued to use its 106-inch wheelbase and 170-cubic-inch engine, but it was no match in price for either the Model T or the Chevrolet Four, nor was it a match in value for the popular Dodge Four. Despite its wavering appeal, Buick tried to enhance the 4-cylinder line by introducing a small sedan and a delivery truck in the series. The sedan was a failure, and only 700 were built. However, the truck was a moderate success, and 2,410 were sold. The sedan, which was expected to sell primarily in the cities, used 23 x 3.5 inch tires. The truck and all open models, which were very popular in rural areas, continued to use the 31 x 4 inch tires, which were more at home on the muddy roads of the time than were the smaller wheels.

In the 6-cylinder line, all models were now on a newly designed 118-inch wheelbase, and were powered by a redesigned Six of 242 cubic inches. This engine used a bore and stroke of 3-3/8 x 4.5 inches and developed 60 brake or 27.3 SAE horsepower. In August, the E Series was joined by two 124-inch wheelbase seven-passenger vehicles. These were the Model E-49 Touring and the Model E-50 Sedan, with its body by Fisher. The 118-inch wheelbase cars continued to use 34 x 4 inch tires but the 124-inch models used 34 x 4.5 tires.

Buick's most expensive car was the new Model E-50 7-passenger sedan. It cost $2,175 and weighed 3,620, thus also being Buick's heaviest car of the year. Production was 987. The newly delivered car is shown here with its new owners, L.S. Ward and family of Kirkwood, Ill. Mr. Ward, then a nationally known landscape designer, managed to put 85,000 trouble free miles on this car in the next four years. The door posts were removable so that a touring car effect could be obtained in warm weather. Thus, the car, in effect, was Buick's first true hardtop sedan.

A detail view of the Model E-50 7-passenger sedan shows how the door posts could be removed when all of the windows were lowered. In this era, when open touring cars were still by far the most popular vehicle on the road, it was considered definitely advantageous from the point of sales to produce a closed car that could be converted into a type of open tourer. The style was dropped following this model year, and did not reappear until the "hardtop takeover" in the 1950s.

Buick returned to the 7-passenger field this year with the introduction of the Model E-49 Touring and E-50 Sedan. The touring was by far the most popular, with 16,148 being built. Both models used a new 124-inch wheelbase chassis. The touring cost $1,385 weighed 3,075 pounds, and was finished in Buick blue with black fenders. Shown here with his newly delivered model is B.P. Lisenby of Mt. Vernon, Ill., who had used Buick touring cars in his taxi business in that city since 1907. Mr. Lisenby immediately put this car into taxi service.

Shown with his newly delivered Model E-49 Touring is General Swinton, one of America's lesser known generals of World War I. Production figures on the Model E-49 conflict. The most accepted lists show production of 16,148 of these cars, but another Buick list claims production of only 5,643. It is impossible to ascertain which list is correct, but the assumption leans toward the higher figure, as the second comes from a list that is incomplete in many other areas.

In the style department, all open models took on a more modern look through the use of slanting windshields and wrap-around rear curtains, called gypsy tops. The rear window glass on these models continued to be a patent oval produced by the Johnston Company. All models continued to use rear wheel brakes only, with the service brake being of the external contracting type and the emergency-parking brake being of the expanding internal expanding type. Standard equipment on all cars included speedometer and ammeter, clock, electric horn, and demountable rims.

During the year Walter Marr retired. He had been

responsible for the highly successful initial 2-cylinder engine, and for Buick's continued use and improvement of the valve-in-head engine design, which has been a Buick hallmark since its inception. Unlike many of the great names associated with Buick during its early years, Marr had continued with the company since David C. Buick first conceived the car, had shunned publicity, and had quietly and conscientiously produced one fine engine after another, which was one of the main factors in Buick's continued success.

Across the border, the Canadian McLaughlin Company which had been very successful in assembling and selling basically Buick cars under the McLaughlin name, was sold to General Motors. As such, it became the foundation for General Motors of Canada in much the same manner as the American Buick company had become the cornerstone of General Motors. The cars still continued to be called McLaughlins, and still were primarily Buicks with slightly more elaborate and luxurious body work.

Buick's lightest 6-cylinder car was the Model E-44 Roadster, of which 10,391 were built for domestic sales and 275 were built for export. It weighed 2,750 and cost $1,265. Its standard color was Buick green with black fenders and radiator shell. This beautifully restored model is owned by Harold MacGillivray of Clio, Mich. Note the twin portholes in the rear curtain.

Going through a complete style change was the Model E-46 Coupe. The car was now a true coupe with a fixed top, instead of the true convertible that it had been in 1917. The change caused demand to increase by six-fold, and 2,965 were produced. The 3,250-pound car sold for $1,695. The car was described as a 4-passenger model, but in reality, three people was its true capacity.

Buick's most popular car was the Model E-45 Touring, of which 58,971 were built for domestic sales. Available only in Buick green with black fenders and radiator, the 2,850-pound car cost $1,265. This model is shown with its original owner, Miss Cressie Raupp of Decatur, Ill. Miss Raupp gained some renown in her home town after she completed a solo 13,000 mile trip around the country in this car. The car wears an accessory bumper and spotlight.

Buick's least popular car was the E-47 Sedan, of which only 463 were built. Surprisingly, the car weighed 3,230 pounds, or 30 pounds less than the E-46 Coupe. It cost $1,845. This was the first year that Buick used a multiple-disc clutch on all models, rather than the old cone clutch. Carburetors were Marvel, while ignition was Delco.

Shown with his new Model E-44 Roadster is the original owner, T.H. Hanrahan, president of the Buffalo Freight Terminal & Warehouse Co. of Buffalo, N.Y. This was Mr. Hanrahan's first car.

New for the year, and proving to be definitely unpopular, was the Model E-37 Sedan. Only 700 were built. The car weighed 2,420 pounds and cost $1,185. It was of the center door style, which meant all passengers had to enter into the rear compartment, then squeeze to the front.

The Chanslor & Lyon Co. of Seattle, distributors of Lee tires, supplied the new Model E-44 to its salesmen. This car uses a single window in its rear curtain. Note the accessory siren, bumper, and spotlight.

Mr. and Mrs. Phil Miler of Kewanee, Ill., posed proudly with their newly purchased Model E-37 Sedan, shortly before they left on a trouble-free 6,700 mile trip through New England and down the east coast. The trip was a bit remarkable because Mr. Miler had no legs, and had to operate the car with his cumbersome artificial limbs.

Appearing for the last time this year was the 4-cylinder line, the lightest of which was the Model E-34 Roadster, which weighed 1,900 pounds. The car was priced at $795. Buick built 3,800 for domestic use and exported an additional 172. This model is shown with its original owner, a Mr. R.C. Barnes. Note the accessory spotlight, extra leaf spring carried on the running board, and accessory bumper and dual spare tire carrier.

By far the most popular of the 4-cylinder line was the Model E-35 Touring. Buick built 27,125 for domestic sales, and shipped 1,190 more overseas. The car weighed 2,100 pounds, was priced at $795, the same as the roadster, and was available only in black. Its wheelbase was 106 inches.

1918

One of the 3,035 Model E-X-45 Touring Cars built for export wound up in Paris, France, in the form of this attractive open-front limousine. The body work, from the cowl rearward, is strictly of European custom design, though it could not be ascertained which form did the work.

The E-X-45 touring was Buick's most popular export model. A total of 3,035 were built, most with right-hand drive. Here a fleet of these cars arrives on the island of Jamaica. Eventually almost all of them wound up in the taxi business on that island.

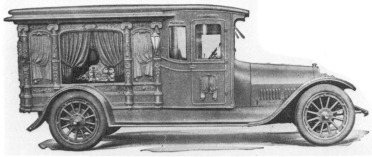

Produced this year only was the Model E-4 Light Delivery Truck, of which 2,410 were built. Fitted as a canopy express, as shown here, it cost $790 and weighed 2,050 pounds. It was also available as an open express or as a stripped chassis. Weather protection was by roll-up curtains all around, and the spare tire carrier was standard equipment. A seat back was provided on the driver's side only, but the seat cushion was full-length across the front.

Miller & Paine of Lincoln, Neb., still a major department store firm, used a fleet of the new Model E-4 Buicks for light delivery work. The trucks were purchased with the standard cowl and windshield, but special delivery bodies were fitted by the owners.

In addition to constructing their own hearse and ambulance bodies, the August Schubert Wagon Co. of Oneida, N.Y., also specialized in rebuilding ornate horse-drawn hearses into motorized vehicles. Here is one such example, built on the Model E-49 chassis. The original body ended just forward of the coach lamps, and has been successfully blended with the new chassis via a Schubert-built cab and roof. The center panel was of plate glass.

Somewhere in Europe, this Buick began its life as a 1915 Model C-4 truck. It was then bought by the French Red Cross, who built the shed-like ambulance body on the rear section. Following use by the French, it was captured by the Germans, who also used it as an ambulance. In 1919, it was recaptured in the condition shown here by the Americans, and was shipped to Washington, D.C., where it was put on permanent display at the American Red Cross Museum. It wears the Croix de Guerre and three other citations awarded to units with which it served.

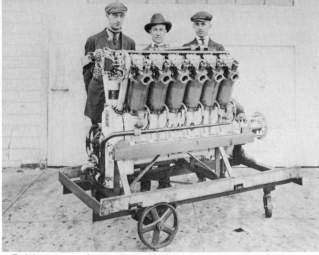

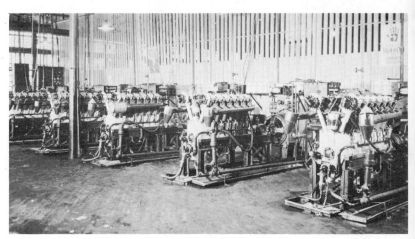

Buick was one of several companies to hold a contract for the production of Liberty aircraft engines for the U.S. Army during World War I. Under a contract shared with Cadillac, the two firms built a total of about 2,500 such engines. Other large producers of these famous and well designed power plants were Ford, Packard, Marmon, and Leyland. It was the production of these engines, and the termination of the contract at the end of the war, which caused Leyland to go directly into the automobile business and start producing the Lincoln cars.

A few of the 2,500 Liberty aircraft engines built by Buick and Cadillac are shown here being run in on their test stands. The Liberty engine turned out to be one of the most efficient and long-lived aircraft engines ever designed up to that time.

Buick's experimental war tractor is shown here undergoing tests at a slag dump in Flint. Buick also had plans for a completely armored cargo carrier version and an armored tank-type fighting version, but after the army lost interest, all plans were scrapped, as were the prototypes.

The front view of Buick's experimental crawler tractor shows some of the detail of the complicated combination brake and clutch devices that would have steered the vehicle. This version was destined to be used on a short wheelbase vehicle, similar to a modern bulldozer. It never went into production.

Buick's president Charles Nash is shown here test driving a long wheelbase war tractor that used Buick's experimental crawler power unit. In this form, the vehicle would have been used to tow heavy artillery pieces or large cargo trailers. However, the military decided that it wasn't interested in the vehicle, and production never went beyond this stage.

With emphasis on World War I, Buick's engineers experimented with several versions of a crawler tractor for use by the military. All used basically the same power unit, shown here in rear view. The gas tank was mounted over the standard 6-cylinder engine, and a conventional clutch and transmission was employed. Steering would have been by the outboard combination brake and clutch mechanisms, controlled by the two side levers.

World War I was ended, and as could be expected, production zoomed upward, hitting a healthy 119,310 in the calendar year. In addition, Willys-Overland, which had held second place in production since 1912, had a disastrous year, and tumbled from second to fifth place. This resulted in the top three automobile producers being Ford, Chevrolet and Buick respectively.

Since the Four was dropped, all of Buick's production was powered by only one engine, a fact that had not occurred in the past dozen years. The engine was the relatively new 252-cubic-inch block introduced on the Series E. Although the engine was unchanged mechanically, it now sported valve, spark plug, and push rod covers which not only gave the parts better protection from dirt and water, but also made the engine a much better looking piece of machinery.

The 1919 line is considered to be the Series H for all practical purposes. Basically these cars were the same as the Series E. The 118-inch wheelbase with 33 x 4 inch tires was used on all five-passenger models, while the seven-passenger cars used the 124-inch wheelbase with 34 x 4.5 tires.

In the styling department, a few more hood louvers were added, but the radiator and hood contour remained the same as on the Series E. New for the year was a Delco combination ignition and light switch with lever controls, which replaced the former pull-type switch. Also new for the year was an illuminated instrument panel.

The Model H-49 Touring and the H-50 Sedan, both 7-passenger cars, used their own exclusive 124-inch wheelbase chassis. This is the Model H-49, of which 6,795 were built. The car weighed 3,175 pounds and cost $1,985. All open models used a slanting windshield. Leather paint saver pads were provided on both doors and body panels front and rear. Upholstery was of black leather, with hair padding.

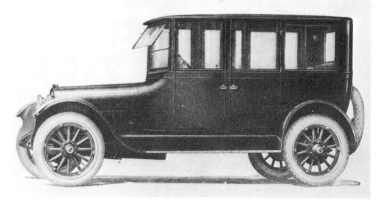

Only slightly more popular than the 5-passenger sedan was the Model H-50 7-passenger version. Buick produced 531. The car was Buick's heaviest and most expensive model this year, weighing 3,736 pounds and costing $2,585. The two auxiliary rear seats disappeared into the back of the full-width front seat when not in use. Silk roller shades were fitted on all rear quarter windows and on the rear window. Reading lights were provided in the rear quarters, while another light by the rear door illuminated both the door and the step.

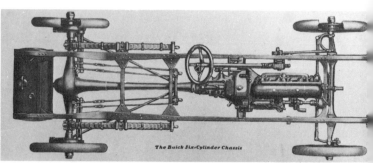

The Buick Six-Cylinder Chassis

Buick's chassis was on par with or better than most other cars in its price class, even though it does look fragile by today's standards. Front springs were semi-elliptic directly under the frame rails, while the rear springs were exceptionally long cantilever type, outboard from the frame. Brakes were still mechanical on the rear wheels only, the service brake being of the external contracting type while the parking brake was of the internal expanding type.

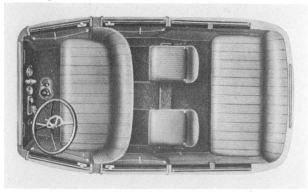

This interior view of the H-50 7-passenger sedan shows that the car was fairly spacious even when the auxiliary seats were in place. As in the 5-passenger version, the door windows were controlled by mechanical risers, while the quarter windows used adjustable straps.

Buick's lightest car this year was the new Model H-44 Roadster, which weighed 2,813 pounds. Described as a 3-passenger vehicle, the car cost $1,595. Buick produced 7,839 for domestic sales and 176 for export. Upholstery was in French pleated leather.

Buick's most popular car this year was the Model H-45 Touring, of which 44,589 were built for domestic sales. The car cost $1,595, and weighed 2,950 pounds. Standard equipment included the leather hand-holds on the top's of each door, the top boot, and side curtains.

Long-distance touring was still no easy matter in 1919. Here Mrs. Mittie Baldwin-Hall and companions take a well-earned breather after driving their new Model H-45 Touring from Seattle to Atlanta, Ga. Note the large tool box mounted on the running board and the tent poles strapped to the side. Spotlight and front bumper were popular accessories.

The lowest production model this year was the Model H-47 Sedan, of which only 501 were built. The 3,296-pound car cost $2,195. New for the year were the solid door posts, which could not be removed as in the 1918 style. Thus the car was now a true sedan, and not a "hardtop" style.

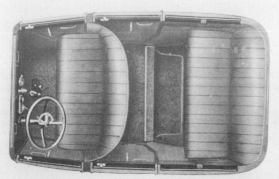

The Wilson Machinery Co. of Denver used Buicks exclusively for their business cars. Here Mrs. Wilson prepares to drive away in the company's new Model H-46. Note the winter gear, consisting of chains on the rear wheels, and a cover over the hood to keep the engine temperature high.

Dr. A.B. Elmer of Rochelle, Ill., proudly accepts delivery of his new Model H-46 Coupe. The 3,100-pound car cost $2,085. Buick built 2,971, all for domestic sales.

An interesting interior design was employed in the Model H-46 Coupe. Two passengers could squeeze into the recessed large seat, while another could perch on the small folding jump seat by the dashboard. The jump seat passenger would have to ride backward, and his head would obviously obstruct the driver's view. The small compartment behind the driver's seat was a tool box, and the space on top of this could be used to store small packages.

Both the interior and exterior of the new Model H-47 Sedan followed very closely the design, workmanship and appointments of the Model H-50 7-passenger sedan, with the main difference being in wheelbase and seating capacity. The door windows were raised or lowered by mechanical risers, while the quarter panel windows were regulated by adjustment straps.

Looking very un-Buick-like is this Model H-44 Roadster, fitted with Houk wire wheels, a "California" padded top, and rakish spare tire carrier. Houk wheels were far superior to any standard wheels of the day, but their high price made them out of reach of many buyers.

Shown here in Mexico's Yucatan is one of the 2,595 Model H-X-45 Touring Cars that Buick built for export. This model, because it was destined for a Mexican buyer, was fitted with left-hand drive, while most export models were built with right-hand control.

Many of the 2,595 Model H-X-45 Buicks built for export were shipped to Australia this year. There, in a series of preformance tests run for all cars, Buick won its class in every test. The chassis, with right-hand drive, were shipped to Australia, and fitted with Australian bodies. In this photo, car No. 9 in the inset won a one-day gasoline consumption run with an average of 30.19 miles per Imperial gallon. The three cars in the main photo won first, second and third place in a 107-mile run over a rugged section of hill country.

One of the stranger things to be built on a Buick chassis was this covered wagon type camper, based on a Model H-49 chassis. The vehicle has been fitted for winter use, via skid chains and a radiator cover of adjustable louvers. Driver visibility must have been exceedingly poor.

A more conventional camping outfit of the era is this unit, shown on a Model H-45 Touring in Glacier National Park. The tent floor hooked directly to the running board, while the tent top was anchored to the floor on one end and to the car top on the other, utilizing the same clips used for the side curtains. The bumper and spotlight were among the most popular accessories.

In the world of numbers, production slipped slightly this year, with 115,176 Buicks being built. However, Buick again dropped to fourth place in the industry, as Dodge went into a tremendous production binge that shot the company not only past Buick but past Chevrolet as well and made it the second place manufacturer behind Ford.

But the slippage, though small on the surface, had very deep roots. General Motors stock had dropped from $400 a share to less than $300 during 1919, even though corporate profits passed $60 million. By 1920, the postwar slump was in effect, and auto prices were being slashed by all companies but General Motors. By mid-1920, carloads of unsold General Motors vehicles stood on railroad sidings across the country. By October, Chevrolet had curtailed all production, and General Motors executives were even considering killing the company for good.

In July, a knife was plunged into General Motors when 00,000 shares of GM stock were dumped on the market at $20.50 per share. Durant personally bought these in an effort to save the company. More and more stock was dumped, and the price kept going down, to a low of $12 per share. Durant used his entire personal wealth to try to save the company. Within the year, Durant's personal fortune went from over $90-million to $2-million in debt.

To keep these Durant shares from sliding back into the panic market, the DuPont family assumed Durant's obligations. The transaction left Durant with a considerable sum of money, but the 3-million shares he held were transferred to the DuPonts. Thus, once more, control of General Motors slipped from Durant's hands. On November 30, a heartbroken Durant attended his final board meeting, and then left General Motors, never again to return.

It has been noted by many writers that on that day, a great many tears were shed by General Motors and Buick executives and employees of every rank and station. Durant was recognized as a genius by virtually everyone. But those who knew him and worked for and with him saw far more than merely a brillant man. Here was a person who would sacrifice everything for that in which he believed, and who would dissipate his own personal fortune in an effort to keep those who trusted in him from losing their investments.

He stood not above his workers and his fellow men, but among them. And thus, in their minds, he soared to the greatest heights imaginable.

With Durant out of General Motors, Pierre DuPont became General Motor's president as well as chairman. Walter P. Chrysler had left Buick late in 1919, and was now considering taking over the shaky Maxwell company. Harry M. Bassett, formerly of Weston Mott Axle Company, a General Motors subsidiary, took over as Buick's new president. Durant, meanwhile, still energetic, started laying the groundwork for still another automotive empire that he would create. This empire also succeeded to a degree, but it was wiped out in the great depression of the late 20's and 1930's. After that, Durant lived in comparative obscurity and modest means until his death in 1947.

On the automotive scene, this year's Buick line was considered the Series K, but for all practical purposes, it was simply the Series H held over. All models continued with virtually no change whatever in either styling or engineering. About the most noticeable change in any model was the use of 34 x 4.5 inch tires on the 118-inch wheelbase Model K-47 Sedan. This was the same size tire used by the 124-inch wheelbase seven-passenger models, whereas all other 118-inch wheelbase cars used 33 x 4 inch tires.

Buick's most expensive, heaviest, and least popular car was the huge Model K-50 7-passenger sedan, built on a 124-inch wheelbase chassis. The car cost $2,695, and weighed 3,736 pounds. Buick built only 1,499, which was still three times its production of the 1919 7-passenger sedan. Shown with his newly delivered car is its owner, Simon W. Baker of Shamokin, Pa.

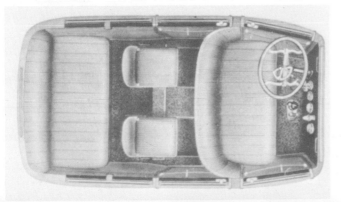

Another view of the Model K-50 7-passenger sedan shows its massive but appealing line. This car is shown with its new owner, Mrs. George Tayloe, wife of the owner of the Tayloe Paper Co. of Memphis, Tenn.

The interior design of the new Model K-50 sedan followed the style set in 1919. Silk roller shades were provided for the rear and quarter windows, and reading lights were provided in each corner of the quarter panel. The auxiliary seats would disappear into the front seat back when not in use. Quarter windows still used straps for raising and lowering.

Still a very popular car was the huge Model K-49 7-passenger Touring, of which 16,801 were produced for domestic sales and another 1,100 were built for export. The car cost $1,785 and weighed 3,175 pounds. It is shown here with its original owner, Mr F.J. Spies Jr., then vice-president of the Bartlesville, Okla., National Bank.

By a wide margin, Buick's most popular car was the Model K-45 Touring. Production hit a record 85,245 for domestic sales and an additional 7,400 for export. The car weighed 2,950 pounds. Shown here with her new car after accepting delivery is Miss Clara Horton, a Goldwin Photoplay star who gained fame for her supporting role in *The Little Shepherd of the Hills.*

The Model K-46 Coupe received a sudden spurt in popularity this year, and production shot up to 6,503, all for domestic sales. The car weighed 3,100 pounds and cost $2,085. Pictured here with her brand new car is Miss Charlotte Pence of Minneapolis, daughter of the Buick distributor in that city. Miss Pence entered her car in the 1920 Minnesota State Fair, where it won first prize for beauty of design and workmanship.

Seen from the back, the Model K-46 Coupe shows the small but functional trunk that had surprisingly spacious luggage capacity for the era. The low-mounted spare allowed easy access to the trunk and also served as a rear bumper. The huge back window was fitted with a silk roller shade. The quarter windows could be lowered, but the rear window was stationary. The wheels shown here are very rare demountable wood-spoke wheels, rather than the demountable rims typically used with wood-spoke wheels. There was no indication as to the manufacturer of these wheels. Today, they would be deemed a very rare and desirable accessory, though they enjoyed virtually no popularity in this era.

Buick's lightest car was the Model K-44 Roadster, which weighed 2,813 pounds. The popular little vehicle had an amazing production run of 19,000 units for domestic sales and 200 more for export. It and its companion Model K-45 Touring were both priced at $1,495.

Just as the coupe climbed in popularity, so too did the new 5-passenger sedan. The Model K-47 this year hit a production run of 2,252, indicating a definite growing acceptance of closed cars in preference to open models. The K-47 cost $2,255 and weighed 3,296 pounds. Shown ready to take a run in their brand new sedan are Harold and Mirian Wagner of Beloit, Wis.

Especially built for Ferdinand of Savoy, Prince of Udine, a member of the Royal Italian family, was this magnificent 5-passenger touring speedster. The full-custom bodywork, done by Alessio, included a novel radiator shell and upper hood panels. The headlights are standard Buick, but appear to have been nickel plated. The car appears to be based on the Model K-45 Touring, of which 7,400 were built for the export trade this year. During this era, Buick was beginning to enjoy a wide reputation overseas for its stamina and dependability, and was being ordered by many royal houses and governments, either in stock form or as chassis for custom bodies.

In Canada, the McLaughlin Buicks were looking more and more like their American cousins. The McLaughlins used a diamond shaped emblem, while U.S. Buicks used the square design. The heavy bumper on this model is an accessory. This well restored car is now in the Sloan Panorama of Transportation in Flint, Mich. The McLaughlin Co. was bought by General Motors in 1918.

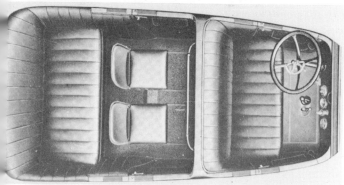

The interior of the Model K-49 Touring was quite different from the Model K-50 Sedan. The front seat has a straight back, topped with a small tonneau cowl, and the upholstery of the rear seat is continued around the quarter panels and into the rear door edge. The interiors were finished in black leather with black carpeting in the rear and hard rubber front floor panels. Note that the open model does not use the tilting steering wheel. The open model also was fitted with a robe rail behind the front seat, but this was not used on the sedan.

One of the few Buicks of this era to be found on the race tracks was this conversion of a 1920 Model K-44. It was built and driven by J.O. Morgan, a mid-western dirt track driver of some local fame. The body features interesting cowl work, but looks strangely chopped because of the lack of any rear body work. Houck wire wheels and a custom hood were used.

Take one old but heavy car, one ingenious mechanic, and the result is one rather different but functional truck. Here a Model 47 has been converted to a log hauler by R.O. Hamill of the Ludington Basket Co. of Ludington, Mich. The car's chassis was welded to the rear end chassis section of a worn out truck, and the rear half of the body was simply sawed off. The conversion gave years of service, making two 70-mile round trips a day between the logging woods and the company's sawmill in all types of weather.

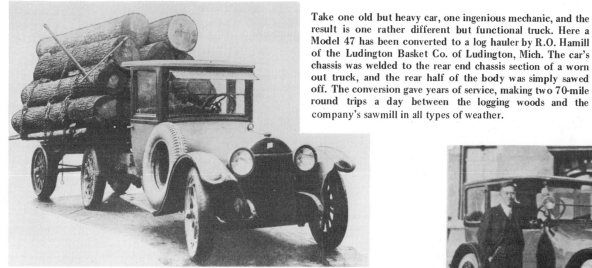

At least one of the 1,100 Model K-X-49 Touring Cars that Buick built for export wound up in China. The car was first shipped to Japan, where this open front limousine body was added. From there the car was shipped to Mukden, Manchuria, where it served as a courtesy vehicle for the Yamato Hotel in that city.

Buick's most expensive, heaviest, and least popular car continued to be the 7-passenger sedan, now designated the Model 21-50. The car cost $3,295, and weighed 3,612 pounds. Only 1,480 were built. It was finished in Buick blue body and black fenders and upper portion, or all black.

Still a popular large car was the Model 21-49 7-passenger touring, of which 6,429 were built for domestic sales and another 366 were built for export. The 3,272-pound car cost $2,060. It was finished in Buick blue with black fenders, or in all black. Shown in the car is Mrs. Z.K. Ayres of San Francisco, who had just won the 1921 San Francisco Women's Driving Championship.

Shown here with its top raised and carrying a full complement of passengers is the popular 7-passenger touring, the Model 21-49. Although open cars still outsold closed models by a wide margin, more and more people were beginning to pay attention to the year-around comforts of closed vehicles, especially as roads became better and average driving speeds increased. New for the year was Buick's large 4-passenger coupe, designated the Model 21-48 and built on the 124-inch wheelbase chassis. Finished in Buick blue with black fenders and upper portion, the 3,397-pound car cost $2,985. Buick built 2,606.

Buick this year changed from a letter designation to a numerical designation for its series, with the new model logically being called the Series 21. The cars sported higher hoods and radiators and had a smoother and less round contour than did the Series K's. But, with this exception, there was little difference between the two series.

The fact that no radical styling was contemplated was due in large part to the economy. The predicted postwar depression had settled down with far more severity than expected, and Buick, along with many other manufacturers, felt the squeeze. Production sagged to 82,930 for the calendar year, but still there were others who were even harder hit. Two of the companies to feel the pressure the most were Chevrolet and Dodge, the latter which had enjoyed an amazingly successful production run in the previous year. Both Chevrolet and Dodge drastically curtailed production, and Buick was again able to regain second place, right behind Ford in the country's list of top auto manufacturers.

All of the production used the 242-cubic-inch Six for power and all models were built on either the 118-inch or the 124-inch wheelbase. All models this year used 34 x 4.5 inch tires. Brakes were still on the rear wheels only, with the service brake still being of the contracting type and the emergency brake being of the expanding type.

New for the year was the Model 21-48 Coupe, a four-passenger car built on the 124-inch wheelbase, and using a Fisher body. All models used a rear-mounted spare tire carrier, but only on the 124-inch wheelbase models could an optional 2-tire rack be installed. All closed models had cowl-mounted parking lights as standard equipment, but these were optional accessories on the open models. After January 1, 1921, cord tires became standard equipment on all Buicks. Also standard on all models were a windshield wiper, dash-mounted gasoline gauge, speedometer, ammeter, electric horn, and demountable rims.

While production was sagging, Buick engineers were busy concocting another new engine. This was to be an improved Four, which it was hoped would allow the company to better compete in the overall market by offering a car for the average man's now squeezed bank account.

1921

Buick's most popular sedan was the 5-passenger Model 21-47, built on a 118-inch wheelbase. Sales reached 3,621. The car weighed 3,397 pounds and cost $2,895. It was available only in black. Silk roller shades were still provided on the rear and quarter windows.

Buick's most popular car was the Model 21-45 5-passenger touring, of which 31,877 were built for domestic use. The car was finished in Buick green body with black fenders and radiator shell and straw yellow wheels and trim. The interior and top were black. The car weighed 2,972 pounds and cost $1,795. This beautifully restored example is owned by Bill Chapman of Flint, Mich.

Weighing only 2,845 pounds, Buick's Roadster continued to be its lightest car. Designated the model 21-44, the car this year was fininshed in Buick green with straw yellow wheels and black top. The attractive car, featuring totally new body styling, sold for $1,795. Buick built 7,236 for domestic use and another 56 for export. Shown shortly after taking delivery of this model is its owner, Dr. J. George Hoffman of Milwaukee, Wis.

Buick this year had two distinctly different 4-passenger coupes, one on a 118-inch wheelbase, and the other on a 124-inch wheelbase. This is the 118-inch model, designated the Model 21-46. Available only in black, the 3,137-pound car cost $2,585. Buick built 4,063. The cowl lights were standard on all closed models this year, but the bumper was still an accessory. The Model 21-47 Sedan still used adjustable straps to raise or lower the quarter windows. The small quarter panel reading lights were removed, and replaced by a single dome lamp. Silk roller shades were still provided for the quarter and rear windows.

The Model 21-44 Roadster offered very conventional seating, but had an interesting little covered parcel compartment behind the seat. Roadsters were not carpeted.

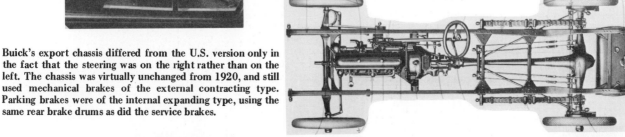

Buick's export chassis differed from the U.S. version only in the fact that the steering was on the right rather than on the left. The chassis was virtually unchanged from 1920, and still used mechanical brakes of the external contracting type. Parking brakes were of the internal expanding type, using the same rear brake drums as did the service brakes.

Just as the Model 21-45 Touring was Buick's most popular car in the U.S., its export counterpart, the Model 21-X-45 was the most popular export vehicle of the year, with 1,192 being built. Proudly displaying his newly delivered export version is A.G. Hillberg, a prominent consulting engineer in Manila, Philippines. The tool box and bumper were accessories.

The Model 21-44 Roadster was fairly popular in the U.S., but its export sales were virtually insignificant. Only 56 were built for overseas shipment. All were virtually identical to the U.S. models, except that most were built with right-hand drive.

Buick wasn't doing much racing on the tracks, but one west coast dealer gained much publicity by racing on the roads. In a standard Model 21-46 Coupe, he raced the Southern Pacific's fastest limited from San Francisco to Portland, Ore. The car, seen here splashing through some of the typical roads of that time, made the 750 mile trip in 29 hours, and thus beat the train's scheduled time.

One of the 366 Model 21-X-49 Touring Cars built for export is shown here after winning the mid-winter 785-mile Swedish reliability run. The car carried a driver, navigator, mechanic and race official, plus a full complement of tools and fuel. The boards on the sides were for getting out of deep mud or snow. Note the large headlights fitted to the cowl, and the extra spare carried on the side, in addition to the two carried on the rear rack.

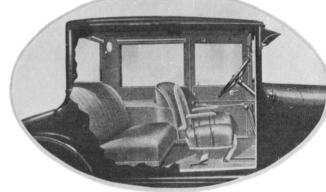

The Model 21-48 Coupe, which used a 124-inch wheelbase featured a forward facing jump seat for the fourth passenger. The folding seat was equipped with double armrests. Also, this model differed from the Model 21-46 in that roller shades were provided for both rear and quarter windows, and quarter panel reading lights were still used.

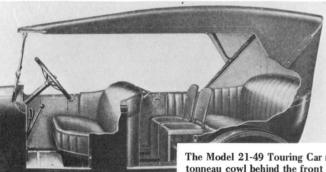

The Model 21-49 Touring Car no longer was equipped with a tonneau cowl behind the front seat, and that seat now curved in the same manner as did the front seats of the sedans. However, the rear seat upholstery was still carried completely around the rear quarters to the door edges. Notice that the open cars continued to use slant windshields while the closed models had vertical windshields. The front compartments of the touring models were not carpeted.

The interior of the 118-inch wheelbase coupe still used a small and uncomfortable rear-facing jump seat for the fourth passenger. The interior design was essentially the same as used in 1918. With the jump seat folded, the car was a fairly spacious 3-passenger vehicle. A silk roller shade was provided for the rear window only.

Buick's new 4-cylinder engine was introduced, and it had the expected effects — production rose to 123,152 as a combination of the Four and Six gave a wider market spread and put Buick within reach of the average middle-class wage earner. Yet, both Chevrolet and Dodge pulled back into gear, and with such force that Buick tumbled back to its fourth place standing, despite its impressive production gains.

The big news car, of course, was the new Four, introduced in August, 1921, as a 1922 model. The engine used a 3-3/8 x 4.75 bore and stroke and developed 18.23 SAE horsepower from its 170 cubic inches. This new block lived in a completely new series of 109-inch wheelbase cars, consisting of a touring car, a roadster, coupe, and a sedan. Tires on these cars were 31 x 4 inches, and all electrical components were Delco.

At the start of the year, the 6-cylinder line was almost identical with the 1921 models. After about two months of production, the spare tire carriers on all models were changed, but since the change was made after 1922 production was well under way, it is impossible to date the cars by the tire carriers. As with the 1921 models only the 124-inch wheelbase cars could mount the optional dual spare tires.

The 6-cylinder line continued to use the well-known 242-cubic-inch block of 3-3/8 x 4.5 bore and stroke, rated at 27.3 SAE horsepower. The engine now featured double heater pipes from the exhaust manifold to the carburetor. As before, Delco electrical equipment and Alemite lubrication were used. The line continued to use both the 118-inch and 124-inch wheelbases, with the 118-inch models again using 33 x 4 tires while the seven-passenger cars used 34 x 4.5 inch tires.

In January, 1922, Buick introduced its Sport Roadster, Model 22-54. This was a sleek-looking maroon car with red Houk wire wheels of 32 x 4.5 inch size. It used the 124-inch wheelbase chassis, was upholstered in red Spanish leather and red wool carpeting, and its instruments

included a Van Sicklen speedometer and clock. In May, its companion was introduced. This was the Model 22-55 Sport Touring, which was finished in the same manner as the Sport Roadster. Essentially, this car was the Model 22-45 five-passenger touring body set on the 124-inch wheelbase chassis and finished in luxurious materials. Appointments included Houk wire wheels and a small leather-covered trunk at the rear. Both the Sport Roadster and Sport Tourer used a rectangular rear window as opposed to the oval rear windows used on the regular touring and roadster models.

Buick's 5-passenger 6-cylinder sedan, the Model 22-47, used the 118-inch wheelbase chassis. But, the car was catching on in popularity, and 4,878 were produced. Available only in black, the 3,425-pound car sold for $2,435. A hand-operated windshield wiper was standard this year.

Surprisingly, Buick's most popular car on the 124-inch wheelbase chassis was not the Touring, but was the 4-passenger Model 22-48 Coupe. Finished in Buick blue, the 3,430-pound car had a production run of 8,903, signifying a definite trend away from open cars to the year-around comfort of closed styles. The coupe cost $2,325.

The 7-passenger Model 22-49 Touring used the 124-inch wheelbase chassis, but otherwise looked very similar to the Model 22-45. Available only in black, the 3,280-pound car sold for $1,735. Buick built 6,714 for domestic sales and 71 for export. Late in the year, the 5-passenger Model 22-55 Touring was introduced. This car used the Model 22-45 body and the 124-inch wheelbase chassis, with an extended luggage rack on the rear. Priced at $1,785 and weighing 3,270 pounds, the car sported an attractive maroon finish. Buick built 900. Also introduced late in the year was the Sport Roadster, Model 22-54. This also was mounted on the 124-inch wheelbase chassis, and was finished in maroon with red wheels. Buick built 2,562. The car cost $1,785, and weighed 3,180 pounds.

Still the heavy weight of the line was the 7-passenger Model 22-50 Sedan, which this year weighed 3,615 pounds. The car was priced at a hefty $2,635, still Buick sold 4,201. All closed cars continued to have cowl lights as standard equipment, while the open models did not.

Buick's lightest 6-cylinder car was the Model 22-44 Roadster, which weighed 2,285 pounds. It sold for $1,495. Buick built 7,666 for domestic sales, but only nine for export.

Buick's most expensive and least popular car was the pretentious Model 22-50-L Limousine. The 7-passenger car was priced at $2,735. Only 178 were built, with buyers having a choice of left or right-hand drive. All tonneau windows were equipped with roller shades, and the tool box, coach grips, and speaking tube were standard equipment.

Again, two 4-passenger coupes were offered, one on the 124-inch wheelbase chassis, and this one on the 118-inch wheelbase chassis. The smaller model, designated the Model 22-46, cost $2,135 and weighed 3,235 pounds. It was available only in black. Only 2,293 were built.

Buick's popularity leader of the year was the 6-cylinder Model 22-45 Touring, of which 34,433 were built for domestic sales and another 449 were produced for export. The 5-passenger car weighed 3,005 pounds and sold for $1,525. A robe rail and leather hand grips on all four doors were standard equipment. The car used the 118-inch wheelbase chassis.

The Rex Mfg. Co. of Connersville, Ind., continued to offer its Rex California Top for both the 5- and 7-passenger touring cars. These tops produced a fairly snug car in winter, while still leaving the owner with an open car for warmer days.

The 7-passenger touring used its extra six inches in wheelbase length to squeeze in two extra seats. However, with the jump seats raised as shown here, rear seat passengers were rather cramped for knee space. The jump seats were as uncomfortable as they looked.

Rather surprisingly, the 4-cylinder Model 22-37 Sedan received a fairly good reception for this type of car, and 3,118 were built. The 2,780-pound cars were listed at prices ranging from $1,395 to $1,650. A switch on the door post controlled the dome light.

In a surprise move, Buick returned to producing 4-cylinder cars. By far the most popular of the 4-cylinder line was the Model 22-35 Touring, of which 22,521 were built for domestic sales. The car weighed 2,380 and is listed at prices ranging from $935 to $975. This restored version, all buttoned up for wet weather, is owned by Rube Wright of Shoemakersville, Pa.

Buick's least expensive car this year was the 4-cylinder Model 22-34 Roadster, which is listed at prices ranging from $895 to $935. The 2,310-pound car had a production run of 5,583. The Fours used the same multiple disc clutch and drive train as did the larger models.

The least popular of the 4-cylinder Buicks was the Model 22-36 Coupe, of which only 2,225 were built. The 3-passenger car was listed at prices ranging from $1,295 to $1,475. It weighed 2,560 pounds. Unlike the larger coupes, this model used a straight bench seat.

Buick's 4-cylinder Touring was not popular overseas, and surprisingly, the Model 22-X-34 export Roadster was even less popular. In fact, only five were built with right-hand drive, apparently all on special order.

The little 4-cylinder touring was popular in the U.S., but not overseas. Buick listed its export version as the model 22-X-35, but only 29 were built. The export version was identical to the U.S. model except that it used right-hand drive.

1922

The full 4-passenger coupe, on the 124-inch wheelbase, retained its forward facing jump seat with armrests. The 118-inch wheelbase model, called a 3 to 4 passenger coupe, still had its small rear-facing jump seat. Quarter panel reading lamps and large roller shades on the rear and quarter panel windows were still standard.

The Roadster continued to feature a small storage compartment behind the seat, in addition to the large compartment in the rear deck. The upholstery was in leather.

The 5-passenger sedan used a single dome light, while the 7-passenger model used quarter panel reading lights similar to those in the large coupe. Both sedans continued to use adjustment straps for the quarter windows, while risers were used for the door windows.

The 5-passenger touring provided ample seating space and leg room for its passengers. All open cars were equipped with small storage pouches in each door.

The new Buick Four chassis was more than ample for the era. Tires were 31 x 4 inches, with the same tread being used on all four wheels. The 6-cylinder line still used non-skid tread on the rear wheels and cord tread on the front tires. The steering wheel was 17-inches in diameter. Service brakes were still of the external contracting type on the rear wheels only.

Buick's new 4-cylinder engine was a nice clean appearing piece of machinery, with all moving parts now protected by covers of various types. The engine ran through a multiple-disc clutch.

Buick's lowest priced truck was the open express, which was priced at $945. All three trucks used the same vestibule cab, and varied only in the design of the cargo area. An Alemite grease gun and a full set of tools were supplied with each truck.

A return was made to the trucking business this year, with the introduction of the S.D.-4 light delivery truck. Only 403 were built and some consider these all 1923 models. The most popular bodies were the panel shown here, an express, and a canopy delivery. The panel, priced at $980, featured a vestibule body and double rear doors. It was finished in blue-black with gold trim. Unlike earlier panel trucks, the sides of this body were of sheet steel on a wood frame.

The canopy delivery version of the new S.D.-4 truck used the same body dimensions as did the panel delivery, but featured a drop-type tailgate and roll-up curtains for the cargo bed. Standard equipment included electric lights and horn, and speedometer and gasoline gauge.

Station wagons were still 50 years from full popularity, yet a large number of small body firms built a wide variety of these bodies for most popular makes. This rather attractive depot hack body is mounted on the new S.D.-4 truck chassis. It appears that a type of alligator hide covering has been used for both the seats and the body panels. Weather protection was by roll-up curtains. Sadly, the maker of this body could not be ascertained.

Yes, it is a 1922 Buick — or at least it started its life as such. This beautiful and very modern raceabout is one of four built on the west coast by a Mr. Battistini, and is the only one still known to exist. It is owned by Jerrol J. Largin of Stockton, Cal. The car features Houk wire wheels and a completely custom body, hood, fenders and radiator shell. Still, the running gear is all 6-cylinder Buick.

Following the postwar depression, a boom time of sorts occurred, and good times were reflected by virtually every auto company in the U.S. Buick enjoyed a record production of 201,572 vehicles this year, which again boosted it up to third place in the industry, beaten only by Ford and Chevrolet. Part of this increase was due to the overall economic conditions, and part was due to the long-awaited drastic price reductions on all models which put Buick in a much better competitive light.

All cars had a more modern look via the use of new crowned fenders and drum headlights and cowl lights. Also new for the year was a built-in lock on the transmissions, and cowl ventilators for all closed models.

The 4-cylinder cars used the same 109-inch wheelbase as used previously. The engine also was basically unchanged except that oil holes were added to the valve covers, as was done on the 6-cylinder line also. The 6-cylinder cars used the same basic engine of 3-3/8 x 4.5 inch bore and stroke. Wheelbases remained 118 and 124 inches, but the tire size was reduced to 32 x 4 inches on 118-inch models and 33 x 4.5 on the 124-inch wheelbase cars. All open sport models used 32 x 4.5 inch wheels.

The 4-cylinder line was increased to six models through the addition of a Sport Roadster and a Touring Sedan, both with nickled radiator shells. The 6-cylinder line remained at nine models, but a Touring Sedan was added as a new model to replace the Model 46 Coupe, which was dropped at mid-year in 1922.

All 4-cylinder open models continued to use an oval rear window, but all 6-cylinder open cars now used the rectangular rear windows similar to those introduced on the Sport Touring and Sport Roadster in 1922. Introduced in January was the companion to the 6-cylinder sport models. This was the 4-cylinder Sport Roadster, Model 23-29, which reflected the same maroon and red trim of its larger brother. The car was available with wood spoke Houk wire, or Tuarc steel disc wheels.

New for the year was a return to the truck field. This was accomplished by the introduction of a one half ton light delivery truck. The vehicle used the 109-inch wheelbase chassis, running gear and engine of the 4-cylinder line. The truck was offered for this year only, and was dropped at the start of the 1924 season.

Across the border in Canada, the fifteen-year agreement between McLaughlin (now part of General Motors of Canada) and Durant drew to a close and as the agreement terminated, the McLaughlin cars were renamed McLaughlin-Buick. This seemed quite logical, as it had been many years since there was any real difference between the Canadian McLaughlins and the U.S. Buicks, either mechanically or in bodywork.

Companion car to the Sport Touring was the model 23-54 Sport Roadster which enjoyed a very favorable production run of 4,501. As was the Sport Touring, the Sport Roadster was finished in maroon with red wheels, used a nickel radiator shell, and featured windwings and motometer. Buyers had a choice of wood or wire spoke wheels. The car used the 124-inch wheelbase chassis. The bars immediately behind the top protected the body when the top was down.

This rear view of the outstanding Model 23-55 of Basil Lewis shows the attractive rear treatment used on the Sport Touring. The trunk, body guards, double spare tire carrier, side curtains, and white wall tires were all standard equipment. Note the guards on the rear panel, to keep the removable trunk from scratching the body.

A beautiful car, enjoying excellent sales, was the Model 23-55 5-passenger Sport Touring, which had a production run of 12,857. The 3,330-pound vehicle was finished in maroon, with red wire wheels and upholstery, and a khaki top. It cost $1,675. Basically, the car was the 5-passenger touring body running on the 124-inch wheelbase chassis, and mounting its own special trunk and double rear spares. This outstanding example is owned by Basil Lewis of Kalamazoo, Mich.

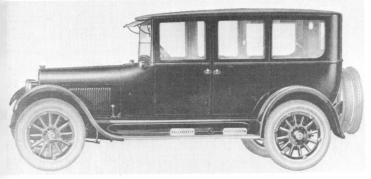

Buick's most expensive and heaviest car continued to be the Model 23-50 7-passenger sedan, which cost $2,195 and weighed 3,670 pounds. It was the only Buick priced over $2,000. There were 10,279 built for domestic sales, but only one special order model was exported. Buyers had a choice of wood spoke or disc wheels, with the disc wheels being at slight extra cost.

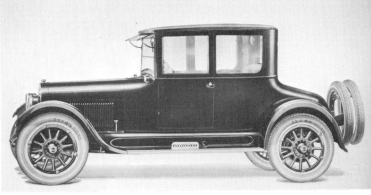

Production of the 4-passenger, 124-inch wheelbase Model 23-48 Coupe climbed again, going up to 10,846 this year. The Fisher-built body was finished in maroon, with black fenders and radiator shell. The car cost $1,895 and weighed 3,440 pounds. Tires were 33 x 4.5 inches.

Slipping slightly in sales appeal was the large 7-passenger Model 23-49 Touring, built on the large 124-inch wheelbase chassis. Buick sold only 5,906 in the U.S. and only 25 overseas. The overall height of the car was decreased this year, giving it much more appealing line. The twin spare tire carrier was standard, as were the step plates. The car cost $1,435 and weighed 3,290 pounds. The sun visor on open models was a new innovation for the year.

The ignition side of the 6-cylinder engine was as uncomplicated a piece of machinery as one could hope to find. This was due to the valve mechanism and spark plug covers that effectively protected these moving parts from dirt. This immaculate engine room is found on the Sport Touring of Basil Lewis of Kalamazoo, Mich.

One of the 25 export versions of the Model 23-49, designated the Model 23-49-X, was purchased in India by Lowell Thomas and used on his famed trip to Afghanistan. Mr. Thomas and the Buick were the first outsiders ever to penetrate the tightly closed and guarded country in an automobile. Mr. Thomas and part of his crew are shown here in the Afghan Desert, surrounded by curious natives. The car was equipped with Goodyear wire wheels and tires.

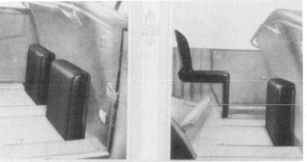

The jump seats of the 7-passenger Model 23-49 Touring folded neatly out of the way, but did not disappear into the front seat back. The small switch on either side of the front seat back was for the step light. Storage pouches were included in each door of all open models.

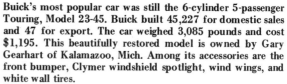

Buick's most popular car was still the 6-cylinder 5-passenger Touring, Model 23-45. Buick built 45,227 for domestic sales and 47 for export. The car weighed 3,085 pounds and cost $1,195. This beautifully restored model is owned by Gary Gearhart of Kalamazoo, Mich. Among its accessories are the front bumper, Clymer windshield spotlight, wind wings, and white wall tires.

The Model 23-44 Roadster continued to enjoy popularity in the U.S., but found little interest elsewhere. There were 6,488 built for domestic sales, but only three special order models were produced for export. The 2,940-pound car utilized the 118-inch wheelbase Light Six chassis. It cost $1,175. This version features accessory bumper, spotlight, and compressed air horn. Cowl lights were standard on all models.

This right-side view of Gary Gearhart's beautiful Model 23-45 Touring shows the most accepted method of carrying baggage in the early 1920's. The running board rack was handy, but luggage took a beating from road dirt, and the rack made one rear door inoperative. The diamond-shaped fender-mounted taillights were an accessory, as was the spare tire cover.

Of totally new design was the Model 23-41 Touring Sedan, a 6-cylinder companion to the 4-cylinder Model 23-38. The 5-passenger car featured a leather covered trunk and rear trunk guards on the body as standard equipment. It cost $1,935 and weighed 3,380. Buick built 8,719.

Still climbing rapidly in popularity was the Model 23-47 Sedan, a 5-passenger car which used the Light Six 118-inch wheelbase chassis. Buick built 7,358. It cost $1,985 and weighed 3,475 pounds. An option on all closed cars and sport models this year were disc wheels.

The 4-cylinder line received some welcome redesigning, and the appearance was much improved over what it had been in 1922. This is the Model 23-35 Touring, which was now priced at $885. It weighed 2,520 pounds, and used the 109-inch wheelbase chassis. Buick built 36,935 for domestic sales, but only 63 for export.

Buick's storm curtains were of a new design this year, which made them a bit easier to install and store. After the curtains were put in place, a weather strip was snapped around the top on the inside, making the cars fairly weather tight. They are shown here on the Model 23-45.

The new and improved side curtains all featured a small flap for the driver for hand signals. On the roadster models, a small triangular curtain had to be provided for the top cutout.

Again Buick's lightest and lowest priced car was the 4-cylinder Roadster. Designated the Model 23-34, it weighed 2,415 pounds, and cost $865. Buick built 5,768 for domestic sales, but only eight on special order for export. Later in the year, the Model 23-39 Sport Roadster was introduced. This car, which had a production run of 1,971 weighed 2,445 pounds and cost $1,025. It was finished in maroon with red wheels, and buyers had a choice of wood spoke, wire, or disc wheels. The Model 23-34 shown here has accessory wind wings and bumper.

The Model 23-36 Coupe featured a Fisher-built body and claimed ample seating space for three passengers. It sold for $1,175 and weighed 2,575 pounds. Sales jumped up to a surprising 7,004. A front bumper was not supplied, but the low-slung spare acted as a rear bumper.

As could be expected, closed models continued their rapid rise in popularity. The 4-cylinder Model 23-37 Sedan this year had a production run of 8,885 for domestic sales, and one special order export model with right hand drive. The car cost $1,395 and weighed 2,875 pounds. It used a Fisher body and utilized the standard 4-cylinder chassis of 109-inch wheelbase.

A totally new design for the year was the 4-cylinder Touring Sedan, Model 23-38. Produced this year only, the style predated what would later become Buick's popular 2-door coach. It cost $1,325 and weighed 2,750 pounds. Buick built 6,025. The small rear trunk was standard equipment.

1923

Continued as a standard production body was the panel truck with vestibule cab, which was priced at $860. The body sides were of steel over a wood frame. A bench seat was provided across the full width of the cab, but only the driver had a seat back.

Entering its first full year of production, and also its last year, was the 4-cylinder Model SD-4 Truck. The stripped ½-ton chassis weighed 2,020 pounds. Although sales totaled 2,740, Buick did not feel the truck had a future, and production stopped shortly after mid-year. Most popular of all the styles was this open express, with a vestibule body. Because of the forward door position, entry from the driver's side was virtually impossible. In this form, the truck listed for $830.

A rather popular truck style of the era was the canopy delivery, which could be converted into a type of closed truck via roll-up curtains. The canopy delivery sold for $855 complete with curtains. It used the same roof as did the panel delivery and the same box as the express.

New for the truck line was the DeLuxe Panel Body, which featured a curved-line design, oval side windows, and many trim refinements. It sold for $960, being Buick's most expensive truck style. As with other Buick trucks, the door on the driver's side was virtually useless.

After watching others produce depot hack bodies for Buick chassis, Buick decided to enter the field this year. The result was this vehicle, called a "combination passenger and express truck." It sold for $935, complete with removable seats for seven and full weather curtains.

New for the year was the screen side delivery, which basically was the canopy delivery with screened sides. It sold for $875 with the price including the side curtains. However, rear door screens were at an extra cost.

1923

To demonstrate the torque power of the new Buicks, this San Francisco dealer pulled a 2½-ton steam roller through the streets of his town. The car is the 118-inch 6-cylinder chassis with body removed. Also removed were the rear springs. The rear axle was blocked directly to the chassis, and several hundred pounds of weight were set on the rear end to provide better traction.

Eureka of Rock Falls, Ill., produced this glass sided hearse to special order on a Buick 124-inch chassis, extended to meet the required dimensions. The extension area can be seen on the rocker panel, just ahead of the rear wheel. The car was painted in pilgrim gray, with light gray drapes. The coach lamps were electric. The unit was built for Clarence R. Huff of Huntington, N.Y.

In addition to its distinctive styling, the Sport Touring and Roadster models offered some exclusive features, such as a rubber heel plate for the driver, carpeted front compartment, and an attractive heavily grained dash. The speedometer dial included odometer, trip meter, and clock.

Shown during a run in 1924 is this 1921 Buick, one of a fleet of Buicks and Cadillacs operated by the Narin Brothers on their famous trail-breaking mail and passenger route between Baghdad and Damascus. The run, which involved 550 miles of hard, roadless desert driving each way, was completed in 24 hours or less by these cars. When setting up the run in 1922, the Narins considered makers of cars from all parts of the world, but finally settled on Buicks and Cadillacs because of their speed and unsurpassed dependability and stamina. Later, because of Arab rebellions, the route was changed to avoid the trouble areas, and the new trail involved 750 miles of mountain and desert driving. These longer runs were made for several years, until the hostilities ended and the original route could be resumed. The runs were made by these cars into the 1930s, when more sophisticated equipment was put into effect. By then, each car had run approximately 250,000 miles, carrying tremendous overloads and operating under unbelievably severe conditions—quite a testimony to Buick (and Cadillac) engineering.

The dash of the 4-cylinder cars was more Spartan than that used on the 6-cylinder models, but was still sufficient for the time. The dash light had a movable hood so that it could illuminate either the oil gauge and ammeter or the speedometer. A trip meter was included.

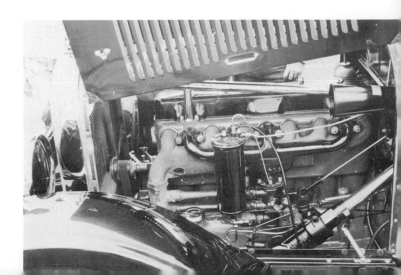

After one highly successful year, Buick production slumped slightly, but the calendar year tally of 160,411 vehicles was still the second highest in the company's history. Still, tremendous production increases occurred at both Dodge and Willys-Overland, and both of these companies shot past Buick, with the result that Buick dropped back to fifth place in the industry.

Both the Four and the Six were continued, but the Four was destined to be dropped at the end of the model year. With the discontinuance of this line, Buick would never again have less than six cylinders to offer its customers, unless one includes the German-made Opel that Buick dealers were authorized to sell beginning in 1958.

The big news of the year was the inclusion of 4-wheel brakes on all models. The brakes were still mechanical, and the service brake was still of the contracting type, though now they were on the front wheels as well as the rear. The parking-emergency brake remained the expanding type, and worked on the rear wheels only.

Also new for the year was a new hood, radiator shell and cowl styling that was considered the most important styling change that Buick had made since 1914. The drastic redesign, with a sharp cornered radiator shell surrounding a Harrison radiator, resulted in lines suspiciously similar to Packard's. In fact, Packard retaliated in its ads by pointing out that "When prettier cars are built, PACKARD will build them."

With the 4-cylinder line destined to be dropped, it was no surprise that mechanically the cars were little changed. The basic 4-cylinder engine was continued, with its major change being the elimination of vent holes in the valve covers. The 109-inch wheelbase was continued, but the series was cut down to four models through the discontinuance of the Sport Roadster and the Touring Sedan.

On the other side of the fence, there was great activity in the 6-cylinder line, where the wheelbases of the cars were now stretched to 120 and 128 inches. The engine size was increased to 255 cubic inches, via a new bore and stroke of 3-3/8 x 4.75 inches. The new block developed 27.3 SAE or 70 brake horsepower. For the first time, aluminum crankcases and removable cylinder heads were used. Other innovations included ball and sockets of the tie rods and cowl ventilators on all models. Wheels on all 6-cylinder cars were now 32 inches, but the 120-inch wheelbase models used 32 x 4 inch tires, while the 128-inch wheelbase cars used 32 x 4.5 inch tires.

In addition to this, the line was expanded to fourteen models through the addition of six new styles and the discontinuance of the Touring Sedan. The new styles were a three-passenger Cabriolet, two Broughams, a Demi-Sedan, a Town Car, and a Limousine. Obviously, Buick was not aiming its new products at the sporty set. Still, one of the prettiest cars of the year was the Model 24-51A Brougham. This was a five-passenger car with oval quarter windows, dummy landau irons, and natural-finish wood-spoke wheels. Its color was Sagebrush Green. Trunks were available for many models. These were supplied by several accessory firms, as Buick did not produce any separate trunks of its own except for the wooden types used in 1923.

New for the year was the 7-passenger limousine, Model 24-50-L, which was really the 7-passenger sedan fitted with a glass partition window and a few interior refinements. The car cost $2,385. Production was 713 for domestic sales and 33 for export.

Buick's heaviest car continued to be the 7-passenger sedan, Model 24-50, of which 9,561 were built for domestic sales and 71 were built for export. Unlike the 5-passenger sedan, this car featured very modern and stylish body styling, with rounded quarter windows and an attractive curve to the rear styling. Finished in cobalt blue with black fenders, it cost $2,285 and weighed 4,020 pounds. Dual rear spares with individual covers were standard equipment.

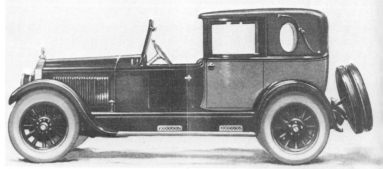

Of totally new design was Buick's lowest production, most expensive, and most attractive car. It was this 4-passenger town sedan with open front compartment, and rather private tonneau with dummy landau irons. It was priced at $2,795 and attracted only 25 buyers. It weighed 3,860 pounds. Surprisingly, it was not available in 7-passenger form.

New for the year was the 3-passenger Cabriolet, Model 24-54-C. The car, introduced late in the season, was slow in drawing attention, and only 1,107 were built. It cost $1,945, and weighed 3,765 pounds.

New for the year and introduced late in the season was the Brougham Model 24-51 Sedan and Model 24-51-A. Finished in Carmine Lake, the car cost $2,235 and weighed 3,940 pounds. The dummy landau irons were standard. Buick built only 24 for export, but turned out 4,991 of the Model 24-51 and 2,295 of the Model 24-51-A. It was impossible to ascertain the difference between the two models, as all specifications, photos, etc., of the two cars seemed identical.

Making good use of the new 128-inch wheelbase chassis was the Model 24-54 Sport Roadster, which this year weighed 3,470 pounds and cost $1,675. The body was finished in maroon and gold, with black fenders. Standard equipment included the visor and windwings, but wire wheels were an added cost accessory this year on both the Sport Touring and Roadster. A single spare was used with wire wheels, but dual spares were carried when wood spoke wheels were mounted. Buick built 1,938 for domestic sales and only 52 for export.

The 4-passenger Coupe, Model 24-48, turned out to be Buick's most popular car on the 128-inch wheelbase chassis, with 13,009 being built for domestic sales. However, only four were built on special order for export. The 3,770-pound car was finished in cobalt blue with black fenders. It cost $1,995 complete with dual rear-mounted spare tires. A new styling innovation for the year was the creased design of the radiator and hood, an attractive concept that highly irritated Packard, which thought it owned an exclusive right to this design. The creases would ride on Buick hoods and radiator shells through the 1927 models.

As the sport touring dipped in appeal, the standard 7-passenger Touring, Model 24-49, climbed in sales. Buick produced 7,224 of these large cars for domestic consumption and 885 for export. The cars were finished in cobalt blue with black fenders. They cost $1,565 and weighed 3,645 pounds.

The Model 24-55 Sport Touring, which had enjoyed excellent sales the previous year, this year dropped substantially, with production being only 4,111 for domestic use and 324 for export. The large car was still finished in maroon with black fenders. A trunk was no longer standard equipment, but the permanent trunk rack was still built into the design. The dual rear spares and nickeled headlights were standard, but the tonneau cover on this version is an accessory. The car weighed 3,605 pounds and cost $1,725.

The Model 24-44 Roadster was finished in cobalt blue with black fenders and headlights. A pretty little car, it attracted 9,700 buyers in this country, but only 68 overseas. Equipped with a rumbleseat, the car cost $1,275 and weighed 3,300 pounds. This little beauty is owned by Bob Poliday of Fenton, Mich. The bumper, windwings and motometer are accessories.

New for the year, and appearing this year only was the Model 24-42 Demi-Sedan or Double Service Sedan. The car was built on the new 120-inch wheelbase, 6-cylinder chassis. The 5-passenger car cost $1,695 and weighed 3,675 pounds. The rear seat was easily removable for hauling packages. Buick built 14,094 for domestic sales and 25 for export. One of those still remaining is this model, owned by Bert Nunneley of Mt. Clemens, Mich.

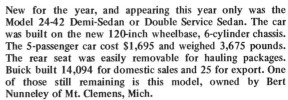

The most expensive car on the 120-inch chassis was the Model 24-47 5-passenger Sedan, which still clung to rather archaic line. Still, it attracted 10,377 domestic and 20 export sales. It was painted in cobalt blue body with black fenders and upper body sections. Weighing 3,845 pounds, the car cost $2,095. The step plates and spare tire cover were standard equipment.

Buick's most popular car remained the 5-passenger Touring, Model 24-45, of which 48,912 were built for domestic sales and 1,561 were built for export. Available only in black, the car cost $1,295 and weighed 3,455 pounds. This version is owned by Arnold Reenders of Grand Haven, Mich. All 6-cylinder models used a nickeled radiator shell and all were equipped with a new innovation for Buick this year—a transmission lock.

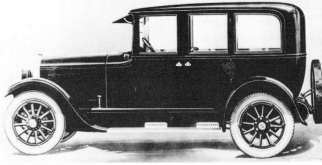

The Buick 6-cylinder engine was a sound piece of engineering, known for its long life and relatively easy maintenance. Buick this year claimed that all of its cars were capable of maintaining speeds of 60 to 70 miles an hour without strain. The pan beneath the carburetor was to catch dripping gas and drain it out of the engine compartment.

Even though Buick did not find the depot hack market large enough to bother with, other companies continued to produce these bodies for use on Buick chassis. This example, on the 128-inch wheelbase chassis, was built by the Cotton Body Co. of Boston. It was rated as a 9-passenger vehicle, with the rear seats removable for carrying cargo. A tailgate was provided for luggage carrying, while side curtains provided weather protection. The side-mounted spare made the left front door useless. Cotton also built similar bodies for use on Essex and Dodge chassis.

1924

The Buick 4-cylinder engine, phased out this year, followed the basic design of its 6-cylinder cousin, but lacked some of the later refinements made to the larger block. Following the demise of this engine, Buick would never again build a 4-cylinder power unit.

Appearing for the last time was the 4-cylinder line, of which the most popular was still the Model 24-35 Touring. Available in black only, the car had a production run of 21,854 for domestic sales and an additional 4,294 for export. It cost $965 and weighed 2,680 pounds. This immaculately restored version is owned by David Stork of Lapeer, Mich.

A major innovation this year was Buick's mechanical 4-wheel brakes. The rear wheel mechanisms were not changed to any great degree, but totally new front units of rather complicated design had to be constructed for the front wheels. Buick still retained its archaic idea of using external contracting brakes for service use and internal expanding of the rear for parking.

The 4-cylinder Model 24-37 Sedan was now finished in cobalt blue body with black fenders and a black upper section. The car was exported for the first time, with 103 being built for the overseas market and 6,563 for domestic sales. It cost $1,495 and weighed 2,955 pounds. All of the 4-cylinder Buicks used painted radiator shells.

New for the year was the Model 24-33 Coupe, a 4-passenger vehicle which replaced both the 2-passenger coupe and the touring sedan in the 4-cylinder line. The 2,845-pound car was finished in maroon with black fenders and radiator shell. It cost $1,395. Buick built 5,479 for domestic sales and 30 for export.

Buick's lightest and least expensive car continued to be the 4-cylinder Model 24-34 Roadster, which cost $935 and weighed 2,570 pounds. Black was the only color available. Buick built 4,296 for domestic sales and 113 for export. This beauty, featuring optional, extra cost white wall tires, is owned by Charles Pergl of Binghamton, N.Y.

Despite the fact that the Four was gone, Buick's calendar year production reached 192,100, making this the second highest production year in its history. Yet, other companies were producing even faster, and Buick slipped to sixth place as Hudson-Essex soared into the top five for the first time.

Not only was the Four gone, but there were now two distinctive 6-cylinder cars. The totally new line was the Standard Six Series, consisting of 114.3-inch wheelbase cars using a new engine of 3 x 4.5 inch bore and stroke. This displaced 191 cubic inches and developed 21.6 SAE or 50 brake horsepower. The series consisted of nine models, all priced over $1,000, representing a substantial jump in price over the 4-cylinder line, which technically the Standard Series replaced. Tires on these cars were now 5:00 x 22.

The new line was the Master Six Series, which in effect was a continuation of the former 6-cylinder line. Engines remained the unchanged Six of 3-3/8 x 4.75 inch bore and stroke and wheelbases remained 120 and 128 inches. Tire size increased on all models to 32 x 5.77 inches, but many buyers took the new optional balloons of 6:00 x 22 size. All cars used Marvel carburetors, Delco ignition, 4-wheel mechanical brakes, and the new enclosed propeller shafts. These enclosed shafts, now famous as the Buick torque tube drive, have been in continuous use on Buicks since this year.

Model range was again expanded in the Master Six line, with a total of sixteen production styles now being offered. Prices on all models were about $100 higher for comparable styles than they were in 1924.

All cars were now finished in DuPont Duce lacquer rather than the old color varnish known as japaning, which

Appearing for the last time this year was Buick's very pretentious 4-passenger Master Six Town Sedan, Model 25-57. Priced at $2,925, it was Buick's most expensive car. It weighed 3,850 pounds. It was also Buick's least popular style, with only 92 being built for domestic sales and one special order model being produced for export. It is shown here at the New York Auto Show.

The driver's compartment of the Model 25-57 Town Sedan was finished in black leather, while the passenger compartment was in broadcloth. The partition window could be lowered, but the electric intercom (or speaking tube) was standard equipment. All tonneau windows were equipped with silk roller shades. The front compartment top and side curtains stored under the front seat.

Buick's Model 25-57 Town Sedan was available in two styles. Buyers had a choice of the oval quarter window, or a blank quarter panel as shown here. However, all production figures are combined, so it is now impossible to tell how many of each style were made. Weather protection for the driver was by a snap-on fabric roof and side curtains.

The passenger's compartment of the Model 25-57 Town Sedan was upholstered in fine broadcloth, with a plush rug. A rear floor heater was standard equipment, as was a smoking set and vanity. Each rear door was equipped with a small storage pouch, and individual reading lights were provided for the rear seat. The oval quarter windows were fixed in place and could not be opened.

was used prior to this year. The Fisher-bodied models used a one-piece windshield for the first time, ending the old horizontally split windshield. Also for the first time, vacuum operated automatic windshield wipers were made standard, replacing the old hand operated variety.

For the first time, two closed cars were the most popular styles in Buick's line, ending forever the public's favor of open touring models. The two styles were the late-entry five-passenger coach in the Master Six line, which turned out to be Buick's most popular model, with over 30,000 being built, and the similar model in the new Standard Six Series, with almost 22,000 being built. Both of these cars used wool broadcloth upholstery.

Standard equipment on all models included speedometer, fuel gauge, ammeter, electric horn, transmission lock, automatic windshield wiper, demountable rims, front shock absorbers, spare tire carrier, heater, rearview mirror, sun visor, dome light on closed models, clock, running board scuff plates, instrument panel light, and headlight dimmer.

The 4-passenger Master Six Coupe, Model 25-48, turned into a very attractive car this year, through the use of a rubberized fabric top, large oval quarter windows, and dummy landau irons. It was finished in cobalt blue with black fenders and top. Buick built 6,799 for domestic sales and four special order models for export. The car sold for $2,125 and weighed 3,770 pounds. It used the 128-inch wheelbase chassis.

New for the year was the Master Six 3-passenger Country Club Cabriolet, Model 25-54-C. This attractive car was equipped with a small door on each side rear quarter panel for access to the rumbleseat or trunk floor. The primary design was for easy access to stored golf bags, but the doors also proved handy for loading small packages without opening the main deck lid. When equipped with a trunk deck, the car offered substantial luggage capacity. The top was solid, covered with black rubberized fabric and decorated with dummy landau irons. Finished in sagebrush green with black fenders, the 3,745 pound vehicle sold for $2,075. Buick built a total of 2,751, divided between trunk and rumble seat models. Step plates and dual covered rear-mounted spares were standard, but the white wall tires were extra. The car used the 128-inch wheelbase chassis.

New for the year was the Master Six Brougham Touring Sedan, built on the 128-inch wheelbase chassis. The car used essentially the same rear quarter design as did the 4-passenger coupe, and was furnished with a trunk rack and dual spares as standard equipment. The bumpers and trunk were still accessories. Designated the Model 25-51, this car had a production run of 6,850 for domestic sales and two special order models for export. Finished in sagebrush green with black fenders, top and trunk, the 3,905-pound car sold for $2,350. The body was built by Fisher. All rear windows were equipped with silk roller shades.

Buick's heaviest car was the 7-passenger Master Six Limousine, which weighed 4,030 pounds. The car was essentially the 7-passenger sedan, fitted with a glass partition between the front and rear compartment. Designated the Model 25-50-L, it cost $2,525. Buick built 768. Of similar design, but built for export only was the Model 25-50-LX. This car differed from the U.S. version of the 7-passenger limousine in that it had a built-in trunk rack and single side-mounted spare in a welled left fender. Available in right or left hand drive, the LX version had a production run of 189.

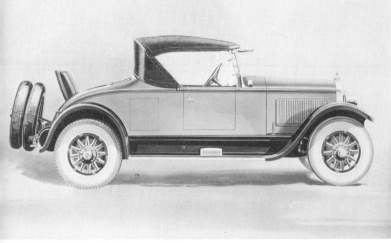

An interesting car was the Master Six Sport Roadster, built on the 128-inch wheelbase chassis. Designated the Model 25-54, the car was available either with a rumble seat as shown or with a trunk. Doors on either side of the body gave access to a separate compartment for golf bags. The car was finished in sagebrush green with orange trim and black fenders and top. It cost $1,750 and weighed 3,485 pounds. Buick built 1,917 for domestic sales and 103 for export.

Arriving late in the year was the Master Six Sport Touring, Model 25-55-S. Finished in sagebrush green, the 3,550-pound car sold for $1,800. It used the 5-passenger touring body on the 128-inch wheelbase chassis, and was equipped with a small trunk rack between the body and the dual rear-mounted spares. The spares, covers, windwings and sun visor were standard equipment. Upholstery was in leather and the floor was carpeted. Buick built 2,774 for domestic sales and 382 for export. Jerome O. Eddy of Pasadena, Cal., the original owner of this model, stands beside his new purchase at time of delivery. The bumpers, spotlight, and white wall tires were accessories.

The 7-passenger Master Six Touring, Model 25-49, used the 128-inch wheelbase chassis. Standard equipment included the dual rear spares and covers and the windshield visor. The car sold for $1,625 and weighed 3,610 pounds. Buick built 2,826. Buick claimed that this car would easily maintain 60 to 70 miles an hour without strain.

MASTER SIX

Why Buick never built this beautiful 7-passenger touring car for domestic sales is unknown. The car is the Model 25-49-X Touring, built for export only. The car featured standard wire wheels with sidemount and a built-in trunk rack. Only 756 were produced.

Using the 128-inch Master Six wheelbase chassis for a base is this hearse, produced by the Cynthiana Carriage Co. of Covington, Ky. Called the Model 85, the body was most often mounted on Dodge or Studebaker chassis, but Buick, Cadillac and other heavy chassis were sometimes used at the buyer's request. The car features landau leather back styling with a small oval window in the padded landau area. The rear compartment windows are of etched glass, framed by velvet drapes and fitted with roller shades.

The 7-passenger Master Six Sedan, Model 25-50 this year was finished in limousine blue with black fenders and top. The large car weighed 3,995 pounds and cost $,425. Buick built 4,606 for domestic sales and another 164 for export. As were all large Buicks, the car was equipped with dual rear spares.

The Master Six Series was divided into two sub-series, of 120-inch and 128-inch wheelbase cars. Most popular of the 120-inch wheelbase models was the 5-passenger Touring, Model 25-45, which had a production run of 5,203 for domestic sales and 701 for export. The car cost $1,395 and weighed 3,465 pounds. This attractive restored version sports accessory wind wings and bumpers. It is owned by Morley Wiederhold of Clio, Mich.

The Master Six 5-passenger Sedan utilized the 120-inch wheelbase chassis. Finished only in limousine blue with black fenders and top portion, the car attracted 4,200 buyers. It cost $2,225 and weighed 3,850 pounds. Bumpers on this model, owned by Lawrence See of Plainfield, Ill., were an accessory, as was the spotlight.

Buick's most popular car this year was the Master Six Coach, Model 25-40, which had an amazing production run of 30,600 for domestic sales, plus an additional 25 for export. Finished in cobalt blue, the car utilized the 120-inch wheelbase chassis. This marked the first time in Buick's history that a closed car outsold the open models. The car cost $1,495 and weighed 3,560 pounds.

Just as the Standard Six Series had its enclosed touring models, so too did the Master Six line. The car was the Model 25-45-A, which was identical to the Model 25-45 except that its top was permanently set on a fixed frame. The car cost $1,475 and weighed 3,540 pounds. Buick built 1,900, all for domestic sales. The glass side panels slid open for ventilation, and the car had a heater as standard equipment. The inside of the top was padded so that the frame didn't show.

Designed for the cold weather country was the Master Six Enclosed Roadster, Model 25-44-A. As was the case with other enclosed versions of the open cars, the glass side panels swung open with the doors, and slid rearward for ventilation. The style was not popular, and only 850 were built before it was dropped. It cost $1,400 and weighed 3,335 pounds.

The concept of the enclosed touring was carried over to the 7-passenger Master Six Touring also, but as was the case with other enclosed open cars, little buyer attraction was present. The 7-passenger version, designated the Model 25-49-A, sold for $1,475 and weighed 3,540 pounds. As with the other enclosed models, the two-piece glass side windows would slide halfway open for ventilation, and both top and windows were permanently fixed on the car. Only 500 were built.

The lowest priced car in the Master Six line was the Roadster, Model 25-44, which was finished in cobalt blue with black fenders and top. The 3,285-pound car sold for $1,365. Buick built 2,975.

Appearing this year only was the Standard Six Demi-Sedan or Double Service Sedan, Model 25-21. The 5-passenger car was upholstered in rather coarse but serviceable material, and was designed primarily for businessmen who used their car both for personal use and for work. Available only in black, it cost $1,475 and weighed 3,185 pounds. Buick built 9,252 for domestic sales and another 56 for export.

Of far less archaic line than the Demi-Sedan was the Standard Six 5-passenger Sedan, Model 25-27. Finished in cobalt blue body with black fenders and top area, the car weighed 3,245 pounds and cost $1,665. Buick built 10,772 for domestic sales and 1,448 for export.

The Standard Six 4-passenger Coupe, Model 25-28, still utilized a jump seat for the fourth passenger. Still, the car retained some degree of popularity, and 7,743 were built for domestic sales while another 119 were built for export. The car was finished in cobalt blue. It weighed 3,075 pounds and cost $1,565.

Buick's second most popular car this year was the new Standard Six Coach, Model 25-20. Production reached 21,900 for domestic sales and another 65 built for export. This marked the first time in Buick's history that closed cars outsold open models. The coach weighed 3,050 pounds and cost $1,295. It was finished in brewster green.

The Standard Six 2-passenger Coupe, Model 25-26, had a blanked quarter panel, rubberized fabric top and dummy landau irons. The attractive car drew 4,398 orders. It was priced at $1,375 and weighed 2,960 pounds. Its companion was the Sport Coupe, Model 25-26-S, of which 550 were built. Both cars offered excellent trunk space for the era.

With the 4-cylinder series gone, the Standard Six line became Buick's economy series. All Standard Six cars used a new 114-inch wheelbase chassis. In a surprise move, the Model 25-25 Touring tumbled from the most popular spot, and slid substantially down the line, with production resting at 16,040. The car, finished in brewster green with black fenders, weighed 2,920 pounds and cost $1,175. The step plates, cowl lights, and spare tire cover were all standard equipment.

Appearing this year only was the Standard Six Enclosed Touring, Model 25-25-A. This car used the same body as did the regular touring, but featured a permanent top fixed on a rigid frame. The side curtains could be removed, but the top could not be lowered. The car sold for $1,250 and weighed 2,970 pounds. Buick built 4,450, all in brewster green. Another touring version to appear for this year only in the Standard Six Series was the Sport Touring, Model 25-25-S. This car, which looks virtually identical to the Master Six Sport Touring shown on Page 92, utilized the 5-passenger touring car body of the Standard Six Model 25-25, but had this mounted on the 120-inch wheelbase Master Six Series chassis. A total of 651 were built, all finished in Buick gray. Standard equipment on this model, as on the Master Six Sport Touring, included dual spare tires with covers, permanent trunk rack, and windwings and sunvisor attached to the windshield.

Built for export only was the interesting Standard Six Model 25-X-25, of which 5,452 were produced. The car featured a sidemount with cover, standard luggage rack, and a completely different top from that found on the U.S. version.

Buick's lowest priced and lightest car was the Standard Six Roadster, Model 25-24. It sold for $1,150 and weighed 2,750 pounds. Buick built 3,315 for domestic sales and 108 for export. Also in the Standard Six Series was the Sport Roadster, Model 25-24-S. These cars, which weighed 2,750 pounds, featured rumble seats, dual spares and a few other refinements not found on the plain roadster models. Only 501 were built, all finished in Buick gray.

Produced this year only was the Standard Six Enclosed Roadster, Model 25-24-A. The car used the regular Standard Six roadster body, but was fitted with a permanent top on a rigid frame, in the same manner as was the top on the enclosed touring shown above. Full side curtains were provided, and these were removable, as shown here. This type of top differed from the conventional "California top" of the era, in that the California tops could be easily removed from the car—even though it too could not be lowered. The Buick enclosed top was built into the body, and was a major effort to remove. The Enclosed Roadster sold for $1,190 and weighed 2,800 pounds. Buick built 1,725. This beautifully restored version, bearing Body No. 1329223 and Engine No. 1346618 is owned by Jimmy W. Dailey of Canton, Tex. In its day, the bumpers, motometer and white wall tires would have been accessories. All Enclosed Roadsters were finished in brewster green with black fenders and aprons, black leather interiors, and khaki top.

One of the Standard Six Touring export models was this famous vehicle, driven on a 16,499 mile run from New York City around the world. It left New York on Dec. 20, 1924, and arrived back in New York on June 23, 1925. The run was made in "driverless" fashion. Each participating Buick dealer would be responsible for driving the car on to the next dealer, who would then drive it on to the next, and so on. The car is shown here in Pittsburgh, Pa., at the completion of the trip.

Not all of the driving of the "Around The World" Special Six Buick was over good roads. Here the car is seen well mired in the middle of an Australian highway. The car was the standard export model, fitted only with large tool boxes on the running boards and with dual spotlights.

Despite the fact that Buick this year offered its "enclosed" versions of the open cars, independent manufacturers continued to produce "California" tops for Buicks. This is the Rex Permanent Top, mounted on a Model 25-49 Touring. The Rex top differed greatly from the Buick permanent top in that the Buick top looked like a touring car with side curtains while the Rex version attempted to make the car look like a sedan.

Buick's chassis was becoming more rigid and strong, a factor which would be a definite asset in future years when several builders of specialized vehicles looked to Buick as a suitable base upon which to mount their bodies. Still retained were the huge cantilever rear wheels and plain cord tread on the front.

The Buick engine was a substantial piece of machinery, using a Marvel carburetor and Delco ignition. This is the large block, running a bore and stroke of 3-3/8 x 4.75 inches. The brake and clutch pedals still were equipped with small tabs on the outer edges to keep the driver's feet from accidently slipping off.

1926

Buick hit an all-time record this year, with calendar year production soaring to 266,753 vehicles. Not only was this by far the highest production in its history, but the company would never again reach this height until 1940. The boost moved Buick into third place in production, passing Hudson-Essex, Willys-Overland, and Dodge.

Both the new Standard Six and the Master Six received more power this year through an increase in displacement accomplished through increasing the bore slightly. The Standard Six now ran a bore of 3-1/8 x 4.5 inches, which gave it a displacement of 207 cubic inches and 23.4 SAE or 60 brake horsepower. The Master Six now had a bore and stroke of 3.5 x 4.75 inches, which gave it a displacement of 274 cubic inches and 29.4 SAE or 75 brake horses. Both engines now used Marvel carburetors equipped with air cleaners for the first time, and two-unit Delco ignition. Gone was the old combination starter-generator, and replacing it was the two-unit system consisting of a Delco starter and an independent Delco generator. The chassis now used Zerk lubrication points throughout.

The radiator, hood and cowl contour remained the same, but the radiator shell edges were more rounded this year. Fisher bodies had double belt moldings above and below the door handles. Headlamp shells were now identical, and were attached to a tie-bar running across the radiator from fender to fender. This did away with the necessity of having to specify left or right shells when replacement was necessary.

Also among this year's innovations was a headlight control arm on the steering column, and a new one-piece brake lining rather than the former two-piece lining. The brake adjustment was now located on top of the drum instead of on the side. Brakes remained 4-wheel mechanical, of the contracting type for service use, and internal expanding on the rear wheels only for the emergency-parking brake.

In the Standard Series, the wheelbase remained 114.5 inches, but the tire size was decreased to 6:00 x 21. However, the ambitious introductory line was reduced from nine to six styles. Disappearing were the Enclosed Touring, the Enclosed Roadster, and the Demi-Sedan. Upholstery in the Standard line was in rough gray wool broadcloth, but this was dropped at the end of the year because, though very durable, it proved too scratchy to the skin. Upholstery in the Master closed cars was either in brown taupe plush or gray mohair plush.

The Master Series continued to use its two wheelbases of 120 and 128 inches and its tires also were 6:00 x 21. However, its line of styles was reduced from sixteen to ten. Among the styles to disappear were the Enclosed Touring and Enclosed Roadster, the seven-passenger Touring, the Town Sedan, and the Limousine.

Standard equipment on all models included speedometer, ammeter, transmission lock, automatic windshield wiper, spare tire carrier, rearview mirror, sun visor, cowl ventilator on open models, ventilating windshield on closed styles, and dome or corner lights on closed cars. The Master Series equipment also included Motometer, front shock absorbers, scuff plates, clock, cigar lighter, heater, and smoking and vanity cases.

On the corporate side, Buick suffered one major loss. That was the death of Harry Bassett, Buick's highly regarded president since 1920. He was replaced as president by E.T. Strong, who had served as sales manager for the past ten years.

One of Buick's most attractive styles was the 5-passenger Master Six Sport Touring, Model 26-55, of which 2,051 were produced for domestic sales and 429 for export. The car used the 128-inch wheelbase chassis. Standard equipment included a built-in trunk rack, wind wings, motometer, and dual spares, though this car has just one spare. It was finished in Buick blue or Texas brown, cost $1,525 and weighed 3,650 pounds.

MASTER SIX

For the first time in Buick's history, a 4-door sedan was the most popular car. It was this Master Six, Model 26-47, of which 53,490 were built for domestic sales and 117 were built for export. The car used the 120-inch wheelbase chassis, and was available either in Buckingham gray or cobalt blue. It cost $1,495 and weighed 3,790 pounds. This nicely restored model, featuring accessory bumper and fog lights, is owned by Frank Norman of Flint, Mich.

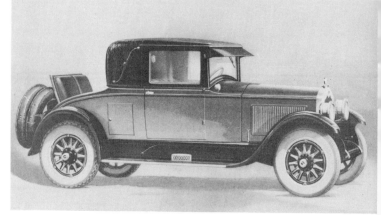

Buick's heaviest and most expensive car was the 7-passenger Master Six Sedan, Model 26-50. The car weighed 4,040 pounds and cost $1,995. It was finished only in lotus blue body with black fenders and upper section. This model is shown with its original owner, Tommy Milton, a famous racing driver of the era. Buick built 12,690 in this style, and turned out another 220 for the Model 26-50-T, which was the same body, but with the interior fitted for taxi work.

Climbing slowly in popularity was the Master Six Country Club Coupe, Model 26-54-C, of which 4,436 were built for domestic sales only. The model was not available for export. Most of the cars were finished in rumble seat form, but a trunk back was optional. Standard equipment included the access doors to the special compartment for golf bags. Finished in Texas brown duotone, the car weighed 3,820 pounds and cost $1,765. The rear quarter and back panels were covered in coarse grain rubberized fabric and decorated with dummy landau irons.

The Master Six 2-door Sedan, Model 26-40, enjoyed good sales, but its popularity did not match that of its Standard Six companion. Buick built 21,867 for domestic sales and 154 for export. The car was finished in cobalt blue, and utilized the 120-inch wheelbase chassis. It weighed 3,655 pounds and cost $1,395. Only one spare was supplied with this model.

A very attractive car was the Master Six Brougham Touring Sedan, Model 26-51, which featured oval quarter windows and dummy landau irons set on quarter and rear panels covered with rubberized fabric. Finished in Texas brown duotone, the car came equipped with a built-in trunk rack, dual covered spares and step plates. Buick built 10,873 for domestic sales. It used the 128-inch wheelbase chassis, weighed 3,945 pounds, and cost $1,925.

The Master Six 4-passenger Coupe, Model 26-48, cost $1,795 and weighed 3,845 pounds. Finished in lotus blue, it used the 128-inch wheelbase chassis and was fitted with dual spares as standard equipment. The motometer was also standard, but the buyer had to pay extra if he wanted bumpers. Buick built 10,028, all for domestic sales. Also produced this year was one experimental version of the Model 27-58 Coupe which would appear in 1927 as the 5-passenger victoria-type vehicle.

In the Master Six line, the 5-passenger Touring, Model 26-45, appeared for the last time. Production was down to 2,630 for domestic sales and 839 for export. The car utilized the 120-inch wheelbase chassis, weighed 3,535 pounds, and cost $1,295. In addition to this style, Buick also built 115 of the Model 26-49-X Enclosed Touring cars for export, and one of the Model 26-49 Enclosed Touring for a special order domestic sale.

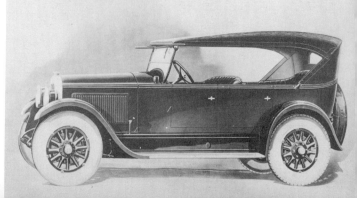

1926

Of much more attractive line than the 2-passenger Roadster was the Master Six Sport Roadster, Model 26-54, which came equipped with a standard rumble seat. On this model, the top could be lowered, but the visor remained in place, attached to the windshield. Dual spare tires, step plates, motometer, and wind wings were all standard equipment. The car used the 128-inch wheelbase chassis, was finished in Texas brown, weighed 3,580 pounds, and cost $1,495. Buick built 2,501 for domestic sales and 67 for export.

Appearing for the last time in the Master Six Series was the 2-passenger Model 26-44 Roadster, which had a production run of only 2,654, all for domestic sales. An interesting feature of the car this year was the fact that the top was built on a solid frame and could not be lowered. Available only in Buckingham gray, the car was built in 2-passenger form only, with no rumble seat options. It used the 120-inch wheelbase chassis, weighed 3,380 pounds, and cost $1,250.

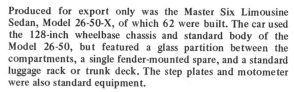

Produced for export only was the Master Six Limousine Sedan, Model 26-50-X, of which 62 were built. The car used the 128-inch wheelbase chassis and standard body of the Model 26-50, but featured a glass partition between the compartments, a single fender-mounted spare, and a standard luggage rack or trunk deck. The step plates and motometer were also standard equipment.

The most popular car in the Standard Six Series was the 4-Door Sedan, Model 26-27, of which 43,375 were made for domestic sales and 636 were produced for export. The 3,210-pound car cost $1,295. As were all Standard Six models, it was available in Buick gray or cobalt blue. Shown with his new Model 26-27 is the original owner, W.R. Woodbury, then public relations director of Buick. The car has accessory bumpers and motometer.

Enjoying almost double the production run of the previous year was the Standard Six Coach, Model 26-20. Production soared to 40,113 for domestic sales and 807 for export. The car cost $1,195 and weighed 3,140 pounds. This finely restored model is owned by Levi Capp of Palmyra, Pa. Both the bumper and the motometer are accessories. The car is finished in cobalt blue.

Buick's least expensive, lightest, and least popular car was the Model 26-24 Standard Six Roadster. The car cost $1,125 and weighed 2,865. Only 1,891 were built for domestic sales. As did the touring, the roadster also came equipped with a visor. It was available in 2-passenger style only, with fairly substantial trunk space, but no rumble seat option.

The Standard Six Touring, Model 26-25, now sported a visor as standard equipment, but its running board step plates were an accessory item. Buyers had a color choice of Buick gray or cobalt blue body, both with black fenders. This year, the Economy Touring suffered a tremendous drop in popularity, with only 4,869 being built for domestic sales and 4,674 being built for export. The car cost $1,150 and weighed 2,920 pounds.

Not only could the top be lowered on the Model 26-54 Roadster, but the rear flap could be removed with the top still raised. The rails just forward of the rumble seat were to protect the body when the top was lowered. Rumble seats of this type just started coming into popular use, and would be considered stylish and practical for the next decade.

The Standard Six Roadster was available in export form, under the designation Model 26-24-X, but only 84 were produced for overseas sales. One of these is this model, featuring an interesting accessory bumper and fender-mounted parking lights, required by British law. The car also has a painted radiator grille, but it could not be determined if this was standard.

Featuring much more attractive body lines than in 1925 was the Standard Six 4-passenger Coupe, Model 26-28. As were all Standard Six cars, it was finished in either Buick gray or cobalt blue, with black fenders and upper body. Buick built 8,271 for domestic sales and another 66 for export. The car cost $1,275 and weighed 3,110 pounds.

The Standard Six 2-passenger Coupe, Model 26-26, soared in popularity this year, with 10,531 being produced in plain form and one Model 26-26 being built on special order with a rumble seat. The car featured much more attractive and modern top treatment, complete with large oval quarter windows and dummy landau irons. The entire top was covered in rubberized fabric. The car cost $1,195 and weighed 3,030 pounds.

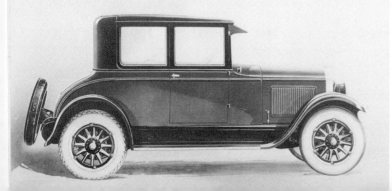

Buick produced only 220 of its new Model 26-50-T taxi bodies, and the entire lot was purchased by the Brown & White Cab Co. of Detroit, which that year changed its name to Detroit Cab Co. Although Buick offered the model to dealers, there were no other cab orders this year.

Buicks were starting to catch the eye of a few custom houses in Europe. This beautiful 7-passenger limousine was built for Lord Byng by the British coach building firm of Kellner, Ltd. The car features dual sidemounts, fender parking lights, coach lights on the windshield posts, and a custom made trunk. The basic body is the Model 26-50-X Limousine.

The E.M. Miller Co. of Quincy, Ill., built this attractive hearse on the Buick Master Six 128-inch wheelbase chassis. The body follows the style of the Limousine Burial Coach, which was quite popular in this era. The same body could be converted for ambulance work.

Eureka of Rock Falls, Ill., started to utilize the large 128-inch wheelbase chassis of the Master Six line for its funeral coaches. This attractive vehicle, designated the Limousine Burial Coach, was built for the Conant Funeral Home of Jacksonville, Fla. It features attractive landau irons and an oval quarter window set into fabric covered quarter panels. The disc wheels on this model were available on all Buicks, but were not a popular option.

The Cynthiana Carriage Co. of Covington, Ky., produced a wide range of semi-custom built ambulances and funeral cars, many mounted on extended Master Six chassis. This is the Cynthiana Model 87, which could be furnished as a funeral car, an ambulance, or a combination of the two. It used a swing-out windshield and a permanent glass partition between the driver and the rear compartment. All rear compartment windows had shades.

All closed cars used the Fisher VV ventilating windshield, which could be raised several inches by the knob mounted directly above the steering wheel near the rearview mirror. Standard equipment included an oil pressure and gas gauge, ammeter, rotating dial speedometer with odometer and trip-meter, and a clock. The instrument light was an accessory.

Whereas years back, Buick had a multitude of moving parts running in the open, it now featured what is referred to as its "sealed chassis and triple-sealed engine." The engine used air, gas, and oil filters. The large cantilever rear springs were still used, as were external contracting service brakes on all four wheels.

Buick was so proud of its new sealed chassis and more powerful engines that it built this cutaway chassis for display at auto shows around the country. It is seen here at the Buick display at the 1926 New York Auto Show. Among the cutaway parts were brakes, radiator, engine, muffler, transmission, clutch, steering unit, and gas tank.

The rear window of the Master Six Model 26-54-C could be lowered so that inside passengers could talk to those in the rumble seat. Although the car looked very much like a convertible, the top was built on a fixed frame and could not be lowered. The landau irons were decoration.

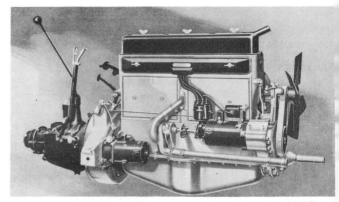

The Standard Six engine now ran a bore and stroke of 3-1/8 x 4.5 inches, displaced 207 cubic inches, and was rated at 60 brake horsepower. Note that the starter was now a separate unit, and not built into the generator-distributor combination. A gear-driven single shaft was used to power generator, distributor, and water pump. All electrical components were by Delco. Wide use of covering pans made the engine easy to keep clean.

After the previous record breaking year, it seemed likely that production would be down. And it was, but not nearly as much as was expected. As a result, 255,160 vehicles rolled from the shop. Still this couldn't hold the line against Hudson-Essex, and thus Buick again slipped to fourth place.

There was virtually no change in engines or running gear of either series, except that the engines now had rubber motor supports. These rubber mounts and new heavier flywheels and counter balanced crankshafts gave rise to Buick's sales slogan of the year — "Vibrationless Beyond Belief."

All cars now used black enameled demountable split rims and blackwall tires. Gone were the optional cadmium rims and whitewall tires. Master Six models of 128-inch wheelbase used an interior heat gauge, while all other models retained Motometers. Replacing the Motometers on the large cars was a radiator cap with a Gothic goddess type of ornament. For the first time, all open models used a one-piece windshield.

The Standard Six Series retained its wheelbase length of 114.5 inches, and the Master Six Series retained its 120-inch wheelbase. Tire size increased slightly to 33 x 6 inches. Both series continued to use Marvel carburetors and Delco ignition. The Standard Series increased its available models to eight styles through the addition of a Town Brougham and a Special Coupe. But, the old Touring and Roadster were gone, their places being taken by a new Sport Touring and Sport Roadster. Upholstery in closed cars in the Standard Series was in brilliant blue mohair plush.

The Master Series continued to list ten styles, but these were changed around a bit. Gone were the plain Touring and Roadster of 120-inch wheelbase, but the sport versions of these cars, on the 128-inch wheelbase, remained. New for the year was a Convertible Coupe and a five-passenger Coupe.

Standard equipment consisted of speedometer, ammeter, electric horn, transmission lock, automatic windshield wiper, spare tire carrier and extra rim (but not the tire), rearview mirror, and sun visor. Most 128-inch wheelbase models also were equipped with front shock absorbers, scuff plates, clock, cigar lighter, heater, and smoking and vanity cases. Open models were equipped with cowl ventilators, while closed models continued to use the Fisher ventilating windshield. Mechanical brakes continued to be contracting on four wheels, with the emergency brake being expanding on the rear wheels only.

THE GREATEST BUICK EVER BUILT

Buick's most popular car again was the Master Six 4-door Sedan, Model 27-47. However, its production slipped a bit, and only 49,105 were built for domestic sales and 322 for export. The car continued to use the 120-inch wheelbase chassis, which seemed sort of an unusual design feature for a 6-passenger car. It cost $1,495 and weighed 3,870. This finely restored model, featuring accessory bumpers, belongs to Victor Belosic of Los Angeles.

Buick's heaviest and most expensive car was the Master Six 7-passenger Sedan, Model 27-50, which weighed 4,115 pounds and cost $1,995. The car, finished in colonial blue with black fenders and upper section, proved surprisingly popular, and 11,259 were built for domestic sales while 233 were built for export. It used the 128-inch wheelbase chassis.

Body by Fisher

Appearing for the last time in the Master Six Series was the 2-door Coach, Model 27-40, which used the 120-inch wheelbase chassis. Finished in Delaware green, the car had a run of 12,130 for domestic sales and 441 for export. It cost $1,395 and weighed 3,750 pounds. Body was by Fisher, with the interior done in walnut, satin and broadcloth.

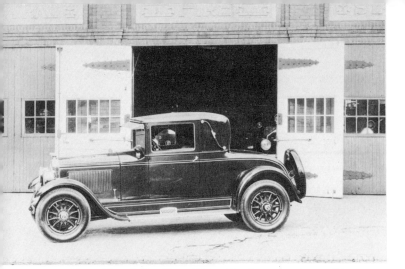

The pride of the Flint, Mich. Fire Department was this Master Six Country Club Special, Model 27-54-C. Painted fire engine red, the car was assigned to the chief. Normally, this model was finished in Paul Revere green with black fenders and upper body. Available only as a rumble seat model, the car weighed 3,905 pounds and cost $1,765. There was an access door on the right lower quarter panel for golf bags. Production was 7,095, all for domestic sales.

An enigma is this coupe, appearing in Buick's archives. Shown with Red Grange, All-American football captain of the University of Illinois team. The car is listed as a Master Six, Model 27-46 3-passenger Coupe. This would be the Master Six companion to the Standard Six Coupe, Model 27-26 (appearing on Pg. 106). However, there is nothing in Buick's records to show that a Master Six Model 27-46 was ever built. The only assumption seems to be that the Model 27-46 was a variation of the Country Club Coupe, Model 27-54-C, and that all production figures were incorporated with the figures for that car. This photo was taken in front of the old Buick Motor Co. showroom and office at 21st St. and Calumet Ave., Chicago.

The Master Six Country Club Coupe, Model 27-54-C, offered attractive rear lines and a rather spacious rear deck. This beautifully restored model is owned by Dick Robey of Cleveland. The paint scheme and trim on the access door are non-standard.

Peter DePaolo, a world famous racing driver of the time and long a fan of Buicks, accepts delivery of his 5-passenger Master Six Bougham, one of several new Buicks that he bought this year. Designated the Model 27-51, the 4,050-pound car sold for $1,925. Buick built 13,862, all for domestic sales and all finished in Paul Revere green. The specially built trunk, which fitted into the built-in trunk rack, was an accessory, as were the bumpers.

Shown in a dealer's garage, awaiting delivery, is one of the 9,350 4-passenger Coupes turned out this year. Designated the Model 27-48, the car used the small 120-inch wheelbase chassis. It cost $1,465, weighed 3,800 pounds, and was finished in Deleware green.

Again Buick offered the Master Six Model 27-50-T Taxi, but only 60 were ordered. The car was basically the Model 27-50 7-passenger sedan, fitted with a more durable taxi interior. The major portion of this year's production was ordered by the Detroit Cab Co. of Detroit, Mich.

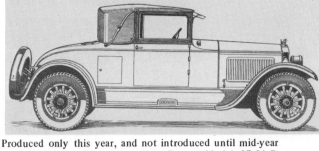

Produced only this year, and not introduced until mid-year was the Master Six Convertible Coupe, Model 27-54-C. Finished in Winchester blue, the car had a production run of 2,354 for domestic sales and 19 for export. The car featured a rumbleseat with folding armrests, access door for golf bags, and a folding top with functional landau irons. It cost $1,925, weighed 3,915 pounds. With its top raised, it was almost identical in appearance to the Country Club Coupe.

New for the year was the Master Six 5-passenger Coupe, Model 27-58. The car used the 128-inch wheelbase chassis and was finished in Colonial blue with a black rubberized fabric top and dummy landau irons. It cost $1,850 and weighed 3,940 pounds. Buick built 7,655. The headlights on the model shown here have caused arguments that the vehicle shown is actually a 1928 model. However, the photo comes from Buick's own photographic archives, and its number clearly indicates that this indeed is a 1927 model, despite the fact that it is wearing 1928 style lamps.

The master Six Sport Roadster experienced a substantial boost in popularity this year, and 4,310 were built for domestic sales and 189 for export. Designated the Model 27-54, the car used the 128-inch wheelbase of the large Master Six models. The rumble seat and front wind wings were standard equipment, but the rear windshield was an accessory made by American Injector Co. of Detroit. Finished in courier cream and green, the attractive car cost $1,495 and weighed 3,655 pounds.

THE GREATEST BUICK EVER BUILT

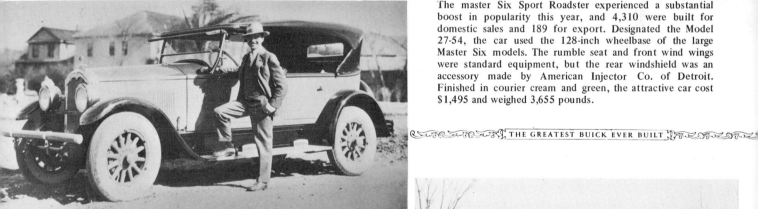

Buick's least popular car was the attractive Master Six Sport Touring, Model 27-55, of which only 2,092 were built for domestic sales and 605 for export. The car was finished in courier brown and courier cream, with black fenders. It cost $1,525 and weighed 3,735 pounds. Standing proudly beside his new model is Peter De Paolo, a world famous racing driver of the era.

Buttoned up for winter weather is one of the Model 27-55 Sport Tourings that the Lee Tire Co. of Conshohocken, Pa., used to test its tires over some of the worst road conditions in the country. The car was replaced only after 100,000 trouble free miles.

The most popular style in the Standard Six line was the 4-door Sedan, Model 27-27. Production was 40,272 for domestic sales and 1,448 for export. Finished in Washington blue with black fenders and upper body, it weighed 3,300 pounds and cost $1,295. Front and rear carpets and a nickeled foot rest in the rear were standard equipment, but the bumper was an accessory.

New for the year was the Country Club Coupe in the Standard Six Series. Designated the Model 27-26-S, the car used the same body as the 2-passenger coupe, but was equipped with a rumble seat and small access doors on the lower rear quarter panel. Buick built 11,688 in this version, and one special order model with a collapsible convertible top. In standard trim, the car cost $1,275 and weighed 3,190 pounds. The body was by Fisher.

New for the year in the Standard Six Series, and introduced only at mid-year, was the Town Brougham, Model 27-29. This attractive example, once owned by Merle Perry of Flint, Mich., is equipped with accessory bumpers. The car was finished in cobalt and Washington blue, with black fenders. It cost $1,375 and weighed 3,305 pounds. There were 11,032 built.

The Standard Six 2-door Coach, Model 27-20, continued to lag behind the more popular 4-door sedan in popularity. Production was 33,190 for domestic sales and 870 for export. Finished in Washington blue with black fenders and upper section, it sold for $1,195 and weighed 3,215 pounds.

A starlet of yesteryear poses with her new 2-passenger Standard Six Coupe, Model 27-26. The car cost $1,195 and weighed 3,110 pounds. Buick built 10,512. The bumpers were still an accessory, but the step plates were standard. The car was finished in Washington blue with black fenders and top. Dummy landau irons and coarse-grain, rubberized fabric decorated the rear quarters.

There was virtually no change in Buick's engine this year, but the transmission went through a major redesign to what is now considered the "standard H" shift pattern. Up until now, Buick had held onto the so-called "Backwards H" shift pattern, which in later years had been used only by Buick and Dodge, and which caused much confusion, clashed gears, and bumper fenders to drivers unfamiliar with these two makes. On the engine, a Delco electric system was used, with generator, distributor and water pump running off of a common gear-driven shaft. A flat leather belt was still used to drive the 4-bladed fan.

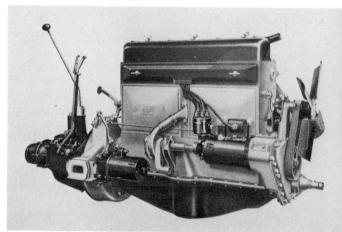

Body by Fisher

This year, the Standard Six 4-passenger Coupe, Model 27-28, was finished in Washington blue with black fenders and upper section. Production slipped somewhat and only 7,178 were built for domestic sales while 94 were built for export. The car cost $1,275 and weighed 3,190 pounds.

The Standard Six Sport Touring, Model 27-25, turned out to be more popular in Europe than in the U. S. There were 4,222 built for export, but only 3,272 built for domestic sales. It was finished in patrol cream with black fenders, a courier brown upper section, and natural varnish wood-spoke wheels. The striking car sold for $1,225 and weighed 3,040 pounds. The step plates and top boot were standard.

It seems that just as long as there have been cars, there have been railroad men desiring to take the cars from the roads and put them on tracks. This Model 27-50 7-passenger sedan was fitted with flanged wheels, a central headlight, railroad tender lamps, and a cow catcher. It was used for many years as an inspection car by the Northern Pacific Railroad.

The lightest car in Buick's line-up was the Standard Six Sport Roadster, Model 27-24, which weighed 2,990 pounds. It was available in rumble seat version only, with the rumble seat this year featuring folding arm rests. The car was finished in the same color scheme as the Model 27-25, and sold for $1,195. Buick built 4,985 for domestic sales and 271 for export. This beautifully restored model, featuring an accessory bumper, is owned by William Belding of Westfield Mass.

Listed as a 1927 Convertible Spider is this creation of the French coachbuilding firm of Jean Henri Labourdette. The car appears in a 1927 French auto magazine, but wears 1928 style headlights. Whether it was actually built on an early 1928 chassis, or whether the headlights were changed is unknown. Though the body is strictly coachbuilt, the lines appear quite similar to those on the 27-54 models. Note the toolbox on the running board.

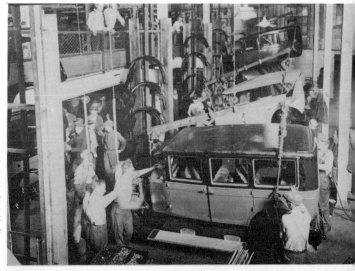

Buick's body drop section was a busy place, with four cars receiving their bodies at a time. Here two 7-passenger sedans and a touring receive their bodies. Front fenders and running boards were attached before the chassis rolled into position, but the rear fenders were put on after the body was bolted into place. The use of black fenders on all models made it unnecessary to color code these parts. The fenders were lowered from the upstairs parts supply.

The Weigande Funeral Home of Barberton, Ohio, used an extended Master Six chassis as the base for this combination hearse and ambulance. The very plain, almost stark body appears to have been built by the Flxible Co.

Not all Master Six 7-passenger Sedans went into private usage. This Model 27-50 was fitted with a large tool box and spent its life serving Culpeper, Front Royal, and Winchester, Va., in daily bus service, making the round trip run four times a day. At the time the picture was taken, the car had completed 52,510 miles of rough riding over the Blue Ridge Mountains, with not one cent spent for repairs or parts.

The Eureka Co. of Rock Falls, Ill., was a popular supplier of hand-crafted hearse and ambulance bodies during this era. One example of their work is this limousine burial coach, featuring a cut glass window insert, velvet drapes, and disc wheels. It was finished in medium gray with black fenders and top section. It could be converted to an ambulance.

Attractive landau irons decorate this combination limousine hearse-ambulance, produced by the Eureka Co. of Rock Falls, Ill., on an extended Master Six chassis. Standard Buick wheels were used on this model. The body was equipped with a partition between the rear and the driver's compartment, but this was fitted with a sliding glass panel. Roller shades were provided for the rear section. The unit was finished in dark gray and black.

The Juckem Co. of Minneapolis produced this attractive limousine hearse on the Master Six chassis, and sold it for $2,250 complete. The car featured a single side-mount, smooth mohair upholstery, and white wall tires. It was finished in Duco Buckingham gray with a black upper section and silver striping.

The Flxible Co. of Loudonville, Ohio, for year was a large user of Buick chassis. Here is one of the company's combination ambulance-hearse bodies, fitted to an extended Master Six chassis. The car was finished in a gray body with black fenders and upper section. The driver's compartment was separated from the rear by a partition fitted with a sliding glass panel.

Production again slipped for the second year in a row, and thus began a downward tumble that would continue at Buick for the next seven years — a financial plague that would hover over the company until the mid-30s. This year, 221,758 vehicles left the plant, which was still a healthy number, but a definite decrease from previous years and a portent of a bad future. In the production race, Buick dropped all the way down to sixth place, being beaten by Willys-Overland-Whippet; Hudson-Essex; and the relatively new Pontiac-Oakland combination.

The cars this year reflected the company's Silver Jubilee celebration by coming in with major style changes in both series. This was accomplished through the use of large plain crown fenders without ridges, bullet-type headlights and parking lights, new radiator, cowl and hood contours, and new chassis of the depressed center type, allowing the bodies to be lower.

However, all major specifications remained the same, with the Standard Six using the 23.4 SAE horsepower engine of 207 cubic inches, a wheelbase of 114.5 inches, and 31 x 5.25 inch tires. The Master Six used the 274-cubic-inch engine of 29.4 SAE horsepower, continued its two wheelbases of 120 and 128 inches, and kept its 33 x 6 inch tires. The 120-inch wheelbase was used only on the 4-door Sedan and its companion, the DeLuxe Sedan.

The Standard Series was reduced to seven styles through the discontinuance of the Special Coupe. The Master Series also was reduced, with only nine styles appearing. Gone were both the Convertible Coupe and the 120-inch wheelbase 2-door Sedan, but the DeLuxe 4-door Sedan was added, so the list of body styles only decreased by one.

Mechanically, this was Buick's first year with a "Standardized H" gearshift. Hydraulic shock absorbers also appeared for the first time as standard equipment, as did an adjustable driver's seat. Cooling was improved through the use of thicker radiator cores, and a new valve design helped to increase horsepower slightly. The Delco and Remy corporations merged this year as subsidiaries of General Motors, and thus all electrical equipment was now Delco-Remy.

All cars used inside heat and gasoline gauges and featured an adjustable steering column that could be adjusted for both height and angle. New stop-reverse taillights were provided, instead of the single tail and stop light. These were made by Guide Lamp Company of Cleveland. Also for the first time, bumpers were made standard rather than being an accessory supplied by the dealer. Wolverine bumpers were selected as the standard line.

Buick still did not offer color options on its bodies, but it changed its color schemes in production several times on the various models, and thus a certain variety of color did actually result.

Optional this year on all 128-inch wheelbase models and the 114.5 inch wheelbase sport models were Buffalo wire wheels and fender wells for either single or dual side-mounts. Still, natural finish wood-spoke wheels continued to be the most popular on the larger cars. Very often, the single rear tire carrier would be modified with the optional dual tire carrier so that two spares could be carried.

THE GREATEST BUICK EVER BUILT

Appearing for the last time was the attractive Master Six Country Club Coupe, Model 28-54-C. Finished in mountain brown with black fenders and a buff top, the car sold for $1,765 and weighed 3,890 pounds. It featured a rumble seat with arm rests and a solid canvas covered top with dummy landau irons. Buick built 6,555, all for domestic sales.

Buick's heaviest and most expensive car continued to be the Master Six 7-passenger Sedan, Model 28-50. It weighed 4,085 pounds and cost $1,995. A fairly popular vehicle, it enjoyed a production run of 10,827 for domestic sales and 206 for export.

A very attractive car was the Master Six 5-passenger Coupe, Model 28-58, which cost $1,850 and weighed 3,925 pounds. Buick built 9,984 for domestic sales and 11 on special order for export. The car was finished in boulevard maroon with black fenders, natural wood wheels, and a beige canvas top. This beautiful restoration is owned by Eugene Rathka of Birmingham, Mich.

A rear view of the Master Six 5-passenger Coupe, Model 28-58, shows the attractive styling of the padded and canvas covered upper body section and the large landau irons. The car offered ample trunk space, but the spare tire made loading the trunk a bit awkward. Buick still used only a single taillight, mounted in the center of the spare. This car is owned by Eugene Rathka of Birmingham, Mich.

Using the 120-inch wheelbase chassis was the Master Six 4-door Sedan, available in plain or DeLuxe versions. This is the plain version, Model 28-47, which sold for $1,495 and weighed 3,920 pounds. Despite its rather stodgy lines, a total of 34,197 were sold in the U.S. and another 378 went overseas.

Utilizing the body of the DeLuxe Sedan, but built on the 128-inch wheelbase chassis, was the Master Six Brougham Touring Sedan, Model 28-51. The 3,980 pound car was priced at $1,925. Buick built 10,258 for domestic sales and 45 for export. Because of the longer wheelbase, the trunk-rack was a standard unit on these cars, with the spare tire mounted behind the rack. However, the matching trunk was an accessory, as were the bumpers. Dummy landau irons and a fabric covered rear upper quarter were attractive styling features on both this and the Model 28-47-S.

Of much more attractive line than the plain sedan was the new Master Six 4-door DeLuxe Sedan, Model 28-47-S, which appeared this year only. The 3,930-pound car cost $1,575, and was also known as the Town Brougham. Buick built 16,398 for domestic sales and seven special order models for export. The car used the 120-inch wheelbase chassis.

Buick's 4-passenger Coupe, Model 28-48, had far less the flair of the country club model, but it offered complete weather protection for all passengers, and thereby gained in popularity. Buick built 9,002, all for domestic sales. Available only in the Master Six Series, the ocean blue car used the 128-inch wheelbase chassis, cost $1,465, and weighed 3,835 pounds.

THE GREATEST BUICK EVER BUILT

1928

Appearing for the last time this year was the very attractive Master Six 4-passenger Sport Roadster, Model 28-54. Buick built 3,835 for domestic sales and 85 for export. All were finished in horizon blue with black fenders, and all were equipped with rumbleseats and folding windshields as standard equipment. The tops were done in buff colored fabric. The car cost $1,495 and weighed 3,655 pounds. This completely original example, in almost perfect shape, is owned by Thurm Kuipers, a Buick dealer in Gilman, Ill. Despite the car's excellent condition, Mr. Kuipers, pictured here with the vehicle, intends to do a full restoration.

Buick's lowest production car of the year was the Master Six Sport Touring, Model 28-55, of which only 1,333 were built for domestic sales. Finished in horizon blue with black fenders, this was Buick's first model to offer dual sidemounts. It cost $1,525 and weighed 3,735 pounds.

Shown with top raised and top lowered is this interesting little 5-passenger custom convertible by the coachbuilding firm of Heinrich Glaser of Dresden, Germany. The interesting design, quite akin to the later day convertibles, was not duplicated in any Buick body styles until 1932 when the first production Buick 2-door phaeton was introduced. Although the car was listed as a 1928 model, it appears that a 1929 chassis, or hood and radiator shell were used.

Only 132 Master Six Sport Tourings, Model 28-55-X, were built for export this year. This one wound up in Saudi Arabia, where it consistently was a center of attraction in that car-poor part of the world. Note the ornate feathered radiator cap. In addition to its production touring cars, Buick also built two Master Six 7-passenger Touring Cars, designated Model 28-49. It cannot be ascertained if these two cars were built strictly for promotional or experimental purposes or if they were special order models. The fact that a model designation was given to the cars indicates that they might have been destined for production, then dropped when it appeared that the market did not warrant production of such a design.

A highly attractive option on the Master Six Sport Roadster were the wire wheels with dual sidemounts. Both the roadster and the touring models featured fold-down windshields of very attractive design. These could be folded down flat across the cowl as seen here. Sport Roadsters were available in rumble seat form only. Shown here with his newly delivered car is Peter DePaolo, a world famous racing driver of the era. A new innovation for Buick this year was a combination ignition switch and settring column lock. This type of lock was continued for 11 years, appearing for the last time on the 1939 models.

With the coach gone from the Master Six Series, the Standard Six Coach, Model 28-20 became Buick's only model of this type. The car was finished in parkway green body with black fenders and upper body section. It cost $1,195 and weighed 3,310 pounds. Buick built 32,481 for domestic sales and 61 for export. This nicely restored model is owned by Bruce Moffett of Flint, Mich. The bumpers continued to be accessories. The interior was of two-tone plush trimmed mohair. The motometer on this car is not standard, as a radiator cap was used this year.

Buick's most popular car was the Standard Six 4-door Sedan, Model 28-27, which enjoyed a production run of 50,224 for domestic sales and 1,863 for export. The car cost $1,295 and weighed 3,370 pounds. Buick was very proud of its narrow windshield and door posts.

An attractive but not too popular car was the Standard Six 5-passenger Town Brougham, Model 28-29. Buick built 10,840. It cost $1,375 and weighed 3,400 pounds. The car featured dummy landau irons set on quarter panels covered in course grain rubberized fabric.

STANDARD SIX

Designed for the businessman was the Standard Six 2-passenger Coupe, Model 28-26, which was available only with a trunk. It cost $1,195 and weighed 3,215 pounds. Buick built 12,417, all for domestic sales. The dummy landau irons were standard equipment. This was the last year that Buick would use the old style wood-rimmed steering wheel.

THE GREATEST BUICK EVER BUILT

The Standard Six Touring, Model 28-25, continued to drop in popularity, with production this year reaching only 3,134 for domestic sales and 2,741 for export. The car was finished in trail green with black fenders and a buff top. It cost $1,225 and weighed 3,140 pounds.

Slightly more popular than the 2-passenger coupe was the Standard Six Country Club Coupe, Model 28-26-S. Buick built 13,211, all for domestic sales. The car cost $1,275, weighed 3,300 pounds, and was available only in rumble seat form. Attractive features included the rumble seat arm rests, dummy landau irons, padded rear quarter panels, and golf club access door.

Buick's own in-plant fire department used this 4-passenger Standard Six Sport Roadster, Model 28-24, for its chief's car. The Roadster was Buick's lightest car, weighing 3,090 pounds. It cost $1,195, and followed the Sport Touring's color scheme of black fenders, trail green body and buff top. It was available only in rumble seat form. Buick built 4,513 for domestic sales and 251 for export. The sport models used the Master Six chromed headlights.

Across the border in Canada, McLaughlin Buicks continued to be turned out in force, with both production bodies and in chassis form for the addition of specialized coachwork. One such specialized unit was this very attractive 3-way funeral car. The wide door opening and rotating casket table allowed loading from either side or from the rear. There was no centerpost for the door latches. Instead, the rear doors latched into the roof and sill, while the front doors latched into the leading edges of the rear doors. This year, Buick had a completely new chassis of the depressed center type, which lowered the height of all bodies about three inches, regardless of whether they were production or coachbuilt models. Large cantilever springs were still used in the rear, but these were now equipped with hydraulic shock absorbers.

Buick's engines remained basically the same as they had been in 1927, but the new gearshift was the first time that Buick used the standard "H" pattern. The Standard Six line used the 207-cubic-inch block, while the Master Six Series had 274-cubic-inch displacement.

Buick built only one truck this year. It was this experimental model which never went beyond the prototype stage. Following use by the design department, it was turned over to Buick's mail department, where it saw years of service. Note that the body does not use a cowl, as did the hearse and ambualnce bodies. This resulted in the sidemount blocking the driver's door and making entry from the left impossible.

Buick's 2-millionth car rolled from the factory this year. It was a Master Six 5-passenger Coupe, Model 28-58, fitted with a top of black rubberized fabric. Here watching the car being assembled is E.T. Strong, then president and general manager of Buick, shown holding his hat. The rear fenders were attached after the body was bolted in place.

1928

The North Wildwood, N.J., Fire Department ordered this limousine-type ambulance on a Master Six chassis. The body was built by the Flxible Co. of Loudonville, Ohio. It uses a leaded glass rear quarter window, and was equipped with dual spotlights, bumpers, and dual sidemounts. The vehicle was finished in white with black fenders and top.

THE GREATEST BUICK EVER BUILT

Lagerquist Auto Co. of Des Moines, Iowa, was a small producer of attractive special commercial bodies. This limousine style was popular because it could be used for both hearse and ambulance work. Built for the Jones Funeral Home of Boone, Iowa, the car used an extended Master Six chassis with disc wheels. The car is rigged for a sidemount, but since a welled fender is not used, the tire would have blocked the driver's door.

Coming into increasing use in the funeral car field was the "side-way" burial coach, in which the casket was loaded onto a turntable mounted within the car and then rotated into the body. Such a design necessitated both doors opening wide, with no centerpost. This version, mounted on an extended Master Six chassis, was built by Eureka of Rock Falls, Ill. The rear door locked into the sills, and the front door locked into the rear door.

The Flxible Co. of Loudonville, Ohio was one of the major specialty body builders to use Master Six chassis for a great number of their vehicles. Shown here is the Flxible limousine funeral coach, which used the same basic body of the limousine ambulance. A partition separated the driver's compartment from the rear compartment.

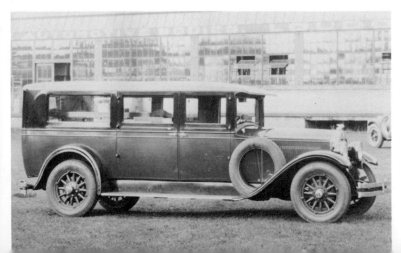

The Knightstown Body Co. of Knightstown, Ind., produced a wide range of medium-priced funeral coaches and ambulances, many of them based on extended Master Six chassis. Known as the Silver Knightstown, this model could be ordered in funeral coach form as shown here, or with ambulance equipment. It used double opening doors, without a centerpost.

Production was again down, this time dipping to 96,104 for the calendar year. Still, other companies were suffering in the early years of the worst depression to ever hit the country, and thus Buick was able to hold its sixth place in company ranking.

Offered this year were three totally new series, replacing the former Standard and Master Series. These were the Series 116, which essentially replaced the Standard, the Series 121, which replaced the former 120-inch wheelbase Masters; and the Series 129, which replaced the former 128-inch wheelbase Master models.

For the first time, color options were available on all models. In all, forty-three shades in a wide variety of combinations were available, all in DuPont lacquer. Body lines this year only were of the "bulge body" or "pregnant" school, a style that the public was still not quite ready to accept.

The 116 Series was built on a brand new 116-inch wheelbase chassis, equipped with 20 x 5.5 inch tires. The engine was a newly designed Six of 239 cubic inches, running a bore and stroke of 3-5/16 x 4-5/8 inches. It developed 74 brake horsepower at 2800 RPM. The model range of the 116 Series consisted of five styles.

The 121 Series also used a redesigned chassis, having a wheelbase of 121 inches and being equipped with 20 x 6.5 inch tires. It was powered by a completely new 309.6-cubic-inch Six running a bore and stroke of 3-5/8 x 5 inches which developed 91 brake or 31.5 SAE horsepower at 2800 RPM. The line consisted of six body styles.

The 129 Series used the same 309.6-cubic-inch engine as did the 121 Series, but its eight body styles were built on a new 129-inch wheelbase chassis which used 32 x 6.5 tires.

For the first time, all engines were equipped with a gasoline pump. Marvel carburetors and Delco-Remy ignition were used on everything. Sadly, the 1929 Buicks soon gained a reputation for being huge "gas guzzlers," a reputation not completely without merit, as many owners found that 10 to 12 miles per gallon was all that could be coaxed from the large engines in the 129 Series.

All closed cars featured slanting, non-glare windshields, adjustable front seats, double electric windshield wipers, and side cowl ventilators as standard equipment. Brakes were still 4-wheel mechanical, with the service brake still being of the contracting type, while the parking brake was of the expanding type on the rear wheels only.

All roadster and touring models had a full ventilating windshield, with the upper part adjustable when the top was raised. With the top lowered, the whole windshield could be folded forward across the cowl. On these cars, equipment consisted of a single hand-operated windshield wiper. Special-finish leather upholstery was used on all open models.

Again, all cars featured hydraulic shock absorbers front and rear, centralized chassis lubrication, an adjustable steering wheel, controlled headlight beams, and a combination stop-taillight-back-up light assembly.

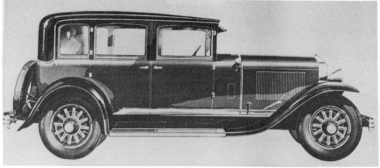

Surprisingly, the Series 129 5-passenger 4-door Sedan, Model 29-57, received a very cool response from the public, and as a result, only 5,175 were built. The car cost $1,935 and weighed 4,260 pounds. It is shown here in standard trim, except for the bumpers which were accessories.

A slightly larger rear end bulge differentiated the Series 129 7-passenger Sedan, Model 29-50, from the 5-passenger version. The car weighed 4,360 pounds and cost $2,045. Buick built 8,058 for domestic sales and 319 for export. Its most popular colors were a classic blue body with black fenders and upper body section.

Buick's most expensive, heaviest, and least popular car was the new Series 129 Limousine, Model 29-50-L. It cost $2,145, weighed 4,405 pounds, and had a production run of only 736 for domestic sales and 169 for export. The car used the same body and seating arrangement as did the Model 29-50, but was fitted with a glass partition between compartments, a richer interior, and small coach-type reading lamps in the rear quarter panels. The wire wheels were an accessory.

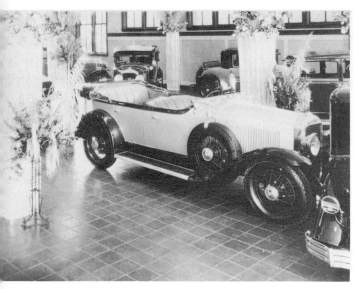

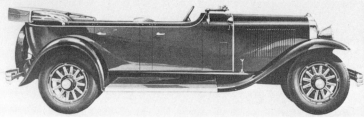

After years of ignoring the 7-passenger open cars, Buick came back with a 7-passenger touring. It was the Model 29-49 in the Series 129. Priced at $1,550 and weighing 3,990 pounds, the car attracted 1,530 buyers and 633 overseas customers. It is shown here with the standard spoke wheels, but wire wheels and sidemounts were a popular option.

A beautiful car, when fitted with the optional wire wheels and dual sidemounts, was the Series 129 5-passenger Sport Touring, Model 29-55. Its most popular color combination was ledo green body with black fenders, wheels and trim, a natural leather interior and natural canvas top. The car cost $1,525 and weighed 3,905 pounds. Buick built 1,122 for domestic sales and 311 for export. Many of these models were also fitted with disc wheels.

A popular style of this era was the close-coupled sedan, and Buick was right in there, offering the style in both the Series 121 and the Series 129. This is the Series 129 version, Model 29-51, which weighed 4,230 pounds and cost $1,875. Production was 7,014 for domestic sales and 105 for export. Its most popular color combination was lido green body with a Boise green upper section. On this model, the trunk, rack, sidemounts, bumpers, and artillery wheels were extra.

The on-again-off-again convertible temporarily reappeared this year in the form of the Series 129 4-passenger Convertible Coupe, Model 29-54-CC. It cost $1,875 and weighed 4,085 pounds. Buick built 2,021 for domestic sales and 91 for export. It was available in rumble seat form only. The most popular colors were nomad tan or storm brown. This model is wearing the accessory artillery spoke wheels and sidemount. An access door was provided in the right quarter panel, and both the rumble seat and the adjustable driver's seat were finished in leather.

The new Series 129 5-passenger Coupe, Model 29-58, no longer sported its beautiful landau irons or canvas top. Built on the 129-inch wheelbase chassis, the large car weighed 4,145 pounds and cost $1,865. Buick built 7,311, with the most popular color being Cairo green. This well restored model, wearing extra cost bumpers and white walls, is owned by Ken Maxwell of Beachwood, N.J. Dual windshield wipers were standard on all large closed models this year.

1929

Despite its new body lines, the Series 121 4-door Sedan, Model 29-47, ended up with rather severe lines. Still, the car was a popularity leader, with 30,416 being built. It cost $1,520 and weighed 4,175 pounds. Regular spoke wheels were standard, but wide-spoke artillery wheels, wire wheels, or disc wheels could be purchased as extra cost options.

The Series 121 Sedan was popular in the U.S., but its overseas sales were not too good, and only 335 were built for export. One of the export models is seen here on a tea plantation in Ceylon. It is wearing the accessory disc wheels. In addition to the exporting of complete cars, Buick also shipped 168 stripped Series 121 chassis overseas.

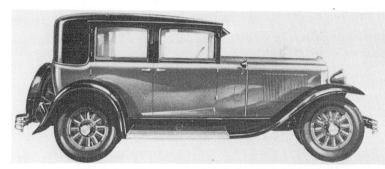

The new welled fenders added an appealing and sporty touch to all models. Welled fenders and sidemounts were an accessory on all models, but were used most often on the open cars or were ordered by buyers who wanted the optional luggage rack on the rear. A wing-nut held the tire at the top, while a tumbler lock secured it at the bottom and prevented theft.

The Series 121 Close-coupled Sedan, Model 29-41, used a blanked-in quarter panel, and featured rather pleasing lines overall. Still, it commanded nowhere near the popularity of the regular sedan, and only 10,110 were built, all for domestic sales. It cost $1,450 and weighed 4,180 pounds. The most popular color of the sedans was Boise green body with black upper section. Ashtrays were provided in both rear doors, but the spare tire and bumpers were added cost items.

More popular than the 2-passenger coupe was the Series 121 4-passenger Special Coupe, Model 29-46-S. The 4,055-pound car cost $1,450 and was equipped with a rumble seat and access door on the right quarter panel. The trunk rack, sidemount, bumpers and wood artillery wheels were accessories. Production, all for domestic sales, was 6,638. Also introduced this year was the Series 121 4-passenger Coupe, Model 29-48, which cost $1,445 and weighed 4,010 pounds. Buick built 4,255. The most popular body color of both coupes was boulevard maroon.

Designed primarily for businessmen who wanted something above average was the Series 121 2-passenger Coupe, Model 29-46. It cost $1,395, weighed 3,990 pounds, and offered substantial trunk space. Buick built 4,339, all for domestic sales. A very popular color for this model was chermonte cream with black fenders and upper body.

Enjoying surprisingly good sales was the new Series 121 Roadster, Model 29-44. The rumble seat equipped car had a production run of 6,195 for domestic sales and 184 for export. It cost $1,325 and weighed 3,795. Its most popular color combinations were chermonte cream or atikes blue body with black fenders and a black or buff canvas top. This beautiful restoration is owned by Gene Amber of Akron, Ohio. It has accessory bumpers, driving lights, and whitewalls.

Wearing the beautiful but not too popular accessory wire wheels is this Series 121 Roadster, Model 29-44. It is shown here on prominent display in a dealer's show room, equipped with dual sidemounts and accessory bumpers. All Series 121 cars used the 121-inch wheelbase chassis.

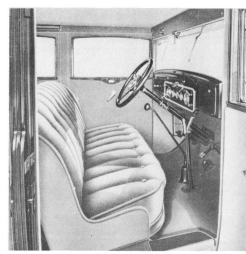

One of the Series 121 chassis built for export was fitted with this unusual coupe body of definite European line. The photo on file in the Detroit Library, gave no indication as to who the coachbuilder was, though styling and equipment are of the British school.

The interior of the new Buicks was impressive for cars in this price range, with all trim being in polished walnut. Roller shades were still provided for the rear doors and windows of sedans. A new style starter and gas pedal was used, and the instrument cluster was of new design, as was the totally new one-piece steering wheel. This new wheel was of molded rubber, and replaced the old steel spoke, wood rimmed wheel used in various forms since Buick started in 1903. The throttle and spark levers and the headlight switch were located in the center of the steering wheel hub, adjacent to the central horn button.

Buick was as proud of its chassis as it was of its new bodies, and built several of these cut-away versions for display at various auto shows and in the showrooms of major dealers. Buick still used canitlever springs on the rear and external contracting service brakes.

The new Buick engine featured improved intake and exhaust manifolds, a new gasoline pump, and a stronger crankcase. Buick continued to use the torque tube drive concept, which required only one universal joint located directly behind the transmission. An updraft carburetor was used.

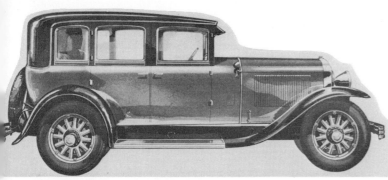

Buick's most popular car this year was the Series 116 4-door Sedan, Model 29-27. Buick built 44,345 for domestic sales and 3,262 for export. The car used the 116-inch wheelbase chassis, weighed 3,630 pounds, and cost $1,320. Its most popular finish was a cynosure blue body with black fenders and top section. The car featured a robe rail and polished foot rest for rear seat passengers, but the bumpers and spare tire were considered added cost accessories.

The 2-door Coach appeared only in the Series 116. Designated the Model 29-27, it cost $1,220 and weighed 3,525 pounds. Buick built 17,733 for domestic sales and 90 for export. Its most popular color was scaraba green or cynosure blue. This restored version features accessory bumpers and step plates. Fenders and upper body were finished in black.

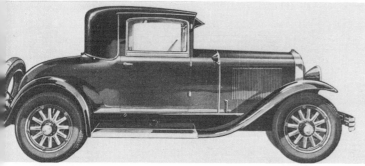

Buick's lowest priced car was the Series 116 Business Coupe, Model 26-26. It cost $1,195 and weighed 3,465 pounds. Buick built 8,745 for domestic sales and one special order version for export. Both bumpers and spare tire were added cost accessories. New for the year were ashtrays and lighters on the door panels. The side access door was no longer used.

More popular than the Business Coupe was the Series 116 Special Coupe, Model 26-26-S. Also known as the Sport Coupe, the car featured a rumble seat with arm rests and an access door for golf bags. The most popular color of the coupes was a pharo gray body with a Tunis gray upper section. The Sport Coupe weighed 3,520 pounds and cost $1,250. Buick built 10,308. Bumpers, sidemount, trunk rack, and wood artillery wheels were added cost accessories.

Buick's lightest car this year was the Series 116 Sport Touring, Model 29-25. Also known as the Phaeton, the car weighed 3,330 pounds and cost $1,225. Buick built 2,938 for domestic sales. The windshield folded forward, and the interior was in special-finish leather. Bumpers, sidemount, trunk rack, and wood artillery wheels were all added cost accessories.

THE GREATEST BUICK EVER BUILT

Buick's Series 116 Sport Touring proved to be more popular overseas than it was in the U.S. The export version, known as the Model 29-25-X, had a production run of 3,024. It is shown here with its British family, hooked to an early type camper trailer. Except for the right-hand drive, the U.S. version in standard form would have looked exactly like this car.

1929

The Flemington, N.J., Post 159 of the American Legion operated the ambulance service in that city, and this year took delivery of a new Flxible ambulance. The vehicle was mounted on an extended Series 129 chassis, and was equipped with leaded glass rear windows, spotlight, side-mount, siren and bumpers. It was finished in two-tone gray with black fenders.

Using the same body as the Flemington ambulance was this Flxible ambulance built for the DuPont Co. of Wilmington, Del. However, since this unit was used strictly as an industrial ambulance, it lacked many of the frills of the units built for public usage. Roller shades were used on all rear compartment windows, and fans were installed in the rear quarter panels. A sliding glass partition was used between compartments. Flxible of Loudonville, Ohio, built many varieties of ambulances and hearses on Series 129 chassis, all using the same basic body.

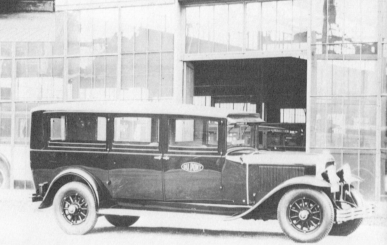

The Eureka Co. of Rock Falls, Ill., mounted many of their 3-way-loading burial coach bodies on extended Series 126 chassis. In this type of car, the casket could be loaded from either the left or the right side, or from the rear. This model is fitted with the Buick accessory artillery wheels, dual sidemounts, bumpers, and extra-large dual taillights.

The Knightstown Funeral Car Co. of Knightstown, Ind., built several versions of funeral cars and ambulances on Series 129 chassis, extended to 155-inch wheelbases. Their economy model was the Knightstown, a rear-loading limousine hearse with side access doors. A solid partition with two fixed windows separated the driver from the rear compartment.

The top of the line hearse built by Knightstown Funeral Car Co. of Knightstown, Ind., was the Silver Knightstown, mounted here on a Series 126 model with extended chassis. The unit was of the side-loading type. Both doors on the right side opened wide, with no center post being used, and the casket was placed on a self-guiding turntable which slid it into the rear compartment. Front and rear compartments were not separated on side-loading hearses, and a folding seat had to be used on the passenger's side to allow for the turning of the casket when the car was loaded.

Production was down again, this time taking a great fall to 119,265 for the calendar year. New blood was needed, and it was already on the drawing boards in the form of a totally new overhead valve Straight 8 which would appear in 1931. Still, though Buick was suffering, other manufacturers appeared to be suffering even more from the depression, and thus Buick managed to float up to third place as rampant chaos was the word of the day in auto plants across the country — and for that matter, around the world.

Meanwhile, Buick completely restyled its entire line, and much modified its "pregnant" body styling. Among the major changes were the three new series that were introduced to replace the three former series of 1929. Likewise, both engines were increased in bore, radiators received thermostatically controlled shutters, and the 4-wheel brakes were now internal expanding with Servo-Mechanical assist units. Marvel carburetors and Delco-Remy ignition was used on all cars, as were Lovejoy-Duodraulic shocks. Standard wheels were the wood spoke type, but disc wheels or wire wheels with sidemounts were available as accessories.

Succeeding the former Series 116, was the new Series 40. The car was on a brand new 118-inch wheelbase chassis, and stood on 19 x 5:00 tires, which resulted in a much lower and far more modern appearance. The engine size was increased to 257.5 cubic inches through a new bore and stroke of 3-7/16 x 4-5/8 inches. This raised the power output to 28.4 SAE or 80.5 brake horsepower at 2800 RPM.

The new Series 50 succeeded the former Series 121. These models grew three inches via a new chassis with a 124-inch wheelbase. Tires were 19 x 6.50. The Series 60, which succeeded the former Series 129, also enjoyed a three inch growth via a new chassis of 132-inch wheelbase. Tires here were 19 x 6.50.

Both the Series 50 and Series 60 were powered by an expanded Six of 331.5 cubic inches, having a bore and stroke of 3.75 inches. The new engine developed 33.75 SAE or 98 brake horsepower at 2800 RPM.

Introduced with a huge fanfare was the ill-fated Marquette, which was supposed to be Buick's answer to the depression slump. The "Baby Buick" was built on a 114-inch wheelbase chassis, with 28 x 5.25 inch tires. It used its own special L-head Six of 212 cubic inches, which had a bore and stroke of 3-1/8 x 4-5/8 inches. It developed 23.4 SAE or 67.5 brake horsepower at 3000 RPM. As did the rest of the Buick line, the Marquette had 4-wheel mechanical brakes with a Duo-Serve assist unit, and used a Marvel carburetor and Delco-Remy ignition. Production, all of which was classed as 1930 design, began June 1, 1929, with an ambitious program of six body styles. Wood-spoke wheels were standard, but wire wheels and sidemounts were available accessories.

Production reached 37,829 in the U.S. and 3,418 in Canada. All Canadian production was of 4-door sedans only, with no other styles being built in that country. However, by mid-1930, Buick management decided that going the "economy car" route with the Marquette was not the answer to Buick's depression problems. There were just too many good 6-cylinder cars around in the low-price market without Buick walking in and trying to compete for the rapidly disappearing customer dollar. And, many of these other 6-cylinder low-price cars were equally as good as the Marquette, had much lower price tags, and were much better known to the public than was the Marquette. By mid-year, management was convinced that it would go nowhere in the Marquette, and thus the car died at the end of 1930, along with its parent 6-cylinder Buick.

In a completely different area, for the first time in seventeen years, Buick was once again at the Indianapolis Memorial Day Classic. The car was a heavily reworked Buick Six entered and driven by Harry Butcher. Starting thirty-eighth in a field of thirty-eight, and barely qualifying at 87 MPH, the car managed to run the entire race, though not the entire 500 miles. Butcher was flagged into fourteenth place at the end of his 127th lap, still running, though 182 miles behind the winning Miller-Hartz Special.

The Series 60 7-passenger Phaeton again used a thin tonneau cowl behind the driver's seat, finished in the same color as the body. The complete interior was carpeted, while both seats and doors were upholstered in hand-buffed leather. Storage pouches were provided on all four doors, and the windshield would fold flat across the cowl.

A decidedly unpopular car, which had slightly more overseas buyers than domestic customers, was the attractive Series 60 7-passenger Phaeton, Model 30-69. Buick produced 807 for domestic sales and 811 for export. The 4,100-pound car cost $1,595. The wire wheels and accessories on this well restored model are accessories. The car's most popular color was boulevard maroon with black fenders, natural canvas top and natural leather upholstery. This car is owned by Vincent Strauere of Downington, Pa. It is equipped with an accessory chromed grille guard.

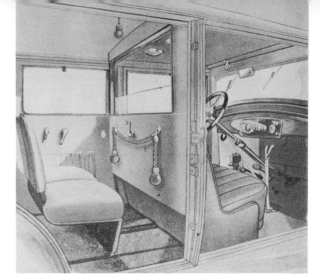

The top of the line models were in the new Series 60, now built on a 132-inch wheelbase chassis. Shown here in the factory staging area are a group of Series 60 7-passenger Sedans, Model 30-60. They weighed 4,415 pounds and cost $1,910. Buick built 6,583 for domestic sales and 67 for export. The wire wheels and sidemounts shown on these cars were factory installed accessories.

The interior of the Series 60 Limousine shows the rich fittings built into the compartment divider. Dome lights were provided for the front compartment, while quarter panel reading lights were installed in the rear. All doors featured storage pouches, and all rear compartment windows were fitted with concealed silk roller shades.

Buick's heaviest, most expensive, and lowest production car was the Series 60 Limousine, Model 30-60-L, which weighed 4,475 pounds, cost $2,070 and had a production run of only 690 for domestic sales and 146 for export. It was the only Buick to have a base price of over $2,000. The car used the standard 7-passenger sedan body, fitted with a glass partition between compartments and slightly more elaborate internal fittings. Wire wheels and sidemounts were factory installed accessories, as were demountable wood-spoke artillery wheels. The standard wheel for these cars remained the non-demountable wood spoke style, with demountable rims. In addition to the completed cars, Buick built 840 stripped Series 60 chassis for domestic sales and 84 for export sales. This outstanding example of the Model 30-60-L is owned by Nicola Bulgari of New York City and Rome, Italy. The car is part of his extensive Buick collection, which is housed in Rome.

Certainly one of Buick's most attractive cars this year was the large Series 60 4-passenger Sport Roadster, Model 30-64. However, only 2,006 were built for domestic sales and only three were built on special order for export. The car weighed 4,015 pounds and cost $1,585. The most popular color was premier green. It was available only in rumble seat form. This excellent example is owned by Clarence Stanbury of New York. Among its accessories are wire wheels, sidemounts, whitewall tires, luggage rack, fog lights and windwings.

The most popular car in the Series 60 line was the 5-passenger 4-door Sedan, Model 30-61, of which 12,508 were built for domestic sales and 49 were built for export. It cost $1,760 and weighed 4,330 pounds. This well restored model, featuring accessory fog lights, sidemounts, and matching-color wire wheels, is owned by Paul Kennedy of Mechanicsburg, Pa.

Buick again discontinued its convertible models, and offered only roadsters or coupes in the 2-4-passenger model range. Looking very similar to a convertible because of its fabric covered top and dummy landau irons was the Series 60 Country Club Coupe, Model 30-64-C. The car was built in rumble seat form only, and was equipped with an access door on the side and a special golf bag compartment. It sold for $1,695 and weighed 4,225 pounds. Buick built 5,370 for domestic sales and 11 for export. This beautiful example, wearing accessory wire wheels, sidemounts, whitewalls, and step plates, is owned by Richard Allen of Nanticoke, Pa.

Jack Dempsey, the world-famous heavy weight boxer, accepts delivery of his new Buick. It is a Series 60 5-passenger Coupe, Model 30-68, which cost $1,740 and weighed 4,200 pounds. This model has the accessory wire wheels, but the standard rear mounted spare. Buick built 10,216, all for domestic sales. The most popular color was LaTorquet green.

The interior of the Series 40 Roadster featured attractive all-leather upholstery, with the doors fitted with storage pouches. The same dashboard was used in all models. Rubber floor mats were used in the Series 40, but all other series had carpeted front and rear compartments. Open models used only a single windshield wiper, while closed cars had two wipers.

An adjustable driver's seat was installed in all Buicks this year, much to the relief of extra tall or short owners. Here a salesman demonstrates the new seat in a Model 30-46 Business Coupe. Note that the Series 40 used rubber floor mats, while all other series had carpeted interiors.

Buick's rumble seats still used the rather quaint folding armrests, but these were set too far back and were too short to be of any real comfort. This is the rear section of the Series 40 Roadster, fitted with accessory wire wheels and luggage rack. Only one step was used, as designers felt the bumper served as a satisfactory first step.

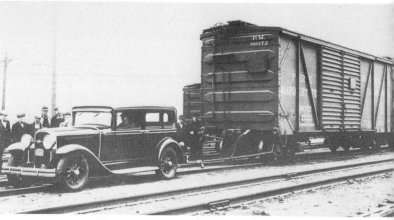

Determined to show the power of the new Series 50 Buicks, a Detroit dealer tied his Model 30-57 to two empty box cars and towed them for several hundred feet. Chains were used on the rear wheels to give the car better traction.

Enjoying less than half the popularity of the Series 40 Sedan was the new Series 50 4-door Sedan, Model 30-57, which was built on a 124-inch wheelbase chassis. Buick built 22,926 for domestic sales and 213 for export. The car weighed 4,235 pounds and cost $1,540. This nicely restored model is owned by Francis Hurley of Flint Mich.

THE GREATEST BUICK EVER BUILT

Only two cars were in the new Series 50. They were the 4-door Sedan and this 4-passenger Coupe, Model 30-58. It cost $1,510 and weighed 4,120 pounds. Buick built 5,275, all for domestic sales, with the most popular color being cynosure blue. For this year only, all chassis were equipped with semi-elliptic front and rear springs. Semi-elliptical front springs had been used on all models since 1916, and would be continued through 1933, with knee-action taking over the front suspension in 1934.

One of only two Series 60 7-passenger Sedans imported into Australia was this model, currently owned by Bruce Lord of Broken Hill, N.S.W. Of the two, one went to Sydney, where all record of it was lost, and the other went to F.J. Potter of Broken Hill, who subsequently sold it to Mr. Lord. The car was, and is, finished in black lacquer with blue wool cord upholstery.

The last of the Canadian McLaughlin Sixes looked identical to the U.S. Buicks, but used a slightly different front bumper. This model, produced for export to England, used right-hand drive and a single windshield wiper. It wears standard spoke wheels, but is fitted for sidemounts. The car compared to the U.S. Series 50 4-door Sedan, Model 30-57.

Buick's lightest line was the Series 40, which used a new 118-inch wheelbase chassis. This is the Series 40 2-door Sedan, Model 30-40, which cost $1,270 and weighed 3,600 pounds. Production was 6,101 for domestic sales and 43 for export. Its most popular color was traverse blue.

Buick's most popular car this year was the Series 40 4-door Sedan, Model 30-47, which had a production run of 47,294 for domestic sales and 202 for export. It cost $1,330 and weighed 3,700 pounds. In addition, Buick produced 2,056 Series 40 Sedan chassis for export.

THE GREATEST BUICK EVER BUILT

The Series 40 Business Coupe, Model 30-46, was built in 2-passenger form only, with substantial trunk space but no rumble seat option. It cost $1,260 and weighed 3,540 pounds. There were 5,695 built for domestic sales and 21 for export. The rear top panels were covered in rubberized fabric, as was the back panel.

Fred Brennan, left, then acting chief of the San Francisco Fire Department, accepts delivery of three new Buicks for his department. The cars are Series 40 Roadsters, Model 30-44, which were available in rumble seat form only. They cost $1,310 and weighed 3,420 pounds. There were 3,476 built for domestic use and 163 for export, with the most popular color being mentone tan. The San Francisco Fire Department had standardized on Buicks for all official cars starting in 1925. These models were painted fire engine red with black fenders.

The Series 40 Sport Coupe, Model 30-46-S, used the same body as did the business coupe, but was equipped with rumble seat, rear quarter access door on the left side, and dummy landau irons. The wire wheels and trunk rack were accessories. In basic form, it cost $1,300 and weighed 3,600 pounds. Buick built 10,719 for domestic sales and 29 for export.

An attractive car of only limited appeal was the Series 40 Phaeton, Model 30-45, of which only 972 were produced for domestic sales and 128 were built for export. The wire wheels and sidemounts were accessories. The car weighed 3,410 pounds and cost $1,310. In addition, Buick produced 72 Series 40 Phaeton chassis for domestic sales, and 1,160 for export.

A pleased purchaser accepts delivery of his new Marquette Roadster, Model 30-34, in front of a Buick showroom laden with Marquette posters. The roadster cost $1,020 and weighed 2,640 pounds. It was available in rumble seat style only, and featured a folding windshield and access door to the rear compartment. Production was 2,397 for domestic sales and 230 for export. All were powered by an L-head Six, the only time that Buick had ever used an L-head engine design.

Marquette produced two versions of its basic coupe body. They were the 2-passenger version, Model 30-36, and this Sport Coupe, Model 30-36-S. The Sport Coupe was equipped with rumble seat and side panel access door. The Sport Coupe had a run of 1,909 for domestic sales and 121 for export. The 2-passenger version, equipped with a trunk deck, had a production run of 2,475 for domestic sales and none for export. The 2-passenger model weighed 2,760 pounds. The 2-passenger model cost $990, while the sport model cost $1,020. The wire wheels and sidemounts shown on this model were accessories.

Sporting a set of accessory wire wheels and sidemounts is the new Marquette 2-door Sedan, Model 30-30, which weighed 2,850 pounds and cost an even $1,000. The Marquette was readily identified by its herring-bone grille. Model 30-30 production was $4,630 for domestic sales and 92 for export.

The least popular of the unpopular Marquettes was the 5-passenger Phaeton, Model 30-35, of which 889 were built for domestic sales and a surprising 1,281 were built for export. The car weighed 2,670 pounds and cost $1,020, but the wire wheels and sidemounts were extra.

The most popular Marquette was the 4-door Sedan, Model 30-37, of which 15,795 were built for domestic sales and 328 were built for export. It cost $1,060 and weighed 2,925 pounds.

Built in Australia for Australians were these versions of the Marquette 4-door Sedan, featuring padded rear quarter panels and dummy landau irons. The bodies were built by the Holden Co. In addition to its regular production run, Buick this year built 972 stripped Marquette chassis for domestic use, and 1,404 for export.

The Eureka Co. of Rock Falls, Ill., continued to offer its popular but expensive 3-way funeral coach, now mounted on a Series 60 extended chassis. This model is shown finished in black and wearing attractive chromed wire wheels and sidemounts. New for this model was an automatic right front seat, which slid forward on its own rails when the casket turntable was moved for side loading. The racks in the rear quarter windows were for carrying flowers. No center posts were used in this style hearse, as these would have blocked the casket loading area.

Built on one of the 2,056 Series 40 Sedan chassis produced for export was this attractive British Piccadilly Coupe. The design used a fabric covered solid top with blank quarter panels and chromed dummy landau irons. The large, removable rear trunk has a top upholstered in the same fabric as the car's top. Fender mounted running lights were required by British law.

The Flxible Co. of Loudonville, Ohio, used the same basic body for both its ambulance and hearse models, and preferred to mount these bodies on Buick Series 60 chassis. This is the funeral coach version, considered a limousine burial coach. It was rear loading, with full-width rear doors in addition to the four side doors. All rear compartment windows had shades.

American Legion Post 15 of East Greenwich, R.I., operated that city's ambulance service. New to the corps this year was this Flxible ambulance, mounted on a Buick Series 60 chassis extended to a 155-inch wheelbase. This model is fitted with a sliding glass partition between compartments, leaded glass rear quarter windows, and shades on all rear compartment windows.

The Flxible Co. of Loudonville, Ohio, continued to use the Series 60 chassis, extended to 155-inch wheelbase, for its ambulance and funeral car bodies. This is the ambulance version, one of several built for the U.S. Public Health Service. It was assigned to Marine Hospital. The car used leaded glass rear quarter windows, shades on all rear compartment windows, and a solid glass partition between compartments.

Buick's big news of the year was the series of new overhead valve 8-cylinder engines — an excellently designed power plant that in various forms would serve Buick admirably for the next twenty-two years. Still, the new engines were not enough to stave off the horrendous depression that was gnawing deeper and deeper into all facets of the American economy. Production fell again, dropping to 88,417. This marked the first time in the past ten years that Buick had produced less than 100,000 vehicles in a year. The reduction caused Buick to slip into fourth place in manufacturing rank, as the low price Plymouth, which had been climbing steadily since 1928, came into the top three where it was destined to remain until 1954.

It is often noted that Buick introduced its Straight Eight in 1931. Actually, it came out with three distinct 8-cylinder engines, and used these in its Four series.

The Series 50, which was now the lowest priced line, used a 77 brake horsepower version with a bore and stroke of 2-7/8 x 4.25 inches and displacing 220 cubic inches. The Series 50 used the 114-inch wheelbase formerly used on the now discontinued Marquette.

The Series 60, which used the 118-inch wheelbase chassis formerly used by the Series 40, was powered by a 272-cubic-inch version of the new engine. This model had a bore and stroke of 3-1/16 x 5 inches, and was rated at 90 brake horsepower. The Series 80, which used the 124-inch wheelbase chassis of the former Series 50, and the Series 90, which used the 132-inch wheelbase of the former Series 60, both used a 104 brake horsepower version of the new engine. In this form, the block was rated at 344 cubic inches and ran a bore and stroke of 3-5/16 x 5 inches.

In addition to the brand new engines, the other gre[at] engineering innovation was the use of Synchro-mes[h] transmissions in all but the Series 50 cars. Other engin[e]eering improvements included an oil temperature reg[u]lator, thermostatically controlled radiator shutters, and a[n] emergency brake that activated the shoes on all fo[ur] wheels.

While the spotlight was on engineering, the stylin[g] department was virtually asleep, and only very min[or] changes distinguished the 1931 styling from the 193[0] version. Options for all models and series included woo[d,] disc, or wire wheels; dual rear-mounted spares; du[al] sidemounts; and trunk racks and trunks. Interiors we[re] finished in mohair plush, broadcloth, and whipcord in [a] variety of colors, and some Series 90 models even ha[d] velvet carpeting in the rear compartments.

Not too long after the new engines were introduced, th[e] acceleration of the new Buicks was being recognized b[y] the automotive world. The cars were able to go from 10 t[o] 60 MPH in about 25 seconds and hold a steady 80 MP[H] which for the time was no small feat.

At Indianapolis, not one but two Buicks showed up fo[r] this year's Classic 500. Harry Butcher again entered [a] highly reworked model, as did Phil Shafer. Both cars use[d] the new Straight 8, but Butcher's car was running on [a] reworked Buick chassis while Shafer's used a Riglin[g] chassis. Shafer qualified at 105.1 MPH and thus starte[d] twenty-third out of a field of forty. He completed his 20[0] laps at an average speed of 86.3 MPH to win twelfth plac[e.] Butcher, however, qualified at only 99.3 MPH and starte[d] in thirty-third place. He completed only six laps before [a] spin-out wreck ended this year's race for his car.

The Series 90 was a line of impressive looking cars using a 132-inch wheelbase chassis. One of the most massive appearing of this series was the 7-passenger sedan, Model 90, which weighed 4,435 pounds and cost $1,935. Buick built 4,159 for domestic sales and 43 for export. Also produced were 636 stripped Series 90 chassis for domestic use and 36 for export. This Model 90, featuring white walls and spoke wheels, but using the rear mounted spare, is owned by Craig Solliday of Port Huron, Mich. Mr. Solliday has the front fitted with accessory fog lights and a chromed grille guard.

The only car to have a base price over $2,000 was the Series 90 7-passenger Limousine, Model 90-L. The car cost $2,035 and weighed 4,505 pounds. Buick built 514 for domestic sales and 106 for export. As before, the car used the Model 90 body, but with a partition between compartments and somewhat richer interior fittings. The wire wheels and sidemounts were an accessory used on the vast majority of these cars.

Slightly less rear overhang of the body marked the only exterior difference between the Series 90 5-passenger Sedan and the 7-passenger models. The 5-passenger style, designated Model 91, sold for $1,785 and weighed 4,340 pounds. Buick built 7,853 for domestic sales, but turned out only five special order models for export. Again, the wire wheels and sidemounts were extra.

The least popular car in the Series 90 line was the 7-passenger Phaeton, Model 95. Buick built only 392 for domestic sales and 68 for export, but produced another 290 of this model, without body, for export sales. The car cost $1,620 and weighed 4,125 pounds.

The Series 90 4-passenger Sport Coupe, Model 96-S, used completely different top treatment than did the Model 96-C, although the dummy landau irons on the Sport Coupe gave the appearance of a convertible. Built in rumble seat form only, the Sport Coupe weighed 4,250 pounds and cost $1,720. Buick built 2,990 for domestic sales and three special order versions for export. This model uses accessory wire wheels and the accessory dual rearmounted spares.

A beautiful car of only limited appeal was the huge Series 90 Roadster, Model 94, of which only 824 were built for domestic sales and 19 for export. The car was available in rumble seat form only, and featured an interior completely finished in fine grain leather. As was the case with all open models, the windshield folded flat across the cowl. The car weighed 4,010 pounds and cost $1,610, but the wire wheels, sidemounts and luggage rack were extra.

Introduced at mid-season was the new Series 90 Convertible Coupe, Model 96-C. Built in rumble seat version only, it sold for $1,785 and weighed 4,195 pounds. Buick built 1,066 for domestic sales and four special order models for export. Hand-crushed leather upholstery was used throughout, and the top was of double-texture canvas. The attractive chrome landau irons were functional, and braced the wooden top bows when the top was raised. The windshield could be folded flat across the cowl. Luggage rack, sidemounts, and wire wheels were extra.

Enjoying surprisingly good sales was the Series 90 5-passenger Coupe, Model 96, which had a production run of 7,705 for domestic sales and ten special order models for export. The attractive style, which featured built-in trunk space, weighed 4,260 pounds and cost $1,765. This well restored example is owned by Barbara McDonald of Howell, Mich. It is equipped with the accessory wire wheels, sidemounts, and luggage rack with matching trunk. Silk roller shades were provided for the back and rear quarter windows.

The Series 80 line consisted of only two models, a 4-door sedan and this 4-passenger Coupe, Model 86. Based on a 124-inch wheelbase chassis, the fairly large car cost $1,535 and weighed 4,120 pounds. The front passenger seat could be folded under the dashboard when not in use. Buick built 3,579, all for domestic sales.

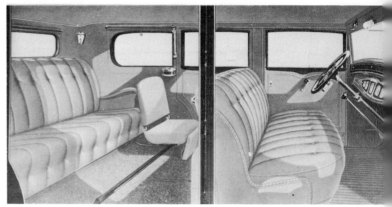

The interior of the Model 90 7-passenger Sedan was in highly refined taste, with heavily stuffed seats upholstered in button-style plush mohair. A smoking set was provided on each side of the rear seat, and silk roller shades were used on the rear and rear quarter windows. Coach-style reading lights on the quarter panels were used in place of a dome light. Also new for the year was a bottom-hinged foot-length accelerator pedal such as in use today. This replaced the former button and bar type accelerator that Buick had used for years.

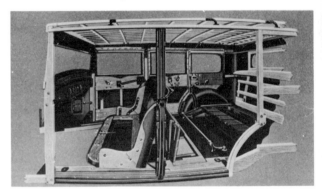

The Fisher Body Co. still used a tremendous amount of wood in its bodies, as can be seen in this cutaway view of the Model 90 7-passenger sedan. The roof was of the slat-and-bow type of construction, with wood slats being supported by small metal bows.

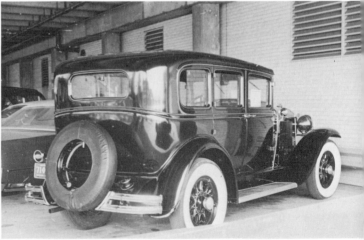

The popular car in the relatively unpopular Series 80 line was the 4-door Sedan, Model 87, of which 14,731 were built for domestic sales and 38 for export. The car cost $1,565 and weighed 4,255 pounds. This attractively restored example is owned by Arthur Reenders of Grand Haven, Mich. It is in completely standard form except for the white wall tires.

The 2-passenger Business Coupe enjoyed slightly more popularity in the Series 60 line than it did in the Series 50, and 2,732 were built, all for domestic sales. Designated the Model 66, the car cost $1,285 and weighed 3,615 pounds. The car was finished in mohair plush or cloth, and was available only with a trunk. The rubberized fabric top was carried over the rear roof quarter panels in both models.

Ann Pennington, an internationally famous dancer of the time, takes possession of her new Series 60 5-passenger Phaeton, Model 65 from a Detroit dealer. The fairly large car cost $1,335 and weighed 3,525 pounds. Buick built only 463 for domestic sales and only 32 for export. But, an additional 184 Phaeton chassis, without body, were produced for export only.

A very attractive car with fairly decent sales was the Series 60 4-passenger Sport Coupe, Model 66-S. Buick built 6,489 for domestic sales and 12 for export. Available in rumble seat form only, the car was trimmed with matching-color top fabric and dummy landau irons. It cost $1,325 and weighed 3,695 pounds. Again, the wire wheels and sidemounts were accessories. The rear window could be lowered to permit conversation between those in the front and in the rumble seat.

The most popular car in the Series 60 line was the very practical 4-door Sedan, Model 67, of which 30,665 were built for domestic sales and 110 were built for export. The car weighed 3,795 pounds and cost $1,355. This well restored version, in completely stock trim, is owned by Philip Jocksom of Toronto, Canada. It is actually a Canadian version, built by the McLaughlin firm, but identical to the U.S. model. In addition to the Series 60 production listed here, Buick built 1,392 stripped Series chassis for domestic sales and 300 for export.

A very attractive car was the Series 60 4-passenger Roadster, Model 64, which was available in rumble seat form only. The car cost $1,335 and weighed 3,465 pounds. Buick built 1,050 for domestic sales and 28 for export. As can be seen, the windshield folded over the cowl. Wire wheels and sidemounts were an accessory. Upholstery was in grained leather, trimmed in plain style, with matching pockets in each door.

A pretty little car was the Series 50 4-passenger Special Coupe, Model 56-S. Built were 5,733 for domestic sales and 24 for export. The car was available only in rumble seat form, but the wire wheels, sidemounts, and white walls shown here were accessories. It cost $1,055 and weighed 3,155 pounds.

Most popular of the Series 50 models was the 4-door Sedan, Model 57, which had a production run of 33,184 for domestic sales and 174 for export. The car cost $1,095 and weighed 3,265. Interior fittings included mohair plush or cloth in button style, arm rests, foot rest, rear compartment carpet, assist cords, dome lights and screened ventilators. In addition to the cars listed here, Buick built 292 Series 50 Phaeton chassis for export; 1,248 stripped Series 50 chassis for domestic sales, and 468 Series 50 Sedan chassis for export.

Enjoying no great popularity was the Series 50 Business Coupe, Model 56, which had a production run of only 1,726, all for domestic sales. It cost $1,025 and weighed 3,055 pounds. The car was built in 2-passenger form only, with substantial trunk space and additional luggage space in a separate compartment behind the front seat.

Introduced at mid-year was the very beautiful Series 50 Convertible Coupe, Model 56-C. Built in rumble seat version only, the car featured a weather-tight top, folding windshield, and chromed functional landau irons. It cost $1,095 and weighed 3,095 pounds. Built were 1,531 for domestic sales and nine special order models for export. This beautiful restoration is owned by John Gerstkemper of Annaheim, Cal. It is fitted with the accessory wire wheels and sidemounts, grille guard, and luggage rack with matching trunk.

This rear view of John Gerstkemper's beautiful Model 56-C Convertible shows the appealing line formed by the accessory luggage rack and trunk. The sidemount covers and trunk cover, in the same material as the top, were accessories for the accessories. Rumble seats no longer used the unique but rather worthless folding armrests.

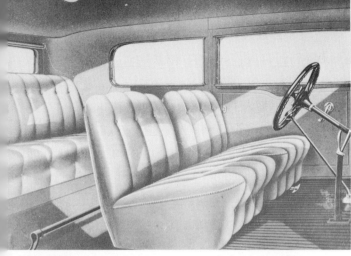

The interior of the Series 50 2-door Sedan was quite pleasing for a car in its price class. The rear compartment was carpeted, but the front used a rubber floor mat. Only the driver's seat was adjustable. The rear compartment was fitted with a foot rest and rear window shade. The steering wheel now had only a throttle and headlight switch on the hub, as the new vacuum operated spark advance made the former spark lever unnecessary. However, an emergency spark lever was still included on the dash for die-hards who didn't trust the newfangled automatic spark.

With the Marquette discontinued, the Series 50 became Buick's lowest priced line. Surprisingly, the Series 50 2-door Sedan, Model 50, had a very poor showing, with only 3,616 produced for domestic sales and 11 special order versions being built for export. The car cost $1,035 and weighed 3,145 pounds. Upholstery was in mohair or cloth, and a tool box was located under the front seat.

A great engineering improvement in this year's Buicks was the new synchromesh transmission, shown here in cutaway view. The synchromesh finally allowed relatively easy shifting and did away with the need for double clutching. The transmission was used in all but the Series 50.

The lowest production car in the Series 50 line was the 5-passenger Phaeton, Model 55, of which only 358 were built for domestic sales and 30 for export. The car cost $1,055 and weighed 2,970 pounds. Standard equipment included an all-leather interior, carpeted rear compartment, large pockets in all doors, and a robe rail and foot rest for the rear compartment. This model is shown with accessory wire wheels and dual sidemounts, white wall tires, and wind wings.

The lightest Buick this year was the Series 50 Roadster, Model 54. It weighed 2,935 pounds and cost $1,055. Available in rumble seat form only, the car had a run of 907 for domestic sales and 70 for export. The interior was fully upholstered in leather, and all trim was in chrome or nickel. This restored version is owned by David Cummings of Crank & Hope Publications, Blairsville, Pa.

The big news in the automotive world was Buick's new Straight Eight engine, built in three distinct horsepower and displacement ranges. The engine used an updraft carburetor, V-belt for the fan, and aluminum oil pan. The generator was still gear driven. Totally new was the automatic vacuum operated spark advance, which did away with the former spark lever mounted on the steering column.

Flxible Co. of Loudonville, Ohio, was becoming one of the major users of extended Buick chassis for their specialized commercial and professional cars. Here is a Flxible ambulance, built on an extended Series 90 chassis. Finished in light gray trim, the car uses dual sidemounts, wire wheels, and leaded glass rear quarter windows. The interior was in black leather, with a divider partition between compartments.

The Flxible economy ambulance was this model, mounted on an extended Series 60 chassis. The car uses the same basic body as used on the other Flxible cars shown here, but had far more Spartan fittings. Standard wood spoke wheels and a single sidemount kept down cost, as did the lack of drapes and shades, and a reduction of other refinements. All of this kept the car's price at a relatively low $2,695.

Flxible's limousine hearse used the same basic body as did the ambulance, but was fitted for funeral use. This is the expensive version, mounted on an extended Series 90 chassis and using wire wheels, dual sidemounts, and heavy velvet draperies, silk shades, and plated flower racks.

The Eureka Co. of RockFalls, Ill., came up with a first in the funeral car trade. It was this beautiful Town Hearse, built to order for the Didesch Funeral Home of Dubuque, Ia. Built on a Series 90 chassis with a greatly extended wheelbase the car could be loaded from either side or from the back. The rear quarter windows contained racks for flowers. A detachable top provided weather protection for the driver. The car was finished in black lacquer with chrome wire wheels, chrome and gray sidemount covers, and chrome landau irons.

One of the 468 Series 50 chassis built for export this year was fitted with this interesting drop head coupe body by the Mayfair Carriage Co. of England. The car uses a modified hood, without louvers, a fixed windshield, and the mandatory fender-mounted parking lights.

A few of the Series 90 Export chassis wound up in the Glaser factory in Germany, where at least one model of this attractive cabriolet was produced. The car uses a divided window between compartments, and a roll-up top over the driver's seat. The rear compartment top appears to be on a rigid frame, though its canvas covering and landau irons give the impression that the top could be folded. Disc wheels and heavy hubcaps were favored by Glaser.

The depression was rampant this year, and all auto companies were hurting to the core. Buick production was cut by more than one-half, and only 41,522 cars were built during the calendar year. This dropped Buick to seventh place, as Hudson-Essex, Pontiac, and Studebaker-Rockne all moved up the list to pass Buick.

Since 1931 was the year of big mechanical changes, 1932 was destined to be the year of large styling changes. The entire line was vastly improved in appearance, though performance remained about the same as in 1931. Included in the styling changes were new front end treatment, outside horns, more slanting windshields without exterior visors, and hood louver doors, all in the General Motors styling idiom. Still, by comparison with many other cars of the day, Buick was on the ultra-conservative side. Its styling reflected the slow and costly cars of yesterday, and this connotation attracted few buyers in the penniless depression days.

Both the Series 50 and 60 used the old 114- and 118-inch respective wheelbases, but the Series 80 had a new chassis with a wheelbase of 126 inches while the Series 90 grew on its new chassis with a 134-inch wheelbase.

Mechanically, all engines except those in the Series 50 retained their old bore and stroke measurements. The Series 50 engines had the bores increased to 2-15/16 inches, which resulted in a new displacement of 230 cubic inches and a new brake horsepower rating of 3000 RPM. Capitalizing on this horsepower increase in a rather subtle way, Buick now had its speedometer designed with a top speed reading of 90 MPH.

The largest mechanical innovation of the year was Wizard Control, a relatively complicated combination of free wheeling and automatic clutch. This, when engaged, allowed the driver to shift the synchromesh transmission from second to third without using the clutch. This year also, the "Silent Second" synchromesh transmission was adopted for all cars, with or without Wizard Control. In addition, for this year only, cars were equipped with manually controlled ride regulators. These adjustable snubbers were replaced in 1937 by regular hydraulic shock absorbers.

Corporatewise, due to the depression, things were in a bad way throughout General Motors. Buick, though down greatly in sales, was still considered rather stable as compared with the rocky road being run by both Pontiac and Oldsmobile. Therefore, Alfred Sloan approved a plan whereby B.O.P. (Buick-Oldsmobile-Pontiac) was formed. This was to be a manufacturing and sales organization having jurisdiction over all activities of the three auto producers, plus a few other GM operations. Buick dealers hated the move, and many refused to abide by the mandatory orders to sell Pontiacs. Most Pontiac and Oldsmobile dealers felt the same way, and ignored the more expensive Buicks and concentrated their sales on the lower-priced Pontiac and Oldsmobile models. After eighteen months, the plan was dropped, but not before over one-quarter of the previous Buick dealers had gone out of Business.

Meanwhile, E.T. Strong, tired of fighting a good but thankless fight, retired from his presidency. His place was taken by Irving J. Reuter, who had been manager of Oldsmobile.

On the racing scene, Phil Shafer again entered his Buick powered Rigling at the Indianapolis 500. He qualified for twenty-sixth starting place in a field of forty by running at 110.7 MPH. He was on his 197th lap when the checkered flag signaled that he had won eleventh place.

Appearing in all series except the Series 80 was the new 5-passenger Convertible Phaeton. This is the Series 90 version, designated the Model 98. It cost $1,830 and weighed 4,550 pounds. Buick built 268 for domestic sales and one special order version for export.

A huge yet attractive car was the Series 90 7-passenger Sedan, Model 90, which now used a new chassis of 134-inch wheelbase length. The car cost $1,955 and weighed 4,695 pounds. Buick built 1,368 for domestic sales and 19 for export. In addition, it produced 192 stripped Series 90 chassis for domestic sales and 24 for export.

It took a sharp eye to tell the Series 90 5-passenger Sedan from the 7-passenger version — unless one counted seats. This is the 5-passenger version, Model 97, of which 1,485 were produced, none for export. It sold for $1,805 and weighed 4,565. This was the first year that Buick used dual taillights, probably to balance the beautiful dual horns.

New for the year was the Series 90 5-passenger Club Sedan, Model 91. The style was of the close-coupled sedan type, with a large built-on trunk as standard equipment, in addition to the folding luggage rack. The attractive car sold for $1,820 and weighed 4,620 pounds. Production was 2,237 for domestic sales, but only one on special order went overseas. This beautiful example, with accessory whitewalls and fog lights, is owned by David Crow of Upper Sandusky, Ohio. It features a chromed grille guard and dual sidemount mirrors.

The Series 90 5-passenger Victoria Coupe gained from the new wheelbase length in that two inches were added to the rear seat leg room. Designated the Model 96, the 4,460 pound car cost $1,785 and attracted 1,460 U.S. buyers. None were exported. Appointments included a folding center armrest and plush velvet carpets for the rear compartment. Shades were still provided for the rear and quarter panel windows.

Of only limited appeal was the Series 90 Convertible Coupe, Model 96-C. Only 289 were built for U.S. buyers and none were exported. The 4,460-pound car was available in rumble seat form only. It cost $1,805. The windshield could be folded flat across the cowl.

A 134-inch wheelbase plus an attractive color combination makes this Series 90 Sport Coupe a very attractive vehicle. Designated the Model 96-S, this style was sometimes referred to as the Close Coupled Coupe. Available in rumble seat version only, it cost $1,740 and weighed 4,470 pounds. Buick built 586, all for domestic sales. This beautiful example is owned by John Sullivan of Livonia, Mich. The spotlight, fog light and running lights are accessories.

The lowest production car in the Series 90 line was the 7-passenger Limousine, Model 90-L, of which only 164 were built for U.S. sales and 26 for export. It weighed 4,810 pounds, and at $2,055, was the only Buick to have a base price over $2,000. This year, wire wheels and sidemounts were standard on all Series 90 cars, but wood spoke wheels could be ordered.

With the top and windshield lowered, the Series 90 7-passenger Sport Phaeton looked as if it were a mile long. Designated the Model 95, it suffered from only limited sales appeal, and only 131 were built for domestic sales and 15 were built for export. It weighed 4,470 pounds and cost $1,675. It featured an all-leather interior and small tonneau cowl on the front seat.

The Series 80 still consisted of only two styles, both built on a new exclusive 126-inch wheelbase chassis. The least popular style was the 5-passenger Victoria Coupe, Model 86, which featured totally new lines and a large independent trunk. Only 1,800 were built, all for domestic sales. The car cost $1,540 and weighed 4,335 pounds.

Totally new for the year was the 5-passenger Convertible Phaeton style. Here it is in the Series 60 line, designated the Model 68-C. It cost $1,310 and weighed 3,880 pounds. Buick built 366 for domestic sales and 16 for export. The sidemounts and wire wheels were standard.

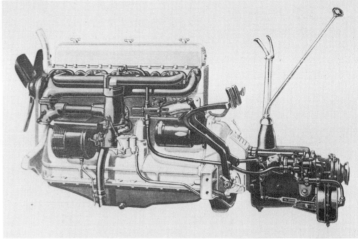

A highly complicated accessory that was soon phased out was Wizard Control. This was a combination of free wheeling and automatic clutch, operated by vacuum and mechanical linkage. It is seen here on the Series 50 engine, with the vacuum tank near the rear of the transmission. When it worked, the driver could shift between second and third without using the clutch, and the car would also automatically go into free wheeling on downgrades.

The more popular of the two Series 80 styles was the 5-passenger Sedan, Model 87, which had a run of 4,089 for domestic sales and three special order versions for export. It cost $1,570 and weighed 4,450 pounds, with wood spoke wheels and a rear spare being standard.

The Series 60 5-passenger Sport Phaeton, Model 65, enjoyed beautiful lines but virtually no buyers. Only 79 were built for domestic sales, and 24 for export. The car cost $1,390 and weighed 3,795 pounds. Buyers had a choice of wood spoke or wire wheels, with dual sidemounts and luggage rack being standard equipment.

The interior of the Series 60 Convertible Phaeton differed somewhat from that of the Series 50. The Series 60 model featured ashtrays in each rear panel, plus a center folding armrest. The interior is shown here in natural leather, with brown leather piping. Only the dirver's seat was adjustable, but both front seats folded for access to the rear compartment.

The most popular car in the Series 60 line was the 5-passenger Sedan, Model 67, which had a run of 9,013 for domestic sales and 47 for export. The large car weighed 3,980 pounds and cost $1,310, with the sidemounts being extra. Upholstery was in gray or taupe mohair or gray whipcord, with heavy velvet carpeting in the rear compartment. Other rear compartment appointments included a folding robe rail, foot rest, assist cords, arm rests and ash trays on each side of the rear seat.

The Series 60 4-passenger Convertible Coupe was a very attractive car, but sales were way down, and only 450 were built for domestic sales while two special order versions were built for export. Designated the Model 66-C, this car sold for $1,310 and weighed 3,795 pounds. It was available in rumble seat version only, with functional landau irons, and a small storage compartment reached through the side access door. This beautiful example is a Canadian production model, but white walls, spare tire covers and large trunk were accessories. The car is owned by W.A. Henderson of Kempville, Ontario, Canada. It is seen here at the 1972 Hershey meet.

New for the year was the 5-passenger Victoria Coupe on the 118-inch Series 60 wheelbase chassis. Designated the Model 68, the car had a run of 1,514, all for domestic sales. It weighed 3,875 and cost $1,290. Woodspoke wheels and a rear mounted spare were standard. In addition to the production listed here, Buick also built 372 Series 60 stripped chassis for domestic sales and 36 such chassis for export.

Occupying quite beautiful surroundings is the rather plain Series 60 4-passenger Special Coupe, Model 66-S, which was basically the rumble seat version of the business coupe. Priced at $1,270 and weighing 3,860 pounds, the car drew 1,678 domestic orders, but only six were produced on special order for export. Buyers could have wire or wood wheels, with a rear-mount.

Again appearing in the Series 60 line was the 2-passenger Business Coupe, Model 66. The car, which weighed 3,796 pounds and cost $1,250, had its lines enhanced by its 118-inch wheelbase chassis and the new quarter windows. Still, only 636 were built, all for U.S. sales.

The dashboard of the new Buick became very attractive, but the instruments were a bit on the small side. This year the cars offered glove compartments in addition to door pouches. This interior is the Series 60 Convertible, done in all-leather, with a rubber floor mat. For the first time, Buick steering wheels had only three spokes instead of the traditional four. The two levers at the hub were for lights and throttle.

An attractive car, bearing lines very similar to the Chevrolet Confederate Series, was the Series 50 Convertible Coupe, Model 56-C. The car was built in rumble seat form only, and featured large functional chromed landau irons, and storage space behind the front seat, with access through the door in the quarter panel. It cost $1,080 and weighed 3,335 pounds. Buick built 630 for domestic sales and 13 for export. Dual sidemounts, luggage rack, and a choice of wood spoke or wire wheels were standard. This beautifully restored version, with accessory white walls, is owned by Murray Rodd of Brooklyn, Ontario, Canada.

The Series 50 Business Coupe, Model 56, was a cute little 2-passenger vehicle, available in trunk-back form only. Buick built 1,726, all for domestic sales. The 3,275-pound car was Buick's least expensive model, costing $935 in basic form. Wood spoke wheels and a rear mounted spare were standard equipment. Rear quarter windows were a new innovation on this model, which formerly had top and quarter panels covered in rubberized fabric.

With the depression bearing down hard on Buick's sales, the most popular car of the year had a production run of only 10,803 for domestic sales. It was the Series 50 4-door Sedan, Model 57, which cost only $995 and weighed 3,450 pounds. Wire wheels were an accessory on this car. Silk shades were provided on the rear and quarter windows. This nicely restored example is owned by Gerald Woods of Charlotte, Mich. In addition to regular production, Buick built 504 Series 50 stripped chassis for domestic sales and 140 for export, and also produced 20 body-less Series 50 Phaetons for export.

Almost as popular as the standard Series 50 Sedan was the Series 50 Special Sedan, Model 57-S, which had a production run of 9,766 for domestic sales and 175 for export. The car used the same body as the Model 57, but featured richer appointments. Buyers had a choice of wire or wood wheels, but the dual sidemounts were extra. Other refinements included dual taillights, chromed headlight brackets, horn motor covers and taillight brackets, and a rear compartment fitted with assist cords, ash trays, folding robe rail, and a chrome folding foot rest. Weighing 3,510 pounds, the car cost $1,080.

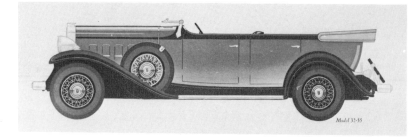

Buick's lowest production car this year was the Series 50 5-passenger Sport Phaeton, Model 55. Only 69 were built for domestic sales and 37 for export. The attractive car sold for $1,155 and weighed 3,270 pounds. Upholstery was in a choice of colored leather with contrasting-color piping trim. The rear compartment was fitted with side armrests, a folding center armrest, and velvet carpeting. Standard equipment included dual sidemounts, a choice of wire or wood spoke wheels, and a luggage rack. Still, the car could not attract buyers.

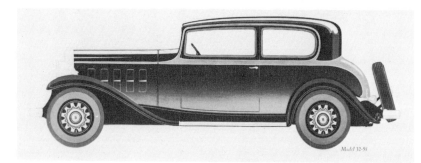

New for the Series 50 was the 5-passenger Victoria Coupe, Model 58. The style, which weighed 3,420 pounds and cost $1,060, appeared this year only in the series. Production was 2,194 for domestic sales and two special order versions for export. Upholstery was in whipcord or mohair plush, and storage space was provided under the rear deck. Only the driver's seat was adjustable. Wood spoke wheels and rear mounted spare were standard.

The Series 50 4-passenger Sport Coupe, Model 56-S, also used the new quarter windows. Available in rumble seat form only, the car cost $1,040 and weighed 3,395 pounds. Luggage space was located behind the front seat and in a compartment reached through an access door on the right quarter panel. Buyers were offered a choice of two shades of mohair or one of whipcord upholstery, and an all-leather interior was available at extra cost. Sidemounts and luggage rack were standard equipment. Buick built 1,905 for domestic sales and nine for export.

Approaching today's concept of the convertible was the totally new Series 50 5-passenger Convertible Phaeton, Model 58-C. The car featured a weather-tight folding top and roll-up windows with a removable centerpost. It cost $1,080 and weighed 3,425 pounds. Buick built 380 for domestic sales and 20 for export. Buyers had a choice of upholstery, either hand crushed leather in either tan or black, or whipcord. Standard equipment included the weather-proof trunk, wire or wood spoke wheels, and dual sidemounts. Only the driver's seat was adjustable.

The interior of the new Model 58-C 5-passenger Phaeton shows refined appointments. This is the all-leather interior, with both seats and side and door panels covered in either black or natural leather with matching color piping.

Buick was back at Indianapolis this year, in the form of this attractive and fine performing Rigling racer with the new Buick Eight under the hood. The driver-owner was Phil Shafer, who qualified for the Memorial Day Classic at 110.7 and placed 11th in the race. From there he went on to win an important road race at Elgin, Ill.

1932

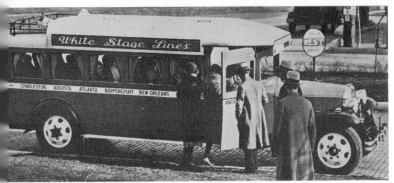

Buick had long been out of the truck business, but the Flxible Co. of Loudonville, Ohio, kept Buicks in the bus business for years, by producing long-distance bus bodies for extended Buick chassis. White Stage Lines, which operated through the deep south as far west as Los Angeles, used many of these Flxible-Buick buses on its long hauls. All were built on extended Series 90 chassis. Some were fitted with dual rear wheels. Capacity was 21 passengers.

In addition to building standard and long-haul buses on Buick chassis, the Flxible Company of Loudenville, Ohio, also produced this interesting limousine style bus. Its anticipated use was primarily for resort hotel service and as a sedan-type bus for low volume, long-range routes. The car, fitted similar to a modern airport limousine, held 10 passengers plus the driver, with luggage stored under the canvas covered roof-top rack. Dual wheels were used in the rear, with truck-type rims used throughout.

The Flxible Co. of Loudonville, Ohio, long preferred to work with Buick chassis for both its hearse, ambulance, and bus bodies. In its literature, Flxible claimed that the Buick Series 90 running gear was the most efficient, longest lived, and best designed of anything in its class. This is the Flxible limousine hearse, which was strictly a rear-loading vehicle. A solid partition separated the front and rear compartments. The same basic body was used for Flxible ambulances.

In Canada, the McLaughlin Buick chassis proved to be as popular with specialty car builders as the Buick chassis was in the U.S. This attractive funeral coach was built by the Mitchell Hearse Co. of Ingersoll, Ontario, on special order for the C. L. Eeoy Funeral Home of Tavistock, Ontario. A special feature on this car was the etched glass design, which formed a frame for all of the side windows, even those in the front door.

Van den Plas of Brussels, Belgium, a world renown coachbuilding firm, turned out this very attractive convertible on a Series 90 chassis. Buick's large wheels and the wide white-walls belie the fact that this car used the standard 134-inch wheelbase chassis. The 4-passenger car was of 3-window design, with the top blanking in the rear quarters when raised. Refinements include the four heavy hinges on each door and the unusual flare of the running boards into both front and rear fenders. Functional landau irons were used.

It started out life as one of the 47 Model 67-X Sedans that were built for export, but it wound up during W.W. II wearing this rather different body. The conversion was made at the direction of the Ancient Order of Foresters, who then donated the vehicle to the British Salvation Army, to use as a mobile canteen in wartime London. The car is wearing the blackout headlights mandatory in Britain during the war, and is painted in military camouflage.

A low point in Buick's later day history occurred this year, with only 40,620 vehicles being built. Not since 1914 had so few Buicks left the factory. Production ranking was down to eighth place, a spot not seen by Buick since 1906. Passing Buick in production this year were Chevrolet, Ford, Plymouth, Dodge, Pontiac, Studebaker-Rockne and Hudson-Terraplane. Something new was needed, both within the company and within the economy. And, in a sense, the start of that something would occur late in the year.

Buick's styling for the year was greatly modified via the use of valanced front fenders, a new and very attractive V-type of radiator shell and grille, and a gracefully rearward curved rear panel called a "veavertail". This new beavertail appeared on the sedan bodies only. The trailing sweep successfully hid the gas tank, and blended in perfectly with the new graceful rear fender lines. Running boards were likewise gracefully styled and the door edges now met the running boards, doing away forever with the old running board apron. Mechanically, there were also some great improvements. The horsepower

The only Buick to exceed $2,000 in base price was the Series 90 Limousine, Model 90-L, which cost $2,055. The 4,780 pound car was available in 7-passenger form only, and was fitted with a glass partition between compartments. Buick built 299 for domestic use and 39 for export.

Buick claimed that more than 1 million people visited dealers' showrooms during the first two days of its presentation. Here they are viewing the new Series 90 5-passenger Club Sedan, Model 91, that turned out to be the most popular car in the series. Buick built 1,637 for domestic sales, but only two special order models for export. It cost $1,820 and weighed 4,520 pounds. Paint trim included harmonizing colors for the fenders and upper body panels. The interior was in mohair plush, whipcord or cloth at buyers option. Fittings included side and folding center armrests, small auxiliary folding seats, thick velvet pile carpets in the rear compartment, robe rail, carpet-covered foot rest, and concealed silk window shades.

of the Series 50 engine was raised to 86 at 3200 RPM, and the Series 60 horsepower was raised to 97 at 3200 RPM.

In size, the cars grew again, with only the Series 50 retaining its 114-inch wheelbase. But the Series 60 now was on a wheelbase of 127 inches, the Series 80 grew to 130 inches, and the already large Series 90 grew four more inches to a huge 138-inch wheelbase. All frames were now of the new and much stronger "X" crossmember design.

A new option this year, and one that really enhanced the appearance of the sporty models was the use of chrome wire or chrome artillery type wheels. All standard wheels were now either painted wire or painted steel artillery type, the wooden wheels having been discontinued at the end of the 1932 model run.

Other new innovations were the use of one key for all locks, a dash mounted starter button, and regular shock absorbers to replace the former manually controlled ride regulators. The free wheeling unit was modified so that the driver could instantaneously switch back to the regular drive train whenever he desired.

In the bodies, the big news was the introduction of Fisher No-Draft ventilation, with small vent windows in the front doors and in the rear quarter windows of sedans.

Still, conditions remained bad at Buick. Of the more than 2,000 exclusive Buick dealers that had been spread country-wide in the mid-1920s, there were only seventy such dealers in 1933. There were still over 2,000 dealers operating under the B.O.P. scheme, but many of these were paying little attention to Buick and were concentrating more on selling the less expensive Pontiac and Oldsmobile models.

It was at this point that William Knudsen made the decision that was to save Buick. After disbanding the much disliked B.O.P. structure, Mr. Knudsen went to another General Motors subsidiary, the AC Spark Plug Company, and convinced its president that he should take over as president and general manager of the deathly sick Buick Company. The man was Harlow H. Curtice. He soon replaced I.J. Reuter as president, and Mr. Reuter, with a sigh of relief, appeared content to retire.

Within short order, plans were under way for a really new Buick, which would not only attract the public, but which would put new birth into the failing sales organization. It was a do-or-die move, and Curtice made it work. Not since the days of Durant had a more energetic and dynamic leader been at the helm of Buick. Subordinate management recognized this fact, and Buick was once again on the move.

Buick was on the move at Indianapolis this year also. Phil Shafer this year had two Buick powered Riglings on the entry line, both of which qualified for the field of forty-two. One car, driven by Stubby Stubblefield, qualified at 114.7 MPH for tenth position, while Shafer's own car qualified at 107.9 MPH. However, Shafer's time was not high enough and he was bumped down the line until he was finally out of the race before it started. Stubblefield meanwhile drove a brilliant race throughout, finishing fifth at an average speed of 100.7 MPH.

Of far less appealing line than the club sedan was the Series 90 5-passenger Sedan, Model 97. It cost $1,805 and weighed 4,595 pounds. Buick built 641, all for domestic sales. In addition, it produced 192 stripped Series 90 chassis for the specialty builders.

SERIES 33 NINETY

Appearing for the last year was the Series 90 5-passenger Victoria Coupe, Model 96. Priced at $1,785 and weighing 4,520 pounds, the car drew only 556 domestic orders and one export order. The rear spare was standard equipment, while the more popular sidemounts were at extra cost.

The Series 90 line now used a huge chassis of 138-inch wheelbase, which resulted in these Buicks being among the most massive cars on the road. This is the 7-passenger Sedan, Model 90, of which 890 were built for domestic sales and 12 were produced for export. It cost $1,955 and weighed 4,705 pounds. Most Series 90 cars were equipped with sidemounts, but these were extra cost items.

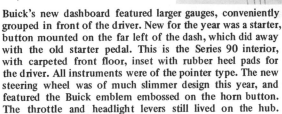

The Eureka Co. of Rock Falls, Ill. continued to build their excellently designed line of funeral cars on Buick chassis. However, this model is a bit of a puzzle, as it features 1933 fenders and lights, but is equipped with a 1934 style hood. Possibly it is a late 1933, and the hood was installed by Eureka to update the appearance. Eureka would custom build bodies for any chassis but specialized in using Buick gear for its "production" models. This is a three-way coach, meaning that it could be loaded from the rear or from either side. No center pillars were used on the doors, and the driver's and attendant's seat would slide up almost flush with the dash to facilitate turning of the movable casket table and loading of the vehicle. Mohair upholstery and velvet drapes were used throughout.

Buick's new dashboard featured larger gauges, conveniently grouped in front of the driver. New for the year was a starter, button mounted on the far left of the dash, which did away with the old starter pedal. This is the Series 90 interior, with carpeted front floor, inset with rubber heel pads for the driver. All instruments were of the pointer type. The new steering wheel was of much slimmer design this year, and featured the Buick emblem embossed on the horn button. The throttle and headlight levers still lived on the hub.

VanDenplas of Brussels, a world famous custom coach builder, used a Series 50 export chassis as a base for this very attractive Coupe Cabriolet body. The landau irons were functional, and the top could be folded back. Swing-arm turn indicators are mounted on the windshield posts. The body lines seem spoiled somewhat by the huge external door hinges.

As was expected, the Series 80 4-door Sedan, Model 87, drew the most orders, but still these totaled only 1,545. The car weighed 4,505 pounds and cost $1,570. The dual horns provided very attractive trim for all Buicks.

Appearing for the last time was the Series 80. It consisted of a five model line, with no export production. This is the Series 80 5-passenger Victoria Coupe, Model 86, of which 758 were built. It cost $1,540 and weighed 4,420 pounds.

The Series 80 line had no business coupe, but it did offer a Sport Coupe, Model 86-S, equipped with a rumble seat. The 4,355-pound car cost $1,495 and drew 401 orders. As in the other series, buyers had a choice of wire or steel-spoke artillery wheels.

SERIES 33 EIGHTY

All Buick chassis were now of the very strong X-frame design, which helped in making these units a favorite with builders of specialty and professional cars, such as ambulances, hearses, etc. This is the Series 80 chassis, of which 90 were sold in this form. It is shown here equipped with welled fenders, but lacking hood and cowl, which would be attached later.

The Series 80 followed the basic model run of the other series, but with the cars on a new chassis of 130-inch wheelbase. This is the Convertible Coupe, Model 86-C, of which only 90 were built. It was equipped with rumble seat, but the side panel access doors were no longer used. It weighed 4,325 pounds and cost $1,575, with the sidemounts and luggage rack being extra. Note that doors of the open cars opened at the leading edges, while closed models opened at the trailing edges.

The Series 80 5-passenger Convertible Phaeton was now a 4-door car of very appealing line. Designated the Model 88-C, it weighed 4,525 pounds and cost $1,845. Buick built 124. Upholstery was in special whipcord or hand-buffed leather in colors to match the exterior finish. The rear seat was fitted with armrests on each side and a folding armrest in the center.

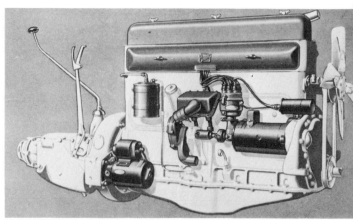

By the time the 1933 blocks started leaving the plant, Buick had built more than 2.7-million engines during its 29 years of production. This year the horsepower ratings of both the Series 50 and the Series 60 engines was raised to 86 and 97 horsepower respectively.

The Series 60 5-passenger Convertible Phaeton, Model 68-C, drew only 183 orders this year. The car cost $1,585 and weighed 4,110 pounds. No Series 60 models were built for export.

The Series 60 Victoria Coupe, Model 68, used Buick's latest styling innovation, the vent windows. However, unlike the 4-door models that used vent windows both front and back, the 2-door styles used them only in the front, and the open models did not use them at all. The Victoria cost $1,310 and weighed 4,005 pounds. Buick built 2,887, and in addition turned out 399 stripped Series 60 chassis for the growing market of specialty and professional car builders.

The interior of the Series 60 Victoria was nicely done in plush mohair. Refinements included a carpeted rear compartment with carpeted foot rest, assist cords, armrests, and concealed roller shades on the rear and quarter windows. Pockets were provided in the backs of the front seats, but door pockets were no longer used.

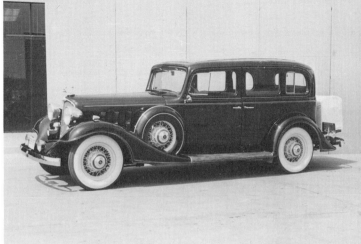

As could be expected, the most popular car in the Series 60 line was the 5-passenger Sedan, Model 67, which had a production run of 7,450. The car cost $1,310 and weighed 4,115 pounds. This beautiful example is owned by Tom Patterson of Howell, Mich. It uses the accessory sidemounts and luggage rack, and is fitted with an original canvas-covered trunk and fog lights.

An unusually short top design gave the Series 60 Convertible a rather chopped look. Designated the Model 66-C, the style drew only 152 orders. Available only in rumble seat form, it cost $1,365 and weighed 3,940 pounds. The windshield was now on rigid frame and could not be lowered. This beautiful example is owned by Russell Wilkin of Bluffton, Ind.

Using the same basic body as the convertible coupe was the Series 60 Sport Coupe, Model 66-S, of which an even 1,000 were built. It cost $1,270 and weighed 3,975. This restored version, owned by Bill Snook of Bowling Green, Ohio, is equipped with steel spoke artillery wheels and accessory sidemounts, luggage rack and trunk. It has been fitted with non-standard sealed beam headlight inserts and dual fog lights.

The new Series 50 Business Coupe, Model 56, again was produced without quarter windows. Using the 119-inch wheelbase chassis, the car was available in trunk form only, with an outside rear-mounted spare. Priced at $995, it was the only Buick with a base price below $1,000. It weighed 3,520 pounds. Buick built 1,321, all for domestic sales.

The most popular car in the Series 50 line was the 4-door Sedan, Model 57, which had a run of 19,109 for domestic sales and 150 for export. Available in 5-passenger form only, it cost $1,045 and weighed 3,705 pounds. Carpets were in color harmonizing with the interior trim, but were used in the rear compartment only. Also in the rear compartment were arm rests assist cords, ash trays on each rear panel, a folding robe rail, and a carpeted foot rest. The sidemounts and luggage rack were accessories, but buyers had a choice of wire or steel spoke artillery wheels.

SERIES 33 FIFTY

The 4-passenger version of the Series 50 coupe was the Sport Coupe, Model 56-S, which was built in rumble seat version only. It cost $1,030 and weighed 3,585 pounds. Ten were built for export and 1,643 were built for U.S. customers. In addition, Buick built 681 stripped Series 50 chassis for domestic use and 189 for export sales.

An attractive but unpopular car was the Series 50 4-passenger Convertible Coupe, Model 56-C. Only 346 were built for U.S. sales, and four special order models were built for export. The car cost 41,115 and weighed 3,525 pounds. Wire wheels were standard, sidemounts an accessory. The car was available in rumble seat form only.

Enjoying fairly respectable sales was the Series 50 Victoria Coupe, Model 58, of which 4,118 were built for U.S. sales and five were turned out on special order for export. It cost $1,065 and weighed 3,605 pounds. The trunk and rear spare tire cover, both in body color, were standard.

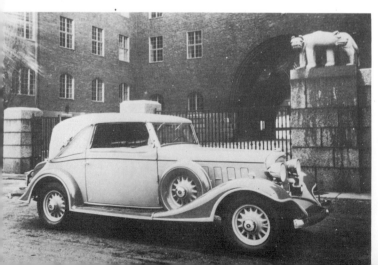

Gustat Norberg of Stockholm used Buick chassis to produce a small annual run of very beautiful and brightly painted semi-custom models. This is the Touring Cabriolet, of which 12 were built. The large landau irons were functional, and the top could be lowered. The car was finished in light and medium blue with a white top.

A slight shot was given to Buick late in the year, in the form of the Series 40. Via this, Buick's production rose to 8,757, not a tremendous rebound but one that was almost double the production of the previous year. Still, Buick remained in eighth place, as all other auto companies, by one form or another also managed to raise their production.

The Series 40 was an outgrowth of Harlow Curtice's idea that a totally new low price car was needed as soon as possible. An arrangement was worked out with Chevrolet and Fisher Body whereby a body of Chevrolet size but with Buick character would be provided for the new series.

The new Series 40 was quickly acknowledged to be one of the hottest performers of the year for its size and price. Based on a 117-inch wheelbase chassis, it housed a new 233-cubic-inch Eight with a bore and stroke of 3-3/32 x 3-7/8 inches which produced 93 horsepower at 3200 RPM.

All engines except the 344-cubic-inch block of the Series 90 were changed this year. The old-line Series 50 used a new block of 235 cubic inches, with a bore and stroke of 2-31/32 x 4.25 that produced 88 horsepower at 3200 RPM; and the Series 60 used a new block of 278 cubic inches, with a bore and stroke of 3-3/32 x 4-5/8 inches that produced 100 horsepower at 3200 RPM. The Series 80 was dropped, but the Series 90 was retained as the prestige line. Here the engine retained its same specifications, but horsepower was raised to 116 at 3200 RPM.

The Series 50 received a needed lengthening, and grew five inches to a 119-inch wheelbase. The Series 60 also grew an inch, now being built on a 128-inch wheelbase, but the Series 90 was reduced somewhat, dropping down to a 136-inch wheelbase chassis.

All cars including the Series 40, used the new knee-action front suspension, which incorporated Delco-Lovejoy shock absorbers and a rear sway bar called a Ride Stabilizer. It is interesting to note that the famed Rolls Royce company was so impressed by this new suspension of Buick's that it acquired at considerable cost the license from General Motors to use this system in its new V-12 Phantom III, which would enter production in 1935. All models still used mechanical brakes, but the Series 90 was equipped with Bendix vacuum power boosters. Offered for the first time this year was a car radio, which could be ordered either as a factory or a dealer installed accessory. Another new innovation this year was what would become Buick's famed combination starter and accelerator pedal. With this unit, when the accelerator was depressed fully, or the hand throttle pulled out fully, the starter was engaged. This innovation was continued through the 1960 models.

At Indianapolis, Phil Shafer again appeared at the Memorial Day 500 with his two Buick powered Riglings, and placed admirably. His own car qualified at 113.8 MPH to gain a sixth starting position out of a field of thirty-three. Its sister car, piloted by Al Miller, qualified at 113.3 MPH to gain eighth starting position. Miller ran an excellent race and finished sixth with an average speed of 98.2 MPH, but Shafer again ran into hard luck and had to retire with a broken camshaft drive after 130 laps.

A truly massive car was the Series 90 7-passenger Sedan, Model 90, which was still huge even though the series was now built on a new chassis with a wheelbase shortened to 136 inches. The car was up in price to $2,055. It weighed 4,906 pounds and had a run of 1,151 for domestic sales and 83 for export.

The interior of the Model 90 7-passenger Sedan was the epitome of good taste, with its deeply upholstered seats, and folding jump seats all done in mohair velvet plush. Concealed silk roller shades were provided for the rear and rear quarter windows, and reading lights were installed in the rear quarter panels. Each rear door was equipped with a storage pouch.

The Series 90 7-passenger Limousine, Model 90-L, is shown here in standard form, with a rear mounted spare. However, most were built with dual sidemounts and a rear luggage rack. Still, production only reached 262 for domestic sales and 166 for export. The car cost $2,175 and weighed 4,876 pounds. A glass divider partition between compartments was standard.

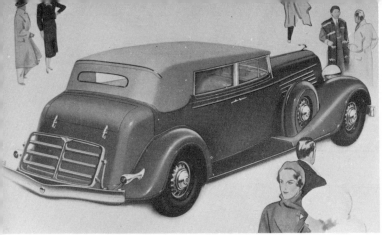

A very attractive car was the large Series 90 Convertible Phaeton, Model 98-C, which sold for $2,145. It weighed 4,691 pounds. It was the only Series 90 model on which the covered sidemounts and luggage carrier were standard equipment. The gas filler on this model was off to the side and not blocked by the luggage rack. Buick built 119 for domestic sales and 19 for export.

Reappearing in the Series 90 line was the huge 4-passenger Convertible Coupe, Model 96-C. The car was built in rumble seat version only, with a separate luggage compartment entered through an access door on the right rear quarter. It cost $1,945 and weighed 4,511 pounds. Only 68 were built for domestic sales and only five special order versions went overseas. One of the few surviving examples is this excellently restored model owned by Ernie Anderson of LaCrosse, Wis. The luggage rack, trunk, and sidemounts are accessories. Rather than using the regular accessory metal spare tire covers, this car uses very attractive canvas covers, which match both the top and the trunk cover.

After being gone for a year, the Series 90 5-passenger Victoria Coupe, Model 98, reappeared. It cost $1,895 and weighed 4,571 pounds. Buick built 347 for domestic sales, but only one on special order for export. Note that the trunk opened fron the leading edge, in rumble seat fashion, which must have made it quite difficult to load. This model features the accessory sidemounts and luggage rack, but the rack effectively blocked the gas filler and had to be pulled down each time the car stopped for gas – which was quite frequently on the Series 90.

After dropping out of sight, the Series 90 Sport Coupe, Model 96-S, reappeared this year, priced at $1,875. The huge coupe weighed 4,546 pounds, and was available in rumble seat form only, with a special luggage space between compartments. Luggage was loaded into this space through a small access door just forward of the rear fender. Only 137 were built, all for domestic sales. The car is shown here in standard form, with rear-mounted spare.

The most popular car in the Series 90 line was the very attractive and practical 5-passenger Club Sedan, Model 91, which featured a built-in trunk and close-coupled seating. The car drew 1,477 domestic orders and 30 for export. It cost $1,965 and weighed 4,696. This model is equipped with accessory luggage rack and sidemounts, but not the accessory spare covers.

The Series 90 5-passenger Sedan, Model 97, simply couldn't draw orders in the face of its companion models, the club sedan and the 7-passenger sedan. Only 635 were built for domestic sales and 19 for export. It cost $1,945 and weighed 4,691 pounds. This example is one of the export models, living in Victoria, Australia. It is identical to the U.S. models except that it is right-hand drive. The sidemounts were accessories.

The new Series 60 Club Sedan was a larger car than last year, now being built on a chassis with a 128-inch wheelbase. Designated the Model 61, it drew 5,395 orders in the U.S. and 234 overseas. It cost $1,465 and weighed 4,318 pounds. The very pretty car was featured in many Buick ads. The luggage rack and sidemounts with matching color wheel covers were accessories.

The Series 60 5-passenger Victoria Coupe offered vent windows in its rear quarter windows as well as in the front doors. Designated the Model 68, the car cost $1,395 and weighed 4,213 pounds. Buick built 1,935, all for domestic sales. Also built were 97 Series 60 chassis with cowl for domestic use. They cost $995 and weighed 3,378 pounds. In addition 620 such chassis in various forms were shipped overseas.

The lowest production car in the Series 60 line was the Convertible Coupe, Model 66-C. The car had a run of only 235 for domestic sales and 10 for export. A rumble seat was standard equipment, as was the rear mounted spare. Buick still offered wire spoke wheels as an option, but there were very few who wanted the "archaic" wire spokes as opposed to the "modern" steel spokes.

The only Series 60 model to use sidemounts and a luggage rack as standard equipment was the attractive 4-door Convertible Phaeton, Model 68-C. The car cost $1,675 and weighed 4,353 pounds. Buick produced only 444 for domestic sales and another 143 for export. In addition to the luggage carrier, the car had a built-in trunk of fairly spacious size.

The Series 60 4-door Sedan, Model 67, proved to be a relatively popular car, with sales reaching 5,171 in the U.S. and 194 overseas. It cost $1,425 and weighed 4,303 pounds. The most popular color of the 4-door sedans was black, though many other color options were available.

The Series 60 Sport Coupe was a large car of only limited appeal, which is understandable in that most people buying 2-passenger models of this type were looking more for economy than size. Designated the Model 66-S, it had a run of 816 for domestic sales and only nine special order versions for export. It cost $1,375 and weighed 4,193 pounds. A rumble seat was standard.

As before, the most popular car in the Series 50 line was the 4-door Sedan, Model 57, of which 12,094 were built for domestic sales and 711 for export. It cost $1,190 and weighed 3,852 pounds. In addition, Buick built 19 Series 50 chassis with cowl. These cost $885 and weighed 2,942. Also built were a total of 1,748 Series 50 chassis and cowls for export.

The interior of the Series 50 sedan was a bit more elaborate than that of the Series 40. Rear seat passengers had concealed silk shades for the quarter windows, assist straps, a carpeted foot rest, robe rail, and storage pouches on the doors. Window trim was in walnut grained metal.

The Series 50 and larger Buicks continued to use dual exterior horns, while the Series 40 used a hidden horn. This is the Series 50 Business Coupe, Model 56, which cost $1,110 and weighed 3,682 pounds. Buick built 1,078 for domestic sales and four on special order for export. The Series 50 now used a totally new chassis with a 119-inch wheelbase.

Using the same basic body as the business coupe, but fitted with a rumble seat, was the Series 50 Sport Coupe, Model 56-S. It cost $1,145 and weighed 3,712. Buick built 1,150 for domestic sales and 42 for export. Buick this year claimed that both the Series 40 and the Series 50 could attain and hold a steady 85 MPH without strain.

A very attractive but not very popular car was the Series 50 Convertible Coupe, Model 56-C, of which only 506 were built for domestic sales and 83 for export. It cost $1,230 and weighed 3,692 pounds. Steel spoke artillery wheels were used on all cars this year.

It was called a touring sedan in the Series 40 line, but in the Series 50 line the style was known as the Victoria Coupe, Model 58. It cost $1,160 and weighed 4,316 pounds. Buick built 4,316 for domestic use and 89 for export. The car featured a built-in trunk, with the gas filler on the left side of the spare tire. The tire cover was standard equipment.

Buick's lowest priced car was the Series 40 Business Coupe, Model 46, which cost $795 and weighed 2,995 pounds. There were 1,806 built for domestic sales. Buick's knee action front wheels and coil spring suspension was claimed to be the smoothest riding front end on the road. Safety glass was used in the windshield and vent windows, but plate glass was used for the side windows. However, safety glass all around could be ordered at extra cost.

New for the year was the Series 40 line, which was a full run of economy priced Buicks using a 117-inch wheelbase chassis. The most popular car was the 5-passenger Club Sedan, Model 41, which sold for $925 and weighed 3,175 pounds. It featured a built-in trunk and quarter windows that opened vent-style. Buick built 10,953 for domestic sales and 542 for export.

The 4-passenger version of the Series 40 coupe was the Sport Coupe, Model 46-S, built with a rumble seat instead of trunk. It cost $855 and weighed 3,085 pounds. Buick built 1,232 for domestic sales and 47 for export. Upholstery was in whipcord, tan leather, or mohair velvet.

The Series 40 4-door Sedan, Model 47, enjoyed surprisingly good sales, despite the fact that its lines were not nearly as pleasing as those of the Model 41, Buick built 7,425 for domestic sales and 380 for export. It cost $895 and weighed 3,155 pounds. This Pennsylvania-registered survivor is owned by James Gordon Jr. It sports an accessory right-hand windshield wiper and the new Buick accessory—a dealer installed radio. The white walls and two-tone paint job would also have been extra cost items.

In a sense, the Series 40 2-door Sedan was simply an off-shoot of the former Victoria coupe. The car had a built-in trunk, but no rear vent windows. The sidemounts were at extra cost, as was the luggage rack. Designated the Model 48, the car had a run of 4,688 for domestic sales and 91 for export. It cost $865 and weighed 3,120 pounds. An assist strap was provided only on the right side of the rear compartment, but both front seats folded forward for entry to the rear. An ash tray was provided on each side of the rear seat. Only one windshield wiper was used.

Shown being crated for shipment overseas is one of the 542 Model 41 Sedans that Buick built for export this year. This one uses left hand drive, so was probably destined for Europe or South America, but not England, Japan of Australia, where left hand drive was not used. In addition to the car styles, Buick built 37 bare chassis Series 40 units for domestic sales. These sold for $615 and weighed 2,410 pounds. Also built were 1,690 Series 40 bare chassis units for overseas sales.

Buick offered these Series 40 Taxis this year, but only 12 were built and all were bought by the Yellow Cab Co. of Flint, Mich. Designated the Model 47-T, the cars were the standard 5-passenger Sedan with leather interiors. Some or all may have had small jump seats, but this could not be ascertained.

The interior of the new Model 41 Sedan was quite finely appointed for a car in its price class. Refinements included twin sun shades, upholstery in mohair velvet or whipcord, a rear ashtray, armrests for both front and rear seat passengers, rear seat assist straps, and a footrest and robe rail for the rear compartment. Rear doors had large pouch pockets.

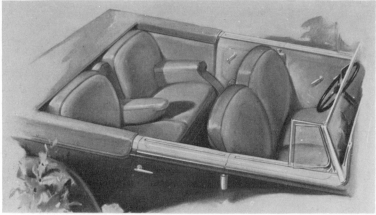

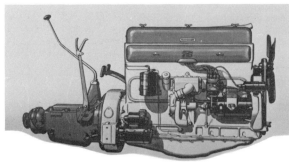

The Buick engine changed slowly in external appearance, even though the new models were a far cry from those of only a few years earlier. A single gear driven shaft still ran the generator and water pump, but the distributor was now mounted independently of these units. The tank directly above the starter is the oil filter. A soleniod starter control was now used.

The Interior of the Series 60 Phaeton was done entirely in natural hand-buffed leather. Side armrests and a folding center armrest were provided for rear seat passengers, but not in the front seat. Front doors on all open models continued to open from the leading edge, being hinged at the training edge, while just the opposite door design was used on the closed cars. Open models also used windshield wipers mounted in the cowl, while the closed models had the wipers mounted over the windshield.

The Gustat Nordberg Co. of Stockholm continued to produce its beautiful bodies, basing many on Buick chassis. This convertible cabriolet is one of 12 such cars produced by the firm. The large landau irons are functional. It is based on what appears to be the Series 60 chassis.

Battered but still in use is this Series 50 chassis, one of 1,748 built for export. Living in England, it wears a custom body produced by Carlton. The style is of the drophead coupe design, where the top can be folded back just over the front seat, or completely back as in a regular convertible. This style was quite popular in Europe, but never took hold in the U.S. The car wears wire wheels, a seldom bought accessory in the U.S.

1934

The A.J. Miller Co. of Bellefontaine, Ohio, was an old line hearse builder who started turning to the sturdy and powerful Buick chassis as bases for it professional cars. This is the Miller limousine hearse mounted on an extended Series 60 chassis. The car was rear loading only, with wide rear access doors. The compartments were divided by a partition.

Still in vogue in some sections of the country, expecially in areas of large European populations, were the carved hearse bodies, featuring heavily lacquered carved wood or cast metal panels. This version, built by the A.J. Miller of Bellefontaine, Ohio, is on an extended Series 90 chassis, fitted with dual sidemounts. It is equipped with small coach lights.

Not only did American builders consider the large Buick chassis excellent for hearses and ambulances, but so too did some British companies. This British hearse utilizes one of the 325 Series 90 chassis built for export. Its body is slab-sided, with large glass panels extending from the door edge to the rear. The doors open at the leading edge.

The Flxible Co. of Loudonville, Ohio, was still a large user of Buick chassis for its limousine-type hearse and ambulance bodies. This is the Flxible ambulance, built on an extended Series 90 chassis. A partition with sliding glass separated the compartments. The color scheme was light gray with black fenders and sidemount covers. This was the last year that Flxible would use fabric on its tops — beginning in 1935, the tops would be all-metal.

The massive Series 90 chassis was a well built piece of machinery, which with radiator, hood, cowl, and front fenders weighed 3,591 pounds and sold for $1,195. Buick built 70 of these for domestic sales and 325 for export. Knee action was used on the front end, and conventional semi-elliptic springs were used on the rear.

One of the prestige hearse builders of the time was the Eureka Co. of Rock Falls, Ill. The top of the line Eureka hearse was the Chieftain, shown here on an extended Series 90 chassis. This model featured the handy but expensive 3-way loading facility, which required that both side doors on each side be able to swing wide as shown. Note how the driver's seat automatically moved forward as the casket table was turned and extended.

A highly attractive car was the Limited Club Sedan, Model 91, which featured a built-in trunk. This model wears a highly unusual accessory for the time – wire wheels. With the new steel spoke wheels being standard equipment, and being considered very modern, few buyers wanted the "archaic" and expensive wire wheels. The car cost $1,965 and weighed 4,666 pounds. Buick produced 573 for the domestic market and only seven for export.

A beautiful car, but one phased out early in the year, was the Limited Convertible Phaeton, which was fitted with standard sidemounts and luggage rack. Only 38 were produced for domestic sales, while five were exported on special order. Unlike the Series 60 Phaeton, this car used exceedingly large chromed door hinges. The centerpost was removable. The car cost $2,145 and weighed 4,661 pounds.

Model year production this year was only 53,249, but calendar year production soared, with 107,611 vehicles leaving the factory. This figure was 3.3% of the total automotive industry, but it was not due to production of 1935 cars. Instead, it was due to a tremendous surge of production at year end, all of which were the new and revolutionary 1936 cars. The increase moved Buick up to seventh place in the industry, as Hudson-Terraplane took a tumble of three places.

But, while most concentration was on the coming 1936 Buicks, something had to be put on the market for 1935. It was; but for all practical purposes, the 1934 Buicks were simply produced for one more model year under new Series names, but nevertheless, still 1934 Buicks. In fact, it takes a real Buick expert to tell one year from the other today. About the only major change of the year was the inclusion of automatic chokes on all models, and the placing of armrests in the rear seat back seats of the Series 60 closed cars.

The new series designations appeared this year. They were the Special, Super, Century and Limited. However, the Super Series would appear this year only, and then be dropped until its re-introduction in 1940. Missing from the well-recognized list was Roadmaster, which would appear in 1936 upon the discontinuance of the Super Series.

Model year production by series was: Special, 38,520; Super, 6,536; Century, 6,238; and Limited, 1,955.

At the Indianapolis 500 this year, only one Buick appeared. This was one of Shafer's Buick powered Riglings, but it was driven by Cliff Bergere. Bergere qualified at 114.1 MPH, taking sixteenth starting position out of a field of thirty-three, and drove an excellent race until the 196th lap when the car simply quit — out of gas!

Also destined to disappear from the Limited Series was the 4-door 5-passenger Sedan, Model 97. Only 117 were produced for domestic sales, and two special order models were exported. Of these, one survives in England, wearing painted headlight pods, fender mounted parking lamps, turn signals mounted on the windshield posts, and right-hand drive. Otherwise, it is identical to the U.S. models. In the U.S., the car cost $1,945 and weighed 4,661 pounds.

Since it was obvious that buyers of 2-passenger cars were not interested in the huge Limited variety, these models were quickly dropped. Among those to go was the Sport Coupe, Model 96-S, which was equipped with rumble seat and rear spare. Only 41 were built for domestic sales, while one special order model was exported. It cost $1,875 and weighed 4,516 pounds.

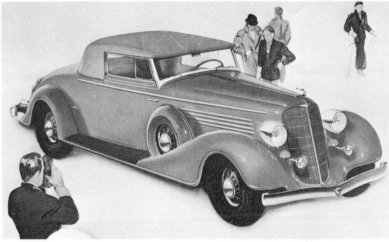

Appearing for the last time in the Limited Series was the huge and beautiful Convertible Coupe, Model 96-C. Buick produced only 10 of these cars for domestic sales and only one export model. The car cost $1,945 and weighed 4,481 pounds.

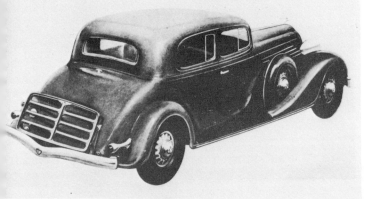

The Limited Victoria Coupe, Model 98, was phased out of production after only 32 had been built. All were sold in the U.S. The car cost $1,895 and weighed 4,541 pounds.

The former Series 90 now became the Limited Series. It continued to offer its massive cars on a 136-inch wheelbase chassis, but because of the depression, buyer resistance was tremendous. The most popular Limited was the 7-passenger Sedan, Model 90, of which only 609 were built for the domestic market and 42 were produced for export. It cost $2,055, and weighed 4,766 pounds. The sidemounts shown here were an added cost item.

Buick's prestige car continued to be the Limited Limousine, Model 90-L. Equipped with a partition between compartments and jump seats, the car cost $2,175 and weighed 4,846 pounds. There were 191 built for domestic sales and 105 for export. The rear-mounted spare was standard.

Buick produced 21 Limited chassis for domestic buyers and 160 for export. Several of these were bought by the Flxible Co. of Loudonville, Ohio, for use as a base on such ambulances as this model. The car was one of several built for the Medical Department of the U.S. Navy. Flxible now used a solid steel top on all of its ambulance and hearse models, pre-dating Fisher's Turret Top by one year. This model was finished in gloss navy gray.

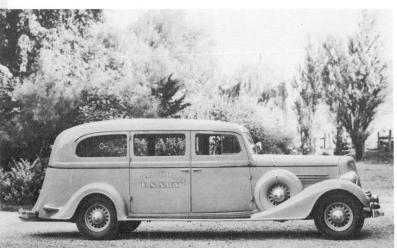

The least popular Century model was the Convertible Coupe, Model 66-C, of which only 111 were built, all for domestic sales. The car came equipped with a rumble seat, cost $1,495 and weighed 4,103 pounds. Its companion model was the Century Sport Coupe, Model 66-S, also built in rumble seat form only. It cost $1,375 and weighed 4,163 pounds. Buick built 257 for the domestic market and produced four special order export versions.

The new Century Series replaced the former Series 60. One of the most attractive sedans of the year was the new Century Club Sedan, Model 61. It is seen here in a New York dealer's showroom, sporting the accessory sidemounts and covers and a luggage rack. The car cost $1,465 and weighed 4,288 pounds. Buick built 2,762 for domestic sales and 92 for export.

The only Century model to offer covered sidemounts as standard equipment was the Convertible Phaeton, Model 68-C. The car cost $1,675 and weighed 4,323 pounds. Production was 256 for domestic sales and 52 for export. In addition, Buick produced 94 Century chassis for domestic sales and 215 for the export market.

Appearing for the last time was the Century 4-door Sedan, Model 67, which used a sloping trunkless back and a rear-mounted spare. Production was only 1,716 for domestic sales and 76 for export. The car cost $1,425 and weighed 4,273 pounds. All series except the Special used both chromed headlight pods and chromed twin exterior horns.

One of the 92 Century Club Sedans built for export was this British version. The car, which uses right hand drive, is finished in attractive yellow and black. As far as could be ascertained, all of Buick's export models used painted headlight pods similar to those used only on the Special Series in the U.S.

The Century 5-passenger Victoria Coupe, Model 68, differed from the lighter 2-door styles in that it used vent windows both front and rear. It cost $1,395 and weighed 4,183 pounds. Buick produced 597 for the U.S. but only six on special order for export.

The Victoria Coupe cost $1,160 and weighed 3,737 pounds. Its production was 1,589 for domestic sales and 29 for export. In addition, Buick shipped 197 Super chassis overseas, to be fitted with foreign-made bodies.

Appearing this year only was the Super Series, of which the 2-passenger Business Coupe, Model 56, was the least expensive style. It cost $1,110 and weighed 3,652. Only 257 were built, all for domestic sales.

Also included in the Super Series were the 4-door Sedan, Model 57, shown here, and the 5-passenger 2-door Victoria Coupe, Model 58. The sedan cost $1,190 and weighed 3,822. Production was 3,778 for domestic sales and 220 for export.

D'Ieteren was a famous European coachbuilder who did some work on Buick chassis. This convertible was built on a Special Series export chassis. With the top raised, it looks stubby and high, but has very attractive lines with the top lowered. The sidemounts seem strange on a Special.

The lowest production style in the Super Series or Series 50 was the Convertible Coupe, Model 56-C. Only 170 were built for domestic use and 17 were built for export. The car cost $1,230 and weighed 3,662 pounds. This particular model, though identical to the U.S. version, is actually a McLaughlin-Buick, built in Canada for export to Great Britain. It varies from U.S. production only in the fender mounted parking lights (required by law in England) and in right-hand drive. Both the 2-tone paint scheme and the sidemounts were added cost options. Note that the car uses canvas spare tire covers rather than the more costly steel covers.

The Super Series replaced the former Series 50. Included in its line was the Sport Coupe, Model 56-S, which was the business coupe body fitted with a rumble seat. It cost $1,145 and weighed 3,682 pounds. Production was only 268 for domestic sales and 11 for export.

Flxible Corp. of Loudenville, Ohio, a major professional car and bus manufacturer, claimed the jump on its particular industry this year by announcing a new all-steel top for its funeral coaches and ambulances. The surprising note is that this top pre-dated this type of construction by any automobile manufacturer by one full year. Flxible built 71 such units this year, all mounted on Buick Series 60 chassis. This unit is finished in two-tone gray with black fenders and sidemounts. It sports dual spotlights and a windshield-mounted "Ambulance" sign.

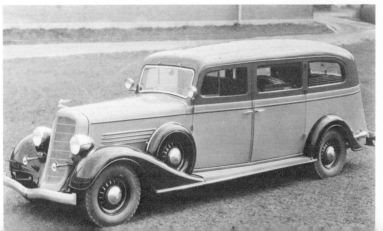

Virtually identical to the 1934 models was the new Special Series. This is the 5-passenger Club Sedan, Model 41, of which 18,638 were sold in the U.S. and 535 went overseas. It cost $925 and weighed 3,210 pounds. The Series 40 did not use the pretty chrome exterior horns.

New for the year was the Special Convertible Coupe, Model 46-C. The car turned out to be the least popular of all Series 40 models, having a run of 933 for domestic sales and 67 for export. It weighed 3,140 pounds and cost $925. It was available in rumble seat form only. Upholstery was in tan leather or tan Bedford cloth, at the buyer's option. In addition, Buick produced the Model 46-S Sport Coupe, unchanged from 1934. It cost $855 and weighed 3,090 pounds. Production was 1,136 for domestic sales and 64 for export.

Destined to disappear for one year was the Special 5-passenger Sedan, Model 47. The car would not appear in 1936, but would reappear in 1937. This year it cost $895 and weighed 3,180 pounds. Buick produced 6,250 for domestic sales and 391 for export.

Buick's least expensive car again was the Special Business Coupe, Model 46, priced at $795. It was built in 2-passenger form only, with fairly substantial trunk space. The 3,020-pound car had a run of 2,850 for domestic sales and eight special order versions for export.

The Special chassis, in stripped form, was offered in several varieties, such as with fenders, with just cowl, hood, grille, and front fenders, or in drive-away form, minus body. Buick sold 173 such chassis on the domestic market, and shipped 2,448 overseas.

A very attractive closed car was the Special 2-Door Touring Sedan, Model 48. It cost $865 and weighed 3,160 pounds. Buick produced 4,957 for domestic sales and 70 for export. The new Special Series replaced the Series 40 of 1934, but the cars were virtually identical.

1936

This was the year that put Buick back on the road. The long-awaited, totally new Buicks were finally unveiled, and public acceptance was overwhelming. Designed by Harley Earl, head of General Motors styling, the new cars carried the GM theme, but still were unmistakable Buicks. They featured bodies with all rounded corners, the new Fisher all-steel turret top, sweptback windsheilds and rear styling, a large cast grille, smoothly rounded and very modern fenders, and a spare in the trunk on some models. By comparison with the classic lines of the 1935 models, the new Buick was really a new and modern car.

And the public responded. Calendar year production was 179,533, which was 4.8% of the industry. This moved Buick up to sixth place, passing Pontiac in the process. Model year production was 168,596, divided over the four series. By series, this production was: Special, 120,714; Century, 25,980; Limited, 4,811; and the new Roadmaster, 17,091.

The Special now used a 118-inch wheelbase; the Century had a 112-inch wheelbase; the new Roadmaster used a wheelbase of 131 inches; and the prestige Limited returned to its huge chassis with the 138-inch wheelbase.

Powering most of the beauties was a totally new Eight featuring aluminum pistons. This was a 320-cubic-inch engine with a bore and stroke of 3-7/16 x 4-5/16, developing 120 horsepower at 3200 RPM. In the relatively light Century, this engine could hold the car at a steady 100 MPH, a feat that few cars of this price class could equal.

The new engine was used in all but the Special Series, with that line having to contend with the 93 horsepower, 233-cubic-inch block of the previous year. All models were now equipped with hydraulic brakes, full synchromesh transmissions, and built-in knee action.

For the first time, the throttle lever and light switch were not mounted on the steering wheel hub. Instead, these were now of the pull-type, and were located on the dashboard. The steering wheel itself was again of totally new design, with spokes of fine rods of spring steel running from the hub to a rim of black molded hard rubber. The hub was much smaller than previously, and contained only a large steel horn button embossed with the Buick emblem. Also for the first time, the hand brake lever was moved from the center of the floor to the left side, and was located under the dashboard, suspended from the firewall area, rather than jutting from the floor. For some strange reason, Buick this year did away with its push-button door locks, which it had instituted in 1933. However, the buttons were reinstalled in the 1937 models, and have been in use ever since.

Far removed from the U.S. capitalistic system was the fledgling Russian Communist system. Yet, as Russia began to produce its own luxury cars for its political leaders, it looked to the U.S. for guidance. The prewar models of the famous ZIS, which went into production late this year, used a Straight 8 engine that was almost a carbon copy of Buick's popular block.

The Limited Series used a new chassis, with a return to the 138-inch wheelbase. In this series were four 4-door models, all using the same basic body. The most popular of these was the 6-passenger Sedan, Model 91, which had a run of 1,713 for domestic sales and 13 for export. It cost $1,695 and weighed 4,477 pounds. All Limiteds used a left hand sidemount, with the popular dual sidemounts being at extra cost.

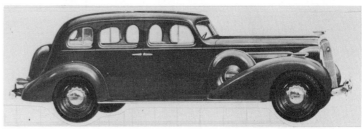

The 8-passenger Sedan, Model 90, was the same basic Limited sedan, but equipped with two jump seats behind the front seat. It cost $1,845 and weighed 4,517 pounds. Buick built 1,590 for domestic sales and 119 for export.

Buick's prestige car was the Limited Limousine, an 8-passenger vehicle fitted with a glass partition between the compartments. Its price of $1,945 marked the first time that the limousine ever had a base price under $2,000. The 4,577-pound car had a run of 709 for domestic sales and 238 for export.

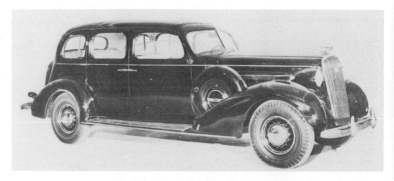

New for Buick was the Limited Formal Sedan, Model 91-F. This was the basic 6-passenger design, but fitted with a limousine-type glass partition between compartments. It cost $1,795 and weighed 4,487 pounds. Only 74 were built for domestic sales and just one special order model was exported. In addition to these sales, Buick produced 25 Limited chassis and cowl units for domestic sales and 329 for export.

Buick probably reached its highest point of notoriety this year, when the last Duke of Windsor, then King Edward VII ordered this custom bodied limousine. The car was a Canadian built McLaughlin-Buick, utilizing the standard Limited Model 90 body with custom bodywork done by the McLaughlin factory in Oshawa, Ontario. The car gained much publicity during the King's romance with American-born Mrs. Wallis Warfield Simpson, which led to his eventual abdication of the throne, and though it was actually a Canadian-built car, most people the world over assumed it was an American vehicle. The car is shown here in front of Buckingham Palace, upon its delivery.

Some bitter irony lies in this pre-delivery photo of the King's custom Buick Limousine. The photo was taken in front of the London showroom of Lendrum & Hartmann, Buick's British distributor in London. The King's car has just arrived, and has not yet been fitted with the Royal standards. Parked directly behind the King's car is a standard McLaughlin-Buick Model 90-L limousine, which came in on the same shipment. This car was ordered by Ernest Simpson for his wife, Wallis Warfield Simpson—who would soon become the King's wife. Note that both cars have been fitted with dual foglights, but that the King's car wears chrome beauty rings on its wheels.

Parked in front of McLaughlin-Buick's factory in Oshawa, Ontario, is the custom-built Model 90-L limousine constructed at the factory for England's King Edward VIII. With the exception of the solid rear quarter panels and the fully custom and lavishly appointed interior, the car differs little from the standard Canadian or American Limited Limousine. All of the custom work was performed by McLaughlin's own staff. One amazing factor in the purchase of these and subsequent Buicks by the Royal Family is that these cars were selected over an ample supply of Rolls Royce, Daimler, Bentley, and other prestigious British cars that were readily available. Had England at the time been a car-poor country, the purchases could have been more understandable, but in this case, the Buicks had to compete with what were considered to be the best cars in the world. Possibly Buick's slogan of this era should have read, "When better Buicks are built—Royalty will buy them."

The interior of King Edward's custom Buick was lavishly fitted, but in typical British quiet good taste. Where the rear quarter windows normally would have been was a mirrored panel containing light and flexible reading lamp. The compartment divider held a wide array of items in four swing-down compartments. Included here was a hot water hearing system, vacuum ice container, bar set, six liquor bottles, smoking set including tobacco and cigarette boxes, London telephone book, lunch basket, and various other units of comfort. The upper compartment doors swung down flush to form luncheon trays, while the lower doors opened hamper-like as shown. A silk shade for the tiny rear window was motor driven, but the glass partition between compartments was operated by hand. Obviously, being designed for British usage, the car utilized right-hand drive.

New for the year was the Roadmaster Series, which based its models on a 131-inch wheelbase chassis. The best looking and least popular of the 2-model series was the Convertible Phaeton, Model 80-C. Buick built 1,064 for domestic sales and 165 for export. It cost $1,565 and weighed 4,228 pounds. A single sidemount was standard. Note that both doors on this model open at the trailing edge, as opposed to the center opening doors used on all other 4-door cars. This model is one of the export versions, identical to the U.S. models except for having left hand drive. It was imported directly into Australia, where it still lives. Holden, an Australian subsidiary of General Motors, was now building bodies for Buick chassis, buy never offered this style.

The Century 5-passenger Victoria Trunk Coupe, Model 68, had nowhere the sales appeal as did its sister car in the Special line. Only 3,762 were built for domestic sales and 37 for export. It cost $1,055 and weighed 3,730 pounds. This year Buick sold 1,110 Century chassis and cowl units to U.S. specialty car manufacturers, but shipped only five such units overseas.

Offering a lot of car for the money was the new Century 4-door Sedan, Model 61. It was the best selling Century, with production being 17,806 for domestic sales and 397 for export. It cost $1,090 and weighed 3,780 pounds. This beautiful example, wearing accessory fog lights and white walls, belongs to Gary Pake of Burton, Mich.

The only other model in the new Roadmaster Series was the 4-door Trunk Sedan, Model 81, which enjoyed a run of 14,985 for domestic sales and 343 for export. It cost $1,255 and weighed 4,098 pounds. This beautiful example is owned by Don Hackenbrunch of Detroit, Mich. In addition to these two models, Buick sold 12 Roadmaster chassis and cowl units in the U.S. and shipped another 522 such units to its overseas plants.

As could probably be expected, the least popular Century was the Convertible, Model 66-C. It was available in rumble seat form only, with a left fenderwell and sidemount being standard, and dual sidemounts being optional. Buick built only 717 for domestic sales and 49 for export. It cost $1,135 and weighed 3,775 pounds. All Century models used a 122-inch wheelbase chassis.

The Century Series offered two versions of the Sport Coupe. The 3-passenger Model 66-SO had a trunk, internal spare, and small opera seat behind the front seat, while the 2-passenger Model 66-SR used a rumble seat and left sidemount. Both cost $1,035. The Model 66-SR, which weighed 3,635 pounds, had a run of 1,001 for domestic sales and 17 for export, while the Model 66-SO, which weighed 3,625 pounds, had a run of 1,078 for domestic sales and one special order for export. This beautiful Model 66-SR features the accessory dual sidemounts, dual fog lights, and an interesting and original grille grard. It belongs to Ron Stimson of Fairview Park, Ohio.

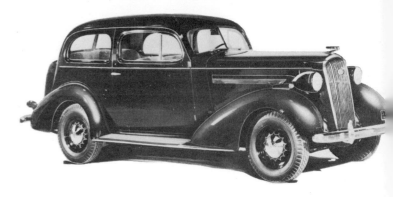

The Buicks for 1936 were a totally new ball game. Series names and model numbers remained the same, but that was about all. The most popular in the entire Buick fold turned out to be the Special 4-door Trunk Sedan, Model 41, of which 77,007 were produced for domestic sales and 1,796 were built for export. It cost $885 and weighed 3,360 pounds. For the first time, the spare tire lived in the trunk.

Buick's second most popular car was the Special Victoria Trunk Coupe, Model 48, which was really a 2-door coach or sedan. Production was 21,241 for domestic sales and 82 for export. It cost $835 and weighed 3,305 pounds. In addition to these sales, Buick sold 150 Special cowl and chassis units in this country, and shipped 5,263 such chassis to its various overseas assembly plants.

Considering the response that sporty cars had been faced with during the drab depression days, the Special Convertible did fairly well, with 1,488 being sold in the U.S. and an additional 162 being for export. It was available in rumble seat form only, with a standard left hand sidemount. Twin sidemounts were extra. It cost $820 and weighed 3,190 pounds.

Appearing to come out of a scene of extreme foreign intrigue is this view of Nicola Bulgari's Special 2-passenger Sport Coupe, with King Edward VIII's limousine lurking in the background on this lonely Italian highway. The sport coupe used the same basic body as did the business coupe, but was fitted with a rumble seat. Designated the Model 46-SR, the car was equipped with a lefthand sidemount as standard equipment, but the righthand sidemount was an accessory. Production reached 1,390 for domestic sales and 104 for export. Later in the Season the Special 3-passenger Sport Coupe, Model 46-SO, was introduced. This car used the same body as the sport and business coupe, had a trunk and internal spare, but was fitted with an extremely small and uncomfortable opera seat behind the regular seat. Buick built 1,086 of these for domestic sales and 17 for export. At the end of the year, both models were dropped. Both cost $820 and weighed 3,190 pounds.

The Special Series, using a 118-inch wheelbase chassis, attracted many new buyers who wanted something better than an economy car, but did not want to spend the hard found depression dollars to enter the medium price class. Filling the bill perfectly was Buick's lowest priced car, the Special Business Coupe, Model 46. It cost only $765 and weighed 3,150 pounds. It was available in trunk form only, and its spare lived in the trunk. Buick built 10,912 for domestic sales and 16 for export.

The Brewster Co., a renowned coachbuilding firm located in Long Island City, N.Y., designed this proposed town car body for use on the Limited Chassis. It is believed that none were built.

Since all Buick's except the Special used the same engine, and since all chassis would have to be extended anyway, most of the builders of professional cars this year purchased Century chassis for their bodies. Among these builders was the Flxible Co. of Loudonville, Ohio, which had long favored Buick chassis. This is the new Flxible ambulance, built in limousine style and using an all-steel body. Note that the hood, cowl, radiator shell and grille have all been raised in order to accommodate the taller body.

The Eureka Co. of Rock Falls, Ill., continued to offer their prestige funeral cars, but also came out with the Chieftan line of quality built ambulances. Eureka would fit these bodies to any chassis, but had a definite preference for Buick and LaSalle units. The Chieftain ambulance was of the 4-door limousine type, but the doors used a centerpost, and the compartments were separated by a partition. A Century chassis and dual sidemounts were used.

The Sayers & Scovill firm of Cincinnati, Ohio, still one of the nation's top producers of ambulances and funeral cars, turned their attention to Buicks for the first time this year. One of their many models was this elaborately carved hearse, called the Romanesque. The heavy body panels were of cast aluminum. The chassis is the Century Series, fitted with dual sidemounts, but Sayers & Scovill made a practice of removing all traces of the car's name, disguising its grille and hood, and inserting S&S emblems in place of the nameplates.

Wearing a slightly modified grille and S&S hubcaps, this Century chassis is serving as the base for the Claremont, a new economy line hearse introduced by the Sayers & Scoville Co. of Cincinnati. The body is of the limousine-type, with a partition between compartments. Unlike Flxible, Sayers & Scoville did not change the height of the hood and cowl.

New in the offerings of Flxible of Loudonville, Ohio, was the Funeral Service Car. This vehicle was used to transport bodies to the funeral home, haul furniture and flowers, and do a multitude of other tasks for which a hearse was really not necessary. Yet, if needed, the car could be used as a hearse. It used the same basic body and raised front end as did the Flxible ambulance, but had rear door and quarter windows blanked in. A partition separated the compartments. It was available with single or dual sidemounts.

For those automotive experts who expected Buick to rest on its laurels this year, 1937 proved to be a shocker. The new Buicks came in, even bigger, better, and more beautiful than before. In fact, in the estimation of many, Buick reached a definite high point in styling with the 1937 and 1938 models.

Again the public showed its acceptance. Calendar year production shot up to 227,038 or 5.8% of the total market. Still, Buick held sixth place in the industry, but Pontiac and Oldsmobile switched places on either side. Model year production was 220,346. By series, this amounted to: Special, 163,349; Century, 35,093; Roadmaster, 17,231; and Limited, 4,673.

Both the Special and the Century models grew substantially. The Special now used the 122-inch wheelbase chassis that had been used on the Century in 1936, and the Century used a new 126-inch wheelbase chassis. Both the Roadmaster and Limited Series retained their respective chassis of 131- and 138-inch wheelbases.

In the styling department, locks were greatly enhanced by new fenders with very attractive squared-off ends, and by a totally new horizontal-line grille, hood, and headlights which gave Buick a distinguished look all of its own, matched by no other car in the GM stable or by virtually no other American car on the road that year.

In the engineering department, the 1937 Buick was as changed and improved as was the exterior. The Special received an all new and larger engine of 248 cubic inches, running a bore and stroke of 3-3/32 x 4-1/8. This developed an even 100 brake horsepower at 3200 RPM.

The other models continued to use the same size bore stroke and displacement as before, but the new engines had a power booster camshaft, a counterweighted crankshaft, improved crankcase ventilation, full-pressure lubrication, and a new carburetor called the "Aerobat." These carburetors, supplied by both Stromberg and Marvel, gave Buick maximum performance under virtually any driving situation. These improvements boosted the engines' performance to 130 horsepower at 3400 RPM.

The 1936 models had been considered hot – the 1937 Models were definitely hotter. The Specials could go from 10 to 60 MPH in only 19.2 seconds; the Century could do the same in 18.5 seconds; while the larger Roadmasters and Limiteds would respond to this test in just slightly over 20 seconds – and for 1937, this was really quick.

Other innovations for the year were new hypoid gears, improved generators, running board radio antennas, windshield defrosters, and better ride control through stabilizer bars both front and rear.

At Indianapolis, the story at the Memorial Day Classic was the same this year as it was in 1936. A Buick powered car was entered and its driver, Emil Andres, qualified at 116.2 MPH. But this was not high enough to hold a place in the race, and the car was eventually bumped.

The Limited Series again consisted of four models, all based on the same 4-door sedan body and using the 138-inch wheelbase chassis. The most popular style was the 8-passenger Sedan, Model 90, which had a production run of 1,592 for domestic sales and 118 for export. It cost $2,240 and weighed 4,549 pounds. Standard equipment included a fender well and sidemount on the left, but dual sidemounts were extra.

The lowest priced Limited was the 6-passenger Sedan, Model 91, which cost $2,066 and weighed 4,469. Buick produced 1,229 for the U.S. market, 13 for export. Only the left sidemount was standard, and a right fender mount was at extra cost. In addition, Buick built two Limited chassis and cowl units for U.S. sales and eight for export, and shipped 588 unassembled Limited chassis overseas for assembly.

Appearing for the last time this year was the 6-passenger Formal Trunk Sedan, Model 91-F. This was the Limited 6-passenger sedan fitted with a disappearing glass partition between compartments. It cost $2,240 and weighed 4,409 pounds. Buick built 156 for U.S. sales and two special order versions for export.

Buick's most expensive car continued to be its Limited Limousine, Model 90-L, available in 8-passenger form only, and featuring a standard sidemount and disappearing glass partition between compartments. It cost $2,342 and weighed 4,599 pounds. Only 720 were built for the domestic market and 245 for export.

Unlike any other 4-door Buick, the new Roadmaster Convertible Phaeton, Model 80-C, used doors that all opened from the trailing edge. In addition, it was the only Roadmaster that had sidemounts as standard equipment. Although it doesn't show in this photo, the car used the trunk-back design. It cost $1,856 and weighed 4,214 pounds. Buick produced 1,040 for domestic sales and 115 for export. The center posts were removable when the top and windows were lowered. In addition to the car production, Buick built eight Roadmaster cowl and chassis units for domestic sales and ten for export, and shipped an additional 588 unassembled Roadmaster chassis overseas.

The large Roadmaster 6-passenger Sedan retained its 131-inch wheelbase chassis, but still was a massive car. Designated the Model 81, it was available only in trunk-back style, with the sidemounts being an accessory item. It cost $1,518 and weighed 4,159 pounds. Buick built 14,637 for domestic sales and 344 for export. This model, wearing non-standard wheel covers, dual fog lights and a "sharks tooth" type grille guard, is owned by Clay Courtney of Churchill, Tenn.

New this year was the Roadmaster 6-passenger Formal Sedan, Model 81-F. It was really the 6-passenger sedan fitted with a disappearing glass partition between compartments — great for when the kids start fighting. It cost $1,641 and weighed 4,299 pounds. Buick produced 452 for the domestic market and 37 for export.

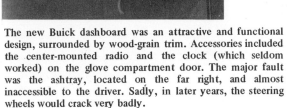

The new Buick dashboard was an attractive and functional design, surrounded by wood-grain trim. Accessories included the center-mounted radio and the clock (which seldom worked) on the glove compartment door. The major fault was the ashtray, located on the far right, and almost inaccessible to the driver. Sadly, in later years, the steering wheels would crack very badly.

American farmers weren't the only people who made a practice of converting old sedans into light trucks. Here an export model of the Roadmaster sedan has been rebuilt into an attractive pickup by its British owner. The body work appears well done and rather attractive.

As before, the most popular car in the Century Series was the 4-passenger Touring Sedan, Model 61, of which 20,679 were built for domestic sales and 461 built for export. The car cost $1,233 and weighed 3,720 pounds. This attractive restoration is owned by Donald Duchene of Grosse Pointe Shores, Mich. It used an original grille guard on the front bumper.

A group of prospective customers inspect the new Century 4-door Sedan, Model 67, prominently displayed in a dealer's showroom. The car reappeared this year after a one-year absence. Built in fast-back style, it cost $1,207 and weighed 3,750 pounds. Buick produced 4,750 for domestic sales and 21 for export. The car had a trunk, but not nearly as spacious a one as did the trunk back models. As in other models, the spare was stored flat in its own sub-compartment.

Drawing surprisingly few customers was the Century 2-door Touring Sedan, Model 68, which used a trunk back. Only 2,874 were built for domestic sales and 23 for export. It cost $1,197 and weighed 3,750 pounds. A feature of all Buicks this year was a tool trough that was located just behind the trunk deck and ran the width of the car. This allowed access to tools and jack without removing luggage or the spare. Sometimes, especially in the coupe models, persons desiring better traction would fill this trough with lead, iron, or even cement.

Produced this year only was the Century 2-door Sedan, Model 64, built in swept-back style. It cost $1,172 and weighed 3,720 pounds. Buick built 1,117 for domestic sales, but only one special order model for export. In addition to the regular production, Buick built 69 Century cowl and chassis units for domestic sales and eight for export, and produced 949 unassembled Century chassis for export to overseas assmembly plants.

Reappearing in the Century Series was the 4-passenger Sport Coupe, Model 66-S. However, the car did not use a rumble seat, but was fitted with two small folding opera seats behind the front seat. Thus, Buick's two convertible coupe models were the only ones to use rumble seats this year. The sport coupe weighed 3,660 pounds and cost $1,187. Production was 2,840 for domestic sales and 33 for export. The sidemounts were an accessory.

One of the 58 Century Convertibles built for export is this model, still living in England. It has been fitted with right-hand drive, and the typically British swing-out turn arrows are mounted on the door hinges. Sidemounts with dual rearview mirrors complete the conversion.

One of the fastest and sportiest cars on the road this year was the Century Convertible, Model 66-C, which cost $1,269 and weighed 3,715 pounds. Still, only 787 were built for domestic sales and 56 for export. This version is shown attached to a Curtiss Aerocar trailer, a very well built and luxurious travel trailer of the 1930s. Its hitch mounted in the rumble seat compartment, and thus its use was regulated strictly to coupe styles with either trunks or rumble seats. This model uses sidemounts, probably so that the trailer would not have to be unhitched to reach the spare tire. No sidemount covers are used, probably because they would not fit on the oversized tires with which this car is equipped. The car is fitted with trunk-type turn signals on the front fenders, a novelty for the era, and has dual fog lights and a single spotlight.

New for the Century Series was the 5-passenger Convertible Phaeton, Model 60-C, which cost $1,524 and weighed 3,840 pounds. Not nearly as popular as the Special version, it had a run of only 410 for domestic sales and 11 for export. The Century wheelbase was increased to 126 inches.

A beautiful and unusual vehicle was this creation of the Bohman & Schwartz Co. of Pasadena, Cal., a well-known west coast custom house. The car was built on a Century chassis for use in the Topper movies, and was fitted with trick controls so that it could be driven by an unseen person. Since its initial construction, the car has been rebuilt twice, and is now mounted on a Chrysler chassis. It is believed this is the original version.

The new Buick engines looked virtually the same on the exterior, but those used in the Special Series now boasted 100 horsepower, while the larger models had an improved camshaft and counter-weighted crankshaft, in addition to improved crankcase ventilation.

Buick's most popular car was the Special 4-door Touring Sedan. Production of this model soared to 82,440 for domestic sales and 2,755 for export. Designated the Model 41, the car cost $1,021 and weighed 3,490. Shown here is the car as it was newly delivered to the home of Merle Perry of Flint in 1937. Mr. Perry is now with the Sloan Museum of Transportation in Flint. Two dealer accessories are the bug guard around the grille and the large single fog light.

The Special 2-door Touring Sedan, Model 48, featured a trunk back that Buick referred to as "a jumbo luggage compartment." In standard form, the spare tire would lie flat on the trunk floor, under a special plywood luggage floor. But, when the attractive but costly dual sidemounts were used, as shown here, the entire trunk could be used for luggage space. In basic form, the car cost $895 and weighed 3,480 pounds. Buick built 15,936 for domestic sales and 98 for export. A beautiful example of this car survives in the collection of Nicola Bulgari in Rome, Italy. It is one of 17 Buicks that Mr. Bulgari has in his collection.

The interior of the Special Touring Sedan was roomy and certainly well in keeping with other cars in its price range. Buyers had a choice of whipcord or mohair upholstery. Rear passengers had assist cords and a cord robe rail. Armrests were provided front and rear. Once again, pushbutton door locks were incorporated on all doors. The steering wheel was similar to the one used in 1936, but the rim was now of yellow molded plastic. This material looked very nice when the car was new, but had a bad tendency to crack and shrink after a few years of service.

Reappearing was the Special 4-door Sedan, Model 47, which used a swept-back rear design. Its limited trunk space was greatly increased by the use of accessory dual sidemounts. In standard form, its base price was $995 and its weight was 3,510 pounds. Production was 22,312 for domestic sales and 205 for export.

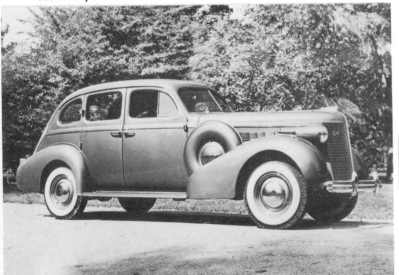

New for the year was the Special 5-passenger 2-door Sedan, Model 44, which used a plain sloping back. The car cost $959 and weighed 3,490 pounds. Buick built 9,330 for domestic sales but only 12 for export. In addition to this production, Buick built 257 Special cowl and chassis units for domestic sales and 110 for export, and produced 6,493 disassembled Special chassis for shipment to its overseas plants.

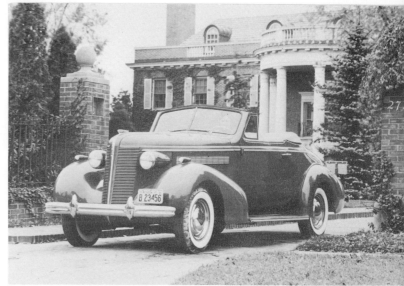

The Special Convertible Coupe used interesting rear treatment. The top deck lid opened for the standard rumble seat, but below this was a second deck lid, behind which lived the spare tire and a very small luggage area. This original model is still in daily use in Santa Barbara, Cal.

A truly beautiful car of only limited appeal was the Special Convertible Coupe, Model 46-C. Only 2,265 were built for domestic sales and 134 for export. It cost $1,056 and weighed 3,480 pounds. All models this year used cowl mounted windshield wipers.

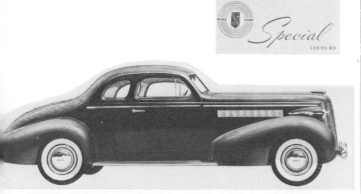

The Special 2-passenger Business Coupe, Model 46, picked up greatly in popularity, with 13,742 being built for domestic sales and 31 for export. Priced at $913, it was Buick's least expensive car. It weighed 3,380 pounds and offered substantial luggage space. The spare tire lived in the trunk, beneath a plywood partition upon which the luggage was placed.

The Special 4-passenger Sport Coupe, Model 46-S, no longer used a rumble seat, but was fitted with two small opera seats behind the front seat. The trunk space on this car was fairly large, but was enlarged even more when the accessory twin sidemounts were used. The car cost $975 and weighed 3,445 pounds. Production was 5,059 for domestic sales and 225 for export.

New for the year was the Special 5-passenger Convertible Phaeton, Model 40-C. Weighing 3,630 pounds and costing $1,302, the car had a surprisingly good reception for a style of this type. Buick produced 1,689 for domestic sales and 256 for export. Sidemounts were an accessory. This model had its doors opening from the centerpost, in a style similar to the 4-door sedans. Featuring dual sidemounts and dual fog lights, this beautiful example is owned by Elaine Amman of Chesaning, Mich. The top folded into its own compartment, and did not overhang the upper edge of the body.

Based on the Special chassis was this Carlton Drop Head Coupe, of very typical British line. This model also was of the drop head type, which allowed the top to be rolled back as far as the landau irons, or put down completely. The landau irons were functional. Slight modification has been made to the grille, and the headlights are non-Buick.

At least one of the 245 Limited Limousines produced for export still survives. It is this English model, fitted with right-hand drive and wearing a set of very non-Buick headlights and hub caps. It uses dual sidemounts and dual fog lights.

Shown in the early stages of restoration is this unusual Limited, sporting a British Sedanca DeVille body. Weather protection for the driver was by a removable leatherette top, with the front compartment provided with roll-up windows. It had left-hand drive.

The Brewster Co. of Long Island City, N.Y., designed a town car for the 1936 Buick, and actually produced one on the 1937 Limited chassis. It is believed that this is the only such car it built, and this very poor photograph is the only one that could be found of the car. From the cowl back, all bodywork is strictly Brewster's. The grille is partly covered by a leatherette windshield, a popular item of the era, used in cold weather to keep the engine temperature high enough to force heat from the hot water heater.

Buicks were becoming very popular overseas, where a wide variety of special bodies were fitted to the chassis-cowl units. This Special model features a British Alvemarle Drop Head Coupe body, with a top that could be folded either half-way or completely back. The landau irons were functional. The car used dual sidemounts, but has rather unusual extended rear view mirrors mounted on the fenders. It also used top-mounted wipers instead of the cowl-mounted units.

A huge car is this Limited chassis mounting a special limousine body by Thrupp & Maberly, a British coach building firm. The rather high design resulted in the car losing some of its original long, sleek appearance. Non-Buick hubcaps have been used.

As could be expected, the Flxible Co. of Loudonville, Ohio, continued to build substantial numbers of hearses and ambulances on Buick chassis. The majority of these used the basic Flxible professional limousine body, seen here, which still necessitated a raising of the cowl, hood and grille to meet the high body line. This is the combination model, which could be quickly and easily converted to either hearse or ambulance, depending on the need.

The economy hearse in the Sayers & Scoville line was the Manchester, also mounted on an extended Century chassis. The car was of the limousine hearse type, and was rear-loading only. The quarter windows were fitted with flower racks, and heavy drapes were installed in all back compartment windows. A glass partition separated front and rear compartments. As usual, this car has disguise bars on the grille and wears S&S hubcaps.

Sayers & Scoville Co. of Cincinnati, still a major hearse and ambulance builder today, continued to mount its prestige hearse on Buick Century chassis. Called the Romanesque, the car used huge carved panels of cast bronze. The S&S company continued to disguise the Buick grille and hood, and mounted S&S emblems on the car in place of the Buick emblems.

For some reason, possibly because of the improving economic conditions in the country, the carved hearses started to make a comeback. This carved model, featuring hidden rear doors and functional coach lights, was built by the A.J. Miller Co. of Bellefontaine, Ohio. It is mounted on an extended Century chassis. A partition separated the compartments. Loading was via the back door.

Eureka of Rock Falls, Ill., continued to offer its quality built funeral cars on Buick chassis. This limousine hearse, of the rear loading type, was built specially for Perrott's Funeral Home of Newburgh, N.Y. It uses an extended Century chassis. The same style body was used for the Eureka ambulances, and some units were built as combination cars that could be converted to either ambulance or hearse by the owner.

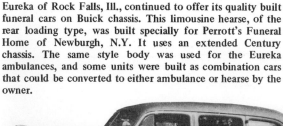

1938

The most expensive Buick continued to be the huge Limited Limousine, Model 90-L, which cost $2,453 and weighed 4,653 pounds. This flagship of the Buick line used the Model 90 body, but was fitted with a glass partition between compartments. Despite its lower price, the Buick could compare favorably with any other American luxury limousine, and many of the exclusive foreign makes produced that year. This beautiful example lives in Rome, in the collection of Nicola Bulgari.

Buick's prestige line continued to be the Limited Series, of which the most popular model was the 8-passenger Touring Sedan, Model 90. Still, only 644 were built for domestic sales and 62 for export. It cost $2,350 and weighed 4,608 pounds. The Limited Series used a newly designed chassis of 140-inch wheelbase length — one of the largest on the road that year.

The lowest priced Limited was the 6-passenger Touring Sedan, Model 91. It used the same basic body as did the other two Limited models, but lacked jump seats and/or divider partition. It cost $2,074 and weighed 4,568 pounds. Buick built 437 for domestic sales, but only four special order versions for export.

Buick styling hit a high point in 1937, and in 1938 it hi its highest point. The 1938 Buicks today are the undis puted kings of the Buick line among antique car buffs, an well-preserved or well-restored 1938 Buick will comman higher prices and more respect than any other similar styl Buick of post-1920 vintage. In a word, these cars wer "absolutely beautiful." Actually, the styling was not tha different than found on the 1937 models, but what fev changes were made were in complete harmony with th styling, and end result was superb.

Calendar year production was only 173,905, but th drop was due to a major slip in the economy this year, an all other manufacturers slipped, too. Thus, though pro duction was down, Buick still accounted for 8.6% of th total cars produced in the U.S., and moved up to fourt place in the industry, passing both Pontiac and Dodge Model year production amounted to 168,689. By serie this was: Special, 141,301; Century, 19,287; Roadmaste 6,100; and Limited, 2,001.

Whereas styling changed only little, the engineerin changes were tremendous. Primarily, these changes in volved three major areas — suspension, engine, an transmission. In the suspension department, all Buicks nov featured coil springs all around — another industry first The coils were much softer and more resilient than th former leaf springs, and these were bolstered by shoc absorbers roughly four times the size of any absorber o the road.

Under the hood lived the new "Dynaflash" Eight, whic featured "turbulator pistons" of Buick's exclusive design The Dynaflash engines retained the same displacemen bore and stroke of the previous two engines, namel 3-3/32 x 4-1/8 inch bore and stroke and 248-cubic-inc displacement for the Special, and 3-7/16 x 4-5/16 inc bore and stroke and 320-cubic-inch displacement for al other models; but horsepower was raised to 107 at 340(RPM in the Specials and 141 at 3600 RPM in all othe models. Also under the hood there now lived the battery – another Buick innovation.

The third important engineering development turne(out to be a complete flop as far as Buick was concerned but Buick didn't want the thing in the first place. Cadillac and Oldsmobile engineers had for some time been workin on an automatic transmission which they felt was per fected in time for the 1938 season. But neither company had the production facilities to manufacture this unit, anc therefore the job was given to Buick. And, since Buick was building the transmissions, GM top management fel that these units should be offered as an option on Buick cars, despite the pessimism shown by the majority o Buick engineers.

The Derham Co. of Rosemont, Pa., an old and highly respected builder of fine custom bodies, designed this town car style for the Limited chassis. There is conflicting information as to whether or not any of these cars were ever built. The lower portion would have used the standard Limited body, but from the window sills upward, the car would have been strictly Derham's work.

1938

Buick did offer the transmissions, but as an option on the Specials only. The semi-automatic shifter worked on a 5-speed principle, using a first and second in low range and a first, third and direct dirve fourth in high range. But the unit's breakdown record was horrendous, and a steady stream of irate customers convinced both Buick and GM management that this idea should be discarded before the end of the 1938 season.

Although Oldsmobile and Cadillac went on to perfect the automatic transmission within a few years, this experience so soured Buick on such units that it wasn't until 1948 that a small torque converter type of transmission known as Dynaflow was finally approved as being suitable for Buick cars.

In 1937, the Specials and Centurys grew in size. This year it was time for the Roadster and Limited to grow. The Special retained its 122-inch wheelbase, and the Century retained its 126-inch wheelbase, but the Roadmaster and Limited models each grew two inches to new wheelbases of 133 inches and 140 inches respectively.

And, for the third year in a row, the Indianapolis Memorial Day story was one of disappointment for Buick fans. Charlie Crawford piloted a Shafer Buick to a qualifying time of 112.7 MPH, but this was too slow to stay in the field, and the car was bumped. This marked the last time that a Buick would appear at the 500 until Mickey Thompson entered a Buick powered special in 1962.

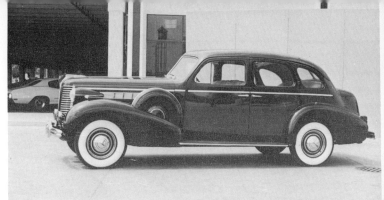

As was the case in the lower price lines, the Roadmaster 4-door Touring Sedan, Model 81, was the most popular car in that series. Buick built 4,505 for domestic sales and 199 for export. Built in trunk-back style, it cost $1,645 and weighed 4,245 pounds. This fine restoration, wearing dual sidemounts and dual fog lights, is owned by John Rocne of Baltimore, Md.

A very beautiful car of very limited appeal was the Roadmaster Convertible Phaeton, Model 80-C. Only 350 were produced for domestic sales and 61 for export. Priced at $1,983, it was the most expensive Roadmaster model. It weighed 4,325 pounds.

A surprise move was made when the new Roadmaster Sport Sedan, Model 87, was introduced. The surprise was due to the fact that this style was fast falling from popularity in the other series, and yet Buick introduced still another version of the unpopular style in the realtively high-priced series. Still, only 466 were built for domestic sales only. The car cost $1,645 and weighed 4,245 pounds.

A style with only little appeal was the Roadmaster Formal Sedan, Model 81-F. Only 247 were built for the domestic market and 49 for export. The car was the Roadmaster Touring Sedan fitted with a disappearing glass partition between compartments. It cost $1,759 and weighed 4,305 pounds. Sidemounts were an accessory of all Roadmaster models.

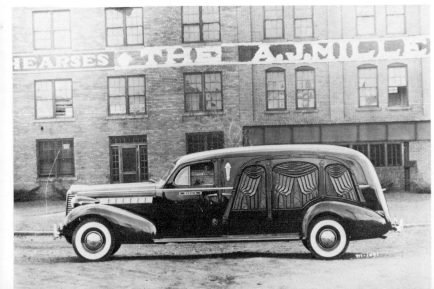

One of the most beautiful professional vehicles to appear on a Roadster chassis this year was the carved panel hearse produced by the A. J. Miller Co. of Bellefontaine, Ohio. These very formal and very expensive carved-panel cars used concealed rear doors and functional coach lamps as standard trim. Buick continued to supply numerous chassis cowl units, complete with front fenders, and sidemounts when ordered, for a multitude of specialty builders, primarily the hearse and ambulance manufacturers. This year its chassis-cowl sales were: Century Series, 73 for domestic sales and five for export; Roadmaster Series, four for U.S. sales and 15 for export; Limited Series, four for domestic sales and nine for export. In addition, Buick shipped to its overseas plants 684 Century, 204 Roadmaster, and 167 Limited chassis in unassembled form. All Buicks now featured coil springs all around, another industry first for a large mass produced car.

As could be expected, the most popular model in the Century Series was the 4-door Touring Sedan, Model 61, which used the trunk-back style. Buick built 12,364 for domestic sales and 309 for export. It cost $1,297 and weighed 3,780 pounds.

Appearing for the last time was the Century 4-door Sport Sedan, Model 67, which was phased out after 1,515 were built for U.S. sales and one special order version was constructed for export. Built in fastback style, it cost $1,272 and weighed 3,785 pounds. Buick still claimed that its Century models were the fastest U.S. production cars on the road — a claim not without good foundation.

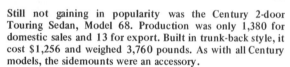

Still not gaining in popularity was the Century 2-door Touring Sedan, Model 68. Production was only 1,380 for domestic sales and 13 for export. Built in trunk-back style, it cost $1,256 and weighed 3,760 pounds. As with all Century models, the sidemounts were an accessory.

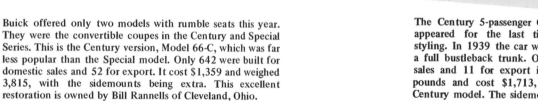

The Century 5-passenger Convertible Phaeton, Model 60-C appeared for the last time with fastback or trunkless styling. In 1939 the car would reappear, but would feature a full bustleback trunk. Only 208 were built for domestic sales and 11 for export in 1938. The car weighed 3,950 pounds and cost $1,713, making it the most expensive Century model. The sidemounts were added cost accessories on all Buicks this year.

Buick offered only two models with rumble seats this year. They were the convertible coupes in the Century and Special Series. This is the Century version, Model 66-C, which was far less popular than the Special model. Only 642 were built for domestic sales and 52 for export. It cost $1,359 and weighed 3,815, with the sidemounts being extra. This excellent restoration is owned by Bill Rannells of Cleveland, Ohio.

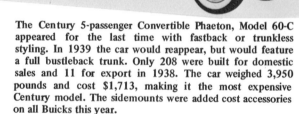

The Century 4-passenger Sport Coupe, Model 66-S, used the same small and uncomfortable opera seats as did the similar model in the Special Series. It cost $1,226 and weighed 3,690 pounds. Buick built 1,991 for domestic sales and 39 for export.

Buick's most popular car continued to be the Special 4-door Touring Sedan, which used the trunk back. A total of 79,510 were built for domestic sales and 2,681 for export. It cost $1,047 in basic form and weighed 3,560 pounds. Dual sidemounts were an attractive but expensive accessory.

The interior of the Century Touring Sedan was smartly finished, with dashboard and window edges being in wood-grained metal. Armrests were provided on both front doors and at either side of the rear seat. A robe rail and assist straps still added class to the rear seat. Another Buick first occurred this year, with the introduction of the horn ring. The steering wheel was virtually unchanged, but the rims were now of maroon plastic, a material carried through the 1939 model year.

Appearing for the last year was the Special Sport Sedan, a 5-passenger 4-door using the fastback styling which was falling from favor. It cost $1,022 and weighed 3,535. Buick built 11,265 for domestic sales and 76 for export.

The Special 2-door Touring Sedan, Model 48, used the trunk back styling which was rapidly gaining favor over the fast back models. It cost $1,006 and weighed 3,520 pounds. Buick built 14,153 for U.S. sales and 60 for export. The sidemounts were an accessory.

Appearing for the last year was the Special 2-door Sport Sedan, Model 44, which used the fast-back design. It cost $981 and weighed 3,515 pounds. Only 5,943 were built for domestic sales and eight were built for export, as the majority of buyers favored the trunk-style models with their greatly increased luggage space. This attractive restoration, with dual fog lights and original grille guard, is owned by Tom Cronin of Fremont, Neb.

The least expensive Buick was the 2-passenger Business Coupe, Model 46. It cost $945 and weighed 3,385 pounds. The car featured vast luggage space, both in the trunk and behind the driver's seat. Production was 11,337 for U.S. sales and 31 for export.

Far less popular than the business coupe was the Special Sport Coupe, Model 46-S. Production was 5,381 for domestic sales and 193 for export. The car used the same body as the business coupe, but was equipped with two small and uncomfortable opera seats behind the main seat. It cost $1,001 and weighed 3,425 pounds. This original model is equipped with the accessory dual sidemounts, dual fog lights and a radio.

A very attractive car was the Special Convertible Coupe, Model 46-C, which held a fairly steady production run of 2,473 for domestic sales and 152 for export. The 3,575-pound car cost $1,103. It continued to use double rear deck lids, with the upper one for the rumble seat and the lower one for the spare tire and small luggage. There was also luggage space behind the driver's seat. This car is wearing accessory oversized balloon tires.

The new Dynaflash engine featured turbulator pistons of Buick's exclusive design, which gave a significant increase in horsepower without increasing the bore, stroke or displacement. The Specials now had 107 horsepower while all other models were rated at 141 horsepower at 3600 RPM.

Appearing for the last time this year was the Special Convertible Phaeton, Model 40-C. The 5-passenger car had a production run of 776 for domestic sales and 170 for export. It cost $1,406 and weighed 3,705 pounds. In addition to the figures shown for the models, Buick built 455 Special chassis and cowl units for domestic sales and 109 for export, and shipped 6,528 unassembled Special chassis to its overseas assembly plants.

The Gustat Nordberg Co. of Stockholm, Sweden, continued to produce limited numbers of exotic bodies for Buick chassis. One such design is this touring model. Nordberg built six in the 4-door style shown here and another six in 2-door style.

One of the 52 Century Convertible Coupes built for export still lives in England. It is this right-hand drive model, wearing dual sidemounts and dual fog lights.

Australia was becoming a good market for Buicks, expecially since the G.M.-owned Holden Co. of Australia was now producing their own bodies for the unassembled Buick chassis that were being imported. This is the Holden 4-door sedan body, which differed in many subtle ways from the American style. It is mounted on a Century chassis.

From the rear, the Fernandez & Darrin town car exhibits styling of unmistakable European flair. It used dual sidemounts, dual fog lights and dual spot lights. The color is black with cream body inserts and wheels. The small rear compartment is for tools and jack.

One of the most unusual and attractive vehicles ever to be based on a Buick chassis is this town car by Fernandez & Darrin of Paris. Built on the 140-inch wheelbase Limited chassis, the car uses virtually no exterior Buick parts except for the head, tail and parking lights. The grille is in the Rolls Royce tradition. Built for use in France, the car uses left-hand drive. It is owned by Jim Robbins of Dearborn, Mich.

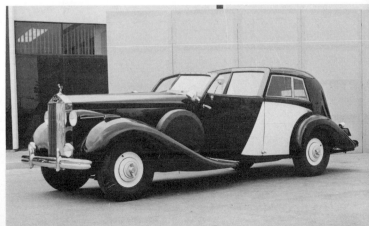

The New York Worlds Fair Corp. set its standards for what ambulances would be used on the grounds, and the contract fell to the Flxible Co. of Loudonville, Ohio, for the bodies and Buick for the chassis. The chassis were extended Century models with the cowl, hood, and grille raised to meet the tall Flxible body. The vehicles were operated at the fair only one year, and then were turned in on new models.

The carved hearses were making a comeback during the late 1930s, and the Buick chassis were right there waiting to act as bases for these oddly interesting vehicles. The A.J. Miller Co. of Bellefontaine, Ohio, produced this version on an extended Century chassis. It uses hidden rear doors and functional coach lamps. Note that the chrome side trim appears before and after the cast carved panel. A partition separated the compartments.

Flxible Co. of Loudonville, Ohio, came out with a new style of carved hearse this year, and mounted many of them on extended Century chassis. The carved panels, cast in bronze or aluminum, were even carried over to the rear door. The hearse was a 4-door model, or 5-door if the rear door is counted, but the two rear side doors were well hidden in the carved panel work.

A.J. Miller Co. of Bellefontaine, Ohio, was noted for its fine hearses, but it also built ambulances. This is the 1938 version, mounted on an extended Century chassis. The same basic body was easily converted to limousine-hearse style.

The Eureka Co. of Rock Falls, Ill., started turning out its version of the carved hearse, for use on Buick chassis. On this model, the carved panels were carried right down to the running board. This model was of the 2-door style, with all loading being via the back door. In addition to Buick, Eureka also made heavy use of La Salle and Cadillac chassis.

The 1939 Buicks rolled onto the scene and again came as a complete surprise to everyone. With Buick's styling of 1937-38 so highly acclaimed by the automotive world, it seemed reasonable to expect this basic design to continue for a year or two longer. But such was not the case. The 1939 Buick was a completely new animal, featuring a waterfall grille, long flowing lines, and functional use of ornamentation.

Total calendar year production was 231,219, which was 9% of the industry, and certainly sufficient to keep Buick in fourth place. Model year production was 208,259, which by series read: Special, 175,568; Century, 24,415; Roadmaster, 6,489; and Limited, 1,787.

Two new styling innovations appeared this year. The first was the use of "Streamboards" which were an optional replacement for runningboards, while the other was the availability of a sun roof on several closed models. Sidemounts were still available, but were decreasing in popularity. Buick used two distinct types of mounts this year. The Roadmasters and Limiteds used the conventional style tire covers which fitted into the top edge of the fenders. But the Special and Century models used rather novel mount designs with the cover draping well below the top fender line. These mounts gave the impression that the outside spare was located beyond the actual fender line.

Wheelbases remained the same on all models except the Special Series, which was reduced by two inches to a new length of 120 inches. Visibility on the Specials and Centurys was increased by 26% over the 1938 models through the use of larger windows and more narrow roof posts.

For the first time, there were no rumble seat models. Both the coupes and convertibles that had rumble seats in 1938 were now equipped with small (and uncomfortable) opera seats.

As an industry first, Buick made turn signals standard equipment on all models, with the flasher lights being an integral part of the Buick trunk emblem. But, there were no front turn signals. The pretty bullet shaped fender lights were still available as an accessory on all models, but surprisingly, these well-designed lights were not popular.

Other new innovations included having the gearshift mounted on the steering column, a first time for Buick, but not an option, as there were no floor shift models. Also for the first time, the Buick "Sonomatic" optional radios offered push-button tuning.

The former airplane type shock absorbers were discontinued in favor of the refillable type. New channel type strut rods were used on the rear axle, and the frames were now two inches closer to the ground.

Interiors were offered in broadcloth, bedford, or a variety of colored leather. Standard equipment on the models 90 and 90-L included a cigarette lighter in one armrest and a vanity case and notebook holder in the other.

In the speed department, the Special would go from 10 to 60 MPH in 18.2 seconds; the Century would do it in 16 seconds; the Roadmaster in 18 seconds; and the Limited in 18.3 seconds.

Buick's most expensive car was the Limited Limousine, Model 90-L, now priced at $2,453. The huge car, weighing 4,653 pounds, had a run of 423 for domestic sales and 120 for export. It was fitted with an adjustable glass partition between compartments, and had a speaking phone between the rear and the chauffeur's compartment. It came in 8-passenger form only.

The popularity leader in Buick's prestige Limited Series continued to be the 8-passenger Sedan, Model 90. The car cost $2,350, weighed 4,608 pounds, and used a new chassis of 141-inch wheelbase. Buick built 650 for domestic sales and 36 for export.

Still attracting some buyers was the massive Limited 6-passenger Sedan, Model 91. Buick built 378 for domestic sales and four special order models for export. It cost $2,074 and weighed 4,568 pounds. This car had a fairly large luggage locker, built behind the front seat in the same place where the jump seats were installed in the other Limited models. In addition to finished cars, Buick built two Limited chassis-cowl units for U.S. sales and six for export, and shipped 168 unassembled Limited chassis overseas.

New for the year was the Roadmaster Sport Phaeton, Model 81-C, which was built in trunk-back style. Unlike its sister Model 80-C, this version enjoyed some popularity, with 311 being built for domestic sales and 53 for export. It cost $1,938 and weighed 4,932 pounds. The upper portions of the centerposts could be removed when the top was lowered.

The prestige vehicle of the Roadmaster Series was the Formal Sedan, Model 81-F. This car, which cost $1,758 and weighed 4,312 pounds, used the basic 6-passenger sedan body, but was fitted with a disappearing glass partition between compartments. Only 393 were built for domestic sales and 37 for export. In addition to completed cars, Buick built two Roadmaster chassis-cowl units for U.S. sale and nine for export, and shipped 132 unassembled chassis overseas.

The highest production style in the Roadmaster Series was the 4-door Touring Sedan, Model 81. Buick built 5,460 for domestic sales and 159 for export. The car used a 133-inch wheelbase chassis, weighed 4,247 pounds, and cost $1,543. The sidemounts on this model were an accessory, as were the whitewall tires.

Apparently some of Buick's management team felt that the fastback style still had hope, and so the Roadmaster Sport Sedan, Model 87, was offered again. However, the car was built on special order only, and the orders didn't come in. Only 20 were produced for U.S. sales. They cost $1,543 and weighed 4,247 in basic form, with the sidemounts being extra.

Offered on special order only was the attractive Roadmaster Convertible Sport Phaeton, Model 80-C. However, the orders weren't there, and only three such models were built. They cost $1,983 and weighed 4,362 pounds. This model retained the fastback styling of 1938.

Produced in Canada for the first Royal visit were two virtually identical models of this beautiful custom-fitted McLaughlin-Buick, seen here in a later day parade honoring Canadian flying aces of World War II. The cars were hand-built by McLaughlin employees on Series 49 Limited chassis, stretched to 155-inch wheelbases. Measuring over 20 feet in length, they were the largest passenger cars ever built in Canada. Both cars were finished in Royal Maroon, but one had maroon upholstery, while the other was finished in beige. Both cars were fitted with tops of superfine duck, and these were built seven inches higher than the tops of regular Buick convertible sedans, to allow for the high headgear, often favored by the royal party. The cars honored the first time a King and Queen of England had ever visited Canada. After the visit of King George VI and Queen Elizabeth, the cars continued to be used as official parade and courtesy vehicles by the government of Canada.

Still sagging drastically in sales was the Century 2-door Touring Sedan, Model 68. Only 521 were produced for domestic sales and only four special order models were exported. The car cost $1,205 and weighed 3,757 pounds. In addition to completed cars, Buick built 55 Century cowl-chassis units for domestic sales and seven for export.

The Century Sport Coupe, though designated a 4-passenger vehicle, was really comfortable for only two or three passengers. The additional seating in this car continued to consist of small and uncomfortable folding opera seats behind the front seat. Designated the Model 66-S, it cost $1,175 and weighed 3,687. Buick built 3,408 for domestic sales and 62 for export. This model, living in Rome, Italy, is owned by Nicola Bulgari.

Faring only slightly better than the Sport Phaeton was the Century Convertible Coupe, Model 66-C, which had a run of 790 for domestic sales and 60 for export. As did the Special Convertible, the Century model also did away with the rumble seat and made room for extra passengers in two small folding opera seats behind the main seat. The car cost $1,343 and weighed 3,762. Buyers had a choice of streamboards, shown here, or running boards.

Still just barely making it in production was the attractive Century Convertible Phaeton, Model 61-C, which now used trunkback styling. Only 249 were built for domestic sales and 20 were built for export. The car cost $1,713 and weighed 3,967 pounds. The accessory sidemounts of both the Special and Century Series overhung the outer edge of the front fenders.

James Witherspoon of Maryland shows off his Century 4-door Touring Sedan, Model 61, at Hershey. As before, the Century sedan was the most popular model in the series, with 18,462 built for domestic sales and 321 going for export. In base form, the car cost $1,246 and weighed 3,832 pounds. Although this car is fitted with the traditional running boards, stream boards were also available for this model, as were sidemounts with the very unusual over-hanging covers used on this year's Century and Special models.

One of the 321 Century Touring Sedans built for export was this model. It was the lead car of the Thaw Asiatic Expedition, which traveled throughout southeast Asia shooting travelog movies. The car was fitted with a special sunshine top over the rear compartment, so that movies could be made while the car was in motion. It was finished in Java Sea blue with a silver top and blue leather upholstery. The trailer was finished in the same color combination.

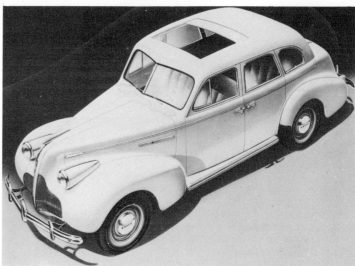

Buick's most popular car took a real jump in sales this year, with production going up to 109,213 for the domestic market and 2,260 for export. The car, of course, was the Special 4-door Touring Sedan, Model 41, priced at $996. It weighed 3,547 pounds. This flawless restoration is owned by John L. Teets of Livonia, Mich.

Appearing for the first time this year on Buicks was the Sunroof option, a styling feature just now coming into popularity. The sliding roof was available on all Special and Century 4-door and 2-door Sedan models. It is shown here installed on the Special Sedan. Since no records were kept of the number of cars built with this option, it is impossible to tell how many were made. But a safe guess would be that very few such cars ever left the factory.

The 2-passenger Business Coupe, Model 46, continued to appear in the Special Series. It was Buick's least expensive model, selling for $849. It weighed 3,387 pounds. Buick built 14,582 for domestic sales and 27 for export. This excellent restoration is owned by Tom Priebe of Cleveland, Ohio.

The Special Convertible Coupe was no longer a rumble seat model, but was fitted with two small folding opera seats behind the regular seat. Designated the Model 46-C, the car carried a base price of $1,077 and weighed 3,517 pounds. Buick produced 4,569 for domestic sales and 240 for export. This excellent restoration, owned by Ron Kucharski of Flushing, Mich., carries a wide range of original accessories, including steamboards in place of running boards, fender skirts, the unusual dual sidemounts, and the fender-mounted parking lights.

The interior of the Special 4-door Touring Sedan retained its good taste, a factor which probably contributed heavily to the popularity of the car. Rear seats had armrests and ashtrays on either side, and a robe rail was still provided. The rear quarter windows now slid back, rather than being of the swing-out type used in 1938.

New for the year was the Special Convertible Phaeton, Model 41-C, which now used a trunk-back style rather than the fast back used in 1938. It was the lowest production model in the Special Series, with only 724 built for domestic sales and 106 built for export. It weighed 3,707 pounds and cost $1,406, and thus was also the most expensive car in the Special line.

Picking up percentage points in sales was the Special 2-door Touring Sedan, Model 48, which this year had a production run of 27,218 for domestic sales and 72 for export. It cost $955 and weighed 3,482 pounds. In addition to the sales of completed cars, Buick built 295 Special chassis-cowl units for domestic sales and 66 for export, and shipped 5,820 unassembled Special chassis to overseas plants for completion.

The Special Sport Coupe, Model 46-S, picked up substantially in sales, with production standing at 10,043 for domestic sales and 233 for export. The car still used small folding opera seats behind the regular seat for extra passengers. It cost $950 and weighed 3,437 pounds.

Probably the most famous experimental car ever built was the Y-Job, which Buick unveiled this year. Actually, the car is built on a 1938 Roadmaster chassis. Rebuilt many times since its first introduction, it served Buick for over 10 years as a show piece and test vehicle. Near the end of World War II, a major wire service erroneously carried a picture of this car as a "sneak preview" of the post-war Buick.

A rear view of the Y-Job shows the interesting boattail design that was employed on this car but never put into production on any Buick models. The exhaust now exits under the bumper in normal fashion, but at one time was directed out of twin vents just inside of the fender lines.

The front end of the famous Y-Job has undergone many changes since its original unveiling. Today it is fitted with fixed headlights, whereas originally it used disappearing headlights in the fenders. Both the grille and bumper have been changed since the original car was built.

During its last major rennovation, the Y-Job was fitted with a 1949-style dashboard and steering wheel. The car is finished in black lacquer with an attractive use of chrome ribbing on the fenders. It can be seen today in the Sloan Museum of Transportation in Flint, Mich.

The Buick Dynaflash engine was unchanged this year, simply because there was no reason to make a change. The engine was still one of the most powerful and efficient on the highways, and Buicks were known for being just about the fastest production cars on the road.

In Australia, the Holden company was busy producing sedan bodies for unassembled Buick chassis that were being imported into that country. The forward portions of the bodies were quite similar to those built in the U.S., but from the centerpost rearward, the styling differed substantially. All Holden Buicks were right-hand drive. This attractive restoration belongs to G. Howarth of Geelong, Victoria.

Flxible bodies and Buick chassis again were named as the official ambulances for the New York Worlds Fair. The bodies were the standard Flxible limousine ambulances, painted in blue and orange, the official colors of the fair. Venitian blinds were used in the windows, marking one of the first times that such blinds had been used in vehicles of this type.

All Buicks had a totally new dash this year. All cars were equipped with column mounted gearshifts, because unlike many other makes, Buick did not leave the floor mounted shift optional. Mounted on top of the gearshift lever was the signal light control, marking the first time that a production car was fitted with the relatively new signal lights as standard equipment.

The Flxible Co. of Loudonville, Ohio, continued to turn out fine funeral car and ambulance bodies on Buick Special and Century chassis. They also continued to raise the cowl, hood, and grille lines to compensate for the higher line of their bodies. In so doing, this year they also had to raise the headlights on extended pods. This is the Flxible funeral service car, built on an extended Special chassis. Such cars were used for moving equipment, carrying bodies to the funeral home, and for long distance transportation of caskets, and could be pressed into service as a hearse when the need arose.

Finally Buick did what was expected for years. It produced a line of cars that differed little from the year before. But that is the story that the automotive experts told. As far as the average person was concerned, the 1940 Buick was as different from the 1939 models as the 1939 cars had been from the 1938 models.

The mirror trick was done through a skillful and very artistic reworking of grille and fender design, which gave the car a completely different appearance. The grille was much larger and consisted of heavy horizontal bars, and the headlights moved down into pods integral with the front fenders. Small parking lights rode on top of these pods.

In addition, there were two series introduced. The Super Series was instituted as an intermediate car between the Special and the Century, and its popularity is attested to by the fact that it outstripped every other series in sales. The Roadmaster 70 Series was instituted as an intermediate line between the Century and the former Roadmaster 80 Series, which remained for this year only but was renamed the Limited 80 Series.

Calendar year production reached an all-time record of 310,995 vehicles. This was 8.3% of the entire industry and Buick was thus firmly entrenched in fourth place. Model year production was 283,204, which by series was: Special, 117,355; the new Super, 130,851; Century, 9,878; the new Roadmaster 70 Series, 18,775; the Limited 80 Series, 4,451; and the Limited 90 Series, 1,894.

The only car to show any growth was the Special Series, which went from its 120-inch wheelbase classis to a 121-inch wheelbase. It now shared the same chassis with the new Super Series. Both the Century and the new Roadmaster 70 Series used the same 126-inch wheelbase chassis, while the Limited 80 retained the 133-inch wheelbase chassis of the former Roadmaster line. The Limited 90 Series kept its own huge 140-inch wheelbase.

Under the hoods, the engines remained the same relatively new Dynaflash models that had been introduced in 1938. The Special and Super Series used the 107 horsepower blocks of 248 cubic inches, while all other models used the 320-inch engines of 141 horsepower. One significant change was that oil filters were now standard on all engines.

New for the year were the unusual "Torpedo" bodies without running boards or even the hint of such. These styles turned out to be a top hit, and became a strong factor in Buick styling for the next several years. With sales

A truly huge line of vehicles was the Series 90 Limited line, which used a 140-inch wheelbase chassis and a basic sedan body style of vast interior dimensions. The most popular car in the series was the 8-passenger Touring Sedan, Model 90, of which 796 were built for domestic sales and 32 were produced for export. This beautiful restoration, owned by Sonny Abagnale of Arlington, N.J., starred in the movie *The Godfather*. In basic form, the car cost $2,096 and weighed 4,645 pounds, with the sidemounts being standard equipment.

Still holding appeal was the Series 90 Limited 6-passenger Touring Sedan, Model 91. Buick built 417 for domestic sales and one special order model for export. It cost $1,942 and weighed 4,590 pounds. It used the same body as the Model 90, but in place of of jump seats or divider partition, the rear portion of the front seat held a luggage locker. In addition to finished cars, Buick built one Series 90 chassis-cowl unit for a U.S. customer and one for a European customer, and shipped 12 unassembled Series 90 chassis overseas for assembly.

Buick's prestige car, and most expensive model, continued to be the Series 90 Limited Limousine, an 8-passenger car with a divider partition between compartments. Designated the Model 90-L, it cost $2,199 and weighed 4,705 pounds. Buick built 526 for domestic sales and 108 for export. This beautiful restoration is owned by Terry Dunham of Fresno, Cal.

The only car in the entire new Series 80 Limited line that had a production run in excess of 1,000 was the 4-door Touring Sedan, Model 81. Buick built 3,810 for domestic sales and 88 for export. It cost $1,553 and weighed 4,400 pounds. This attractive version is owned by Jack McCarthy of Flint, Mich. Part of the Buick home office and plant is seen in the background.

Appearing this year only was the Series 80 Limited line, which used a 133-inch wheelbase. One of its most attractive cars was the Streamlined Convertible Phaeton, Model 80-C, built on special order only. The orders didn't materialize, and only seven were built. Priced at $1,952 and weighing 4,550 pounds, the car featured the swept-back rear style and was equipped with dual sidemounts as standard equipment, though a slight price reduction was made if the mounts were not ordered. The chrome centerpost was removable when the top was lowered.

Built on special order only was the Series 80 Limited Streamlined Sedan, Model 87. It cost $1,553 and weighed 4,380 pounds. Only 14 were built, all for domestic sales. This original version is Body #5 of the 14. It is owned by Terry Dunham of Fresno, Cal. The car is wearing non-standard hubcaps and appears to be fitted with tires smaller than specified.

1940

running ahead of production, Buick at mid-year introduced a convertible coupe and a convertible sedan in each series.

At the request of Harlow Curtice, Brunn & Company of Buffalo, which for years had been a highly respected builder of luxurious custom bodies for such prestige makes as Lincoln, Packard, Pierce Arrow, and others, came in and designed a limited line of prestige cars for Buick. Curtice had attempted to have Fleetwood design these bodies, but his plans were thwarted by Cadillac, which was less than enthusiastic about having Buick a competitor for the almost nonexistent prestige market.

The first and only Brunn creation this year was a Town Sedan, built on the new Roadmaster 70 chassis. The car was listed at $3,895; but since none were ordered, it really must be considered in the class of a one-off show model. The car won acclaim of Buick's top management, and the Brunn company busily went to work designing an entire custom series for the 1941 models.

Much more popular than the special order model was the Series 80 Limited Convertible Phaeton, Model 81-C. This car was identical to the Model 80-C, except that it was built in trunkback style rather than the now relatively unpopular fastback style. Buick produced 230 of these large cars for domestic sales and another 20 for export. It cost $1,952 and weighed 4,540 pounds, with the sidemounts being standard equipment. This example, in catalog color combination, is owned by Nicola Bulgari of Rome, Italy, and New York City. The dual fog lights were an accessory.

Also on special order only was the Series 80 Limited Streamlined Formal Sedan, Model 87-F, which used the same limited production fastbacked body of the Model 87, but was fitted with a glass divider window between compartments. Only seven were built, all in 6-passenger form and all for domestic sales. The sidemounts were an accessory. It cost $1,727 and weighed 4,435 pounds. In addition, Buick produced two Series 80 chassis-cowl units for domestic sales and three for export.

The prestige car of the Series 80 Limited line was the 6-passenger Formal Sedan, Model 81-F, which was basically the Model 81 with a glass divider partition between compartments. It cost $1,727 and weighed 4,455 pounds. Buick built 248 for domestic sales and 22 for export.

Receiving a new numerical designation this year was the Roadmaster line, now officially known as the Series 70. Its top selling model was the totally new Touring Sedan, Model 71, which used the same modern body as did its companion car in the Super Series. These bodies differed considerably from the former sedan bodies both in appearance and in design, with the most noticeable characteristics being their low profile, all doors opening form the trailing edges, and lack of quarter windows. The Model 71 had a run of 13,583 for domestic sales and 150 for export. It cost $1,359 and weighed 4,045 pounds.

The Roadmaster Convertible Phaeton, Model 71-C, retained the basic body styling of the old model sedans, with doors opening from a centerpost, and a much more square trunk compartment. It cost $1,768 and weighed 4,195 pounds. Only 235 were built for domestic sales and three special order versions were built for export. This attractive model features the beautiful but seldom seen accessory sidemounts. The centerposts were removable when the top was lowered.

The Roadmaster Convertible Coupe, Model 76-C, cost $1,431 and weighed 4,055 pounds. Buick built 606 for domestic sales and six on special order for export. All Roadmasters were 214 inches long overall, and had a wheelbase of 126 inches. In addition to completed cars, Buick produced four special order Roadmaster chassis-cowl units for domestic use and 216 for export.

The Roadmaster Sport Coupe, Model 76-S, was the second most popular style in that series, having a run of 3,921 for domestic sales and 51 for export. It cost $1,277 and weighed 3,990 pounds. Front seats in the Roadmaster models were 56 inches wide, and were padded with a combination of springs and Foamtex rubber padding.

This highly unusual vehicle is a one-off Town Car built on a Buick chassis by the famous Brewster Co. of Long Island City, N.Y. The car, which uses a Limited 90 chassis, was sold under the name Brewster, and the Buick name does not appear at all. Other such models were built on Ford and Packard chassis, again with the name Brewster appearing on all exterior surfaces. The company was noted for its fine body work, especially in town cars such as this. For years, its trademark was the heart-shaped grille, snow-plow bumpers, and huge headlights. All body work was custom designed. A few other such models were turned out on Buick chassis this year, but this is the only one to use the Limited 90 chassis. It was originally built for Mr. J. Whitney of the N.Y. Stock Exchange, and is today owned by Noel Thompson of New Vernon, N.J. It is finished in maroon lacquer with black rear fenders and a maroon leather top.

With the introduction of the new Super Series, the Century Series felt a drastic reduction in sales. Its most popular model, the 4-door Touring Sedan, Model 61, had a run of only 8,597 for domestic use and 111 for export. It cost $1,211 and weighed 3,935 pounds. This beauty, wearing the seldom seen accessory sidemounts, is owned by Charles Schmidt of Indianapolis, Ind. The Century 4-door, and the Special 2 and 4-door sedans were the only models on which the sunroof was available.

Appearing for the last year was Century Convertible Phaeton, Model 61-C. Only 194 were built for domestic sales and nine special order models were built for export before the style was phased out of production. It cost $1,620 and weighed 4,050 pounds. The interior was in all-leather, with small step lights provided at the back corners of the front seat. These went on automatically when the rear doors were opened. All Century models were 209 inches overall and were built on a 126-inch wheelbase.

Surprisingly, the least popular car in the Century Series was the 5-passenger Business Coupe, Model 66, of which only 44 were built, all for domestic sales. It cost $1,128 and weighed 3,800 pounds. A Buick option this year was the rotating radio antenna above the windshield.

Appearing for the last year was the Century Convertible Coupe, Model 66-C. It cost $1,343 and weighed 3,915 pounds. Buick built 542 for domestic sales and eight for export. Among the accessories on this model are rear skirts, streamboards, and a side-mounted antenna. In addition to completed models, Buick produced 179 Century chassis-cowl units for domestic sales and 98 such units for export.

Having only slightly more sales than the Century Business Coupe was the Century Sport Coupe, Model 66-S. Only 96 were built, all for domestic sales. The car had a base price of $1,175 and weighed 3,765 pounds. The sidemounts, of course, were accessories.

R. Rustin of Toronto, Ontario, is the owner of this nice example of the new Buick Estate Wagon, Model 59. The style, which was destined to eventually become one of the most popular body types in America, was definitely not a popular car in Buick's line this year. Introduced only in the new Super Series, the car had a run of only 495 for domestic sales and six on special order for export. The all-wood bodied car cost $1,242 and weighed 3,870 pounds. The dual fog lights on this model are an original accessory. Only slightly more popular than the station wagon was the Super Convertible Phaeton, Model 51-C, of which 529 were built for domestic sales and another five were turned out on special order for export. The car, which was identical in styling to the Century phaeton, cost $1,549 and weighed 3,895 pounds. Buyers had a choice of running boards or the more attractive and modern stream boards. Also in the new Super Series was the Convertible Coupe, Model 56-C, which again in styling was virtually identical to the Century convertible. In the Super Series, the convertible cost $1,211, weighed 3,785 pounds, and had a run of 4,764 for domestic sales and 40 for export. This was a fairly good showing for a newly introduced convertible in this era. In addition to completed cars, Buick also produced three special order Super Series chassis-cowl units for domestic sales, and sent overseas a total of 1,321 unassembled Super chassis-cowl combinations. Obviously, these export chassis were fitted with bodies in their country of destination.

New for the year was the Super Series, which consisted of five models, with all but the 4-door Touring Sedan, Model 51, considered in the sporty-type car set. The Model 51 was by far the most popular car in the new series, with 95,875 being built for domestic use and 1,351 for export. It cost $1,109 and weighed 3,790 pounds. This attractive version, wearing accessory fender skirts and streamboards, is owned by Les Raye of New Canton, Ohio.

Called a "Townmaster," this beautiful custom Town Car was built by the Brunn Co. of Buffalo, N. Y., on a Roadmaster chassis. The car was designed to be the first of a limited run of such cars on both Roadmaster and Super chassis, but this was the only model produced this year. Buick used it as a show car for awhile, then placed it into executive limousine service at its home office for about a year. The car used the new sedan body, with a higher roofline and a removable top over the front compartment. The 126-inch wheelbase Roadmaster chassis was unchanged.

Overall, the 1940 Buicks were very well styled cars, and one of the nicest of the lot, in all around proportions, was the Super Sport Coupe, Model 56-S. The car had a full-width rear seat and substantial luggage space. Buick built 26,251 for domestic sales and 211 for export. It cost $1,058 and weighed 3,735 pounds. This excellent example, featuring dual fog lights and streamboards, is owned by Peter Hoogestraat of Warrenville, Ill.

The first Buick owned by the author was this Special 2-door Touring Sedan, Model 48, shown here on the family farm in Upstate New York. The car was purchased in 1953 for $75, used in relatively hard mountain driving for about one year, and was resold for $75, still in fine condition throughout. The Model 48 had a run of 20,739 for domestic sales and 20 for export. It cost $955 and weighed 3,605 pounds in base form. In addition to finished models, Buick this year built 320 Special Series chassis-cowl units for domestic sales, and sent 2,260 such units to its assembly operations overseas.

Richard L. Davis of Glenbeulah, Wis. is the owner of this very rare Special 2-door Touring Sedan, Model 48-A. The poorly accepted "hole-in-roof" was continued this year, and was available only on the Special 2-door and 4-door sedans and the Century 4-door sedans. Buyer disinterest and problems with rain leakage combined to cause the demise of these roofs until the 1970s, when they again began to appear in limited numbers. Buick kept no separate records of how many such roofs were installed, and therefore, it is impossible to ascertain their true popularity—however, it is well known that the number produced was very limited.

As ever, the beautiful Special Convertible Phaeton, Model 41-C, was at the low end of the production list. Only 552 were built for domestic sales and 45 for export. It weighed 3,755 pounds, and at $1,355 in basic form was the most expensive of the Special models. Upholstery was in leather, available in six optional colors, or in optional cloth. Once again Buick settled on yellow plastic for its steering wheel rims, and would continue to use this choice through the 1947 models. This beautiful Special phaeton is owned by Ken Minch of Parma, Ohio. It features the attractive twin sidemounts with attached mirrors, original teardrop skirts, and twin fog lights. The sidemounts by this time had become a very expensive accessory, and thus were very seldom seen on Special Series cars, which were designed primarily for the economy minded.

Appearing for the last time in the special line was the Convertible Coupe, Model 46-C, which cost $1,077 and weighed 3,665 pounds. Buick built 3,664 for domestic sales and 99 for export. For the first time, the car had a full rear seat instead of the uncomfortable rear jump seats. Sidemounts were available on the Special line as an accessory, but were hardly ever ordered.

Surprisingly, though Buick overall hit record production levels this year, the car that was formerly its most popular model took a substantial nosedive in sales this year. The car was the Special Series 4-door Touring Sedan, Model 41, which dropped from over 100,000 to 67,308 for domestic sales and 1,508 for export. It cost $996 and weighed 3,660 pounds. This very attractive version is owned by Leslie Woodrow of Lakewood, Ohio. For the first time since 1928, Buick did away with combination steering column and ignition lock, and accepted the "standard" type of dash-mounted ignition lock.

Using a full rear seat for the first time was the Special Sport Coupe, Model 46-S. It cost $950 and weighed 3,540 pounds. Buick built 8,291 for domestic sales and 110 for export. This nicely restored version, owned by James Basiorka of Dyer, Ind., uses two rarely seen accessories, the large windshield visor and white wheel discs.

The Special 2-passenger Business Coupe, Model 46, continued to be Buick's low price style, costing $895 in basic form. The 3,505-pound car had a run of 12,372 for domestic sales and ten for export. All Specials this year had an overall length of 204 inches, on a 121-inch wheelbase.

Buick made an attempt at entering the taxi market again this year, but the attempt fell flat, and only 48 such vehicles were built. Designated the Special Model 41-T, the car used the basic Model 41 body, but was fitted only with a driver's seat in front, a glass partition between compartments, and a luggage space where the front passenger seat was located in the sedan versions. It also had two small jump seats in the rear.

In addition to building the custom Town Car, the Brunn Co. of Buffalo, N.Y., also proposed this full custom Sport Coupe for the Roadmaster chassis. This model, in hardtop styling, would have used a radically altered body, hidden headlights, and custom fenders. None were built.

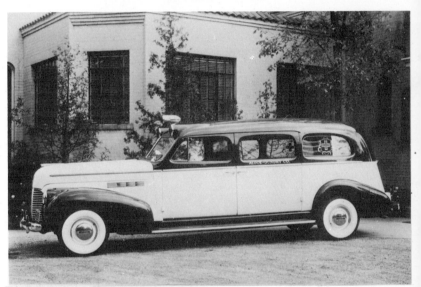

The interior of the new Roadmaster sedan showed excellent taste, in keeping with the traditions of a luxury car. It featured a folding center armrest, ashtrays in the side armrests, assist straps, crank regulated vent windows, and wood-grain metal trim on all window sills.

The Flxible Co. of Loudonville, Ohio, continued to produce ambulance and funeral car bodies for Buick chassis, but still had to raise the height of the hood and cowl to meet the bodies. This year, the raising was accomplished simply by constructing a new hood to match the raised cowl. This attractive ambulance, with built-in red roof lights and roof-mounted siren, was produced for the Angloe-Gundry Co. of Flint, Mich. It uses a stretched Century chassis.

Of far less cost and more popular design than the carved hearse was the limousine hearse. This version, by the A.J. Miller Co. of Bellefontaine, Ohio, features blanked in rear quarters, functional coach lights, decorative landau irons, a leather covered top, and heavy velvet draperies. A partition separated the compartments. It uses an extended Century chassis.

The A.J. Miller Co. of Bellefontaine, Ohio, also continued to be a large user of Buick chassis for their fine hearse models. This heavily carved model, built on an extended Century chassis, is in the French Canadian tradition. It has a cast metal cross and Bible mounted on the roof, functional coach lights, and concealed rear access doors.

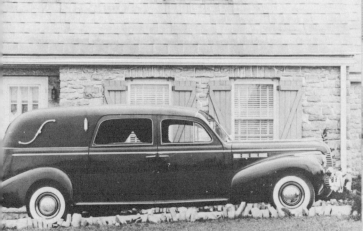

The greatest variety of Buick models in history was offered this year, as twenty-six separate body styles were available in four distinct series. Actually, there were five series, as the Special Series was now divided into the Series 40-A on 118-inch wheelbase chassis, and the Series 40-B on the regular 121-inch wheelbase chassis, which was also shared by the Super Series. The Century and Roadmaster Series retained their 126-inch wheelbases, but the Limited series shrunk slightly to a 139-inch wheelbase.

Not only was the greatest variety of models available, but the most vehicles ever produced in a year were turned out by Buick. The company broke all records by building 316,251 cars during the calendar year. This was 8.4% of the total number of cars produced in the U.S., and Buick remained solidly in its fourth place. Of this production, Buick was second only to Ford in the number of convertibles produced, building 19,087, which was 19.4% of all soft tops built in the U.S. In the new station wagon line, production was 838, which was still 2.5% of all built this year.

Model year production was 377,428, which by series was: Special, 242,089; Super, 95,465; Century, 20,907; Roadmaster, 15,861; and Limited, 3,106.

Stylewise, the 1941 Buicks were quite different from the 1940 models, though a basic grille similarity existed. New fender line treatment provided a much sleeker look and the headlights were now completely enclosed in the fenders, rather than nesting in discernible pods. The grille and hood continued to follow the theme of 1940, but again were made smoother and more flowing. Running boards were gone for good, and the door hinges were hidden. Though the relationship between the models was very obvious, there was no doubt about which was a 1940 and which was a 1941 Buick.

Under the hood there also were some major changes. A brand new engine, called the "Fireball 8" was introduced, as was a new fuel system called "Compound Carburetion." The new Fireball engine was really a variation of the old "Turbulator" piston that would compress the gas vapor into a tight package just before explosion. The compound carburetion was forerunner of the common-place 4-barrel carburetors of today and of the multi-carburetion that has so delighted the hot rod contingent since the end of World War II. Basically, it was two carburetors hooked in unison. At slow speed and at starting, only the first carburetor did any work. But, after a certain speed was attained, or on heavy acceleration, the second carburetor would cut in to provide more fuel flow to the engine.

Between the new piston design and the compound carburetion, horsepower moved up significantly, though neither bore, stroke, nor displacement changed. The small 248-cubic-inch engine used in the Specials and Supers now developed 115 brake horsepower at 3500 RPM in standard form, or 125 horsepower at 3800 RPM with the compound carburetion. The 320-cubic-inch engine, used in the three larger series, now developed 165 horsepower at 3800 RPM with the compound carburetion which was standard on these models. This 165 horsepower engine was the most

The Brunn Co. of Buffalo, long-famous for its fine custom bodies, was commissioned by Harlow Curtice, then head of Buick, to have available on special order a series of custom bodied cars built on the Limited chassis. These cars used the basic Limited body shell, with heavy custom work above the belt line and very regal interiors. One such design was the Town Car, shown here in a catalog illustration with the unusual 7-bar Limited grille that never went into production. It is believed that two or three of this model were built. It used a leather-covered tonneau top and a removable canvas top over the front compartment.

A beautiful Brunn custom was the Limited Phaeton, shown here in a catalog illustration. At least one of this style is known to have been built, and was in use for many years in the vicinity of Baltimore, Md. None of these Brunn creations are known to exist today. Promotion of these cars was stopped by Cadillac management, who feared that Buick was competing too strongly for what little remained of the ultra-luxury market.

The Brunn Limited Landau Brougham combined the features of the town car with the style of the landau. However, the rear section was not convertible, and the landau irons were strictly decorative. The chauffeur's compartment was done in leather. After GM forbid Buick to promote the Brunn customs, the entire idea died. It is known that at least one Limited Landau Brougham was built.

powerful mill that General Motors built in 1941, being rated 15 horsepower higher than the engine used in that year's Cadillac.

Buick's finest, the Limited, this year could be classed as one of the best luxury cars in America, and certainly as the best value in the luxury field — a fact which must have given fits to a good many people in the Cadillac division. The car used a totally new chassis of the "X" cross-member design, featured about the most comfortable seats ever installed in any car, and had every accessory available in any luxury car built up to that time. The only thing it lacked was an automatic transmission, which for the most part anyway, was still considered only a passing novelty by most car buyers. All in all, both Buick and its Limited series reached record production, and for good reason — they were record cars.

The proposed 4-model Brunn Series of special order cars was completed, and in fact, was even illustrated in some early Limited catalogs for the year. But Harlow Curtice suddenly found himself in trouble with top management at General Motors. Cadillac management had apparently complained bitterly about Buick's "pretentious" ideas in the custom luxury line, and Curtice was ordered to squelch the idea. Under a second agreement between Brunn and Curtice, such cars could still be ordered directly from Brunn through Buick dealers, but few dealers were interested in promoting the idea.

Figures on these exotic Brunn customs vary widely. It is known that one custom Town Car was produced and used in some early ads, but ever here there is some suspicion that this really wasn't a new model, but was simply the body of the 1940 Town Car reworked to fit the 1941 chassis. It is also substantiated that at least one Convertible Phaeton was built on the Roadmaster chassis and an additional Town Car and a Convertible Coupe were built on Roadmaster chassis. Still others contend that at least six of each of the special Limiteds were produced. Take your choice.

The Brunn customs were all built on the standard 139-inch wheelbase Limited chassis. This chassis was of new design, with wider and stiffer frames, a longer drive shaft, heavy X-bracing, and a newly designed stabilizer bar. Despite the inherent strength of this chassis, only three Limited chassis-cowl units were sold in the U.S. The Brunn customs were not built up from the chassis, but were reworked from the standard Limited 6-passenger Sedan, Model 91.

An unusual car for the era was the Brunn custom Limited Landau. In true landau style, it had a solid top over the front compartment, which extended half-way back over the rear compartment. The back half of the rear compartment was of the convertible type. No quarter windows were used in this style. It is believed that two were built.

The Brunn Co. of Buffalo designed a radical custom convertible for a Buick chassis in 1940, but never produced the car. This year, it produced a one-off convertible on a Roadmaster chassis, but the car used many more Buick body pieces, and looked much more like a Buick than did the 1940 design. The car was planned for limited production, but only this one model was built. Buick dealers could order the car for their customers at $3,500, but at this price, there were no takers.

Buick's new compound carburetion was basically the forerunner of today's 4-barrel carburetors, and also of the multi-carburetion units so loved by the speed set following World War II. At idle or low speed, only one carburetor operated, but upon acceleration or at very high speed, both units went to work. Compound carburetion was available in the Century, Roadmaster and Limited Series.

With the Series 80 Limited line gone, the 6-passenger Formal Sedan moved to the Series 90 line, where it was designated the Model 91-F. Production was only 293 for domestic sales and three special order models for export. It cost $2,310 and weighed 4,665 pounds. In addition, Buick produced three Limited chassis-cowl units for domestic sales and one for export.

Buick's top of the line car continued to be the Limited Limousine, Model 90-L, built in 8-passenger form only, with a divider window between compartments. It cost $2,465 and weighed 4,760 pounds. Buick built 605 for domestic sales and 64 for export. This nice example is owned by Ken Rodenhouse of Grand Rapids, Mich. It lacks only the rear skirts which were standard on the Limited Series models this year. Directional signals on the trunk deck were standard.

In a surprise turn, the most popular car in the Limited Series this year was the 6-passenger Sedan, Model 91. Production reached 1,223 for domestic sales and eight special order models for export. It cost $2,155 and weighed 4,575 pounds. Of interesting note is the fact that Buick catalogs for 1940 show the Limited Series with its own exclusive 7-bar grille, yet when production began, the car used the same 8-bar grille as used in all other series.

With the Series 80 Limited line phased out after one year, the Series 90 Limited line was Buick's only prestige class. For a change, however, the 8-passenger Sedan, Model 90, was not the most popular car in the series. It fell behind the 6-passenger version in sales, with production being 885 for domestic sales and 21 for export. It cost $2,360 and weighed 4,680 pounds. This beautiful restoration is owned by Henry W. Reus of Baltimore, Md.

The interior of the Limited models was done in high luxury. Plush mohair, usually in blue or gray, was the most common material used. Window trim was in chrome, with a wood-grain under bar. Doors had pouches, and chrome smoking sets were provided in each side of the rear seat base.

One of the most attractive cars in this year's Buick line was the Roadmaster Convertible Coupe, Model 76-C. It weighed 4,285 pounds and cost $1,457 in basic form. Production stopped at 1,845 for domestic sales and 24 for export. A power operated top and outside mirror were considered standard equipment. This outstanding example, garaged in Rome, Italy, is owned by Nicola Bulgari of Rome and New York City.

Using the same basic lower body as the convertible was the Roadmaster Sport Coupe, Model 76-S. It cost $1,282 and weighed 4,109 pounds. Production was 2,784 for domestic use and 50 for export. In addition to completed cars, Buick built 170 Roadmaster chassis-cowl units for domestic sales and another 109 for export. The two-tone paint was at extra cost.

ll 1941 Buicks used the same attractive dashboards, finished two-tone Damascene with heavy use of chrome trim. All ntrols ran vertically on either side of the centrally located dio speaker. The only negative aspect of the compartment as the fact that the plastic steering wheels and gear shift obs had a tendency to crack and separate very badly with e.

The Roadmaster 4-door Sedan, Model 71, continued to use the trunk back styling of the type made popular in 1940. The car lacked quarter windows, but was provided with vent windows in the rear doors. It cost $1,364 and weighed 4,204 pounds. Production was 10,431 for domestic sales and 122 for export. All Roadmasters were 215 inches long overall on 126-inch wheelbases.

Appearing for the last time this year was the beautiful but unpopular Roadmaster Phaeton, Model 71-C. The car was phased out of production after a short run of 312 for domestic use and 14 for export. It cost $1,775 and weighed 4,451 pounds. This beautiful example is owned by Keith LaMoine of Delano, Cal. The interiors were done entirely in natural leather.

The Roadmaster Sedan interior was quite similar in material and trim to the Century interior. The difference in roof line gave the Roadmaster rear seat a bit more headroom, but a little less visibility due to the lack of quarter windows. The vent windows had their own cranks.

The Century Sedan, Model 61, used the new fastback styling and experienced a substantial increase in sales, with production reaching 15,027 for domestic sales and 109 for export. It cost $1,288 and weighed 4,239 pounds. All Century models were 213.5 inches overall.

Appearing this year only in the Century line was the Business Coupe, Model 66, which was built in 3-passenger form only. The design used chrome window trim similar to that used in the Special and Century sedanettes. It weighed 4,093 pounds and cost $1,195. Only 220 were built for domestic sales and two special order models were produced for export before the style was phased out. In addition, Buick built only two Century chassis-cowl units this year, both for domestic sales. The Century Series used a 126-inch wheelbase chassis.

In outward appearance, the Century Sedanet, Model 66-S, was identical to the Business Coupe. Inside, however, a full rear seat occupied what was additional luggage space in the coupe. The car weighed 4,157 pounds and cost $1,241. Production was 5,521 for domestic sales and 26 for export. It cost $1,775 and weighed 4,451 pounds.

The interior of the new Century 4-door Sedan, Model 61, had surprisingly good rear headroom, despite the sloped roof design. Standard equipment included a center armrest, assist straps, wood-grained metal window sills, and chrome door and seat trim. The quarter windows slid open.

New for the year was Buick's two-way hood, that could be opened from either side. The design, which Buick continued to use for many years, had the advantage of giving a clear working area near the firewall. Its big disadvantage was that a person could not work on both sides of the engine at the same time, without constantly switching the hood opening, or removing the hood entirely. A pivot bar on the firewall braced the hood when it was opened.

Buick's new engine was the now-famous Fireball Eight, which developed 165 horsepower with just about the same gasoline consumption of the former 107 horsepower model. The engine was available with a single carburetor or with compound carburetion, as shown here. Buick made no claims as to the top speed of its cars, but pointed out that the engine could cruise all day at a steady 80 MPH and still have plenty of power left for passing.

1941

Buick convertibles, always beautiful cars, were begininning to make a significant dent in the market for sporty cars. The Super version, Model 56-C, had a run of 12,181 for domestic sales and 210 for export. It cost $1,267 and weighed 3,810 pounds. For the first time, Buick used powered tops on this model as standard equipment. This nice example is owned by Bery Stolsmark of Midland, Mich. All Supers were 210 inches overall and used a 121-inch wheelbase.

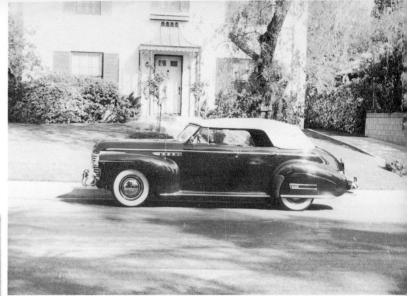

Appearing for the last time this year was the attractive Super Convertible Phaeton, Model 51-C, which now used the same rounded trunk treatment as did the Super sedan. Only 467 were built for domestic sales and 41 for export before the style was phased out of production. It cost $1,555, weighed 4,015 pounds, and featured a factory-installed under-seat heating system, fresh air intake and defrosters. This beautiful example is owned by Jim Moloney of Santa Barbara, Cal.

The most popular car in the Super Series continued to be the 4-door Touring Sedan, Model 51, which had a run of 57,367 for domestic sales and 1,271 for export. It cost $1,185 and weighed 3,770 pounds. Buick claimed this was the country's most popular model at its price. This completely original version was still in daily use in Los Angeles a few years ago.

The Super Sport Coupe, Model 56-S, continued to be an exceptionally good looking car. It was equipped with a full rear seat, but this could be removed, making the entire rear compartment available for luggage. It cost $1,113 and weighed 3,670 pounds. Buick built 19,603 for domestic sales and 273 for export. Also turned out were 220 Super chassis-cowl units for domestic use and 1,380 for export. The Sport Coupe shown here is owned by Jim Krause of Cincinnati, Ohio.

The 3-passenger Business Coupe, Model 56, continued to appear in the Super Series, but only 2,449 were built for domestic sales while three special order models were built for export. It weighed 3,620 pounds and cost $1,031. The large trunk deck was fitted with standard signal lights, a Buick trademark since 1939. This excellent restoration is owned by Jack Jones of Flint.

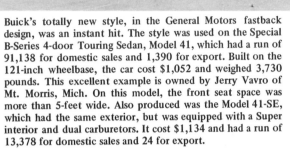

Buick's totally new style, in the General Motors fastback design, was an instant hit. The style was used on the Special B-Series 4-door Touring Sedan, Model 41, which had a run of 91,138 for domestic sales and 1,390 for export. Built on the 121-inch wheelbase, the car cost $1,052 and weighed 3,730 pounds. This excellent example is owned by Jerry Vavro of Mt. Morris, Mich. On this model, the front seat space was more than 5-feet wide. Also produced was the Model 41-SE, which had the same exterior, but was equipped with a Super interior and dual carburetors. It cost $1,134 and had a run of 13,378 for domestic sales and 24 for export.

The Special B-Series Business Coupe, Model 46, was a completely different car than the A-Series model. It used fastback styling similar to that used by the new B-Series Sedanette, but featured completely different window chrome. It cost $935, weighed 3,630 pounds, and was so large that, if used in farm work, it could carry 10 10-gallon milk cans. Buick produced 9,185 for domestic use and 16 for export, but it is unlikely that too many were put to work carrying milk cans. All B-Series Specials were 209 inches overall.

Totally new in the Special line was the 6-passenger Estate Wagon, Model 49, which was part of the Special B-Series. It cost $1,463 and weighed 3,980 pounds. Buick built 838 for domestic sales and 12 for export. In addition, three Special B-Series chassis-cowl units were sold in the U.S., while 1,344 such units were sold overseas.

A completely different type of window chrome quickly set the Special B-Series Sedanette apart from the business coupe. The totally new style, designated the Model 46-S, had a run of 87,687 for domestic sales and 461 for export. It cost $1,006 and weighed 3,700 pounds. This beautiful restoration is owned by William W. Ningard of Baltimore, Md. When the accessory fender skirts were used, the rear fender chrome trim had to be removed. Also produced in this style was the Model 46-SSE. This used the same exterior as the Model 46-S, but had a Super interior and dual carburetors. This version cost $1,063 and had a run of 9,591 for domestic sales and 23 for export.

The interior of the new Special Estate Wagon was tastefully done, considering the fact that the car was still considered in the utility vehicle class, and was not really thought of as a family car. The seats were in tan leather with chrome trim, while the floor mats were black rubber. Framing was of northern white ash, with the exterior panels being mahogany and the interior panels being birch. The roof was of rubberized fabric.

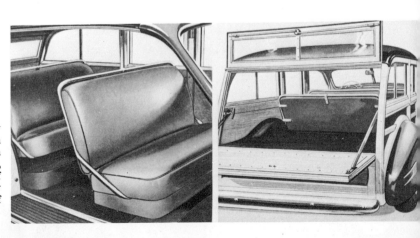

The Special Series was proving so popular that Buick this year divided it into two sub-series, the Series 40-A, on a 118-inch wheelbase and the Series 40-B on a 122-inch wheelbase. In the A-Series, the least expensive car was the 3-passenger Business Coupe, Model 44, which sold for $915 and weighed 3,530 pounds. Buick built 3,258 for domestic sales but only three for export.

Surprisingly, the Special 4-door Touring Sedan was found in both the A-Series and the B-Series, but each was a completely different car. This is the A-Series version, Model 47, which used a trunkback style, and no quarter windows. It cost $1,021 and weighed 3,670 pounds. Buick built 13,992 for domestic sales and 147 for export. This nice example is owned by Briggs Watson of South Pasedena, Cal. Although this is in solid color, two-tone combinations were a popular option on this particular model.

The Special Convertible Coupe, Model 44-C, wound up in the new Special A-Series. It cost $1,138 and weighed 3,780 pounds. Buick built 4,282 for domestic sales and 27 for export. All Buicks this year used concealed running boards.

The 6-passenger Sport Coupe, Model 44-S, appeared only in the Special A-Series. It offered a full-width rear seat, but poor rear leg room. Costing $980 and weighing 3,590 pounds, it had a run of 5,269 for domestic sales and 21 for export. This year, the rubber gravel shields on the leading edges of the rear fenders were standard on all models.

Looking somewhat like a lavish panel truck was this professional car turned out by the Flxible Co. of Loudenville, Ohio, on a Limited chassis. The car, designed primarily for the transport of bodies, caskets, and funeral equipment, could also be used as a secondary hearse when necessary, though its interior fittings were not as plush as those found in true hearses. Custom body work included raising the hood and cowl line to blend in with the higher overall body line. The chassis has been stretched, but standard Buick fenders were used both front and rear. Access doors were located on both sides as well as on the rear. The upholstered divider partition contained a curtained window.

Just starting to come into popularity was the distinctive flower car design. This one, by the Flxible Co. of Loundonville, Ohio, is built on an extended Super chassis. It featured large access doors in the quarter panels, plus a full-width back door. The flower deck could be covered with sliding steel roof panels, and the car could double as a first-call car, or be used for transporting equipment, furniture, caskets, or for long distance transporting of bodies.

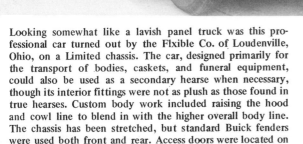

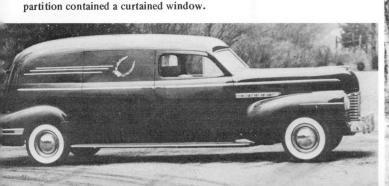

As did all 1942 cars, this year's Buick lacked a certain amount of quality found in previous models. But this was not the fault of Buick, nor was it the fault of any other car manufacturer. With the world in trouble, and threats of a world war becoming stronger and stronger on an almost daily basis, a great amount of material and manpower was being poured into defense production.

World War II did come into being, and by February 2, 1942, all auto production was curtailed. Between January 1 and February 2, which was the end of this calendar year, Buick managed to produce only 16,601 cars. Still, this was 7.6% of the industry's total production, and it was enough to hold Buick in fourth place.

Since 1942 production had actually started in September, model year production was 94,442. Of this, by series, the production was: Specials, 46,715; Supers, 33,917; Century, 4,551; Roadmaster, 8,559; and Limited, 700.

But, despite the hardships imposed by lack of materials and uncertain production schedules, Buick managed to make a substantial change in its 1942 models, and the almost total redesign caught virtually all other auto makers by complete surprise. The new Buick was an extremely modern car, with its massive grille and large bumpers, and its flowing fenders that were the longest of any car on the road.

A major styling innovation was the "Airfoil" fender design used on the Super Century and Roadmaster Series. This marked the first time that a major American car had front fenders sweeping the entire length of the body until they met the leading edge of the rear fenders. In addition, the rear fenders of these models were equipped with standard fender skirts rather than the optional clip-on skirts so popular in that era.

Both the Special and the Limited models used less sweeping front fenders, but still, these also went well beyond the cowl and into the front doors. All models used heavy chrome trim bars on the front fenders and chrome rocker trim. After January 1, 1942, the government prohibited the use of all chrome trim, and thus all trim pieces were painted in matching colors, primarily battle-ship gray, for the remainder of the 1942 calendar year. Known as "blackout models," these chromeless cars, too, were stopped on February 2, 1942, when the government ended all of Buick's auto production for the duration of the war.

As could be expected, both the Fireball engine and compound carburetion were continued. But, in the small block engines, cast iron pistons replaced the aluminum ones of 1941. The large engine, basically unchanged, continued to use aluminum pistons.

The added weight of the iron pistons caused the horsepower of the 248-cubic-inch engine to drop back to 110 at 3400 RPM with single carburetor and 118 at 3600 RPM with the compound carburetion. Since the 320-cubic-inch block was not changed, and since the compound carburetion had been modified much for the better, the big engine still developed 165 horsepower at 3800 RPM. This was still the largest and hottest passenger car engine in production anywhere in the world, and this fact alone made the Century the fastest and hottest stock automobile to be found anywhere.

The Special continued to use its 118-inch and 121-inch wheelbases, but the Super this year had its own exclusive chassis of 124-inch wheelbase. Likewise, the Century kept its 126-inch wheelbase; but the Roadmaster grew, and now used its own chassis with a wheelbase of 129-inches. The huge Limited retained its huge 139-inch wheelbase.

Again the Limited 6-passenger Sedan, Model 91, turned out to be the most popular style in the Limited Series, with 215 being built, all for domestic sales. It cost $2,245 and weighed 4,665 pounds. Although the long flowing lines of this year's Buicks greatly enhanced all of the other series, this styling did not seem to do much for the very formal Limited models.

The lowest production Limited was the Formal Sedan, Model 91-F, which combined the 6-passenger interior styling with the electrically operated division window of the limousine. Only 85 were built, all for domestic sales. It cost $2,395 and weighed 4,695 pounds. No Limited chassis-cowl units were produced this year.

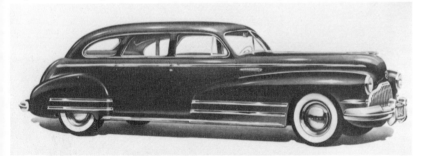

Appearing for the last time was the Limited Series, which still used the 139-inch wheelbase chassis. Its models, all built on the same basic body style, were 226 inches in overall length. Surprisingly, the least popular car this year was the 8-passenger Sedan, Model 90. Only 144 were produced for domestic sales and six for export. It cost $2,455 and weighed 4,710 pounds. The Limited name would appear on a full series just one more time, in 1958, and then would go away for good, except for its use as trim designation on today's Electra models.

The interior of the Limited models was almost identical to that of the 1941 models. The assist straps hung on a chrome bar, which allowed them to be moved the entire length of the quarter window. All Limiteds used this same rear seat and door style, and varied only in the addition or deletion of divider glass, jump seats, leather driver's compartment, and internal luggage compartment, as found on the 6-passenger sedans. For the first time, the parking brake now consisted of a pedal activator and a pull-button release. Both pedal and button were located on the far left of the under-side of the dash.

The Limited Limousine continued to be Buick's most expensive and heaviest car, costing $2,545 and weighing 4,765 pounds. Only 192 were built for domestic sales and 58 for export. This version was used by General Eisenhower at Palm Springs, Cal. It was not owned by him, but was on loan from a friend.

Both the Roadmaster convertible and the Sedanet, Model 76-S, used the new swept-back fenders. The Sedanet cost $1,365 and weighed 4,075 pounds. Production was 2,471 for domestic sales and four special order versions for export. Rear skirts were standard on all Roadmasters. In addition to completed cars Buick produced 86 Roadmaster chassis-cowl units for domestic sales and 48 such units for export.

The Roadmaster 4-door Sedan, Model 71, continued to be built in trunkback form, with the fenders decorated with heavy chrome bars. It cost $1,465 and weighed 4,150 pounds. Production was 5,418 for domestic sales and 21 for export. All Roadmaster models were 217 inches in overall length and used a 129-inch wheelbase chassis.

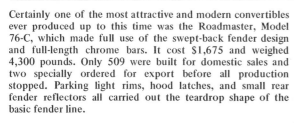

Certainly one of the most attractive and modern convertibles ever produced up to this time was the Roadmaster, Model 76-C, which made full use of the swept-back fender design and full-length chrome bars. It cost $1,675 and weighed 4,300 pounds. Only 509 were built for domestic sales and two specially ordered for export before all production stopped. Parking light rims, hood latches, and small rear fender reflectors all carried out the teardrop shape of the basic fender line.

The 1942 Buicks used the same dash, with minor degrees of refinement between models. This is the Super version, finished in wood-grain, and wearing the accessory clock and radio. Dual ashtrays were provided on each side of the radio dial, and all controls were of the pull type, located vertically on either side of the radio speaker.

The interior of the Century sedan was a bit more impressive than that of the Super model, and included such extras as assist straps and wide wood-grained window edges. However, the practical courtesy lights used on the Super models were not used on the Century sedan. This same interior was available in the Special Series-B sedans for an additional cost.

The interior of the Roadmaster Sedan was attractively done in whipcord and mohair, in several color options. The rear seat was equipped with a center armrest and courtesy lights at each lower corner. The window frames were in matching color to the wood-grained panels.

The interior of the Super 4-door Sedan was in fairly luxurious trim, considering the car's price class. The rear seats were fitted with courtesy lights at each corner, and a center armrest. However, the side armrests could give a person a mean bump when entering or leaving.

Appearing for the last time was the Century Series, which would not be reactivated until 1954. The series now consisted of only two models, a sedan and a sedanet. This is the 4-door Sedan, Model 61, which had a run of 3,312 for domestic sales and seven for export. It cost $1,350 and weighed 4,065 pounds. Both Century models were 212 inches overall and used the same basic bodies as used on the Supers, though the Century wheelbase was 126 inches while the Super was built on a 124-inch wheelbase chassis.

The Century Sedanet, Model 66-S, used the same basic body as used on the Super version, but lacked the beautiful and highly unusual swept-back fenders of the Super model. In the Century Series, the sedanet cost $1,300 and weighed 3,985 pounds. Only 1,229 were built for domestic sales and three special orders were exported. No Century chassis-cowl units were sold this year.

1942

One of the most attractive and totally different cars on the road this year was the new Super Convertible, Model 56-C, which used Buick's new swept-back fender styling, decorated with heavy chrome sidebars. It cost $1,450 and weighed 4,025 pounds. Production was 2,454 for domestic sales and 35 for export. The top was electrically operated; fender skirts were standard.

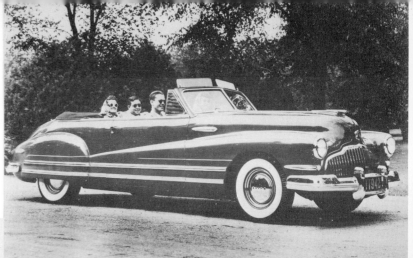

Ranking second on Buick's popularity roll this year was the Super 4-door Sedan, Model 51, of which 16,001 were built for domestic use and 264 were built for export. The car cost $1,280 and weighed 3,890 pounds. All Super models were 212 inches in overall length.

Also using the swept-back fender design was the new Super 6-passenger Sedanet, Model 56-S. This car had a run of 14,579 for domestic sales and 50 for export. It cost $1,230 and weighed 3,800 pounds. In addition to completed cars, Buick also produced 30 Super chassis-cowl units for domestic sales and 504 units for export.

A very attractive vehicle this year, which probably would have had a substantial increase in sales had it not been for W.W. II, was the Special Series-B Estate Wagon, Model 49. Built in 6-passenger form, it had a run of only 326 for domestic sales and one export order. It cost $1,450 and weighed 3,925 pounds. The rear seat was removable. In addition to completed cars, Buick built 175 Series-B chassis-cowl units for domestic sales and 828 for export.

The Special line continued to be divided into two sub-series, the Series-A on 118-inch wheelbase chassis, and the Series-B on 121-inch wheelbase chassis. Buick's most popular car was the Series-B 4-door Sedan, Model 41, of which 17,187 were built for domestic sales and 310 were built for export. It cost $1,120 and weighed 3,760 pounds. It was built in fastback style. Also built was the Model 41-SE, which used the same exterior, but had Century internal equipment, including compound carburetion and Century interior trim. This version had a run of 2,286 for domestic sales and two special orders for export.

The Special Series-B Sedanet came in a variety of forms this year, but all versions used identical exteriors. The most popular version was the Family Sedanet, Model 46-S, which was a 6-passenger style. It cost $1,075, weighed 3,705 pounds, and had a run of 11,856 for domestic sales and 77 for export. Next in popularity was the Model 46-SSE, which also was a 6-passenger version, but using Century interior trim and dual carburetion. This version had a run of 1,809, all for domestic sales. The least popular was the 3-passenger Business Sedanet version, Model 46, which was fitted with a large luggage compartment behind the front seat. This model cost $1,020, weighed 3,650 pounds, and had a run of 1,406 for domestic sales and two special orders for export. All Series-B Specials were 208 inches in overall length.

The only Buick this year to have a base price under $1,000 was the Series-A Special Utility Coupe, Model 44, which cost $990 and weighed 3,510 pounds. Only 461 were built, all for domestic sales. The car was built in 3-passenger form only, with substantial luggage space behind the front seat. All Series-A Special models were 202 inches in overall length.

The Series-A Special Convertible, Model 44-C, used the same basic body as the utility coupe, but was a far more appealing car. A total of 1,776 were built for domestic sales and 12 were built for export. The car used an electrically operated top. It cost $1,260, weighed 3,790 pounds.

Unlike the utility coupe, the Series-A Special 3-passenger Business Sedanet, Model 48, used fastback styling. But, like the utility coupe, there was no back seat, and the entire rear compartment was fitted as a cargo area. It cost $1,010 and weighed 3,555 pounds. Only 559 were built before W.W. II ended all auto production.

The Series-A Special 6-passenger Family Sedanet, Model 48-S, used the same body as the business version, but was fitted with a rear seat and trimmed rear compartment. It continued to use different window chrome than did the business version. Weighing 3,610 pounds and costing $1,045, the car had a run of 5,981 for domestic sales and nine for export.

The Series-A Special 4-door Sedan, Model 47, used the 118-inch wheelbase chassis and trunkback styling. It cost $1,080 and weighed 3,650 pounds. Production was 1,611 for domestic sales and 41 for export. This example, owned by John Gibbons of Ann Arbor, Mich., has been painted to resemble a Japanese staff car of W.W. II. Although this particular car has never been outside the U.S., the mock-up is authentic and quite logical, since the Japanese confiscated or captured many American autos at the start of the war, and used them as military staff vehicles.

Looking almost like a deluxe panel truck was this Flxible Funeral Service Car, built on an extended Super chassis. The car used the basic body of the Flxible hearse, but had blanked in side panels. Access was by the two very wide rear side doors or the back door. The hood and cowl were extended to meet the high beltline. Service cars such as these were used for transporting caskets and funeral equipment, long-distance transportation of bodies, and as first-call cars. They could also be used as hearses if necessary. This model was finished in white with a maroon interior and chrome trim.

The Flxible Landau Hearse was an attractive but high vehicle. To meet the high beltline, the Buick hoods had to be sectioned and raised substantially. This model, finished in black and silver, used dummy landau irons and rather unusual rear door window treatment.

Flxible Co. of Loudonville, Ohio, was one of the few builders of professional cars to construct any number of vehicles before war restrictions ended production. Virtually all of its production was on Roadmaster chassis, though some Super chassis were also used. This is the 1942 Flxible ambulance, which this year used a different basic body than did the funeral models. It used a back-up light, rear roof marker lights, and dual red flashers in rooftop pods on the front.

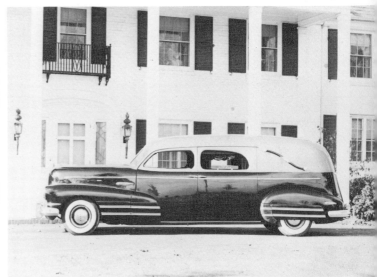

The 1942 Buick chassis was further refined through the use of newly designed shock absorbers, improved weight distribution, and wider wheel rims. This year, stripped chassis-cowl units were produced only in the Special Series-B, Super, and Roadmaster Series. Whitewalls were extra.

The last Buick leaves the factory at the close of auto production, Feb. 2, 1942. From this point on until mid-1945, all auto plants in the nation would concentrate strictly on war production. The car is a "blackout model" Special, with all former chrome trim except the bumpers now painted in pale gray. Buick did not have to resort to painted bumpers because it had enough of the pre-restriction chromed bumpers stockpiled for the length of its 1942 model run.

The last Buick rolled off the assembly line on February 2, 1942, and from then until the first postwar 1946 model rolled off the line on October, 1945, no automobiles would leave Buick's plants. Instead, production was converted to a vast array of war material, and Buick-built military items were represented at virtually every fighting front in World War II.

Buick was assigned more that thirty separate war production operations, ranging from production of the powerful and speedy Hellcat tank destroyers to producing 20 MM. shell bodies. The Hellcats were, to the automotive buff, probably the most impressive and most interesting of all Buick's war production.

Although war production had ended the manufacture of all civilian automobile production, the Flxible Co. of Loudonville, Ohio, was able to purchase a few 1942 Super and Roadmaster chassis and produce some high-priority ambulances. This example was built for the AFL-CIO, and donated to the Trenton, N.J., Defense Council. It is a black-out version of the Roadmaster chassis, with all former chrome parts except the bumpers and siren painted in pale gray, as was the vehicle itself.

Although Buick produced a wide variety of war material, it was probably most famous for its Hellcat Tank Destroyers and its production of Pratt & Whitney aircraft engines. This is the Hellcat, built in a variety of basic forms. It was classed as a tank destroyer, not a tank, and had less heavy armor plate but a much higher speed than did the tanks.

Buick built a total of 2,507 of these monsters at Flint. The Hellcat, officially designated the M-18, was a highly mobile, low silhouette, lightly armored 76 mm. gun-carrying motor carriage. It was designed primarily for gun carriage and tank destroyer use, but later in the war many of these were converted to armored cargo carriers.

The 39,000 pound vehicle carried a crew of five, could hold a steady 50 MPH on level ground, and had a cruising range of 150 miles. Power was by a Continental C-1 or C-4 gasoline engine, while drive was through a torquomatic transmission with three speeds forward and one reverse.

Also produced were 19,428 power trains for other types of tanks, Pratt & Whitney radial engines, over 3-million cylinder heads for Pratt & Whitney aircraft engines, 2,952 mounts for anti-aircraft guns, over 2.5-million steel cartridge cases, and almost 10-million 20 mm. shell bodies. In fact, only a few days after the last Buick was taken off the assembly line, the fender division was busy pressing out the shell bodies.

In addition, other departments assembled and serviced Pratt & Whitney aircraft engines, produced prop-shaft forgings for these and other aircraft engines, produced diesel crankshafts and engine components, and did a wide variety of machining and assembly work for other war material manufacturers.

Actually, much of Buick's war production was begun before the war was actually declared, and was considered "defense production." For example, the contract to build the M-18 Hellcat tank destroyers and 500 Pratt and Whitney engines was let in 1941. Early in that year, Buick had started a crash program to complete a huge assembly plant near Chicago in order to process the aircraft engines. The plant was completed in September of 1941, and tooling for the production of these engines began. Actual engine production began in January of 1942, and by March, the plant was turning out 1,000 of these engines each month.

No sooner had auto production stopped than Buick's fender plant began punching out shell casings and cartridge cases. Here the all-woman assembly line is inspecting and crating the casings. Buick turned out 10-million of these 20mm. shell bodies and 2.5-million cartridge cases.

Workmen on the Buick assembly line are shown putting the final touches on an almost-finished Hellcat Tank Destroyer. The vehicle could maintain a sustained speed of 50 MPH on level ground, but was slowed down to 15 MPH on a 10% grade. It was able to climb a 60% grade in low gear. It had a cruising range of 150 miles from its 165-gallon fuel tank.

A later version of M18 Hellcat is shown here with its new style fenders. The vehicle was powered by a Continental gasoline engine running through a torquomatic transmission with three forward speeds and a reverse. It used torsion bar suspension.

The Hellcat turret, complete with 76mm gun, is guided into place on a half-finished vehicle at the Buick plant. In operation, the driver and assistant driver were seated in the forward part of the hull, while the gunner, loader, and commander occupied the turret. Two escape hatches were provided in the turret and one in the floor. The turret could turn 360-degrees. Headlights and siren were guarded against damage by brush or flying debris.

In addition to the Hellcats, Buick's other major war effort was the production of over 3-million cylinder heads for Pratt & Whitney aircraft engines, and the actual production of these engines. Beginning in January, 1942, in a newly constructed plant near Chicago, Buick produced 1,000 of these Pratt & Whitney engines a month. The engines are shown here on assembly stands, being given their finishing touches.

Some of the 2,507 Hellcat Tank Destroyers produced by Buick are lined up in front of the main Buick plant in Flint, Mich., awaiting shipment. Many of these vehicles went overseas and served with the British army.

One of the 2,507 Hellcat Tank Destroyers built by Buick undergoes testing at the Aberdeen Proving Grounds in Maryland. In Army nomenclature, it was known as the M18. Most often it was fitted with a 76mm gun, and would be called the 76mm Gun Motor Carriage M18.

World War II ended, and all U.S. auto manufacturers made a mad scramble to get their "new" postwar cars before the auto starved American public. Buick, of course, was among these manufacturers. But Buick had one factor in its favor. That was the fact that the 1942 Buick was about the most modern car on the road that year. And, since the "new" postwar cars were really not new at all, but only slightly warmed versions of the 1942 models, Buick stood in good stead by still having about the most modern car on the road in 1946.

Calendar year production was 156,080, which was 7.2% of the industry. Still, Buick dropped to fifth place as Dodge nosed out fourth place by a total of only forty-eight cars. To the calendar year production must be added 2,482 vehicles that actually were produced in late 1945, but were classed 1946 models.

Model year production was 158,728, which by series was: Special, 4,502; Super, 122,135; and Roadmaster, 32,091.

Of primary note was the fact that a much reduced selection of cars was available. The Special Series, which had by far been Buick's largest seller, was now cut down to only two models, both on the 121-inch wheelbase chassis. In 1942 there had been five Special models on the 118-inch wheelbase chassis, and six primary models on the 121-inch wheelbase. Yet, this year the 118-inch wheelbase was not used at all.

The Super Series, on a 124-inch wheelbase, now had four models; and the Roadmaster Series, built on a 129-inch wheelbase chassis, consisted of the same three models as had appeared in 1942. Both the Century and the Limited Series were gone.

The Special and Super models continued to use the 248-cubic-inch block of 110 horsepower at 3600 RPM. The engines, which ran a bore and stroke of 3-3/32 x 4-1/8, were equipped with either Stromberg or Carter carburetors. The Roadmaster models also continued to use their prewar blocks of 320 cubic inches, with a bore and stroke of 3-7/16 x 4-5/16 inches. The engine was rated at 144 horsepower at 3600 RPM, which was less than the prewar rating of 165 horsepower.

An extremely attractive car, in comparison to other makes, was the Roadmaster Convertible, Model 76-C. At $2,347 and 4,345 pounds, it was Buick's most expensive and heaviest model. Production was 2,576 for domestic sales and 11 for export. This fine example is owned by Dr. Marvin Speer of Cleveland, Ohio. It wears accessory spot light and dual fog lights.

Of interest is the fact that the Super and Special model used 6.50 x 16 tires, while the Roadmaster used smaller but wider 7.00 x 15 tires. Also of special interest was the novel "bombsight" hood ornament sported by Buick from this year through 1948. This little ornament was so widely accepted by the public that scores of accessory manufacturers began producing them. And, for the next decade, these Buick bombsights could be seen decorating hoods and fenders of millions of vehicles of all sizes, from Harley Davidsons to Autocar Diesels.

Except for its added length, the Roadmaster Series this year was identical to the Super Series. This is the Roadmaster 4-door Sedan, Model 71, which cost $2,110 and weighed 4,165 pounds. Buick built 20,549 for domestic sales and 267 for export.

Still using the popular fastback styling was the Roadmaster Sedanet, Model 76-S, shown here with the optional two-tone paint job. It cost $2,014 and weighed 4,095 pounds. Buick built 8,226 for domestic sales and 66 for export. In addition, the company produced 180 Roadmaster chassis-cowl units for domestic sales and 168 for export.

The Buick dash was used in all models, but varied in trim between series. This is the Roadmaster Sedan version, trimmed in two-tone wood-grain. In the Specials and in both convertible models, the dash was painted in matching color. Its only bad feature was the cable operated windshield wipers. The cables, which would often jump their grooves were located under the dash, high on the firewall, and were horrendous to replace.

Buick's most popular car this year was the Super Sedan, Model 51, of which 73,991 were built for domestic sales and 3,679 were produced for export. It used the full-length fenders pioneered in 1942, but with much less chrome trim than the pre-war models. It cost $1,822 and weighed 3,935 pounds. The two-tone paint was an added cost option.

Except for a different grille and less chrome trim, the Super Convertible, Model 56-C, was virtually unchanged from the 1942 version. One major change was that the top and power windows were now hydraulically operated rather than electrically. This was fine while the cars were new, but led to problems in later years when the hydraulic cylinders began to leak. The convertible cost $2,046 and weighed 4,050 pounds. Production was 5,391 for the U.S., 56 for export.

The new Buick Estate Wagon moved to the Super Series, where it was designated the Model 59. Considering the new fenders and redesigned body, it was probably Buick's most changed model. It cost $2,594, weighed 4,170 pounds, and had a run of 786 for domestic sales and 12 for export. In addition to completed cars, Buick built 81 Super chassis-cowl units for domestic sales and 3,120 for export.

Ranking second in total popularity was the Super Sedanet, Model 56-S, which had a run of 34,197 for domestic sales and 190 for export. It cost $1,741 and weighed 3,795 pounds. All Super models were 212.5 inches overall and had wheelbases of 124 inches.

The post-war Special Series was no longer divided into two sub-series. In fact, it was reduced to a two-model line of very limited production, with both models using the 121-inch wheelbase chassis and being 207.5 inches overall. One of these models was the 4-door Sedan, Model 41, which cost $1,580 and weighed 3,720 pounds. Only 1,621 were built for domestic sales and one special order model went overseas. The Special Series was the only line to retain the heavy chrome side trim. The other two series had far less chrome than the pre-war cars.

The other model in the reduced Special Series was the Sedanet, Model 46-S, which like the sedan, used the short pre-war fenders and heavy side trim. Buick built only 1,349 for domestic sales, none for export. It cost $1,522 and weighed 3,670 pounds. Fender skirts and rear fender chrome trim were an added cost accessory on all Special models. In addition to the completed cars, Buick built two Special chassis-cowl units for domestic sale and 1,500 for export.

One of the 3,679 Super Sedans built for export is this model, which is still in daily use in England. The car has right-hand drive, and used dual fog lights in addition to a running light.

As could be expected, the Buick engines were unchanged from the 1942 models. The Specials and Supers used a 110-horsepower version, while the Roadmasters used the 144-horsepower model. Compound carburetion was not used on any models.

As could be expected, the Flxible Co. of Loudonville, was back in production almost as fast as Buick could start turning out stripped chassis-cowl units. But, because of the new fender lines of the Super and Roadmaster cars, Flxible had to form its own fender ends this year. This is the Flxible Landau Hearse, on an extended Roadmaster chassis. It varied little from the 1942 version.

The Buick chassis, like the engines, were virtually unchanged from the 1942 models. It was built in three sizes of 121, 124, and 129-inch wheelbases. Tires on the Specials and Supers were 6.50 x 16 while the Roadmasters used 7.00 x 15 tires.

The interior of the Special Sedan was a bit more Spartan than it had been before the war. However, an assist strap was still provided on each rear door post, and the quarter windows were of the sliding type. Window frames were painted in solid colors, not wood grained.

Calendar year production went up to 267,830, which was 7.5% of the industry. This allowed Buick to regain its fourth place spot from Dodge, but it was still a long way from either of the top three which were, respectively, Chevrolet, Ford, and Plymouth. Model year production was 277,134, which by series ran: Special, 34,270; Super, 163,410; and Roadmaster, 79,454.

Buick also led the industry in the number of convertibles produced, turning out 37,743, which was 22.9% of the U.S. total. In many ways, this was a deserved lead, as Buick had one of the best looking convertibles on the road this year, with the convertible lines most certainly enhanced by the full-length fenders and general long, low appearance of the cars. In the station wagon field, it was a different story. Here Buick produced only 2,331, or 2.8% of the U.S. total.

With the exception of a new grille, Buick made very little change this year. This was to be expected, as cars were still a high priority item, and all buyers had to go on lengthy waiting lists and be satisfied almost with whatever happened to come down the pike.

All body styles remained in effect in the three series, but an Estate Wagon was added to the Roadmaster Series. Wheelbases remained 121 inches, 124 inches, and 129 inches for the Special, Super and Roadmaster Series respectively. Likewise, the engines remained the 248-cubic-inch block of 110 horsepower in the Special and Super Series, and the 320-cubic-inch block in the Roadmaster Series.

Buick's second most popular car, by a slim margin, turned out to be the new Roadmaster Sedan, Model 71. It had a run of 46,532 for domestic sales and 621 for export. It cost $2,232 and weighed 4,190 pounds. The two-tone paint and whitewall tires were added cost options.

The Roadmaster Sedanet, Model 76-S, cost $2,131 and weighed 4,095 pounds. Buick built 18,983 for domestic sales and 229 for export. In addition, Buick produced 356 Roadmaster chassis-cowl units for domestic sales and 360 such units for export sales.

For the first time since 1921, Buick had a car with a base price in excess of $3,000. It was the new Roadmaster Estate Wagon, Model 79, which listed at $3,249 and weighed 4,445 pounds. Only 300 were built, all for domestic sales.

Both the Super and Roadmaster convertibles showed an amazing increase in sales this year, reaching heights never before attained for this type of car. In the Roadmaster Series, the Convertible had a run of 11,947 for domestic sales and 127 for export. Designated the Model 76-C, it cost $2,651 and weighed 4,345 pounds.

The most expensive Super model was the Convertible, Model 56-C, which had a base price of $2,333. The 4,050-pound car had an amazing production run of 25,796 for domestic sales and 501 for export. Hydraulically powered top, windows, and seat were standard equipment.

The Super 4-door Sedan, Model 51, continued to be the most popular car in Buick's line, with production being 76,866 for domestic sales and 6,710 for export. It cost $1,929 and weighed 3,910 pounds. The Supers continued to be 212.5 inches overall.

The Super Sedanet, Model 56-S, continued to attract customers, and 46,311 were produced for domestic sales while 606 were exported. It cost $1,843 and weighed 3,795 pounds.

The Flxible Co. of Loudenville, Ohio, continued to use Buick chassis for the complete line of ambulances and hearses. all models this year were built on extended Roadmaster chassis, with hoods and cowl-lines raised to meet the larger bodies. Flxible used the standard Buick front and rear fenders, but bobbed the door pods rather than carrying the sweep to the rear fender.

With production becoming less erratic as supplies became more available, time could be spent in producing additional models of the less popular vehicles. A car to fall into this class was the Super Estate Wagon, Model 59, which this year had a production run of 2,031 for domestic sales but only five special order versions for export. It cost $2,805 and weighed 4,170 pounds. In addition to completed cars, Buick produced 4,584 Super chassis-cowl units which were shipped to various assembly plants overseas. This wagon sports non-standard hubcaps of much later vintage.

The Special Series adopted the new grille of the 1948 Buicks, but otherwise continued to use its 1942 body with the short, heavily chromed fenders. For the first time in Buick's advertising, it referred to the car as a "compact model," a term that would not really enter the general vocabulary until the 1960s. This is the Special 4-door Sedan, Model 41, which cost $1,673 and weighed 3,720 pounds. Production was 17,136 for domestic sales and 1,295 for export.

The Special Sedanet, Model 46-S, was unchanged except for the grille. It cost $1,611 and weighed 3,670 pounds. It was Buick's least expensive car. Production was 14,278 for domestic sales and 325 for export. In addition, Buick built 108 Special chassis-cowl units for domestic sales and 1,128 for export.

Appearing for the last time in Australia were the Holden bodied Buick Specials. Despite the 1946 grille, this is the 1947 version, quite similar to those built by Buick, but with right-hand drive and slightly different interior fittings. Beginning in 1948, Holden would begin producing its own all-Australian cars, which today are by far the most popular vehicles in that country.

Since Buick produced no Super chassis for domestic sales, body builders such as the Flxible Co. of Loudonville, Ohio, had to build their specialty vehicles on Roadmaster chassis. This is the Flxible ambulance. It used a relatively high belt line, which required an extensive raising of the hood to meet the windshield. Flxible still had to reform its fender ends.

1948

The Roadmaster Convertible, Model 76-C, was priced at $2,837 and weighed 4,315 pounds. Hydraulic cylinders were still used for top, windows, and seat, with these components being standard equipment. Production this year was 11,053.

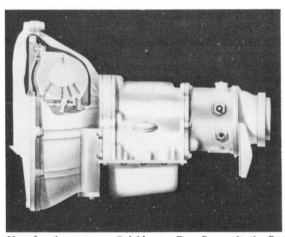

The Roadmaster Estate Wagon, Model 79, continued to be Buick's lowest production model, with only 350 being built. It cost $3,433 and weighed 4,460 pounds. Both the Roadmaster and Super wagons continued to use an all-wood body with a rubberized fabric roof, and leather seats.

New for the year was Buick's new Dynaflow unit, the first automatic transmission that Buick management would consider after the disastrous 1938 attempt. It was available only on the Roadmasters and at extra cost. It was a fairly dependable unit, but quite sluggish.

Buick's second most popular car was the Roadmaster Sedan, Model 71, which had a slight increase in production, with domestic sales going up to 47,569. It cost $2,418 and weighed 4,160 pounds. All Roadmaster models this year were fitted with accessory chrome wheel rims.

Calendar year production went up to 275,503 this year. This was an increase in Buick's production, but other companies were increasing production as well, and Buick claimed only 7% of the total U.S. production. Still, Buick was firmly entrenched in fourth place. Model year production was 229,718, which by series ran: Special 36,187; Super, 112,441; and Roadmaster, 81,090.

Of this production, Buick again led the industry in the production of convertibles, turning out 34,970 of the attractive soft tops, which was 18.9% of all soft tops built in the U.S. this year. Wagons were at the other end of the list, with 2,487 being built, which was 2.2% of the total U.S. production.

The big news for the year was Dynaflow, which many automotive experts consider one of the most important automotive developments since the self starter. It appeared only as an option on Roadmaster cars this year, but the demand for the new torque converter type of transmission was so great that production facilities were doubled, tripled, and then quadrupled. Within two years, 85% of all Buicks built would have Dynaflow.

But, with the exception of Dynaflow, there were virtually no other changes in the Buick line. In fact, external appearance changed even less this year than it had between 1946 and 1947. All wheelbases remained the same; specifically, the Special was 121 inches; the Super, 124 inches; and the Roadmaster, 129 inches. The Special continued to use 6.50 x 16 tires, but the Super now used the smaller but wider 7.60 x 15s, while the Roadmasters used an even fatter 8.20 x 15 tire.

Under the hood, a few changes were made. Both the Special and the Super used the 248-cubic-inch block. But the Special's compression remained 6.3:1, which resulted in a rating of 110 horsepower at 3600 RPM; while the Super's compression was raised to 6.6:1, resulting in a horsepower rating of 115 at 3600 RPM. The Roadmaster continued to use the 320-cubic-inch engine, rated at 144 horsepower at 3600 RPM with standard transmission, or 150 horsepower with Dynaflow.

This year, Harlow Curtice moved up to General Motors as executive vice-president, thus ending another great era of Buick management. But his leaving was not without one unusual turn. In one of his last moves, he conceived for Buick designs the now famous "mouseholes" or ventiports, which on and off through the years have become a Buick hallmark. And, similar to the bombsight hood ornaments, the mouseholes also found quick public acceptance, were widely copied in dummy form by a number of accessory manufacturers, and for years appeared on a wide range of vehicles not even vaguely related to Buick.

Mr. Curtice was succeeded by Ivan Wiles, who had begun his accounting career with Marmon, then moved to Oakland, and later arrived at Buick.

The Roadmaster Sedanet, Model 76-S, followed the theme of the 2-door models in the other series and was built in fastback style. It weighed 4,065 pounds and cost $2,297 in basic form, with the two-tone paint being extra. A total of 20,649 were built. This car, owned by Mrs. H.R. Lammons of Jacksonville, Tex., was one of 17 Buicks entered in the first Carrera Panamerican Mexico, better known as the Mexican Road Race of 1950. The Buicks ranged in age from a 1938 model to eight 1950 cars, but only six of the 17 managed to complete the entire race, and only three of these were within the allocated time limit. The primary reason for Buick's poor showing was not due to its speed or handling capabilities, but to the fact that all Buick entries were driven by amateur drivers. The professional drivers, who set all of the records, were in cars other than Buick, primarily Lincolns, Cadillacs, Oldsmobiles, Packards, and Alfa Romeos.

The Buick interior, as could be expected, was virtually identical to the 1947 version, except for its trim. The window rails and top portion of the dash were now done in the same color as the body, while the lower portion was in matching color. Solid tone was used in the Specials.

Buick's overseas sales dropped substantially this year, with the exception of the Super Series, where 4,140 unassembled cars, primarily 4-door sedans, were exported. This Super, assembled in England, used right-hand drive, and auxiliary fender mirrors and fog light. It is missing the front fender chrome spear.

With Special models no longer being exported to Australia, the production of export models dropped substantially. Only 192 unassembled Special Sedanets were exported, primarily to England. One of them is seen here, virtually identical to the U.S. version except for its right-hand drive. It wears accessory fender mirrors and head light visors.

For the Australian car fancier, a tremendous event took place this year. The Holden Co., a GM subsidiary, started building Australia's first total-Australian high-production car. The 1948 Holden, seen here with much later model mag wheels, was destined to eventually become Australia's most popular car. Actually, this vehicle was designed by Buick in 1938 with the idea of being a compact U.S. Buick for the mid-1940s. W.W.II scrapped the entire project, but the design was sent to Holden, where the original plans were updated and converted for Australian needs and driving conditions. In fact, the first 12 Holdens were hand-built at Buick's plant in Flint and shipped to Australia as prototypes for testing and design modification. Today Holdens outsell Fords by two to one and Chrysler Valiants by three to one in Australia. The 1948 version was powered by an overhead valve Six, which looked suspiciously like a miniature Buick engine.

The only Buick this year to experience a substantial jump in popularity was the Super Estate Wagon, Model 59, whose production reached 7,018. Priced at $3,124, it was the only Super model to have a base price in excess of $3,000. It weighed 4,170 pounds.

The Super Sedanet continued its racy lines and fastback styling, but production slipped to 33,819 for domestic sales. At $1,987, it was the only full-size Buick priced under $2,000 this year. It weighed 3,770 pounds. This attractive example, wearing a host of Buick accessories, is owned by James McDonald of Enfield, Conn. Among the accessories are windshield visor, spotlight, dual fog lights, grille guard, headlight visors, door window visors, and chromed exhaust deflector.

Buick's most popular model continued to be the Super Sedan, Model 51, but its sales were now down to 53,447 in the U.S., plus 4,140 unassembled models shipped overseas. It now cost $2,087 and weighed 3,885 pounds. Supers continued to be 212.5 inches overall, Specials 207.5 inches.

Still one of the most attractive convertibles on the road was the Super, Model 56-C, which this year had a run of 19,017. It cost $2,518 and weighed 4,020 pounds. This fine example is owned by E. Strobtman of Galena, Ill. It wears the heavy accessory grille guard sold by Buick dealers.

The least change that Buick had ever made between annual models, since the 1934 styles were rerun in 1935, occurred this year. About the most major change was a substantial increase in the prices of all models. This is the Special Sedan, Model 41, which now cost $1,809. It weighed 3,705 pounds. Buick built 14,051, all for domestic sales, and shipped 768 unassembled overseas.

The Special Sedanet, Model 46-S, now priced at $1,735, was Buick's least expensive model. It weighed 3,635 pounds. Buick produced 11,176 for domestic sales, and shipped 192 unassembled models overseas. This mint example is owned by Jerry Sims of Kenai, Alaska. It has been issued special Alaskan license plates bearing the word "Buick" instead of the usual numbers. In the summer of 1972, Mr. Sims drove it 4,500 miles from Alaska to Flint, Mich.

1949

Absolutely beautiful. That was the most often used description of the totally new Buicks this year. And in comparison to other cars of the era, the description was quite valid. And the public responded. Buick hit a record production year of 398,482 vehicles. This was 7.7% of the total industry, and Buick remained firmly entrenched in third place.

Model year production was 409,138, which by series was: Special, 92,444; Super, 229,032; and Roadmaster, 87,662. Of this, Buick slipped to third place in the industry in the production of convertibles. It turned out 35,094 soft tops, which was 12.7% of the U.S. total. Wagon production also slipped, with the final count being 3,381 or 1.9% of the U.S. total.

Although Buick had totally beautiful cars in its Super and Roadmaster Series, it made a surprise move by not changing the styling one iota on the Special Series. Then at mid-year, the new Special was introduced, carrying 1950 styling, and for all practical purposes, being a 1950 model car.

Although the styling changed drastically, things were quiet under the hood. The Special, as could be expected, kept its old 248-cubic-inch engine, as did the Super. Both retained the horsepower ratings of 1948; but since the Super was now available with Dynaflow, the engine in these models was rated at 120 horsepower at 3600 RPM via the use of 6.9:1 compression. The Roadmaster Series used the 320-cubic-inch engine, now rated at 150 horsepower at 3600 RPM in all models, whether equipped with Dynaflow or standard transmission.

In addition to giving the cars a totally new look, the styling department came out with a real winner. This was

The big news in the automotive world this year was the Roadmaster Riviera Hardtop Coupe, Model 76-R. Buick claims that this was the first truly modern hardtop, but actually Chrysler turned out seven Town & Country hardtop models in 1946, although these were really Town & Country convertibles fitted with a non-removable steel roof. Still, with a first-year run of 4,343, and tremendous increases in production in 1950, Buick cars take credit for producing the first high-production hardtop models. The car cost $3,203 and weighed 4,420 pounds. It is seen here in its introductory trim. In late June, this side trim was changed to the sweep-spear design, and all subsequent models carried the new trim bars.

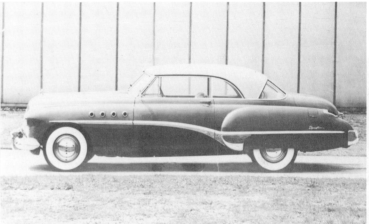

When the Roadmaster Riviera was first introduced, it featured a straight chrome bar as side trim. Then, when production really got rolling in late June, the cars started coming out with the chromed sweep-spear trim shown here. This type of trim was then carried over to the Roadmaster hardtops and station wagons in 1950. In addition, from mid-July on through the end of the 1949 model year, Roadmaster convertibles could also be decked out with the sweep spear trim as an extra cost option.

The only Buick style to have a production figure under 1,000 was the Roadmaster Estate Wagon, of which only 653 were built. At $3,734 and 4,490 pounds, it was Buick's most expensive and heaviest model. Dynaflow was standard in all Roadmasters, optional on Supers this year.

One of the few styles to suffer a setback in sales this year was the Roadmaster Convertible Coupe, Model 76-C. Production was down to 8,244, possibly because its price was up to $3,150. The car weighed 4,370 pounds. Hydraulic top mechanism, window lifts, and front seat control were standard items. From mid-July on, this model could be ordered with the Riviera sweep-spear trim as an extra cost option, though the vast majority of these cars appeared with the standard trim seen here. This beautiful example is the property of Robert L. Toll Jr. of River Forest, Ill. It took first place in its class at the 1975 meet of Buick Club of America at Flint, Mich.

The attractive Roadmaster Sedan, Model 71, experienced a run of 55,242. It cost $2,735 and weighed 4,205 pounds. All Roadmasters were 214 inches in overall length, compared with the Specials, which were 207.5 inches overall and the Supers which were 209.5 inches.

in the form of the Riviera, the first modern hardtop ever not counting the early "California" tops added to roadster and touring models of the teens and twenties. The Riviera was the first truly new body design by General Motors since the war, and its introduction had the automotive press buzzing with excitement. The high-style and immediate acceptance of these models for years gave Buick the reputation of being "the home of the hardtop." Credited with being the creator of all modern hardtops is Edward Ragsdale, who was Buick's general manufacturing manager and the man who instructed the styling studio to come up with a hard roof design for the convertible.

The cars were totally new, but with the exception of the Riviera, there was no change in the number of models available. One change that was noticeable was in the size of wheelbases and in overall length. Even though the new styling made the cars look much longer than the 1948 models, in reality all were several inches shorter. The Super Series was now on the same 121-inch wheelbase chassis that was used on the Special Series, and was only 209.5 inches overall. The Roadmaster now used a brand new chassis with a 126-inch wheelbase, and it was only 214 inches overall.

The most noticeable item on the new Buicks, and that which caused the most publicity, both pro and con, and the most jokes, was the new venti-ports on the front fenders. These ports, known as "mouseholes" and by several other names, had only a negligible functional purpose, but they did more to set Buick apart from the generalities of auto design than did any other single styling feature ever designed for that car. Between the holey Buicks and the fishtail Cadillacs of this year, General Motors made a publicity coup that lasts through today.

Using the same fastback styling as found in the Super Series was the Roadmaster Sedanet, Model 76-S. It cost $2,618, weighed 4,115 pounds, and had a run of 18,537. In addition to complete cars, Buick built 403 Roadmaster chassis-cowl units for domestic sales and shipped 240 unassembled Roadmasters overseas.

Although the Super and Roadmaster models were completely new cars, the 2-model Special Series did not change, but kept its same lines that had been in use since 1942. However, production of both models was stopped after a very short run. The Special Sedan, Model 41, had a run of only 5,940, all for domestic sales. It cost $1,861 and weighed 3,695 pounds.

Buick's lowest priced model was the short-run Special Sedanet, Model 46-S, which cost $1,787. Only 4,687 were built before the series was phased out of production. It weighed 3,625 pounds. This perfect example is owned by Robert Toll Jr. of River Forest, Ill. The Specials were the only Buicks to have a base price of under $2,000.

A record production for a single model was attained this year, when the new Super Sedan, Model 51, attained a run of 136,423. The attractive and unbelievably popular car cost $2,157 and weighed 3,853 pounds. This photo, taken about 20 years ago, shows the author practicing powerslides on a back road near the family farm in upstate New York. The car is fitted with accessory wire wheel discs, and lacks the rear fender skirts.

Buick's second most popular model was the Super Sedanet, Model 56-S, of which 66,260 were built. It continued to use the fastback styling, but with squared off quarter windows. It cost $2,059 and weighed 3,735 pounds. In addition to completed cars, Buick built four Super chassis cowl units for domestic sales and 2,388 unassembled units for export.

Not only did the Super Sedan set a record for single model production, but the Super Convertible, Model 56-C, set a record for production of a convertible style, with 22,110 being built. It cost $2,583 and weighed 3,985 pounds. All Supers were decorated with chrome side molding, stainless steel gravel deflactors, and the three now-famous portholes.

A relatively easy and stylish customizing innovation on the 1949 Buicks was the substitution of 1949 Cadillac taillights and a filling in of the rear fender trough which had held the original units. Such treatment is shown on this Super Convertible, still in use in the Los Angeles area. The car also has accessory back-up lights, but otherwise is in stock trim.

With the new body styling, the Super Estate Wagon, Model 59, did not have much room left for the wooden body. The roof was now all-steel, and the only large expanse of wood was on the tailgate. Rear windows were still of the sliding type, and the quarter windows were fixed in place. The car cost $3,178, weighed 4,100 pounds, and had a run of only 1,847.

The Buick Fireball Eight engine was now rated at 150 horsepower in all Roadmasters, and 115 horsepower in the Super and Special Series. When Dynaflow was added to the Supers, the engine was given a boost to 120 horsepower. All Buicks continued to use the side-opening hood.

All Buicks used the same dash, which was completely new and of rather unusual design. No longer did the pull knobs live on either side of the radio speaker, but were scattered in two horizontal lines under the right hand instruments. This is the interior of the new Riviera, done in a combination of leather and cloth, with a rubber and carpet floor mat. The dashboard, door sills and window edges were painted to match the body color.

The Flxible Co. of Loudonville, Ohio, greatly enhanced the lines of its ambulances and funeral cars by using the new Roadmaster chassis. Rather than bob the fenders as the company had done on previous models, the fender line was extended along with the body lines. This is the Flxible ambulance, which used built in pods above the windshield for the red flasher lights.

The new Flxible funeral service car used the same basic body as did the landau hearse, but lacked the plush trim and the rear door windows. Extending the fender line to meet the chassis extensions and the new body styles must have given Flxible's designers quite a headache at the start, but the end result was a masterpiece of design modification.

Flxible finally lowered the beltlines of its ambulance and hearse models, which ended the need for hood and cowl extensions to meet the higher bodies. This gave the vehicles a much more sleek and modern line, though with some loss of interior headroom. Shown here is the new Flxible landau hearse, of totally new design. It used somewhat unusual but attractive rear door windows, decorative landau irons, and a plush velvet interior.

1950

After producing one totally new and beautiful car in 1949, Buick wasn't content to rest upon its laurels. The 1950 models came out completely different from anything that Buick had yet produced. From the growling and somewhat ugly grille to the squared taillights and rear end treatment, this Buick was totally different from any previous Buick and totally different from anything else in the General Motors stable.

For the second consecutive year, the production record was broken, with this year's production exceeding that of 1949 by an amazing 38%. Model year production was 588,439, while calendar year production was a record 552,827, which was 8.2% of the total U.S. industry. This, of course, kept Buick in a very solid fourth place. Of the model year production, the figures by Series were: Specials, 256,514; Supers, 253,352; Roadmasters, 78,573. Of these, 66,762 were Riviera Hardtops. This represented 24.9% of the total hardtop production in the U.S., and ranked Buick second only to Chevrolet in the number of this type of car produced. In addition, 15,223 of the total were convertibles, which represented 7.4% of the total convertible market; and 2,899 were wagons, which represented only 1.9% of the total U.S. production.

Adding some confusion to the picture was the fact that the multiplication of available styles had once again begun. The Special Series was once more divided into the Special and the Special DeLuxe, with four models in the first sub-series and three, with Dynaflow option, in the DeLuxe one. The Super Series had six models, including a Riviera hardtop coupe and a Riviera Sedan, which was not a hardtop. The Roadmaster Series was also divided, with six models in the Roadmaster sub-series and three in the new Roadmaster DeLuxe sub-series.

The Roadmaster Riviera was available in the plain series as the Model 75-R or in the Deluxe version as the Model 76-R. The exterior of both cars was identical, but the Deluxe version offered power windows and seats, washable leatherette interior, and more deluxe trim. The Model 75-R had a run of 2,300, cost $2,633 and weighed 4,135 pounds. The deluxe version had a run of 8,432, cost $2,845 and weighed 4,245 pounds.

Also using the sweep-spear side chrome of the Riviera models was the mid-year edition of the Roadmaster Estate Wagon. The trim on these wagons was changed in early May, 1950, were fitted with the bar-type trim similar to that used in 1949. Designated the Model 70 and priced at $3,407, the estate wagon was Buick's most expensive car. It weighed 4,470 pounds. Only 420 were built. Also planned was the Roadmaster Deluxe Estate Wagon, Model 79-R. This car was to have cost $3,433 and would have weighed 4,430 pounds, but none were built. This nice looking example of a late production Model 79 is owned by James Kimble of Fort Wayne, Ind.

The Roadmaster Convertible, Model 76-C, used the sweep-spear side trim of the Riviera and Roadmaster Deluxe models, but was not considered part of the Deluxe sub-series. It cost $2,981 and weighed 4,345 pounds. Buick built 2,964. The interiors were again in all leather.

Using the Riviera sweep-spear chrome was the mid-year issue of the Roadmaster Deluxe Riviera Sedan. As was the case with the estate wagon, sedans built up to May, 1950, were fitted with straight bar-type side trim similar to that used in 1949. But all sedans built after May 1 used the attractive sweep-spear. The sedan cost $2,764 and weighed 4,215 pounds. The Riviera Sedan differed from the standard Roadmaster sedan in interior refinements, and in having power windows and power seats as standard equipment.

The Roadmaster Series was also divided this year, into the Roadmaster and Roadmaster Deluxe models. Appearing only in the Roadmaster line was the Touring Sedan, Model 71, which used blank quarter panels and vent windows in the rear doors. It cost $2,633 and weighed 4,135 pounds. Buick built only 6,738, with sales being taken by the new and more elaborate Roadmaster Riviera Sedan.

The Specials and Supers now shared the same 121.5 inch wheelbase, but the Supers were five inches longer overall than the Specials. The Supers measured 209.5 inches and the Specials measured 204 inches overall. Despite the totally new body lines, the Roadmaster continued to be 214 inches overall. The exceptions to these measurements were the new Riviera Sedans. In the Super Series, these cars used their own wheelbases of 125.5 inches; while in the Roadmaster Series, they had their own chassis with a 130-inch wheelbase. All Buicks now used 15-inch wheels, and Easy-Eye glass was offered for the first time.

The engines remained the same 248-cubic-inch model for the Specials and the 320-cubic-inch block for the Roadmasters. But the Specials had an increase in horse-power, going up to 115 at 3600 RPM in the standard models and 120 at 3600 RPM in the Dynaflow equipped models. The Roadmaster engine was now rated at 152 horsepower at 3600 RPM.

The Super Series received a new bored-out version of the old block, which resulted in displacement going up to 263 cubic inches. With a new bore and stroke of 3-3/16 x 4-1/8 inches, and running compression ratios of 6.9:1 and 7.2:1, the new engines were rated at 125 and 128 horsepower at 3600 RPM.

The most popular Roadmaster was the Riviera 4-door Sedan, which was available in both standard and the Deluxe versions. In plain form, the car used straight-line side chrome. It was designated the Model 72, cost $2,738, and weighed 4,220 pounds. Total production in both Deluxe and standard forms was 54,212. The Riviera Sedans used an exclusive 130-inch wheelbase and were 213 inches long overall.

The new Super models were attractive looking vehicles with all models being in the trunkback style. This is the Super Touring Sedan, Model 51, which this year featured a 3-piece rear window. It cost $2,139, weighed 3,745, and had a run of 55,672. The two-tone paint was extra. Its companion car was the 2-door Sedanet, Model 56-S, of which 10,697 were built. The Sedanet cost $2,041 and weighed 3,645 pounds.

New in the Super Series was the Riviera, Model 56-R, which surprisingly, had the highest production run of any 2-door Super model, with 56,030 being built. The hardtop concept had caught on. The car cost $2,139 and weighed 3,790 pounds. All Supers were 204 inches overall.

Appearing only in the plain Roadmaster Series was the Sedanet, Model 76-S, which was the only Roadmaster model to use Jetback styling. It cost $2,528 and weighed 4,025 pounds. Sales stopped at 2,968. All Roadmasters except the Riviera sedan were 208 inches overall.

1950

The Super Convertible, Model 56-C, cost $2,476 and weighed 3,965 pounds. Top, windows, and seat were all hydraulically operated. Buick built 12,259. In addition to this production, Buick turned out 421 Special chassis-cowl units and 1,469 Super units.

Escaping form the public's eye this year was the Super Estate Wagon, Model 59, of which only 2,480 were built. It cost $2,844 a significant reduction from its 1949 price of over $3,000. Weighing 4,115 pounds, it used seasoned natural wood for the upper body sections.

The 1-millionth post-war Buick was built on Sept. 21, 1949. It was this 1950 style Special Deluxe Sedan, Model 43-D, which sold for $1,952 and weighed 3,720 pounds. The car, shown here in the finishing area, has yet to be fitted with its side chrome trim. Buick built 14,335.

New for the year was the Super Riviera Sedan, Model 52. Contrary to what its name implied, the car was not built in hardtop styling, but was an extended and deluxe version of the standard Super Sedan, using quarter windows, its own 125.5-inch wheelbase ﬩ and being 208 inches overall. An amazingly popular car, it had a run of 114,745. It cost $2,212 and weighed 3,870 pounds.

Buick set another single model production record this year, and the car doing the setting was the Special Deluxe Touring Sedan, Model 41-D, which had a run of 141,396. The highly popular car used trunkback styling, and was available in standard shift or Dynaflow. It cost $1,983 and weighed 3,735 pounds. Shown here, in export version, is this Australian model, still in daily use. It had right-hand drive and standard transmission. The chrome bar which encircled the upper half of the grille has been removed.

The Buick chassis continued to use heavy side rails and deep bracing, making it a favorite with several builders of specialty vehicles. This year Dynaflow was standard in the Roadmaster Series, and optional in both the Super and the Special models.

The Super Deluxe Sedanet, Model 46-D, proved far more popular than its plain sister. It had a run of 76,902. In basic form it cost $1,899 and weighed 3,665. This year Buick referred to its fastback models as Jetback styles. When Dynaflow was added, the car was decorated with a rear fender signature signifying the fact.

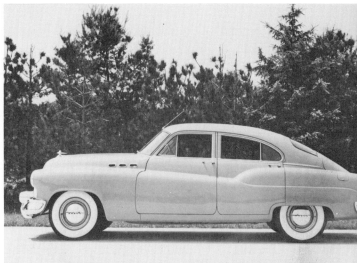

The Special Sedanet, Model 46-S, sold for $1,856 and weighed 3,655 pounds. Buick built 8,124. All Specials were 204 inches overall, and were built on a 121.5-inch wheelbase chassis.

In a surprise move, Buick returned with a 3-passenger business model. It was the Special Business Coupe, Model 46, which turned out to be the lowest priced car of the line. It cost $1,803 and weighed 3,615 pounds. Only the front seat was used, and the rear passenger area was fitted for luggage or cargo carrying. The car proved to have little sales appeal, and the style was discontinued for good after a run of only 1,062.

New for the year was the Special Touring Sedan, Model 41, built in trunkback style. It cost $1,941 and weighed 3,710 pounds. Of the 1,141 produced, many were bought by both the U.S. Army and Navy for use as staff cars.

The Buick Fireball Eight now ran compression ratios ranging from 6.6:1 to 7.2:1 and horsepowers going from 115 in the standard Special and Super models to 152 in the Roadmasters. The large ducts were part of the newly designed WeatherWarden combination vent and heater.

Not only did the new Special Series adopt the styling of all other Buick series, but the line grew into two distinct sub-series, the Special and Special Deluxe. The Special Series was devoid of any side chrome whatsoever. Its leading car was the 4-door Sedan, Model 43, in fastback style, which cost $1,909, weighed 3,715 pounds, and had a run of 13,115.

The new Riviera Sedans differed form the regular 4-door sedans in their use of exclusive wheelbases not shared by any other Buick models. The added length was used primarily in rear seat leg room, and in extending the top in order to provide better head room and to allow space for the interesting little quarter windows, which would swing out for ventilation. All Buick sedans except the Jetback models used a three-piece rear window.

One of the most unusual custom Buicks to come along in years was the El Kineno, built on a Roadmaster chassis for the King Ranch of Texas. It was designed to be used specifically as a hunting and range car. It featured such oddities as rifle racks and ammunition compartments in the front fenders, an outside rear-mounted spare, power winch, and outboard hunting seats.

Another view of the El Kineno, this one with top down, shows the two-tone natural leather interior, and the fold down windshield with special stand-up mirror. To allow for better engine cooling, the upper part of the hood was cut out and filled in with a small grille. In place of the famous Buick bombsight hood ornament, the car wears the King Ranch brand.

The dashboard arrangement was again changed this year, with instruments grouped in two units on either side of and below the centrally mounted speedometer. In this photo, the left instrument group is blocked by the steering wheel. Pull-out knobs under the radio controlled the heater. This is the Special dash, in solid color. Supers and Roadmasters used two-tone. In addition, the Specials continued to use a two-piece windshield while the other Series did not.

The new Flxible Ambulance used a body somewhat different in exterior dimensions from the hearse body. Built on Roadmaster chassis, the car used full door windows and an interesting quarter window. Rather than use a high beltline and necessitate raising the hood and cowl, Flxible used a new raised roof line in order to provide more headroom within the ambulance.

This year Buick built 539 Roadmaster chassis-cowl units for specialty builders such as the Flxible Co. of Loudonville, Ohio. This is the new Flxible Landau Hearse, which this year featured an interesting downward sweep of the fenders plus full-size windows in the rear access doors. All Flxible models used Dynaflow as standard equipment.

Buick's largest car was the Roadmaster Riviera Sedan, Model 72-R, which used its own exclusive chassis of 130.25-inch wheelbase and was 215 inches long overall. It cost $3,044 and weighed 4,240 pounds. Buick built 48,758. The interior was in velvet broadcloth available in duotone combinations or solid gray. Leatherette door panels were extra cost items.

Buick's heaviest and most expensive car continued to be the Roadmaster Estate Wagon, Model 79, which cost $3,780 and weighed 4,470 pounds. Only 679 were built. All Roadmasters except the Riviera Sedan used a 126.25-inch wheelbase chassis and were 211 inches long overall.

After two drastic change years in a row, Buick settled down this year and kept its styling fairly consistent with that of 1950.

Calendar year production reached 404,695, which while not a record, was still the second highest production year in Buick's history. This total represented 7.5% of the total U.S. production, and kept Buick firmly in its now almost traditional fourth place.

Model year production was 404,657, which by series was: Special 165,554; Super, 172,235; and Roadmaster 66,868. Of this amount, 83,929 were Riviera hardtops representing 17.5% of the U.S. hardtop production; and 2,891 or 1.5% of the total market were wagons. Convertible production reached 13,128, or 9.4% of the U.S. total once again resulting in Buick being the third largest manufacturer of convertibles in the U.S.

One major change in this year's cars, and a great improvement in the estimation of most automotive writers, was in the grille. Now a series of twenty-five stamped steel vertical bars located inside the front bumper replaced the walrus face of the previous year.

There was a slight reduction in the number of models available. The Special Series continued to be subdivided into Special and Special DeLuxe, but the Roadmaster DeLuxe sub-series was dropped. Four separate wheelbase sizes were continued, with the Special, Special DeLuxe and Supers being on a 121.5-inch base; the Super Riviera Sedan being 125.6 inches; the Roadmasters, 126 inches; and the Roadmaster Riviera Sedans being 130 inches in wheelbase length.

During the year, a third Special sub-series was considered. This was to be the Custom Special Series 44 which would have used the same general appearance theme of the Special Series, but the bodies would have been the 206-inch overall length units used on the Super Series rather than the 204-inch overall length bodies used on the Special models. Styles to be used in this line would have been a trunkback and a jetback sedan and a Riviera hardtop coupe, but the idea was dropped before production began. Still, this sub-series does appear in a few early brochures, and this creates some confusion today.

Under the hood, the Specials received a new engine. This was the 263-cubic-inch model introduced in the Super Series in 1950. Gone was the old 248-cubic-inch model. The engine was used in both the Special and Super Series, and was rated at 128 horsepower when used with Dynaflow, or 124 horsepower when used with synchromesh. The Roadmaster engine remained unchanged.

The Roadmaster Convertible, Model 76-C, weighed 4,355 pounds and cost $3,283. It had a run of 2,911. All Buicks used the same grille, made up of 25 stamped steel vertical bars. Roadmasters used four portholes while Supers and Specials used three. This attractive example of the Model 76-C is owned by Dick Boyer of Hanover, Pa.

The Roadmaster Riviera, Model 76-R, was an attractive car priced at $3,143 and weighing 4,235 pounds. Buick built 12,901. Also produced was the Riviera Model 76-MR, which used the same exterior but had a less deluxe interior and lacked the hydraulically operated windows and front seat. It cost $3,051, weighed 4,185 pounds, and drew 809 orders.

The Super Riviera, Model 56-R, is shown here in an illustration from the early catalog which shows the unusual and unused parking lights. Priced at $2,356 and weighing 3,685 pounds, the car had an admirable run of 54,512. All Supers except the Riviera Sedan were 206.2 inches in overall length.

For some reason, sales of the attractive Super Convertible, Model 56-C, dropped, with only 8,116 being built. The car cost $2,728 and weighed 3,695 pounds. Standard equipment included hydraulically operated top, windows and front seat. Bombsight hood ornament and fender portholes had by now become accepted Buick trademarks.

Buick's most popular car this year was the Super Riviera Sedan, Model 52, of which 92,886 were built. It cost $2,437 and weighed 3,845. The car used a 125.5-inch wheelbase, as compared with the regular Super wheelbase of 121.5 inches, and was 210.2 inches overall. This model, featuring the extra-cost two-tone paint, was owned by the author and is shown in front of the family farm in upstate New York. It was a substantial and trouble-free car, but due to its Dynaflow transmission, lacked much of the snap and handling characteristics of the author's 1949 Super Sedan.

The only Super to exceed $3,000 in price was the Estate Wagon, Model 59, which cost $3,133. The 4,100-pound vehicle had a run of 2,212. The car still used real wood in its body, with framing being of seasoned ash, exterior paneling being mahogany, and interior being birch.

Appearing for the last year was the Super Tourback Sedan, Model 51. This is an illustration from an early catalog, which shows the never-used fender-mounted parking lights. Priced at $2,256 and weighing 3,755 pounds, the car had a run of even 10,000.

Enjoying a popular place in the market was the Special Deluxe Sedan, Model 41-D, which was in trunkback style. Buick built 87,848. The car cost $2,185 and weighed 3,680, but the two-tone paint and white wheel discs shown here were options. All Specials had an overall length of 204.8 inches and were built on a 121.5-inch wheelbase chassis.

The Special Deluxe Sedanet, Model 48-D, cost $2,127 and weighed 3,615 pounds. A fairly popular car, it had a run of 54,311. This illustration is from an early catalog, and shows the car with unusual fender-mounted parking lights that never were produced.

Appearing for the last time was Buick's last Jetback model, the Super Sedanet, Model 56-S. It cost $2,248 and weighed 3,685 pounds. Only 1,500 were built before the car was phased out of production. The Jetback or fastback style received whirlwind acceptance immediately before and after W.W. II, but fell from public favor just about as quickly as it had been accepted.

New for the series was the Special Deluxe Riviera Coupe, a pretty little hardtop with a price of $2,225. Designated the Model 45-R, it weighed 3,645 pounds and had a run of 16,491. The two-tone paint and white wall tires were accessories. It used a three-piece rear window.

New for the series was the Special Deluxe Convertible, Model 45-C. Despite its price of $2,561, the car had a run of only 2,099. It weighed 3,830 pounds. Even though it was classed as Buick's economy model, the car featured hydraulically controlled windows, top, and front seat. In addition to regular production, Buick produced 1,106 Special chassis-cowl units this year.

This car, spotted in Orlando, Florida by William Hill of Marshalltown, Ia., poses a real problem. The car is the Special 3-passenger Business Coupe, Model 46. The car appears in the early Buick catalogs, but not in the later literature. In addition, Buick's records give no indication that any of these cars were ever built—in fact, the records seem to show that this model was never put into production, but was strictly a drawing board model. Yet, there it is. Another car falling into the same class was the Special Sedanet, Model 48, which would have used the body of the Special DeLuxe Model 48-D. This car too appears in the early-lead catalogs, but there is no indication that any were ever built.

Although the Special DeLuxe line used a one-piece windshield, the super-economy Special sub-series used the split windshield in both 1951 and 1952. This windshield shows quite prominently on the remains of this U.S. Air Force staff car, a Special Model 41. In civilian dress, the car was priced at $2,139 and weighed 3,605 pounds. However, only 999 were built, and virtually all of these were bought by the U.S. government for various military and government motor pools. These cars had no side trim, except for the flaring stone guard on the rear fenders.

Only three models were produced in the Special sub-series. They were this 2-door Sport Coupe, Model 46-S; a 4-door sedan, and a very low production business coupe. The Model 46-S had a run of only 2,700. It weighed 3,600 pounds. The car was Buick's lowest priced model, but its base cost of $2,046, marked the first time that there were no Buicks priced under $2,000. This illustration comes from an interesting first run catalog, which shows all of the cars with attractive fender-mounted parking lights. However, a style change was made after the catalogs were distributed, and the attractive lights never materialized. Although most of the catalogs were recalled, a few escaped and still remain in private collections.

Proposed but never produced was the Special Custom Series. This series would have used the standard Special engine and 121.5-inch wheelbase chassis, but would have been equipped with the Super body shells, having an overall length of 206.2 inches. Planned body styles were this 4-door Sedan, shown here from an early catalog, a Riviera Coupe, and a Jetback Sedanet.

The Buick dashboard again was changed slightly, and now used three dial faces of identical size. The far left one contained gas, oil, heat and ammeter gauges; the center one, adjacent to the radio, was the speedometer; and the one on the far right was the clock, a fairly common option. All pull-knobs once again were in vertical lines on either side of the radio speaker. This is the Special Deluxe dash, with standard transmission. An attractive two-tone paint job was used. The Special sub-series continued to use a two-piece split windshield, while all other models, including the Special Deluxe, used the one-piece style shown here. Steering wheels were now available in black, beige, dark blue or dark green plastic.

The Buick chassis remained a rugged, X-braced piece of engineering, with relatively low center of gravity and rigid torque tube drive. In addition to the Special units, Buick built 3,009 Super chassis-cowl units and 810 such units in the Roadmaster Series.

1951

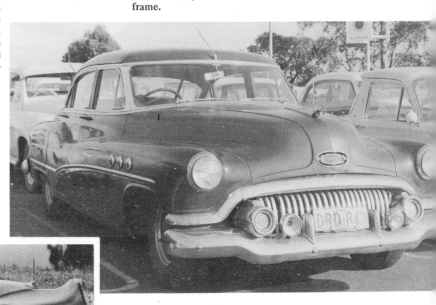

The Flxible Co. of Loudonville, Ohio, was one of several specialty builders who favored the strong Buick chassis for their bodies. The company built on both extended Super and Roadmaster chassis, and built into these bodies a long flowing fender line that matched in perfectly with Buick's own design. This is the Flxible Landau Hearse, in this case built on a Super chassis, but also available on the Roadmaster frame.

The Flxible Ambulance was available on both the Super and Roadmaster chassis, but most often was built on the more powerful Roadmaster. The attractive car was available in either plain form, as seen here, or with red flashers and siren built into roof pods over the windshield. All Flxible ambulances and funeral vehicles were equipped with Dynaflow.

Despite the fact that the all-Australian Holden was gaining rapidly in sales in that country, Buick still found a market for its own cars there. One example, still in daily use in New South Wales, is this Super Riviera Sedan. Except for the right-hand drive conversion, it is identical to the U.S. version.

Buick finally retired its famous Y-Job this year, and constructed two experimental and show cars to take its place. One was the LeSabre, which would give its name to a full series in 1959. The car was built on a 115-inch wheelbase chassis and was 200.8 inches overall. Its 2-passenger body was built entirely of aluminum and magnesium. It was powered by a supercharged experimental V-8 engine of 215 cubic inches which developed 335 horsepower. Surprisingly few of its styling innovations ever appeared in actual production.

Buick's second experimental and show car this year was the XP-300. It too was a 2-passenger model with the body making heavy use of magnesium and aluminum. It was powered by the same type of experimental V-8 as used on the LeSabre. This engine had a square bore and stroke of 3.25 inches, displaced 216 cubic inches, and developed 335 horsepower at 5500 RPM. The car was built on a 116-inch wheelbase chassis and was equipped with Dynaflow. Several of its styling features appeared in modified form on later production models.

Calendar year production dropped to 321,048 due to three primary factors — a crippling steel strike during the year, restricted quotas imposed by National Production Administration, and a lengthy factory shut down to allow changeover to the completely different cars that would appear in 1953. Still, the calendar year production of 321,048 was 7.4% of the industry, and allowed Buick to keep its firm fourth place ranking.

Model year production was 303,745, which by series ran; Special 120,898; Super, 136,404; and Roadmaster, 46,443. Of this, Buick produced 93,492 Riviera hardtops, and thus became America's largest builder of this style car. Also produced were 10,627 convertibles, which continued its third place ranking as a builder of soft tops. As before, wagon production appeared to be little more than an afterthought, with only 2,135 being built. Of interest is the fact that 274,259 Dynaflow units were built this year, and 85% of all Buicks now carried this option. Offered for the first time this year were power steering and airpower carburetion. The power steering caught on; the fancy carburetion did not.

All dimensions remained the same this year, as styling changed very little. The Specials and Supers continued to be on the 121.5-inch wheelbase chassis, with the Specials being 204.8 inches overall and the Supers, 206 inches overall. The Super Riviera Sedan continued to have its own 125.5-inch wheelbase and was 210 inches overall.

Roadmasters used a 126.5-inch wheelbase chassis and were 215 inches overall, while the Roadmaster Riviera Sedan had its own 130.25-inch wheelbase chassis and was 215 inches overall.

Both the Specials and Supers continued to use the 263-cubic-inch engine, rated at 120 horsepower in the Special and 124 horsepower in the Super when equipped with synchromesh. When equipped with Dynaflow, both cars used the 128 horsepower version of this engine. The Roadmaster continued to use the 320-cubic-inch block, now rated at 170 horsepower at 3800 RPM with its new compression ratio of 7.5:1 and its new 4-barrel carburetor and redesigned manifold.

Buick's high-style leader, but one that still was not coming up to anticipated sales, was the Roadmaster Riviera, Model 76-R. Production rested at 11,387. It cost $3,306 and weighed 4,235 pounds. Standard equipment included hydraulically controlled windows and seat.

As could be expected, the most popular Roadmaster style was the Riviera Sedan, Model 72, which had a run of 32,069. It cost $3,200 and weighed 4,285 pounds. The car used its own exclusive chassis of 130.25-inch wheelbase and was 215 inches overall. The window frames and centerpost were chrome plated.

Buick's heaviest and most expensive model continued to be the Roadmaster Estate Wagon, Model 79, which now cost $3,977 and weighed 4,505 pounds. Only 359 were built. In addition to the Special chassis listed, Buick also turned out a total of 1,071 Super chassis and chassis-cowl units in various forms, and 226 such units in the Roadmaster Series.

The attractive Roadmaster Convertible, Model 76-C, had a run of only 2,402 this year. It cost $3,453 and weighed 4,395 pounds. Dynaflow continued to be standard on all Roadmasters. All Roadmasters, except the Riviera Sedan, were built on a 126.25-inch wheelbase chassis and were 211 inches in overall length.

Buick's most popular car again was the Super Riviera Sedan, Model 52, which this year had a run of 71,387. It cost $2,563 and weighed 3,825 pounds. It was built on its own 125.5-inch wheelbase chassis and was 210.2 inches in overall length. This beautiful example, wearing the extra cost chrome wheel discs, is owned by Richard Czaho of Cleveland, Ohio.

A definitely attractive and popular car was the Super Riviera Coupe, Model 56-R, which had a run of 55,400. It cost $2,478 and weighed 3,775 pounds. This year's primary style feature was the sweep spear which started over the front wheel cutout and swept down to form a gravel deflector just forward of the rear wheel cutout. Series identification appeared on the rear fender.

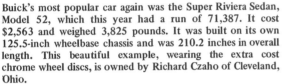

Still drawing only disappointing sales was the Super Estate Wagon, Model 59. Only 1,641 were built this year. Costing $3,296 and weighing 4,105 pounds, the cars still made heavy use of natual mahogany, ash, and birch in their bodies.

Production of all convertible models slipped this year, and the Super Convertible, Model 56-C, was no exception. Only 6,904 were built. The car cost $2,869 and weighed 3,970 pounds. All Supers except the Riviera Sedan were built on the 121.5-inch wheelbase and were 206 inches long.

Although the exterior styling didn't change too much, the dashboard arrangement was given a totally different look, with the speedometer now located in a central pod directly in front of the steering wheel, and the other gauges grouped in two dial faces flanking the speedometer. All pull-knobs continued to live in vertical lines on either side of the radio speaker grille.

The Special Deluxe Sedan, Model 41-D, could be quickly identified from the Standard Special model by its long lower chrome bar running the length of the rocker panel. It was the most popular car in the entire Special Series, with a production run of 63,346. It cost $2,255 and weighed 3,655 pounds.

The Special Deluxe Riviera Coupe, Model 45-R, was popular both in the U.S. and in Australia, where this excellent original model was seen recently in a used car lot in New South Wales. The U.S. version cost $2,295 and weighed 3,655 pounds. A total of 21,180 were built. The Australian model uses right-hand drive and is fitted with non-Buick accessory wheel discs and interesting grilled gravel deflectors over the headlights.

The Special Deluxe Convertible, Model 46-C, proved to have very little sales appeal this year, and only 600 were built. It cost $2,634 and weighed 3,850 pounds. All Specials were 204.8 inches in overall length and used the 121.5-inch wheelbase chassis. In addition to completed models, a total of 744 Special chassis and chassis-cowl units were produced.

The Special 2-door Sedan was supposed to be available in both the Special and the Special Deluxe sub-series, but none were built in the plain Special version. The Special Deluxe version, designated the Model 48-D, cost $2,197 and weighed 3,620 pounds. Buick built 32,684.

The Special Series was again divided into two sub-series, the Special and the Special Deluxe. However, the Special sub-series, sometimes called the Standard Special, was phased out after only a few months. Actually, there was very little difference this year between the two sub-series, and on the exterior both were identical except that the Deluxe models had a one-piece windshield like the other Buicks, while the Standard Specials continued to use the old two-piece split windshield. Also, the Deluxe models had a chrome molding running the length of the rocker panels, while the Standard models did not. The Standard Special Sedan, Model 41, in plain form sold for $2,209 and weighed 3,650 pounds. Only 137 were built before the style was phased out for good. This car, from a Buick catalog, shows the car with the optional extra-cost wheel covers. In standard form it would have used plain, rather ugly, hub caps.

The only model in the Special sub-series that did not appear in the Special Deluxe sub-series was the Tourback Coupe or Sport Coupe, Model 46-S. It cost $2,115 and weighed 3,605 pounds. Only 2,206 were built before the car was phased out of production. It differed from the 2-door sedan in that it used slightly different rear roof and quarter panel styling. It was also listed as being available as a 3-passenger Business Coupe, Model 46, but none were built in that style.

The Flxible Landau Hearse was usually mounted on a Roadmaster chassis, but was also available on extended Super chassis, as seen here. The car was fitted with a sliding glass partition between compartments, used wide full-windowed rear doors, and decorative landau irons.

The Flxible Co., long a believer in Buick, continued to turn out an attractive and well made series of funeral vehicles and ambulances on Buick chassis. This is the Funeral Service Car, shown here on an extended Roadmaster chassis, but also available on the Super frame. The car is of the 5-door type, with access to the rear compartment through either of the side rear doors or the wide back door.

The Buick Fireball Eight continued to be an excellent and long-lived workhorse, known for its dependability. This year the engine was produced in 120, 124, and 128 horsepower versions for the Special and Super Series, and 170 horsepower for the Roadmaster Series. In the Roadmaster version, it displaced 320 cubic inches and used a compression ratio of 7.5:1.

Flxible's Combination Car was a relatively handy vehicle that could be converted for either hearse or ambulance work. It is shown here in hearse form on an extended Roadmaster chassis. The drapes and casket carrier were removable, and an ambulance interior could be fitted.

The interior of the Roadmaster Riviera Sedan was finished in attractive duo-tone broadcloth upholstery and a two-tone dashboard. Armrests were provided on all four doors, and rear seat passengers had a center armrest.

The Flxible Ambulance was usually built on an extended Roadmaster chassis, but was also available on Super chassis, as seen here. Buyers had a choice of a plain top or one fitted with pods for red flashers and siren. Windows could be plain, designed, or frosted glass.

The big news this year was Buick's fiftieth anniversary model, which was a completely new car sporting a completely new V-8 in both the Super and Roadmaster models. The engine was not only a new innovation for Buick, but it sported a 8.5 compression ratio, which was the highest in the industry this year.

Calendar year production reached up to a beautiful 485,353, which was the second highest in Buick's history keeping the make in a firm and virtual traditional fourth place in the industry. This figure represented 7.9% of the total industry, and was a full 50% greater than the 1952 production.

Model year production was 488,755 of which 217,624 were in the Special Series; 191,894 were in the Super Series; and 79,237 were in the Roadmaster Series. Of this total, 172,000 were hardtop models; 15,500 were convertibles; and 2,500 were wagons. Dynaflow was used in 388,086 vehicles or 80% of all Buicks made this year.

In addition, as a way of celebrating its fiftieth year, Buick this year built its 7-millionth car on June 13, and for the first time, attained 8.5% of all the new car registrations in the U.S.

Even though the Special still used the old Straight 8, the new V-8 was used in 270,675 cars, which was 55% of all production. Actually, this engine represented only the fourth major change in engine design in Buick's entire history, and was the first radical engine innovation since the introduction of the first Straight 8 in 1931.

The new engine used a bore and stroke of 4 x 3.2 inches, displaced 322 cubic inches, and developed 164 horsepower at 400 RPM with a 2-barrel carburetor in the Super with synchromesh, 170 horsepower at 400 RPM with Dynaflow, and 188 horsepower at 3000 RPM in the Roadmaster, when using the 4-barrel carburetor.

But not only were a new engine and new styling enough to celebrate the Golden anniversary, but Buick also came up with a totally new limited production car. This was the Skylark, a beautiful $5,000 sports-type convertible which drew the attention of the entire automotive world. In a sense, the car was a harbinger of the wide variety of luxury-sport type of cars that would be turned out by all manufacturers during the next twenty years.

The Specials continued to use a new and improved version of the Fireball Straight 8, still displacing 263 cubic inches, but now rated at 130 horsepower. Both Specials and Supers continued to use their former 121.5-inch wheelbase chassis, with the Super Riviera continuing to have its own exclusive chassis of 125.5-inch wheelbase. However, the Specials grew one inch to a new overall length of 205.8 inches, while the Supers grew over an inch to a new overall length of 207.6 inches, and 211.6 inches for the Riviera sedan.

In a surprise move, the Roadmasters now used the same wheelbase chassis as did the Specials and Supers, while the Roadmaster Riviera sedan used the same wheelbase as the Super model. In addition, the Roadmasters now shared the basic bodies with the Supers, and thus the lengths were the same.

Buick celebrated its 50th anniversary in grand style, by introducing one of its all-time great cars. This, of course, was the very limited production Skylark, which cost a flat $5,000, and had a run of only 1,690. It weighed 4,315 pounds, and was the only Buick not to use the venti-ports on the fender. This perfect example is owned by Len Peterson of Wilton, N.H.

Even with its top raised, the new Skylark was a beautiful vehicle. Wisely, Buick did not call the car a "sports car," which it was not, but simply referred to it as a sport convertible. The wheels each had 40 individually set chromed spokes. Standard equipment included the 188 horsepower engine, Dynaflow, power brakes and steering, easy-eye tinted glass, the Selectronic radio with powered antenna, and white wall tires. This fine example is owned by Jim Krause of Cincinnati, Ohio.

For the first time, the Roadmaster Series shared its chassis with the Super Series. This is the new Roadmaster Riviera, which cost $3,358 and weighed 4,215 pounds. Buick built a total of 22,927. Dynaflow, standard in the Roadmaster, was now installed in 80% of all Buicks built.

Buick's big news in the engineering department was its V-8 engine, the first it had ever built. The new block used overhead valve design, with the pistons at a 90-degree V. It used a bore and stroke of 4 x 3.2 inches and displaced 322 cubic inches. In the Roadmaster Series it used an 8.5:1 compression ratio, while an 8:1 ratio was used in the Super models.

As could be expected, the most popular Roadmaster was the Riviera Sedan, Model 72-R, of which 50,523 were built. It cost $3,254 and weighed 4,100 pounds. All Buick used the sweep-spear side trim, but only the Roadmasters used the chrome rear trim between the spear and bumper.

The Roadmaster Convertible, Model 76-C, was priced at $3,506 and weighed 4,250 pounds. A total of 3,318 were built. Both the Supers and Roadmasters used the new 50th anniversary V-8 of 263 cubic inches, but the Super version was rated at 164 and 170 horsepower, while the Roadmaster version was 188 horsepower. The bottom portion of the front bumper was an air scoop.

The only Buick, with the exception of the Skylark, to be priced over $4,000 was the Roadmaster Estate Wagon, Model 79-R, which has a base price of $4,031. It weighed 4,315 pounds. Only 670 were built. This was the last Estate Wagon to use natural wood in its body. As of the 1954 models, the wagons would have all-metal bodies. This beautiful example is fitted with the very expensive chromed wire wheels and knock-off hubs built for the Skylarks, but available on all models. It was owned by Michael Baker of Flint, Mich.

The second most popular car in Buick's total line was the Super Riviera Coupe, Model 56-R, which had a run of 91,298. It cost $2,611 and weighed 3,845 pounds. This model is shown with the very pretty accessory wire wheel covers which Buick issued specially for its 50th anniversary. This year, Buick air conditioning was available on all Super and Roadmaster models except the convertibles and estate wagons. All Supers and Roadmasters also shared the same dimensions, being 207.6 inches overall except for the Riviera Sedans, which were 211.6 inches overall.

Surprisingly, the Super Riviera Sedan, Model 52, slipped from first place to third place in total sales and production. Buick built 90,685, which placed the car behind the Special Sedan and the Super Riviera Coupe. It cost $2,696 and weighed 3,905 pounds. It shared its 125.5-inch wheelbase chassis and 211.6-inch overall length body only with the Roadmaster Riviera Sedan. This perfect example is owned by Robert Carter of Maryville, Tenn.

Appearing in the Super Series for the last time this year was the Estate Wagon, Model 59. The 6-passenger car, shown here with the optional wire wheel covers, cost $3,430 and weighed 4,150 pounds. Production was 1,830. Natural wood was still used throughout the body.

The Super Convertible, Model 56-C, continued to be a very good looking car, especially when equipped with the accessory wire wheel covers. It cost $3,002 in basic form, and weighed 4,035 pounds. Production was 6,701. In addition to completed cars, Buick produced a total of 1,380 Super chassis and chassis-cowl units this year, and 109 Roadmaster units.

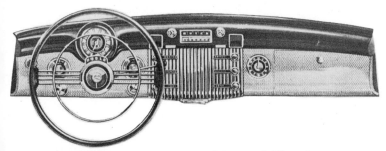

The 50th anniversary dash was one of the most brilliant that Buick had yet designed, with the top portion being in matching color to the body and the lower part being in machined stainless steel. The same basic instrument and clock grouping was used as had been used in the previous year, but the dials were easier to read. Buick still mounted all pull-knobs in vertical rows on either side of the centrally mounted radio speaker grille.

Buick used all-wood bodies in its wagons for the last time this year, but even at that, the amount of wood used was a far cry from that used a few years earlier. The framing was done in seasoned northern ash, with the small panels being in mahogany. The tailgate panel was birch with metal runners. The carpeting was Roxpoint nylon, while the seats were leather.

The new Special Riviera Coupe, Model 45-R, cost $2,295 and weighed 3,705. It had a run of 58,780, which is surprising when it is considered that the car was available only with the straight eight engine. The assumption would be that buyers of a sporty car of this type would have been more inclined to buy the Super or Roadmaster models with their new V-8 engines.

After one relatively slow year, Buick's production shot upwards at an amazing rate. The most popular model in the entire line this year was the totally new Special 4-door Sedan, Model 41-D, which had a run of 100,312. It cost $2,255 and weighed 3,710 pounds.

Buick's lowest priced model was the Special 2-door Sedan, Model 48-D, which cost $2,197 and weighed 3,675 pounds. Buick built 53,796. A redesigned version of the old Fireball Straight Eight was used in all Specials. In addition to completed models, Buick built 504 Special chassis-cowl units. All Specials were 205.8 inches overall, and used a chassis with a wheelbase of 121.5 inches.

After one year of very poor sales, the Special Convertible, Model 46-C, this year had a quite respectable run of 4,282. In standard form it cost $2,553 and weighed 3,815 pounds. This model is wearing the very pretty and rather expensive optional Skylark wire wheel covers.

The interior of the new Wildcat show and experimental car displays a dashboard not too unlike that found on later model Buicks. The body was white fiberglass, with the interior being in green trim with matching green leather upholstery and green nylon carpeting.

Buick's new show and experimental car was the Wildcat, which like the earlier LeSabre, would also lend its name to a full series in later years. The car used a fiberglass body and reportedly was built primarily to test the use of fiberglass for possible future production bodies. Its interior was in green leather. The car was powered by a 188 horsepower version of the new V-8 engine and used the new Twin Turbine Dynaflow. An interesting feature was its front wheel discs with built-in air scoops. The discs remained stationary while the wheels revolved around them. Air scoops were also built into the hood and the front fender tops.

This year's Buicks were roomier, had Panoramic windshields, airplane-type dash indicators, new fenders, and new bumpers and trim. So much for the standard models. But the big news was a new line — the Century Series had returned. And, added to this, there was a V-8 available in every series, and the old Straight 8 was gone for good.

Calendar year production came close to breaking the record, but did not quite make it — still 531,463 Buicks rolled off the line during 1954, and this was 9.6% of the industry. This production resulted in a startling and unexpected move. Buick moved from its fourth place niche and bumped Plymouth out of its third place role in the industry. Plymouth had held third place since 1931, and with the exception of 1946, Buick had been in fourth place since 1938.

Model year production was 444,609, which by series was: Special, 191,484; the new Century, 81,983; Super, 119,375; and Roadmaster, 51,767. Of the above, there was a tremendous growth in hardtop production, with 260,608 being built. In addition, Buick built 19,718 convertibles, and increased its wagon production to 4,000. The hardtop move, though, was hailed as an industry mark, as Buick became the first auto maker to build more than a half-million of this style car.

The new Century followed Buick's prewar philosophy of stuffing a lot of engine into a relatively light car, and really creating a road burner. But unlike the prewar Century Series, the 1954 version was fitted between the Special and Super Series rather than between the Super and Roadmaster Series. Basically, the new Century was the Special chassis, fitted with the Roadmaster engine — and that meant a lot of go.

Again Buick contented itself with only two basic wheelbases, but these were both brand new and were shifted around a bit. Now the separate wheelbases and body sizes that had been used for the Riviera Sedans were gone, and these cars now used the same basic chassis and bodies as were used on other models. The Special and Century models, and the limited edition Skylark, all used a new 122-inch wheelbase chassis, and all were 206 inches overall. The Super and Roadmaster models used a new 127-inch wheelbase chassis and were all 216.8 inches overall.

New for the year, the Special's little V-8 drew much interest. This block had a bore and stroke of 3.65 x 3.2 inches and displaced 264 cubic inches. It developed 143 or 150 horsepower at 4200 RPM, depending on whether or not Dynaflow was used. The higher horsepower engine ran an 8:1 compression ratio, while the lower used a 7.2:1 ratio.

All other models used the 322-cubic-inch block, but with varying horsepowers. In the Super Series, the engine developed 177 or 182 horsepower at 4100 RPM; while in the speedy Century Series, the engine was rated at 195 horsepower with synchromesh. Dynaflow equipped Centurys and all Roadmasters used the largest version of this engine, rated at 200 horsepower at 4100 RPM.

In the engineering department, new steering linkage and newly designed power steering units gave the car substantially improved handling characteristics. At Flint, the Dynaflow plant was expanded to produce 500 units a day, and total Dynaflow production for the year reached 479,802 units. On May 3, the 2-millionth Dynaflow was produced.

The new Skylark, Model 100, used totally new styling that either was or was not an improvement over the 1953 model, depending on personal taste. Appearing for the last time this year, the car had its price reduced to $4,355. It weighed 4,260 pounds and used the Special's 122-inch wheelbase. It was 206.3 inches overall. Only 836 were built. This perfect example is owned by Kermit Svendsen of Mendota, Ill.

Shown with its top up is the Skylark, which used highly modified styling, including the unusual wheel openings which, by optical illusion, made the beautiful chrome spoke wheels look too small. Totally new rear treatment was used, with the trunk deck sloping quite sharply and large chrome taillight pods being set upon the trailing edges of the rear fenders. This original version is owned by John Roth of Chicago, Ill.

1954

The Roadmaster Riviera Coupe, Model 76-R, was a nice looking car but had only one-third the sales of the Super version. Production was 20,404, with the difference probably caused by the Roadmaster's $3,373 base price. It weighed 4,215 pounds. The car is shown here with the standard wheel discs.

The Roadmaster Riviera Sedan, Model 72-R, had its appearance greatly enhanced by the accessory Skylark wheels, but it is doubtful if very many sedans were turned out with these sporty wheels. The car cost $3,269, weighed 4,250 pounds, and had a run of 26,862. Dynaflow was standard.

Buick's most expensive full-size car this year, not counting the Skylark, was the Roadmaster Convertible, Model 76-C, which cost $3,521. With the discontinuance of the Roadmaster Estate Wagon, there were no regular production Buicks with a base price in the $4,000 range. The 4,355-pound convertible had a run of 3,305. Buick claimed that the new panoramic windshield provided 19% better visibility than was found in the 1953 models.

Buick's most popular car this year turned out to be the Super Riviera Coupe, Model 56-R, of which 73,531 were built. It cost $2,626 and weighed 4,035 pounds. All Super and Roadmaster models were 216 inches long overall, and were 80 inches wide. The Skylark wire spoke wheels were a seldom seen and expensive accesory. Each wheel had 40 individually set chrome spokes.

Making good use of its new panoramic windshield was the Super Convertible, Model 56-C. It cost $2,964 and weighed 4,145 pounds. Buick built 3,343. In addition to completed cars, Buick also produced 600 Special chassis-cowl units, one such Century unit, 745 Super units, and 360 Roadmaster units.

The Super Riviera Sedan no longer had its exclusive wheelbase, but now used the 127-inch wheelbase chassis shared by all other Super and Roadmaster models. Designated the Model 52, the car weighed 4,105 pounds and cost $2,711. It had a run of 41,756.

The new Century Convertible, Model 66-C, lacked nothing but buyers. Only 2,790 were sold. The car cost $2,962 and weighed 3,950 pounds. Century models were available with standard transmission or Dynaflow, but the vast majority of buyers chose the automatic transmission.

Buick termed the new Century Series the "highest powered cars in the price range," and in fact, the cars were pretty hard to beat with anything in any price range. Most popular of the Century styles was the Riviera Hardtop Coupe, Model 66-R, which had a run of 45,710. It cost $2,534 and weighed 3,796 pounds. After years of fender skirts and half hidden rear wheels, Buick's new fully exposed rear wheels were an attractive styling innovation.

The Special interior used a different dash than did the other series, in that its speedometer occupied the circular dial on the right of the wheel, while the other instruments were clustered into the left face. The center panel was in cream, the others in body color.

A totally new car in a totally new series was the Century Estate Wagon, Model 69. The all-steel 6-passenger vehicle cost $3,470 and weighed 3,975 pounds. The very attractive and very expensive Skylark wire wheels on this model were a seldom seen accessory. Only 1,563 Century wagons were built this year. The rear quarter windows still could not be opened.

Returning after an absence of 12 years was the Century Series, which used the same chassis and basic body as did the Special Series. However, the car used a 195 or 200 horsepower engine of 322 cubic inches, making it one of the fastest cars on the road this year. This is the 4-door Sedan, Model 61, which cost $2,520 and weighed 3,805 pounds. It had a run of 31,919.

The Super dash was a bit less pretentious than the Road-master version, though the difference was in trim only. The center band was in sprayed silver. Twin ashtrays were used, but the cigarette lighter, located just below the right ashtray, seemed to be stuck there as an afterthought.

The Special Convertible, Model 46-C, was a pretty little car that attracted 6,135 buyers. It cost $2,563 and weighed 3,810 pounds. All Special and Century models used the same 122-inch wheelbase chassis and were 206.3 inches in overall length and 76.8 inches wide.

The Special 2-door Sedan, Model 48-D, continued to be Buick's lowest priced and lightest model. It cost $2,207 and weighed 3,690 pounds. Possibly due to price alone it was a fairly popular car, with production standing at 41,557. This year all Specials used a new V-8 of 264 cubic inches that developed 143 or 150 horsepower.

Buick's second most popular car this year was the Special Riviera Coupe, Model 46-R, of which 71,186 were built. It cost $2,305 and weighed 3,740 pounds. Among the conveniences found as standard equipment in the Specials were cigarette lighter, directional signals, key light, front and rear bumper guards, trip mileage meter, map light, armrests, and twin sun shades.

Buick's most popular car had been the Special 4-door Sedan, Model 41-D, but this year its production slipped down to 70,356 and it wound up in third place on the popularity scale. It cost $2,265 and weighed 3,735 pounds. All Buicks this year, except the Estate Wagons and the Skylark, used the same basic styling of 1953, but with a few refinements in trim.

New for the Special Series was the all-steel Estate Wagon, Model 49. Its base price of $3,163 marked the first time that a Special model had ever been priced over $3,000. The car was available in 6-passenger form only. It weighed 3,905 pounds and had a run of only 1,650.

1954

Buick's latest show and experimental car was the Wildcat II, a cute little sports car with flying front fenders and rear treatment not unlike the current Skylark. Built on a 100-inch wheelbase chassis, the car used a fiberglass body painted in dark tan with a two-tone tan leather interior. The car was only 170 inches long and 35 inches high at the cowl. It used the standard 322-cubic-inch V-8 boosted to 220 horsepower through the use of four carburetors. Dual spotlights were mounted on the doors.

With the new V-8 tucked inside, the engine room of the new Buicks was getting a bit crowded. This is the Super model, with the 322-cubic-inch block. Buick still used the long thin battery design that it had used since the late 1930s.

From the front the new Wildcat II show and experimental car had a grille hinting more of Oldsmobile than of Buick. The flying wing fenders were lined with large chrome panels containing air scoop louvers, and holding the very small headlight pods. Skylark wire wheels were used, and the hood contained the famous Buick ventiports.

The interior of the Roadmaster Riviera Coupe was definitely on the bright side, with upholstery forming large inverted V-patterns in matching color and texture, and chrome headliner bands running from frame to frame. The dash was completely new, and featured four airplane type dials set under a wide-bar speedometer. Pull-knobs were now of the airplane throttle type, set to the right of the steering wheel. The upper and lower portions of the dash were in body color, while the center band was of highly polished, engine-turned stainless steel.

A beautiful show car this year was the Buick Landau. It was built by the GM styling staff on a Roadmaster chassis, and followed the style of the beautiful classic landaus of the 1930s. The rear compartment was in beige leather with mutton carpeting. The chauffeur's compartment was in blue leather, and was sealed off by an electric division window. The padded trunk was closed by leather straps, and the spare lived in a compartment behind the swing-down rear bumper. The rear seat armrest contained a cocktail set and shaker. Windows were electrically operated while the landau top was hydraulically operated. The car still exists today, but the owner requested that his name be withheld.

All Buicks this year used very attractive, if not somewhat heavy, taillight and back-up light combinations, which blended in quite nicely with the attractive squared-off trunk deck. This is the Roadmaster Riviera Coupe, Model 76-R. It cost $3,453 and weighed 4,270 pounds. Buick built 28,071. This perfect example is owned by Gary Klecka of Riverside, Ill.

The Roadmaster Series had the only models which used large chrome gravel shields between the rear wheel well and the back bumper. The most popular Roadmaster style was the 4-door Sedan, Model 72-R, of which 31,719 were produced. It cost $3,349 and weighed 4,300 pounds. Both Super and Roadmaster closed models used rain visors over all doors.

Buick's most expensive and heaviest car was the Roadmaster Convertible, Model 76-C, which cost $3,552 and weighed 4,415 pounds. Production moved up to 4,739. Standard equipment on the Roadmasters included Dynaflow, power steering, back-up lights, windshield washer, non-glare rear-view mirror, parking brake warning light, and custom wheel covers.

This was Buick's year for the world of numbers. Annual production shot up to an all time record of 781,29 vehicles, well entrenching Buick in its new third plac position. In addition, on April 5th, Buick produced it 8-millionth car and the 3.5-millionth since World War I Then, on August 3, it produced its one-millionth hardtop and coupled to this was the one-millionth V-8 mark set o March 16.

Model year production was 738,814. By series, this ran Special, 381,946; Century, 158,796; Super, 133,208; an Roadmaster, 64,864. Of the total, 350,116 of these wer 2-door hardtops; 173,527 were the new and revolutionar 4-door hardtops; 24,898 were convertibles, and 9,801 wer wagons.

Buick's big news car of the year was its new Rivier 4-door, which for the first time was a true hardtop Coupled to this was a great refinement or improvement i styling, and a tremendous increase in interior and exterio color options, with almost 200 different color com binations being available this year.

The Specials and Century models continued to use th 122-inch wheelbase chassis, and were 207 inches overal The Supers and Roadmasters used the 127-inch wheelbas chassis and were 216 inches overall.

In a rather unusual move, Buick cut back on engin options, and used only two redesigned blocks with n options. The Specials used the improved 264-cubic-inc model, now rated at 188 horsepower at 4800 RPM, whi all other models used the 322-cubic-inch model, now rate at 236 horsepower at 4600 RPM. All engines feature newly designed cams, ported manifolds and larger 4-barr carburetors. Compression was 9:1 on the big block, an 8.4:1 on the Specials.

The big engineering news this year was the variable pitc Dynaflow that did away with much of the sluggishnes that had been a plague of Dynaflow since 1948. The ne unit featured movable stator blades which changed pitch the throttle was depressed quickly. This produced muc faster starts and a much quicker passing range without lot of complicated gear changing. Tests now ranke acceleration from stop to 60 in 11.2 seconds, and passin pickup, from 50 to 80 at 10.5 seconds. The top speed o the Century was a true 110, while all other models woul hit and hold a true 105 MPH.

When better automobiles are built Buick will build them

Surprisingly, the Super Series did not receive a hardtop sedan, and therefore its only 4-door was the Model 52, with centerposts. Still, the car had a run of 43,280, which was far from minimal. It cost $2,876 and weighed 4,140 pounds. All Supers and Roadmasters were 216 inches in overall length, were 80 inches wide, and used a 127-inch wheelbase chassis.

As could be expected, the Riviera Hardtop Coupe, Model 56-R, was the most popular car in the Super Series, with 85,656 being built. It cost $2,831 and weighed 4,075 pounds. In addition to completed models, Buick built 697 chassis-cowl units in the Special Series; 745 in the Super Series, and 337 such units in the Roadmaster Series. None were built in the Century line.

Convertible production picked up in both the Special and Century Series, but remained a fairly constant 3,527 in the Super Series. Designated the Model 56-C, the convertible cost $3,225 and weighed 4,280. The interiors were done in two-tone leather with matching vinyl boot.

The 322-cubic-inch engine was now rated at a straight 236 horsepower and was used in all but the Special Series. It used a 4-barrel carburetor and a 9:1 compression ratio.

The Buick chassis, built in only two sizes, continued to use coil springs on all four wheels, and was made quite rigid by its heavy X-bracing and torque tube drive. Helping greatly in the performance department was the new Variable Pitch Dynaflow.

The Roadmaster interior continued to use chrome headliner ribs, and was fitted with chrome scuff plates at the base of each door and a chrome runner around the perimeter of each front seat base and back. The upholstery was in matching color vinyl, while the full carpeting was in matching color nylon. Courtesy lights were located over the centerposts.

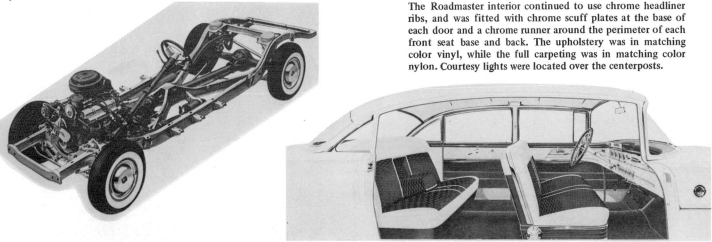

1955

Buick built its 1-millionth hardtop model this year, and it turned out to be the new Century 4-door Riviera. Shown with the car, which rolled off the line on Aug. 9, 1954, are Ivan L. Wiles, then general manager of Buick, and Edward T. Ragsdale, then general manufacturing manager, who is credited with designing the 1949 Riviera, which was America's first successful and high-production hardtop design. The Century 4-door Riviera had an excellent run of 55,088 this year. It cost $2,733 and weighed 3,900 pounds.

For sheer looks, the Century Convertible, Model 66-C, was hard to beat. In performance, it was almost impossible to keep up with, let alone pass. It cost $2,991 and weighed 3,950 pounds. Production rose to 5,588. In addition to the models shown here, Buick also built 280 Century 2-door Sedans, Model 68, but these cars do not appear in any Buick catalogs or price lists for the year. Standard equipment on the Century models included an electric clock, Redliner speedometer, trip meter, 4-barrel carburetor, rear license plate frame, and automatic trunk light. The convertibles were upholstered in leather, had electric windows and seat, hydraulic top, and outside rearview mirrors as standard equipment.

The most popular car in the Century Series was the Riviera Coupe, Model 66-R, which had a run of 80,338. It cost $2,601 and weighed 3,850 pounds. This year, only the Specials used three ventiports in the fenders, while all other series used four of the famous Buick "holes."

The only Century with a base price above $3,000 was the Estate Wagon, Model 69, which cost $3,175. It weighed 3,995 pounds. The car this year used an interesting optional 3-passenger rear seat that could be folded down to 2-passenger size, or 1-passenger size, or completely down to make one continuous cargo floor. Buick built 4,234 Century wagons.

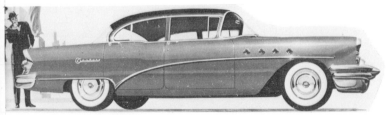

Appearing for the last time in the Century Series was the 4-door Sedan, Model 61, which cost $2,548 and weighed 3,825 pounds. Production slid to 13,269, as sales of the new Century Riviera Sedan skyrocketed. Buick claimed that the Century Series, with its 236 horsepower engine, offered more horses per dollar than any other car in America.

All Special production was increased substantially this year. Included in the increases was the Convertible, Model 46-C, which enjoyed a run of 10,009. The very attractive car cost $2,590 and weighed 3,825 pounds. Standard equipment included an all-vinyl interior and matching top boot.

The Special Series this year had two 4-door sedans, the regular type, Model 41 shown here, and the new Riviera. The standard 4-door was the most popular, having a run of 84,182. It cost $2,291 and weighed 3,745 pounds. All Specials were 206.7 inches in overall length.

Buick's most popular car this year was the Special Riviera Coupe, Model 46-R, which broke all single-model production records with an amazing run of 155,818. The car weighed 3,720 pounds and cost $2,332. Specials were powered by the 188 horsepower V-8.

Buick's least expensive and lightest car continued to be the Special 2-door Sedan, Model 48, which cost $2,233 and weighed 3,715 pounds. Still a popular car, its sales were 61,879. The new mesh grille and heavy bumpers made the 1955 Buicks hard to mistake for any other car.

New for the year was the Special 4-door Riviera, which was now a true hardtop sedan, with no centerpost. It cost $2,409 and weighed 3,820 pounds. Buick built 66,409. Standard Special items included directional lights, side armrests front and rear, sliding sunshades, cigarette lighter, automatic glove compartment light, outside rearview mirrors on convertibles, dual horns, twin rear license plate lamps, and robe cord in sedan models.

The least popular car in the Special Series continued to be the all-steel Estate Wagon, Model 49, which had a run of only 2,952. It cost $2,974 and weighed 3,940 pounds. Options included two-tone paint, Dynaflow, power brakes and steering, Redliner speedometer, and trip meter.

As fast and luxurious as it looked was the Roadmaster Convertible, Model 76-C. Production held at a relatively steady 4,354. It cost $3,704 and weighed 4,395 pounds. This excellent example is owned by David Dieteman of Fort Collins, Col. Offered this year, but hardly ever seen, were the very beautiful and very expensive Skylark chromed wire wheels.

New for the year was the Roadmaster Riviera Sedan, a true 4-door hardtop. Designated the Model 73, it had immediate public acceptance, with orders totaling 24,779. It cost $3,692 and weighed 4,355 pounds. In addition to completed cars, Buick produced 144 Super and 96 Roadmaster chassis-cowl units for builders of specialty bodies.

Appearing for the last time this year was the Roadmaster 4-door Sedan, Model 72, which used centerpost style. It had a run of only 11,804. It cost $3,503 and weighed 4,280 pounds. In addition to completed cars, Buick shipped 672 unassembled Specials, 336 unassembled Supers and 144 unassembled Roadmasters overseas for final assembly.

Buick still held third place in the industry, but this wa its last year of glory. Beginning next year, it would start to slip as a variety of factors entered the business — primarily strikes and smaller cars. But, for this year, calenda production was 535,364, which was a significant drop, bu still high enough to hold third place. The figure repre sented 8.9% of the total industry.

Model year production was 572,024, which represented 9.1% of the industry. Of this, a total of 436,900 were in the Special and Century Series; 81,500 were in the Super Series; and 53,700 were Roadmasters. Also of this total 121,304 were 2-door hardtops; 128,640 were 4-door hardtops; 17,795 were convertibles; and 19,817 were wagons, to which Buick was now paying much more attention than in previous years. In addition, Dynaflow was now installed in 96.7% of all cars.

For the first time, the same size engine was used in al series. This was the 322-cubic-inch block. In the Special Series, it was equipped with a 2-barrel carburetor, and developed 220 horsepower. In all other models, it was equipped with a 4-barrel carburetor and 9.5:1 compression ratio, and developed 255 horsepower. The old 264-cubic inch block was phased out of service.

All cars featured an all-new front end and grille, and a redesigned rear with sporty wheel cutouts. For the first time since World War II, identical instrument panels were used in all models; and overall, a very strong family resemblance was maintained.

Of interest is the fact that all cars were equipped with a foot-operated side-lift jack rather than the conventional bumper jack.

Again the same tow wheelbases were used, with the Special and Century sharing a 122-inch wheelbase chassis, and the Supers and Roadmasters sharing the 127-inch wheelbase model. Although the new lines did not indicate any shrinkage, both the large and small common bodies were smaller than those of the 1955 models. The Specials and Centurys were now 205 inches overall, while the Supers and Roadmasters were down to 213.5 inches overall.

Despite its very attractive lines, the Roadmaster Riviera, Model 76-R, did not fare as well as similar models in the other series. Production totaled only 12,490. The car cost $3,591 and weighed 4,235 pounds. All Buicks but the Specials now used a 9.5:1 compression ratio.

Again the transmission was reworked, and now the Dynaflow had two stator wheels. This gave at least a 10% performance improvement over 1955's really hot performance, and made Buick about the quickest thing on wheels, either from a stop light or cruising wide open across the prairies.

With the new engine changes and the new transmissions, zero to 60 was now rated at 11.7 seconds for the heavy Roadmaster. Passing performance from 50 to 70 occurred in 6.7 seconds, while the maximum speed for all models was in excess of 110 MPH. Dual exhausts were now standard on Roadmasters, optional on all other models, and Dynaflow was now standard on all models except the Special.

During the year, Ivan Wiles moved up to an executive position at General Motors, and Edward T. Ragsdale, credited with being the creator of the modern hardtop, became Buick's general manager.

The Super Riviera Coupe, Model 56-R, was an attractive car with orders totaling 29,540. It cost $3,204 and weighed 4,140. All models but the Special Series again used four fender venti-ports. The Buick bombsight hood ornament, in use in various forms since 1946 disappeared this year.

Appearing for the last time this year was the Super 4-door Sedan, Model 52, which was of the centerpost style. Only 14,940 were built. It cost $3,250 and weighed 4,200 pounds. The wheel covers and two-tone paint job were added cost items.

The least popular model in the Super Series was the Convertible, Model 56-C, of which only 2,489 were built. It cost $3,544 and weighed 4,340 pounds. All Super and Roadmaster models used a 127-inch wheelbase chassis, were 213.6 inches overall, and were 80 inches wide.

New for the year was the Super Riviera Sedan, Model 53, which was built in hardtop style. An immediately popular style, it had a run of 34,029. It cost $3,340 and weighed 4,265. This model is shown on Mackinac Island, Mich., where cars are normally prohibited by law.

The most popular car in the Century Series was the new Deluxe Riviera Sedan, Model 63-D. It had a run of 35,082, cost $3,041 and weighed two tons. The Century Series had no models with centerposts. This perfect example is owned by Gerald Bodden of Wheeling, Ill.

The Century Riviera Sedan this year divided itself into a standard and a deluxe version. The standard model was designated the Model 63. It weighed an even two tons and cost $3,025. Buick built 20,891, including this perfect example, still in use in the Los Angeles area.

Just as the Special wagon took a tremendous jump in sales, so too did the Century version, Model 69. Buick built 8,160 this year. Priced at $3,256 and weighing 4,080 pounds, it was the heaviest and most expensive model in the Century Series. Cargo space with the tailgate and rear seat raised was 44.7 inches, with the rear seat lowered it was 77.8 inches.

The Century Riviera Coupe, Model 66-R, was priced at $2,963 and weighed 3,890 pounds. A total of 33,334 were built. Century models used upholstery and interior trim as bright as the exteriors. Standard equipment included directional signals, front and rear side armrests plus a center rear seat armrest, sliding sunshades, cigarette lighter, map light, automatic glove compartment light, Redliner speedometer, trip meter, dual horns, and outside rear view mirrors on convertibles.

A very fast and beautiful car was the Century Convertible, Model 66-C, which cost $3,306 and weighed 4,045 pounds. Buick built 4,721. The car is shown here parked on the grass by the swimming pool in front of the Grand Hotel on Mackinac Island, Mich. – a place where cars NEVER go.

Buick's second most popular car this year was the Special Riviera Hardtop Sedan, Model 43, which had a run of 91,025. It cost $2,528 and weighed 3,860 pounds. The car is shown here parked by a side entrance of the Grand Hotel on Mackinac Island, Mich.

Buick's most popular car this year was the Special Riviera Coupe, Model 46-R. The attractive hardtop had a run of 113,861. It cost $2,458 and weighed 3,775 pounds. This model, shown brand new in Altadena, Cal., wears the rather unpopular one-color paint job.

Shooting way up in sales this year was the Special Estate Wagon, Model 49, which had a production run of 13,770. The all-steel wagon cost $2,775 and weighed 3,945 pounds. The car used the 4-way rear seat pioneered in the 1955 models. It was available as a 6-passenger model only.

Buick's lowest priced and lightest car continued to be the Special 2-door Sedan, Model 48. It cost $2,357 and weighed 3,750 pounds. A total of 38,672 were produced. Although two-tone paint jobs were at additional cost, the majority of Buick 2-door models and many 4-door models were turned out this year with the attractive matching color schemes.

Still a popular car, despite competition from the year-old hardtop sedans, was the Special 4-door Sedan, Model 41, which had sales totaling 66,977. It cost $2,416 and weighed 3,790 pounds. This perfect example is owned by Frank Denicold of Flint, Mich. The white top was an optional added cost item, as was the chrome gas filler door guard.

The Special Convertible, Model 46-C, cost $2,740 and weighed 3,880 pounds. Buick built 9,712. All Special and Century models used a 122-inch wheelbase chassis, were 205 inches in overall length, and were 75.5 inches wide. Specials used a 220 horsepower version engine.

The standard Buick dashboard this year was an attractive and colorful affair, with a padded vinyl top, machine turned chrome center panel, and matching-color slower portion. The gas gauge and ammeter were located on either side of the bar-type speedometer. When air conditioning was ordered, the vents were located on the outside edges of the lower panel.

Standard equipment in all Buick's this year was a newly patented jack, which worked from the side and lifted the frame rails instead of the bumpers as did most other standard jacks. The unit could be foot operated, as shown, and the handle doubled as the lug wrench.

Buick's main show and experimental car this year was the Centurion, which like the previous LeSabre and Wildcats, would also lend its name to a full series in later years. The car used a fiberglass body and was powered by a 325 horsepower version of the standard Buick engine. Its most unusual feature was the use of a closed circuit TV system in place of rearview mirrors.

Ivan L. Wiles, then general manager of Buick, stands beside the new Centurion show and experimental car. The twin pods at the lower ends of the back fenders served as bumpers and also carried the taillights and exhaust ports. Directly above the large rear decorative bullet was a TV camera which sent closed circuit pictures to a screen on the dash. This replaced the rearview mirror.

All Buick interiors were quite brilliant in their use of matching color upholstery and door panels and wide use of chrome trim. This is the interior of the Super Riviera Coupe, done in nylon and cordaveen. It was available in three standard color combinations and three extra cost combinations. The Roadmaster version continued to use chrome headliner ribs.

The interior of the Centurion featured some rather novel if quite impractical features, such as a TV system replacing the rearview mirror and a free-standing speedometer which used a stationary indicator and revolving dial. A digital clock is centrally mounted above the TV screen.

Buick suffered the greatest loss of any General Motors ~r this year, with a 24% decline in calendar year ~oduction — from 535,364 in 1956 to 407,271 this year. ~he decline dropped Buick from third place in the ~dustry, which it had held only since 1954, to fourth ~ace. Moving back into third place was Plymouth, with its ~dically new and very attractive styling.

Model year production was 405,086, which was a drop ~ 29.2% from the 572,024 of 1956. Of this, the Special ~ries accounted for 220,700; the Century for 66,000; ~per for 70,600; Roadmaster for 33,000; and the new ~oadmaster 75 for 15,000. Of all Buicks built, 61.9% had ~ower steering and 56.1% had power brakes. On November ~ 1956, the 9-millionth Buick was built, obviously a 1957 ~odel.

In retrospect, it is difficult to figure the drastic sales ~rop this year. Pricewise, Buick had one of the widest ~arket coverages of any car. The cars were totally ~designed, with virtually every piece of metal being all ~ew; yet the overall theme was one of continuity with ~revious years.

And under the hood even bigger things happened. All ~ars now had a brand new 364-cubic-inch engine, running a ~ore and stroke of 4.1 x 3.4 inches. The new block used a ~.5:1 compression ratio in the Special Series, where it was ~ated at 250 horsepower at 4400 RPM, and a 10:1 ratio in ~l other models, where it had a rating of 300 horsepower.

Wheelbases remained 122 inches for the Specials and ~enturys, but went up to 127.5 inches for the Supers and ~oadmasters. The Specials and Centurys grew more than

three inches in overall length, now being 208.5 inches long; while the Supers and Roadmasters grew two inches, now being 215.3 inches overall.

New from the design studio was the Caballero, a 4-door wagon with hardtop styling and extremely nice line. Also new was the Roadmaster 75 Series, consisting of a Riviera coupe and sedan, both of which featured as standard equipment leather and fabric interiors and virtually every accessory in the book except air conditioning.

On the negative side, most automotive writers of the time conplained about Buick's too-soft or mushy ride, which certainly didn't help handling or performance characteristics. But since few people bought Buicks for sports car purposes, despite their performance, and since the average person doesn't drive like an automotive writer on a test track, it is logical to assume that neither Buick's engineers nor Buick's buyers were overly concerned about wallowing cornering characteristics.

The Series 75 Roadmaster Riviera Coupe, Model 75-R, was a relatively expensive car that drew only 2,404 orders. It weighed 4,427 and cost $4,373. Standard equipment included Dynaflow, power steering and brakes, dual exhaust, automatic windshield washers and wide-angle wipers, back-up lights, safety rearview mirror, flexible-spoke steering wheel, speed reminder, parking brake warning light, electric clock, deluxe wheel covers, custom interior, and a host of other features.

BUICK *Roadmaster* SERIES 75

New for the year was the Series 75 Roadmaster line, which consisted of two styles equipped with just about every accessory in the book except air conditioning. The new series included Buick's most expensive and heaviest car, the Riviera 4-door Sedan, Model 75-R. It cost $4,483 and weighed 4,539 pounds. It had a surprisingly good run of 12,250.

The interiors of the new Buicks were as totally redesigned as were the exteriors. The new dashboards had all gauges grouped into the same dial face as the speedometer, and the lights and wiper knobs were set in large circles on either side of this face. This is the Roadmaster version, which used a standard padded top and deep-pile carpeting. When air conditioning was installed, the vents would be located in the spear-like designs at the far ends of the dashboard.

1957

Appearing for the last time this year was the Series 70 Roadmaster line, of which the most popular car was the Riviera 4-door Sedan, Model 73. It had a run of 11,401, cost $4,053, and weighed 4,469 pounds. This model used a three-piece rear window with wide divider bars.

New for the year was the Series 70 Roadmaster Riviera 4-door Hardtop, Model 73-A. This car differed from the Model 73 in that it used a one-piece wrap-around rear window. It cost $4,035 and weighed 4,455. A total of 10,526 were built. This example is owned by Glen Anderson of Villa Park, Ill. It lacks the grille centerpiece.

Produced this year only was the Series 70 Roadmaster Riviera Coupe, Model 76-A, which used a one-piece wrap-around rear window. It cost $3,944 and weighed 4,370 pounds. Only 2,812 were built. The car also had a smooth roof, while the Model 76-R used a ribbed roof.

The Series 70 Roadmaster Riviera Hardtop, Model 76-R, used a three-piece rear window, with the pieces separated by rather wide ribbed bars. This ribbing was carried across the roof, ending at the chrome windshield frame. The car cost $3,944, weighed 4,347 pounds, and had a run of 3,826. In addition to this production, Buick shipped 384 unassembled Supers overseas for assembly, and built two Century and 168 Roadmaster chassis-cowl units for sales to specialty body builders.

A rear detail of the new Roadmaster Riviera Coupe, Model 76-R, shows how the distinctive chrome ribs were carried from the windshield post, across the roof, down the window posts, and across the trunk deck. The moldings ended about an inch above the twin trunk grips.

Still keeping its production on an amazingly stable basis was the Series 70 Roadmaster Convertible, Model 76-C, which maintained a production run of 4,363. It cost $4,066 and weighed 4,500 pounds. All Buicks this year featured "low-silhouette" styling, which resulted from a lowering of all hood, roof, and rear deck lines, while retaining precious interior space.

Super SERIES 50

The Riviera Hardtop Coupe cost $3,536 in the Super Series. Designated the Model 56-R, the 4,271-pound car had a run of 26,529. Super's front seat width was 65.3 inches.

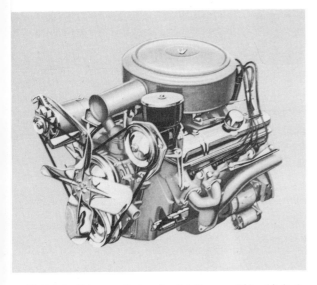

All Buicks this year featured a totally new 364-cubic-inch engine with a bore and stroke of 4.1 x 3.4 inches. It used a 9.5:1 compression ratio in the Special Series, where it was rated at 250 horsepower, and a 10:1 ratio in all other series, where it was rated at 300 horsepower.

Appearing for the last time this year was the Super Convertible, Model 56-C, which was phased out of production after a short run of 2,056. It cost $3,981 and weighed 4,414 pounds. Top and windows were electrically operated as standard equipment, but a power seat was extra.

Making good use of Buick's new Contour-Frame chassis and its resultant lower profile was the Super Riviera 4-door Sedan, Model 53. The car was the most popular in the Special Series, attracting 41,665 orders. It cost $3,681 and weighed 4,356 pounds. All Supers and Roadmasters used a 127.5-inch wheelbase chassis and were 215.3-inches long and 77.6 inches wide.

The Century Convertible, Model 66-C, this year cost $3,598 and weighed 4,234 pounds. A total of 4,085 were built. All Buicks this year used heavy chrome gravel shields extending from the rear wheel cutouts to the rear bumpers. Front bumpers swept back to the front wheel openings.

Experiencing a drastic drop in sales was the very attractive Century Riviera Coupe, Model 66-R. Production was down to 17,029. The car cost $3,270 and weighed 4,081 pounds. Standard equipment included Dynaflow, electric clock, padded dash, and 300 horsepower engine.

An interesting feature of the new Caballero Estate Wagon was the ribbed roof, which consisted of 10 chrome bars extending from a point just over the front seat back to the tailgate. The bars then were carried over the tailgate to the rear window. They were practical as paint savers when a luggage rack was installed, but were strictly decorative without such a rack.

New for the year was the Century Caballero, Model 69, which really was a fancy version of the already fancy Special Riviera Estate Wagon, In Century form it cost $3,706, weighed 4,423 pounds, and drew 10,186 orders. No centerpost wagon was built in the Century Series, but for the first time, a third seat was optional as an accessory.

The second most popular car in Buick's total line turned out to be the Special 4-door Sedan, built in centerpost style. However, all sales were down, and a total of only 59,739 were built. It cost $2,660 and weighed 4,012 pounds. The two-tone paint combination was extra. In addition to completed cars, Buick shipped 504 unassembled Specials overseas for final assembly.

The most popular car in the Century Series was the Riviera 4-door Sedan, Model 63. The attractive hardtop had a run of 26,589. It cost $3,345 and weighed 4,163 pounds. Also built this year was the Century 4-door Sedan, Model 61, which was in centerpost style. This car, which used the Special Sedan's basic body, cost $3,234 and weighed 4,137 pounds. Only 8,075 were built.

New for the year was the Special Riviera Estate Wagon, Model 49-D, which was built in hardtop style, with no centerpost between the doors. Priced at $3,167 and weighing 4,309 pounds, it was the most expensive and heaviest model in the Special Series. Buick built 6,816.

The Special Estate Wagon, Model 49, used the same basic body as the new Riviera style, but had a centerpost between the doors. Both wagons were available in 6-passenger form only. The Model 49 cost $3,047, weighed 4,292 pounds, and drew 7,014 orders. All Specials were 208.4 inches in overall length and were 74.9 inches wide.

Buick's most popular car again was the Special Riviera Coupe, Model 46-R, but with the poor sales showing this year, only 64,425 were built, which was about half of the 1956 production. The car cost $2,704 and weighed 3,956 pounds. Specials used a 122-inch wheelbase.

The Special Convertible, Model 46-C, dropped somewhat in sales, but not nearly as much as other models on a percentage basis. A total of 8,505 were sold. It cost $2,987 and weighed 4,082 pounds. Legroom in the rear seat measured 42.4 inches.

The lowest priced and lightest Buick continued to be the Special 2-door Sedan, Model 48, which was built in centerpost style. It cost $2,596 and weighed 3,955 pounds. Orders totaled 23,180. Options in the Special Series included air conditioning, Dynaflow power steering and brakes, and in the 4-door models only, electric windows and front seat.

The attractive Special Riviera 4-door Sedan, Model 43, took a substantial drop in sales, and only 50,563 were built. It cost $2,780 and weighed 4,041 pounds. All Rivieras used the wide dividers on the three-piece rear windows. Again the Specials were the only cars to use three ventiports.

Edward Ragsdale, general manager of Buick, described this year's styling as "dazzling." And, if one is dazzled by chrome and stainless steel, he was correct. However, in comparison with Buicks before and after, it seemed as if this year's models had just a bit too much of a good thing in chrome, while still being just a bit too sedate in basic styling for the "young-at-heart" market.

But despite the heavy-handed chrome work, the cars were good looking, from the grille which contained 160 chromed squares, free floating within the outer shell, to the rear bumper, which was the largest in the industry. For the first time since 1949, Buick dropped all hint of its mouseholes or ventiports. All engines and wheelbases

BUICK *Limited* SERIES 700

Companion to the Limited Riviera Sedan was the Limited Riviera Coupe, Model 755, which cost $5,002 and weighed 4,691 pounds. Only 1,026 were built. No Limiteds were priced under $5,000.

Buick's least popular car, and also its most expensive, was the Limited Convertible, Model 756. It had a run of only 839, and cost $5,125. It weighed 4,603 pounds. The Limiteds were the only Buicks to use the huge chrome gravel shields between the rear wheel openings and bumper.

remained the same. All cars used the 364-cubic-inch engine, being rated at 300 horsepower at 4600 RPM in everything but the Specials. In the Special Series, it was rated at 210 horsepower at 4000 RPM, or the optional 250 horsepower at 4400 RPM.

Still, calendar year production tumbled to 257,124, and Buick fell to fifth place in the industry, as Oldsmobile moved up to spot number four. Model year production was 241,892, which was only 5.7% of the market. Of this by series the production ran: Special, 133,500; Century 33,000; Super, 42,500; and Roadmaster and the new Limited combined, 21,500. Despite all of the production slips, station wagon production reached a record 11,500.

The Specials and Centurys used a common 122-inch wheelbase chassis, and all other models used the 127.5-inch wheelbase chassis. However, the Specials and Centurys again grew three inches, now being 211.8 inches overall; while the Supers and Roadmasters grew four inches to a new overall length of 219 inches. The new Limiteds were a giant 227 inches overall.

Again the engineers went after the transmission, and a new Flight-Pitch Dynaflow was offered as an option on all but the Roadmaster and Limited, where it was standard. This new transmission now had three turbines, and the stator blades were fully adjustable to match any given performance need.

Optional this year was air suspension, an excellent accessory on the drawing boards, but one that proved to be a rather troublesome nuisance in virtually every make of American car in which it was used — and virtually every make tried it at one time or another.

Of interest is the fact that the 4-millionth car with Dynaflow was built this year, just about ten years to the day of the introduction of Dynaflow in 1948. This year Dynaflow was Buick's most popular option, even outselling heaters, radios, and whitewalls. It was installed in 98.5% of all cars produced, as compared with 97.6% for heaters and 87.6% for radios. In addition, the one-millionth power brake installation was made this year.

In a completely different sales area, Buick dealers this year were authorized to sell the Opel, built by a General Motors subsidiary in Russelsheim, Germany, but having no other relationship to Buick. The car provided Buick dealers with a really low price vehicle and gave them an even wider market spread. The Opels used a 99-inch wheelbase chassis and were 173 inches overall. Power was by a tiny 90-cubic-inch Four that developed 52 horsepower at 3900 RPM and would propel the light car to steady top speed of 77 MPH.

Returning this year only was the Limited Series, which was produced as a three-model line. All Limiteds used the Roadmaster's 127.5-inch wheelbase chassis, but the bodies were extended to 227 inches overall. The most popular car of the new series was the Limited Riviera Sedan, Model 750, of which 5,571 were built. It cost $5,112 and weighed 4,710 pounds. This perfect original example is owned by Ron Wolf of Syracuse, N.Y.

The Roadmaster Riviera Coupe, Model 75-R, was priced at $4,557 and weighed 4,568. It had a run of only 2,368. In addition to completed cars, Buick shipped 1,008 unassembled Specials and 168 unassembled Supers overseas for final assembly.

The lowest production style of the three-model Roadmaster Series was the Convertible, Model 75-C, of which only 1,181 were built. It cost $4,680 and weighed 4,676 pounds. Many automotive experts this year criticized General Motors for its heavy-handed use of needless chrome trim in all of its lines.

With the Series 70 Roadmaster line gone, the Series 75 line became the only line to bear the Roadmaster name — and even this would disappear at the end of the year. The most popular Roadmaster was the Riviera Sedan, Model 75, which had a run of 10,505. It cost $4,667 and weighed 4,668 pounds. The Roadmaster differed from the lower-priced cars in that it used chrome rocker panel covers. The Roadmaster signature appeared on the rear fender trim.

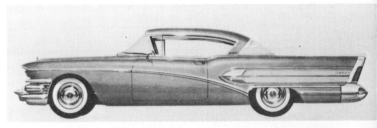

The only other model in the Super Series was the Riviera Coupe, Model 56-R, of which only 13,928 were built. It cost $3,644 and weighed 4,392 pounds. Front seat hip room was 65.7 inches. All Supers and Roadmasters were 219 inches long and 79.8 inches wide.

With its convertible model gone, the Super Series was reduced to a two-model line, consisting of two Riviera styles. The most popular was the Super Riviera Sedan, Model 53, which had a run of 28,460. It cost $3,789 and weighed 4,500 pounds. Rear leg room was 44.5 inches.

Although Limiteds were not exported directly, a few such models found their way overseas via special orders. One such case is this Limited Riviera Sedan, shown here in Victoria. The car has been custom converted to right-hand drive simply because it is now illegal to drive a left-hand drive car in most states in Australia.

The new Century 4-door Sedan, Model 61, was a nice looking car, but its sales were less than half that of its companion Riviera style. Only 7,241 were built. It cost $3,316 and weighed 4,241 pounds. The "Century" name appeared on rear fenders and trunk deck.

An attractive car, but one with little sales appeal this year was the Century Convertible, Model 66-C. Only 2,588 were built. It cost $3,680 and weighed 4,320 pounds. This fine example is owned by Jensen Feather of Claysburg, Pa.

Some of the workings of Buick's new air suspension system are shown here. The compressor was mounted high on the left side of the engine, and was driven by its own belt. Compressed air was fed into the tank located far forward between the frame horns. From here a series of sensors regulated the air to four bags, one for each wheel, which replaced the usual coil springs.

Buick's prestige wagon was the Century Caballero, Model 69, which in effect was a dolled-up version of the Special Riviera Wagon. It cost $3,831 and weighed 4,570 pounds. Production stood at 4,456. In an interesting styling move, Buick returned to a modified bombsight hood ornament in 1957, but this year did away with the hood ornament and created twin bombsights, one for each front fender.

The Century Riviera Sedan, Model 63, attracted 15,171 buyers. It cost $3,436 and weighed 4,267 pounds. Buick claimed that its new headlight design gave a 50% stronger high beam and a 25% stronger low beam. All GM cars this year used dual headlights.

The Century Riviera Coupe, Model 66-R, slid way down in sales, with only 8,110 being built. It cost $3,368 and weighed 4,182 pounds. The new rear side trim, used on all but the new Limited Series, was supposed to represent a flying wing. It carried the series name on the trailing edge.

The new Buick chassis is shown here in Limited version, with the new 3-blade Dynaflow, the unsuccessful air suspension system, and the new dual exhaust units. The exhaust system used two main mufflers, two forward resonators and two rear resonators. It was effective but rather costly to replace. Dynaflow was used in 98.5% of all Buicks built this year.

In a rather surprising turn, Buick's most popular car this year turned out to be the Special 4-door Sedan, Model 41, which had a run of 48,238. In outward appearance, with the windows raised, the car was almost identical to the 4-door hardtop, due to the fact that its very thin centerposts were well hidden behind the door panels and chrome window trim. It cost $2,700 and weighed 4,115 pounds. All Special and Century models were 211.8 inches long overall.

Remaining as Buick's third most popular car was the Special 4-door Riviera, Model 43, which had a run of 31,921. With the windows raised, it was difficult to tell the Riviera from the Sedan, but with the windows down the Sedan had a centerpost while the Riviera did not. It cost $2,820 and weighed 4,180 pounds. This excellent original example is owned by Douglas Baum of Bay City, Mich. All Special and Century models were 78.1 inches wide and used a 122-inch wheelbase chassis.

Despite its attractive, if not somewhat gaudy trim, the Special Convertible, Model 46-C, slid down in sales to 5,502. It cost $3,041 and weighed 4,165.

Buick's lowest priced and lightest car continued to be the Special 2-door Sedan, Model 48. It cost $2,636 and weighed 4,063 pounds. Production was 11,566. No Buick weighed under two tons this year, and only a few Specials had a base price under $3,000.

Dropping from first to second place in the Buick popularity roll was the Special Riviera Coupe, Model 46-R. Production slid down to 34,903, which was 30,000 less than produced in 1957. It cost $2,744 and weighed 4,058 pounds. The name "Special" appeared on the trunk only.

The deluxe wagon in the Special Series was the Model 49-D 6-passenger Riviera Estate Wagon, which was built in semi-hardtop form, with no centerposts between the doors. It cost $3,261 and weighed 4,408 pounds. It had a run of 3,420.

Buick's three wagons all used a basic body, but only the Special Estate Wagon, Model 49, used centerposts between the doors. An interesting styling feature of the wagons was the curved rear window on the upper tailgate, which was attractive but not necessarily practical. The Model 49 cost $3,145 and weighed 4,396. Buick built 3,663.

Buick did not go in for radical show cars this year, but did produce a few slightly modified cars for display at the major auto shows. One such car was the Wells Fargo, a modified Limited Convertible, featuring wood paneling in the flying wing and a solid top boot. It was built to call attention to Buick's sponsorship of the then-popular TV series, Wells Fargo, starring Dale Robertson, who is shown here with the car.

Pinin Farina, Italy's famed auto designer, produced this one-off model on a Buick Special chassis. Called the Lido Coupe, the beautiful car attracted a certain amount of attention, but nothing further ever came of the idea. The roof raised for easy access, but it was not a convertible. The car used chromed wire wheels with functional knock-off hubs.

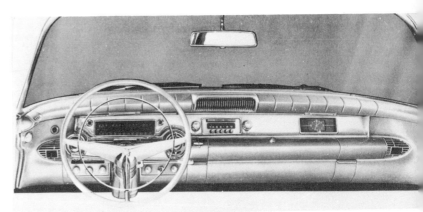

All Buicks used the 364-cubic-inch engine, but the Specials used a 250 horsepower version while all other models used a 300 horsepower model. The lower-powered unit used a 9.5:1 compression ratio, while the higher powered model used a 10:1 ratio and put 12,000-pounds of thrust behind each piston stroke. The unit shown here is equipped with power steering pump.

Buick used a highly decorated exterior this year, and carried the theme into the interior also. This is the Roadmaster dash, done in matching color, chrome and brushed aluminum, with a padded vinyl top. The new steering wheels were of the dished type. Electric window controls were located immediately below the windshield dog-leg, but on the dashboard, not the door.

After extensive testing of various autos built by overseas plants of General Motors, Buick authorized its dealers to handle the German-made Opel cars in an effort to broaden their sales base. The Opels were exported in two basic models, the Caravan 5-passenger wagon, shown here, and the Olympia Rekord 2-door Sedan. The Caravan, designated the Model 29, cost $2,400 and weighed 2,077 pounds. The roof-top luggage rack was an accessory.

The first Opel arrived in the U.S. on Oct. 1, 1957. It was this 1958 model Olympia Rekord 2-door Sedan, which had a base price of $1,988 and weighed 1,911 pounds. The Opels received a fairly warm response from persons receptive to economical little foreign cars.

Credited with being this year's most changed cars, the new Buicks came in four distinctly new series: the 4400 LeSabre, the 4600 Invicta, and 4700 Electra, and the 4800 Electra 225.

Sadly, despite the radically new cars, calendar year production took a substantial nosedive, going from 257,124 in 1958 to 232,579 this year. The dive was not caused by any lack of sales personality in the totally new cars, but was the fault primarily of a major steel strike that resulted in all Buick production ceasing for more than a month in late fall. This, of course, affected all 1960 Buick production. The trouble knocked Buick all the way down to seventh spot being beaten respectively by Ford, Chevrolet, Plymouth, Rambler, Pontiac, and Oldsmobile.

Model year production was 285,089, which was 5.1% of the market. By series, this ran: LeSabre, 157,300; Invicta, 57,600; Electra, 44,200; and Electra 225 Series, 22,400. Wagon production was 13,500 and convertible production still accounted for 11% of Buick's total sales.

As mentioned, the new Buicks were completely new cars, resembling nothing that ever rolled out of Flint before, and having no common ties with other General Motors styles. The cars made their debut on September 16, the earliest that a brand new car had ever been introduced since World War II. The name switch on the series was in line with management's determination to make a complete break from the past and to reduce the number of series available for easier handling and supply at both plant and dealer level — wonder whatever happened to that concept?

Both the LeSabre and the Invicta shared the same 123-inch wheelbase chassis and bodies, with the overall length being 217.4 inches. All chassis were totally new and of the K-type frame with boxed siderails replacing the former X-type.

The Electra and Electra 225 Series both used the same 126.3-inch wheelbase chassis, but the bodies were 220.6 inches overall for the Electras and 225.4 inches overall for the Electra 225.

All models except the LeSabre used a brand new 401-cubic-inch V-8 that developed 325 horsepower at 4400 RPM. It had a bore and stroke of 4.18 x 3.64 inches. The LeSabre used the old 364-cubic-inch V-8 that developed 250 horsepower at 4400 RPM from its bore and stroke of 4.1 x 3.4. Both engines used a 10.5:1 compression ratio.

Both power brakes and power steering were standard on the Electra Series, but cost a total of $150 extra on other models. Air conditioning was $430 extra. The air suspension units, always of dubious value and limited appeal, were available only on the rear axles this year, while coil springs remained standard on all four wheels.

In the spring of the year, Edward Ragsdale retired, and the new general manager was Edward T. Rollert, who had been in engineering all his life, not only in cars, but in spark plugs, watches and clocks, and radiators.

ELECTRA 225

The most popular car in the Electra 225 Series was the 4-door Hardtop, Model 4839, which had a run of 10,491. It cost $4,300 and weighed 4,641 pounds. Unlike the Electra 225 Riviera Sedan, this model used the new Buick hardtop sedan styling, with huge wrap-around rear window.

Replacing both the Roadmaster and Limited Series in one shot was the new Electra 225 Series. It used the same 126.3-inch wheelbase chassis as did the Electra Series, but had its own bodies with the overall length of all models being 225.4 inches. This is the Electra 225 4-door Riviera Sedan, Model 4829, which used the basic roofline of the other new sedans, but was built in hardtop style. This is the only Buick that kept the Riviera name. It cost $4,300 and weighed 4,632 pounds. Buick built a total of 6,324.

The Electra 225 Convertible, Model 4867, drew a surprising total of 5,493 orders. It cost $4,192 and weighed 4,562 pounds. Tires were 8.00 x 15.

Replacing the former Super Series was the new Electra Series, which consisted of two 4-door models and a 2-door. This is the Electra 4-door Sedan, Model 4719, which cost $3,856 and weighed 4,557 pounds. A total of 12,357 were built.

The most popular car in the three-model Electra Series was the 4-door Hardtop, Model 4739, of which 20,612 were built. It cost $3,963 and weighed 4,573 pounds. All Electra models used a 126.3-inch wheelbase chassis and were 220.6 inches overall.

ELECTRA

The Electra Hardtop Coupe, Model 4737, cost $3,818 and weighed 4,465 pounds. A total of 11,216 were built. Power brakes and steering were standard on all Electra models.

Buick came out with a really attractive show car this year, and the only puzzle seems to be why such an attractive car never was put into production. Called the Wildcat III, and referred to as a "toy convertible" the pretty little 4-passenger car used a 110-inch wheelbase chassis, and was 190.5 inches overall. It was finished in red with a red leather interior.

The cockpit of the Wildcat III show and experimental car was in excellent taste and surprisingly functional for a show car. The interior was done in red leather and red vinyl floor mats. The car used the Twin Turbine transmission and was powered by a 280 horsepower Special V-8.

Replacing the former Century Series was the new Invicta Series, which shared the same basic bodies and 123-inch wheelbase chassis with the LeSabre Series. This is the Invicta 4-door Sedan, Model 4619, which cost $3,357, weighed 4,331 pounds, and had a run of 10,566.

INVICTA

Drawing almost twice the orders of the Invicta 4-door Sedan was the new Invicta 4-door Hardtop, Model 4639. Buick built 20,156. It cost $3,515 and weighed 4,373. The hardtop used completely different top styling than did the sedan models.

The Invicta Hardtop Coupe, Model 4637, cost $3,447 and weighed 4,274. Production totaled 11,451. On the exterior, the Invictas differed from the LeSabres in their use of chromed rocker panels. The Invicta signature appeared on the leading end of the front fenders and on the back panel.

The Invicta Convertible, Model 4667, had a run of 5,447. It cost $3,620 and weighed 4,317 pounds. Standard in the Invicta Series were the new Wildcat engine and the Twin Turbine transmission.

Edward T. Ragsdale, then general manager of Buick, presents the 2-millionth Buick hardtop to his wife, Sarah, who is credited with giving Mr. Ragsdale the inspiration for creating the first high-production hardtop in 1949.

The heaviest and most expensive Invicta was the Estate Wagon, Model 4635, which weighed 4,660 pounds and cost $3,841. Buick built a total of 5,231.

LeSABRE

Drawing excellent sales, in comparison to previous years, was the new LeSabre Convertible, Model 4467, of which 10,489 were built. It cost $3,129 and weighed 4,216 pounds. Buicks this year were painted in a new hard-surface high gloss lacquer called Magin-Mirror finish.

Buick's most popular car was the totally new LeSabre 4-door Sedan, Model 4419, which had a run of 51,376. Technically, the LeSabre Series replaced the old Speical Series. The car cost $2,804 and weighed 4,229 pounds. LeSabres were 217.4 inches in overall length.

The most expensive, heaviest, and least popular car in the new LeSabre Series was the Estate Wagon, Model 4435. It cost $3,320 weighed 4,565 pounds, and had a run of only 8,286. It was available in 6-passenger form, and used centerposts between doors.

The only 2-door sedan in the entire Buick line-up was the Model 4411, which appeared in the LeSabre Series. It cost $2,740 and weighed 4,159 pounds, and thus was Buick's least expensive and lightest model. Production was 13,492.

Far more popular than the 2-door sedan was the LeSabre 2-door Hardtop, Model 4437. Orders amounted to 35,189. It cost $2,849 and weighed 4,188 pounds. The Buick 2-door models this year were noted for their huge rear windows in addition to the very radical overall styling.

Running a close second in popularity to the new LeSabre Sedan was the LeSabre 4-door Hardtop, Model 4439, which had a run of 46,069. It cost $2,925 and weighed 4,266 pounds. Except for four LeSabre models, all Buicks had a base price over $3,000. All weighed in excess of two tons.

The totally new Flxible Landau Hearse was fitted to the extended Electra chassis, with standard equipment including automatic transmission and power steering and brakes. In addition to completed cars, Buick this year sent 672 unassembled LeSabres; 48 unassembled Electras and 120 unassembled Electra 225 models overseas for assembly.

The Opel Rekord Caravan, also built in 2-door style, was a rather handy little 5-passenger wagon. Designated the Model 29, it cost $2,293 and weighed 2,077 pounds.

The Flxible Co. of Loudonville, Ohio, still major builders of hearse and ambulance bodies, were quick to change their styling to fit the totally new Buicks. This is the totally new Flxible ambulance, mounted on an extended Invicta chassis.

Showing increasing popularity was the Opel Olympic Rekord, Model 28, still priced at $1,988. The 1,911-pound car was built in 2-door form only, was basically unchanged from 1958, but now offered a much wider selection of colors and upholstery options.

The 1-millionth Opel imported into the U.S. arrived in May, less than two years after the first Opel arrived. The plain but peppy little cars had definite sales appeal.

ELECTRA 225

The new Electra 225 Series was unmistakably identified by wide chrome rocker panels and aluminum trim panels extending from the rockers to the centerline chrome strip. This is the Electra 225 4-door Hardtop, Model 4839, which was priced at $4,300 and weighed 4,650 pounds. Buick built 5,841. All Electra 225 models were 225.9 inches in overall length, and 55.6 inches high.

Appearing for the last time was the Electra 225 Riviera Sedan, which used the roofline of the 4-door sedan, but was built in hardtop style, without centerpost. It cost $4,300 and weighed 4,653 pounds. A total of 8,029 were built, making it the best selling car in the Electra 225 Series.

Up slightly in sales was the very attractive Electra 225 Convertible, Model 4867, which this year had a run of 6,746. It cost $4,192 and weighed 4,571 pounds. This example, in beautiful original shape, is owned by Peter Novak of Orland Park, Ill.

In Buick's production history, 1960 was a dismal year. Calendar year production was 307,804, which in itself wasn't too bad. But, when compared to the tremendous increases made this year by all other manufacturers, Buick's production was awful. The result was that Buick tumbled all the way down to ninth place in the industry, the lowest point it had ever been since 1905. Buick was now behind Chevrolet, Ford, Rambler, Plymouth, Pontiac, Dodge, Oldsmobile and Mercury in production.

Model year production was 253,999, which was only 4.2% of the total market. Of this, by series, production ran: LeSabre, 144,700; Invicta, 40,300; Electra, 35,700; and Electra 225 Series, 20,600. Of this, wagon production accounted for 12,600. In October, the Special was introduced as a 1961 model. Actually, there were 36,733 Specials built during calendar year 1960, but all were considered 1961 models.

Of the 1960 cars, from dash to mufflers and from brakes to heaters, it was the engineers and not the designers who had a field day. Among the new innovations were separate heater controls for rear seat passengers, a new device called Mirrormagic, which allowed the driver to adjust the angle of the instrument dials, and a Twilight Sentinel that automatically turned on the car's headlights at dusk or turned them off at dawn. Vented wheels and wheel covers were designed for greater gear dissipation, and the exhaust system was completely redesigned.

On the surface, the cars continued to reflect the new style, with a more simplified and practical design. With the exception of some trim movement, there was virtually no change in series or styles, with the exception of a new 8-passenger 3-seat version of the Estate Wagon in both the LeSabre and Invicta Series.

Wheelbases remained 123 inches for the LeSabre and Invicta Series, but overall length for these cars was increased slightly to 217.9 inches. Wheelbases also remained 126.3 inches for the Electra Series, but the Electra's overall length increased to 221.2 inches while the Electra 225 grew to 225.9 inches.

The LeSabre continued to use the 364-cubic-inch V-8 of 250 horsepower at 4400 RPM, while all other models used the 401-cubic-inch V-8 of 235 horsepower at 4400 RPM. However, compression ratios of both engines were reduced to 10.25:1.

Power steering and brakes remained standard on the Electras, but cost a total of $150 more on the other series. Air conditioning continued to cost $430.

In England, Bernard Rogers Developments received permission to use the Buick V-8 in prototype sports cars that were seriously being considered for production under the name Warwick. However, the project was scrapped after only a few experimental models were built.

The Electra 2-door Hardtop, Model 4737, cost $3,818 and weighed 4,453 pounds. Buick built 7,416. All Electra and Electra 225 models used four of the decorative venti ports, a return in effect, to the old mouse-holes that had been almost a Buick trademark since 1949.

ELECTRA

The Electra 4-door Sedan, Model 4719, was priced at $3,856 and weighed 4,544 pounds. Buick built a total of 13,794. Power steering and brakes were standard equipment. All Electras were 221.2 inches in overall length and used a wheelbase of 126.3 inches. Glass area amounted to 5,119 square inches on this model, while all Electra windshields were 1,804 square inches.

The Flxible Co. of Loudonville, Ohio, came out with a new vehicle this year. It was the Flxette, a relatively short hearse built on a standard Electra chassis of 126.3 inch wheelbase. The car used all of the luxury trim of the standard Flxible hearses, but the cost was kept down by the unmodified chassis and far lower-cost body.

The most popular Electra was the 4-door Hardtop, Model 4739, which had a run of 14,488. It cost $3,963 and weighed 4,554 pounds. All Electras were 55 inches high and 80 inches wide.

Flxible's prestige ambulance was this landau model, built on an extended Electra chassis and using the wide chrome rocker panel covers of the Electra 225. This model, done in white, used a white vinyl top with blanked in quarter windows and the large chrome landau irons.

The Invicta 4-door Hardtop, Model 4639, used the same attractive styling found on all Buick 4-door hardtops this year. With the huge wrap-around rear window and the compound curved windshield, this model had a total of 4,408 square inches of glass area. It cost $3,515 and weighed 4,365 pounds. Buick built 15,300.

The Invicta 2-door Hardtop, Model 4637, was an attractive car, but sales amounted to only 8,960. It cost $3,447 and weighed 4,225 pounds. The two-tone top and rear deck were at extra cost. Surprisingly, the 2-door, with its huge rear window, had greater glass area than the 4-door hardtop, with 4,875 square inches of glass surrounding the passenger compartment.

INVICTA

Appearing for the last time this year was the Invicta 4-door Sedan, Model 4619. It cost $3,357 and weighed 4,324 pounds. Only 10,839 were built before it was phased from production.

The Invicta Convertible, Model 4667 was a very attractive car that held a fairly stable sales figure of 5,236. It cost $3,620 and weighed 4,347 pounds. All Buicks this year had newly designed front and rear suspension, chair-high seats, and a lowered drive shaft tunnel.

The Invicta Series, as did the LeSabre Series, received a new Estate Wagon, in the form of the 3-seat model. Equipped with a rear-facing third seat, the car was designated the Model 4645. It cost $3,948, weighed 4,679 and had a run of 1,605. Also available was the 2-seat version, Model 4635, which cost $3,841, weighed 4,644 pounds, and had a run of 3,471.

Running second in Buick's popularity roll was the LeSabre 4-door Hardtop, Model 4439, of which 35,999 were built. It cost $2,991 and weighed 4,269 pounds. Leg room was 44.2 inches in the front, 41.1 inches in the rear, while hip room was 65.4 inches in the front and 66 inches in the rear.

Appearing only in the LeSabre Series was the 2-door Sedan, Model 4411, which used a top design similar to the hardtops, but was equipped with centerposts. It cost $2,756 and weighed 4,139 pounds, and thus continued to be Buick's lightest and least expensive car. Production was 14,388. All LeSabres were 217.9 inches long and used a 123-inch wheelbase chassis.

LESABRE

Again far more popular than the 2-door Sedan was the LeSabre 2-door Hardtop, Model 4437, which had a run of 26,521. It weighed 4,163 pounds and cost $2,915, with the two-tone paint being extra. All LeSabres except the convertible were 57.2 inches high. All were 80 inches wide.

Buick's most popular car continued to be the LeSabre 4-door Sedan, Model 4419, which had a run of 54,033. It weighed 4,219 pounds and cost $2,870, but the two-tone paint shown here was added cost. Headroom was 34.7 inches in the front, 33.9 inches in the rear.

The LeSabre Estate Wagons were now produced in two and three seat versions. The new 3-seat version was designated the Model 4445, cost $3,493 and weighed 4,574 pounds. Production was 2,222. The 2-seat style was designated the Model 4435, cost $3,386 and weighed 4,568 pounds. Production was 5,331. Both cars were identical on the outside. The third seat faced rearward.

The LeSabre Convertible, Model 4467, had a small but nice increase in sales, with production going up to 13,588. It cost $3,145 and weighed 4,233 pounds. The convertible was 55.4 inches high. LeSabre windshields had 1,755 square inches of glass area. A return was made to the venti-port concept this year, with LeSabres and Invictas having three decorative ports.

To show the speed and dependability of the new Buicks, a team of cars and drivers drove a pair of Invicta hardtops 10,000 miles in 5,000 minutes at Daytona Beach. The cars ran steadily for 3½ days at 120 MPH average speed, with speeds often exceeding 125 MPH.

Buick's totally new chassis, introduced on the 1959 models, was of the "K" type, with broad side rails replacing the former X-frame chassis. The cars used dual exhaust, but an unusual engineering move was to route both exhausts through a large single muffler just behind the rear axle. In addition to completed cars, Buick this year shipped 144 unassembled LeSabres, and two dozen each unassembled Electra and Electra 225 models overseas for assembly.

The Opel Caravan, a 5-passenger, 2-door wagon, continued to use its one-piece swing-up tailgate, which helped keep cost down, but was not the most practical rear hatch. The car, increasing in popularity each year, cost $2,293 and weighed 2,077 pounds.

For the 10,000 mile Daytona run, Buick engineers took a lesson in refueling on the fly from the Air Force, and came up with this interesting rig. The fuel car would follow the test car, and supply the fuel through the long flexible snout.

During a quick pit stop during the Daytona Beach 10,000 mile run, Buick technicians check under the hood and replace tires while a relief driver scampers in on the left and the relieved driver exits on the right. Doors were sealed for safety. The special jack lifted all four wheels off the ground at the same time. Special hood latches also were a safety item, as were roll bars.

Still virtually unchanged was the Opel Olympia Rekord, Model 28. The little 2-door sedan was still priced at $1,988 and weighed 1,911 pounds.

This was a big change year for Buick, with new styles, new mechanics and a totally new car divided into two sub-series being introduced. The new lines were the Special and the Special DeLuxe. This marked a return to the name Special to designate the low-price line, as was done for years past. The return of the name "Special" caused many long-time Buick buffs to hope the company would also return to the old and familiar Super, Century, Roadmaster and Limited designations, but such was not the case.

Calendar year production dropped to a total of 291,895. Still, other manufacturers also dropped this year, and as a result, Buick made a better showing in the total market. Its sales for the year accounted for 5.28% of total calendar year U.S. production, as compared with 4.65% in 1960, and this allowed Buick to pass Dodge and climb up to eighth place.

However, model year production of the large Buicks was only 189,982, which represented only 3.5% of the total market. Production of the Specials was 87,44, which was 1.6% of the total market. Of these figures, production by series was: LeSabre, 105,300; Invicta, 28,700; Electra 225 Series, 20,900; large wagons, 8,000; Special cars, 68,800; and Special wagons, 18,600.

The new Special series consisted of three basic styles, varied by trim and interior options. All models used a 112-inch wheelbase chassis and were 188.4 inches overall.

Power was by a brand new 215-cubic-inch V-8, rated at 155 horsepower at 4600 RPM. The engine had a bore and stroke of 3.5 x 2.8 inches and a compression ratio of 8.8:1. Tires were 13-inch, while all other Buicks used 15-inch rims.

The LeSabre and Invicta models continued to use a 123-inch wheelbase, but the overall length was reduced to 213.2 inches. No new models were added to either series, but the 4-door sedan was dropped from the Invicta Series. The LeSabre continued to use the 364-cubic-inch engine of 250 horsepower, while the Invicta and Electra Series continued to use the 401-cubic-inch engine of 325 horsepower.

The Electra Series used a new 126-inch wheelbase chassis for both the Electra and Elactra 225 models, and the overall length of both sub-series was reduced to 219.2 inches. No new models were added to either series, but the 4-door sedan was dropped from the Electra 225 Series.

Again, power steering and brakes were standard on the Electras, but cost $150 more on other models. Air conditioning retained its extra price of $430.

Buick's main show car this year was the Flamingo, which really was just a trimmed Electra 225 Convertible painted a brilliant flamingo pink. Its major claim to fame was a reversible front passenger seat, so that the passenger could face rearward to converse with rear seat passengers.

A very attractive car was the new Electra 225 Convertible, Model 4867, which had a fairly decent production run of 7,158. It cost $4,192 and weighed 4,441 pounds. Electra 225 and Electra models used the same 126-inch wheelbase chassis and all were 219.2 inches in overall length.

Buick' most expensive car this year was the Electra 225 Riviera Sedan, Model 4829, which cost $4,350 and weighed 4,417 pounds. Despite its relatively high price, it had a fairly good run of 13,719. The car used the same roof line as the Electra 4-door Sedan, but was minus the centerpost. Only the two Electra 225 models used the large chrome gravel guards, with exhaust louvers, which ran from the rear wheel opening to the bumper.

Destined to be dropped at the end of the year was the entire Electra Series, of which the most popular car was the 4-door Sedan, Model 4719. It cost $3,825 and weighed 4,298 pounds. Buick built 13,818. The sedan version used rear quarter windows, and had a much smaller rear window than did its companion 4-door hardtop. It also was fitted with centerposts.

ELECTRA

Far less popular than the Electra Sedan was the Electra 4-door Hardtop, Model 4739, which had a run of only 8,978. It cost $3,932 and weighed 4,333 pounds. As of 1962, all Electra models would be absorbed by an expanded Electra 225 Series.

The least popular of all the Electras was the 2-door Hardtop, Model 4737, of which only 4,250 were built. It cost $3,818 and weighed 4,260 pounds. Both the Electra and Electra 225 Series used four decorative ventiports on each front fender, with series signature on the leading edges of the front fenders. However, Electras did not use the rear fender chrome gravel shields.

The Invicta 4-door Hardtop, Model 4638, was the most popular car in its series, with sales moving up slightly to 18,398. In fact, it was one of the few models to show a sales increase this year. It cost $3,515 and weighed 4,179 pounds.

INVICTA

The Invicta 2-door Hardtop, Model 4637, this year had a run of only 6,382. It cost $3,447 and weighed 4,090 pounds. Both Invictas and LeSabres used the three ventiports as fender trim, and were identified by signature plaques on the leading edge of the front fenders. Also available in the Invicta line was the Convertible, Model 4667, which cost $3,620 and weighed 4,206 pounds. Only 3,953 were built.

The LeSabre 2-door Hardtop, Model 4437, used a much more swept-back roof line and rear window than did the 2-door sedan model. It cost $3,153 and weighed 4,054 pounds. Buick built 14,474. In addition to completed cars, Buick shipped 576 unassembled Specials and 96 unassembled LeSabre chassis overseas for final assembly.

The new LeSabre Sedan, Model 4469, now used a top style similar to the hardtop models, but with a centerpost and rounded rear door corners. The car turned out to be Buick's second most popular model, with 35,005 being produced. It cost $3,107 and weighed 4,102 pounds.

Buick's most popular style this year was the LeSabre 4-door Hardtop, Model 4439, which had a run of 37,790. It cost $3,228 and weighed 4,129 pounds. All LeSabres were 213.2 inches overall, and shared both bodies and 112-inch wheelbase chassis with the more expensive Invicta line.

Three LeSabres appeared in the series for the last time this year. They were the convertible and the two wagon models. The convertible, Model 4467, cost $3,382, weighed 4,186, and had a run of 11,951. The wagons were the 3-seat version, Model 4445, shown here, which had a run of 2,423, cost $3,730 and weighed 4,483; and the 2-seat version, Model 4435, which cost $3,623, weighed 4,450 pounds, and had a run of 5,628. The roof rack shown here was an accessory.

The only full-size Buick with a base price under $3,000 was the LeSabre 2-door Sedan, Model 4411, which cost $2,993 in basic form. The 4,033-pound car had a run of 5,959. It was the only full-size Buick 2-door model to use a centerpost.

LESABRE

The chassis of the Electras was of completely new design, with no side rails, but simply a heavy X-frame spreading widely at front and back for the bumper horns. Again, a large transverse muffler was used, but the torque drive was done away with. This marked the first time since 1907 that Buick did not use torque tube drive. Power steering and brakes were standard on all Electra and Electra 225 models, cost $250 extra in the other series. New for the year was a starter switch combined with the ignition switch on the dash, doing away with the accelerator mounted starter that had been in use since 1934.

The most popular car in the totally new Special line was the 4-door Sedan, available in both Standard Special and Special Deluxe versions. The Standard line was the Model 4019, which cost $2,384, weighed 2,610, and had a run of 18,339. The Deluxe version was the Model 4119, which cost $2,519, weighed 2,632, and had a run of 32,986. The lowest priced car in the Special Series was the Standard 2-door Coupe, Model 4027, which cost $2,330, weighed 2,579 pounds, and had a run of 4,232. All Specials used three ventiports as side decoration.

A totally new concept for Buick was the Special Series, a complete line of small and somewhat economical cars designed to compete for the buyers who wanted an economy car a little larger than the foreign imports and a little better than the current domestic compacts. As can be seen from the front and rear views of the Special Deluxe Sedan, the new line bore definite style similarities to the full-size Buick line. Specials were 188.4 inches overall.

The Specials were powered by an all-new light V-8 of 215 cubic inches that developed 155 horsepower at 4600 RPM. It had a compression ratio of 8.8:1 and used a bore and stroke of 3.5 x 2.8 inches.

Introduced at mid-year was the Special Deluxe Skylark Coupe, Model 4317, which differed in many respects from the other Specials. It used a different grille and different taillight and rear panel treatment, was fitted with a vinyl top, and was powered by a 185-horsepower version of the 215-cubic-inch engine. It cost $2,621, weighed 2,687 pounds, and had a run of 12,683.

The new Special Series offered three wagon models, all using the same exterior, but fitted with interior differences and trim options. In the standard line were two of the wagons, the Model 4045, a 3-seat version which sold for $2,762, weighed 2,844 pounds, and had a run of only 798, and the Model 4035, a 2-seat version, which cost $2,681, weighed 2,775 pounds and had a run of 6,101. The Special Deluxe version, Model 4135, had a run of 11,729 in 3-seat version only.

The Opel Rekord was a totally new car this year, and a rather attractive one, compared with other imports of the era. This is the 2-door Sedan, Model 11, which still cost $1,988 and weighed 1,966 pounds. It was 177.8 inches long overall and used a 100-inch wheelbase chassis.

The interior of the new Opel Sedan was rather attractive and well furnished considering the price of the car. A carpet was provided in the rear compartment, but rubber mats were used in the front. Interior colors were matched to the exterior paint in both the sedan and the wagon.

The new and improved lines of the Opel Rekord enhanced the sedan and definitely made the 5-passenger Caravan wagon a better looking car. Designated the Model 14, the wagon cost $2,293 and weighed 2,109. The roof-top luggage rack was an accessory. Both the Opel and the new Special wagons used a one-piece hatch-back rear gate, hinged at the top section.

The large Flxible ambulance also used an extended Electra chassis. It was available in either plain paint or with a matching color insert, as shown. This example was done in white with a red center panel. The flashers in the rooftop pods, siren, and roof-top "crazy" light were installed at the buyer's option.

In the economy range, the Flxible Co. produced the Flxette ambulance, which used a standard Electra chassis.

The Flxible Co. of Loudonville, Ohio, came in strong on Buick chassis this year, with a series of totally new bodies in both the ambulance and hearse lines. The showpiece of the Flxible line was its Premier Landau Hearse, which was built on an extended Electra chassis. It used blanked quarter panels and a vinyl covered top, sporting the decorative chromed landau irons.

The Flxible Flxette Hearse was a short-wheelbase version of the Premier Landau Hearse. It used a standard Electra chassis and relied heavily on basic Buick body parts. As did its much larger and more expensive brother, the car had blanked in rear quarters and a rough-grain vinyl top with decorative landau irons.

1962

With the Electra Series gone, the Electra 225 Series was the only line to use the large chassis of 126-inch wheelbase. The cars were 220 inches long overall. This is the Electra 225 4-door Sedan, Model 4819, which cost $4,051 and weighed 4,304 pounds.

Buick's most expensive car continued to be the Electra 225 Riviera Sedan, which used the same styling as the 4-door sedan, but lacked centerpost and door frames. It cost $4,448 and weighed 4,390 pounds. Never popular, it was dropped at the end of the model year.

Using its own top with blank rear quarters was the Electra 225 4-door Hardtop, Model 4839, which cost $4,186 and weighed 4,309 pounds. Electras used four ventiports on the front fenders, compared with all other Buick series which used only three.

After one relatively large change year, it would seem that things would remain quiet in the Buick stable. Not so this year, however. There was a radically new engine introduced, a relatively wild scrambling of series and models, and, of course, the expected sheet metal changes.

All of this proved advantageous in Buick's marketing. Calendar year production was 415,892, which moved Buick past Mercury and into sixth place. Model year production for the large cars was 245,683, or 3.7% of the market; while model-year production of the Specials was 154,467, or 2.3% of the total market.

Of the Buick production, by series it ran: LeSabre, 127,200; the new Wildcat, 43,300; Electra, 62,500; wagons, 13,700; Special cars, 133,900; and Special wagons, 20,600.

The new and well received Special line was now broken into three distinct sub-series. They were the Special Standard, the Special DeLuxe, and the Special Skylark. In addition, Buick came out with a radically new engine. This was, of all things, a V-6 of 198 cubic inches. The introduction of this engine marked the first time that a V-6 was ever used in a major make of American car. The little block developed 135 horsepower at 4600 RPM. It used a cast iron block with a bore and stroke of 3.62 x 3.2 and a compression ratio of 8.8:1. The new engine was available only in the Special Standard series, and in some Oldsmobile models, and yet, 59,200 of these blocks appeared in Specials this year.

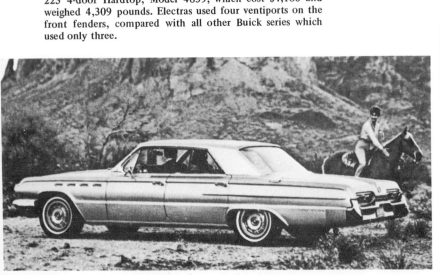

One of the cleanest automotive designs this year was the Electra 225 2-door Hardtop, Model 4847. It cost $4,062 and weighed 4,235 pounds. All Electra models used a ribbed gravel guard just forward of the rear bumper. The Electra 225 signature rode between this guard and the wheel opening.

One of the most luxurious upper-middle price convertibles on the road this year was the Electra 225 Convertible, Model 4867. It is shown here equipped with the optional central console and bucket seats. In standard form, it cost $4,366 and weighed 4,396 pounds.

The Special DeLuxe Series used the year-old 215-cubic-inch engine of 155 horsepower at 4600 RPM, but its compression was raised to 9:1. The Special Skylark Series used the same block, but it was heated to develop 190 horsepower at 4800 RPM, using an 11:1 compression ratio. All Special models had a 112.1-inch wheelbase chassis and were 188.4 inches overall.

The LeSabre and Invicta Series were continued on a 123-inch wheelbase chassis, but all models grew to 214.1 inches overall. Some mixing of models occurred, with the new Wildcat Coupe appearing as the big news car in the Invicta Series. But the LeSabre Series was reduced through the loss of its station wagon models and its convertible. The wagons were picked up by the Invicta Series, but since that series already had its own convertible, the LeSabre convertible simply disappeared.

Dropped from production was the 364-cubic-inch block, formerly used only in the LeSabres. This year the LeSabres used a de-tuned version of the 401-cubic-inch mill, rated at 280 horsepower at 4400 RPM. The Invictas and Electras used the same engine, but rated at 325 horsepower at 4400 RPM. The compression ratio on this block remained 10.25:1.

Dropped completely was the Electra Series, with all previous Electra styles now being incorporated into the expanded Electra 225 Series. That series continued to use the 126-inch wheelbase chassis, but its outside dimensions now grew to 220 inches overall.

Again, power steering and brakes were standard on the Electra 225 Series, but cost $150 more on the other large Buicks and $130 extra on the Specials. Air conditioning on the Specials was $350 extra, while on the large Buicks it was $430 extra.

Buick made a return to Indianapolis this year, but not under Buick sponsorship. Mickey Thompson used a heavily reworked Buick V-8 in his Harvey Aluminum Special which Dan Gurney successfully piloted through ninety-two laps of the Memorial Day Classic before a burned out rear end gear forced the car from the race. The car had qualified at 147.88 MPH, which resulted in its starting in eighth position.

In Italy, the Apollo company received a license from Buick to manufacture a line of small sports cars powered by 215- or 300-cubic-inch Buick engines. The cars were to be made in Italy with final assembly in California. About ninety such cars were produced from 1962 to 1964, when assembly shifted to Dallas, and the car became known as the Vetta Ventura. U.S. production appears to have fizzled out about 1966, when the assembly was returned to Italy and a new model was put out bearing the name Torino and using primarily Ford components.

New for the year was the Invicta Wildcat Coupe, Model 4647. It weighed 4,150 pounds and sold for $3,927, thus being the most expensive car in the Invicta line. Standard equipment was a special vinyl interior with bucket seats, vinyl top, and its own special side trim and identity signatures. In 1963, the Wildcat would be a series of its own, virtually replacing the Invicta Series.

The Invicta Sport Hardtop, Model 4647, used the same styling as the new Wildcat Coupe, but lacked the vinyl top and fancy interior. Its roof contained decorative rib lines pressed into the metal, hinting of the rib lines in a convertible top. The car cost $3,733 and weighed 4,077 pounds.

Buick's mid-range ragtop was the Invicta Convertible, Model 4667, which cost $3,617 and weighed 4,217 pounds. All LeSabres and Invictas were 214.1 inches overall and used the same chassis of 123-inch wheelbase. The primary difference between the two cars was under the hood.

1962

The Invicta 4-door Hardtop, Model 4639, cost $3,667 and weighed 4,159 pounds. Its standard engine was the 325 horsepower 401-cubic-inch block. Invictas were identified by a rectangular signature block on the leading edge of the front fenders.

INVICTA

The Estate Wagons this year moved from the LeSabre Series to the Invicta Series, where they could be equipped with the more powerful engine at no increase in base price. The wagons still came in two basic styles, the 2-seat version, Model 4635, which cost $3,836 and weighed 4,471, and the 3-seat version, Model 4645, which cost $3,917 and weighed 4,505 pounds.

New for the wagon line was a bucket seat option, which could be ordered for either the 2-seat or 3-seat models. It is shown here on the 3-seat version. The third seat still faced rearward.

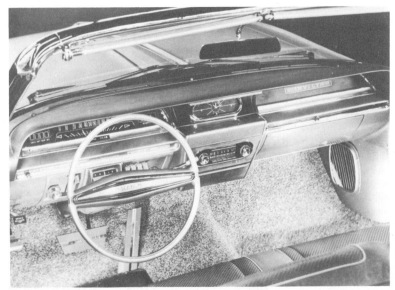

Buick this year had a very refined and attractive dashboard, with the instruments well hooded to prevent windshield glare. Warning lights were used for temperature, generator, and oil. This is the Invicta Convertible interior, which used carpeting throughout, with a rubber heel pad.

1962

Both the LeSabre 4-door Hardtop, Model 4439, and the 4-door Sedan used similar roof lines, but the hardtop lacked both centerposts and door frames. It cost $3,369 and weighed 4,156 pounds. Standard equipment included Turbine Drive and the new fin-cooled aluminum brake drums.

Featuring new top styling was the LeSabre 2-door Hardtop, Model 4447. Its metal roof now contained three pressed rib lines to give it a convertible-like appearance. The car cost $3,293 and weighed 4,054 pounds. LeSabre buyers were given Turbine Drive and a heater-defroster as standard equipment, but could order a 3-speed manual transmission at a price reduction of $108.

The LeSabre 4-door Sedan, Model 4469, continued to be a popularity leader for those who wanted Buick design and workmanship coupled to a relatively low price. It cost $3,227 and weighed 4,104 pounds. Both LeSabres and Invictas used the three ventiports on the front fenders.

The lowest-priced car in the full-size Buick line was the LeSabre 2-door Sedan, Model 4411, which cost $3,091 and weighed 4,041 pounds. Buyers could select either the high compression engine which used premium gas, or the low compression version which would burn regular gas.

The new Special Skylark now developed into a sub-series of its own, consisting of two styles. They were a convertible and this 2-door Hardtop, Model 4347, which cost $2,593 and weighed 2,648 pounds. In a rather unusual move, this year's Specials used a total of four different taillight styles, with wagons, 4-door models, 2-door models, and Skylarks each using a different type of taillight and trim. However, this year both Specials and Skylarks used the same grille.

The most expensive Special, and the only one with a base price over $3,000, was the new Skylark Convertible, Model 4367, which cost $3,012 and weighed 2,871 pounds. The Special Series kept the pointed front fenders which were used on all Buicks in 1961.

The lowest priced car in Buick's entire list was the Special Standard 2-door Coupe, Model 4027. It cost $2,304 and weighed 2,638 pounds. In 8-cylinder form, it could be ordered with standard 3-speed, dual-path turbine drive, or 4-speed floor shift transmissions.

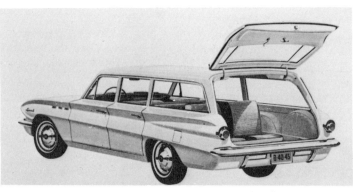

Again the Special Series offered three wagon models, but the 3-seat version shown here was available in the Special Standard sub-series only. Designated the Model 4045, it sold for $2,736 and weighed 2,897 pounds. In 2-seat version, it was designated the Model 4035 and sold for $2,655, and weighed 2,876 pounds. The rear seat continued to face backwards. The spare tire lived on the right rear panel and was hidden with a vinyl cover matching the interior color.

New in the Special Series was the Convertible, which appeared in both the standard and the deluxe sub-series this year. This is the standard version, Model 4067, which lacked the side chrome trim of the deluxe models. It cost $2,587 and weighed 2,858 pounds.

The Special Deluxe Station Wagon, Model 4135, was available in 2-seat form only. It cost $2,890 and weighed 2,845 pounds, with the roof-top luggage rack being extra. All Special wagons continued to use a one-piece hatch-back rear gate, with hinges at the top.

Appearing for the first and last time was the cute Special Deluxe Convertible, Model 4167, which cost $2,879 and weighed 2,280 pounds. All Special Deluxe models offered buyers a choice of three engines and three transmissions, but the new V-6 was available only with a 3-speed manual shift.

As before, the 4-door Sedan was available in the Special Standard and Special Deluxe sub-series. It is shown here in deluxe form, with the side chrome trim running from the front bumper to the rear. The deluxe style was designated the Model 4119, cost $2,593 and weighed 2,468 pounds. In standard form it was designated the Model 4019, cost $2,358, weighed 2,666 pounds.

The Flxible Co. of Loudonville, Ohio, still a major producer of fine buses, and in 1962 still known for its excellent ambulance and hearse bodies on Buick chassis, also produced these interesting special order 8-passenger linousines on extended Electra 225 chassis. The air conditioned vehicles used the basic Electra 225 4-door Hardtop body, much modified to accompany the special-production center section. The top was covered in black rough-grain vinyl, and an electric-powered divider window was included. This exceptionally good looking original model is owned by Roger Hannay of Westerlo, N.Y.

Because of Buick's new body styling, the Flxible Co. of Loudonville, Ohio, again had to change the bodywork of its impressive lines of hearses and ambulances. This is the new Flxible ambulance, built on an extended Electra 225 chassis. Front and rear flasher lights were optional.

The Premiere Landau continued to be Flxible's top of the line hearse, with its body lines comforming to Buick's new lines. It used an extended Electra 225 chassis, and again featured huge blanked in quarters, rough-grain vinyl top and chromed landau irons.

Still being produced were the economy sized Flxette styles of ambulances and hearses built by the Flxible Co. These cars used a regular Electra 225 chassis of 126-inch wheelbase, and carried smaller versions of the large ambulance and hearse bodies. This is the hearse version, which like the large model, used tremendous blanked rear quarters, vinyl top, and landau irons.

The first rear engine American V-8 car to run at the famed Indianapolis 500 race turned out to be a Buick. The car was the Mickey Thompson-Harvey Aluminum Special, owned by Mickey Thompson Enterprises and driven by Dan Gurney. A qualifying speed of 147.8 miles an hour put the car in eighth starting position. However, in the 92nd lap, a rear end gear gave out, and Gurney had to settle for 20th place in the finish. The car did not reappear in 1963. This was the first time since 1938 that a Buick engined car had competed at Indy, and it would also be the last time that Buick saw the famous Brick Yard, with the exception of pacing the 1975 race.

Buick's big-news car this year was the totally new and radically different (for Buick) Riviera, in no way related to the Riviera Hardtops of bygone days. This was the first entrance of Buick into the newly designated upper medium price "personal luxury" market, which for the past several years had been almost the exclusive territory of Thunderbird.

Calendar year production was 479,399, which was a substantial improvement over 1962, but not enough to hold the line against production increases by other makers. Thus, Buick slipped back to seventh place in the production race.

Model year production on the large Buick was up to 309,068, or 4.2% of the total market; but the Special's production was down to 149,538, or 2.1% of the total market. By series, production ran; LeSabre, way up to 161,700; Wildcat, down to 35,700; the new Riviera, 40,000; Electra 225, down to 58,700; wagons, 13,000; Special cars, down to 132,500; and Special wagons, down to 17,000. Of the Specials, 60,900 had the V-6 engine.

The new Riviera had totally different styling, unlike anything else in the Buick lineup, or unlike anything coming out of General Motors this year. It utilized its own 117-inch wheelbase chassis, was 208 inches overall, and was available only as a hardtop coupe with very deluxe appointments.

Powering the new Riviera was the standard 401-cubic-inch engine used in the other large Buicks, rated at 325 horsepower at 4400 RPM. However, a bore-out version of this engine, rated at 425 cubic inches, was available for an extra $50. This engine developed 340 horsepower at 4400 RPM, had a bore and stroke of 4.312 x 3.64 inches and a compression ratio of 10.25:1, as compared with the 401-cubic-inch model with its bore and stroke of 4.18 x 3.64.

Also new for the year was the Wildcat Series, which had been a single model within the Invicta Series last year. The new Wildcat Series absorbed all of the former Invicta styles, leaving the Invicta as a one-model series consisting only of the Estate Wagon.

In a turnabout, the LeSabre Series was expanded once again, with the new models consisting of two wagons and convertible. The LeSabre, Invicta, and Wildcat models a used a common 123-inch wheelbase chassis, and all wer 215.7 inches overall, a growth of 1.6 inches from the 196 models. All used the same 401-cubic-inch block, but th LeSabre Series used a de-tuned version rated at 28 horsepower at 4400 RPM, while the Invicta and Wildca Series used the same 325 horsepower model found in th Electra 225 and Rivieras.

The Electra 225 Series received some style changes, an two newly designed 4-door hardtop sedans. One of thes was a six-window version and one was a four-window style The series continued to use its own 126-inch wheelbase but all models now grew to a new length of 221.7 inche overall.

The Special models received some fairly substantia design work, and even though the 112-inch wheelbase chassis was retained, the overall length was now stretched to 192.1 inches. The year-old V-6 engine was retained unchanged but was now available in the Special DeLuxe models as well as in the Special Standards.

The Special Skylarks continued to be available only with the 215-cubic-inch V-8. However, this engine had compression ratio of 9:0 and was rated at 155 horsepower at 4600 RPM when used in the Special DeLuxe models but had a compression ratio of 11:0 and was rated at 200 horsepower at 5000 RPM when used in the Skylarks.

Power brakes and steering were standard on all large Buicks except the LeSabre Series, and could be obtained for $150 extra on LeSabres or $130 extra on Specials. Air conditioning cost $350 on the Specials, $430 on all other models.

Totally new for the year was the beautiful and luxurious Riviera Sport Coupe, Model 4747, which was designed to compete in the personal-luxury market dominated by the Ford Thunderbird. The 3,998-pound car cost $4,333. It used its own exclusive chassis of 117-inch wheelbase, and was 208 inches overall. This beautiful example is owned by John Sisler of Morgantown, W. Va.

The interior of the totally new Riviera was beautifully done in natural leather with vinyl side panels and headliner. Bucket seats and a central console were standard. Carpeting was carried half-way up the doors and up the kick panels. Radio, adjustable steering wheel and electric windows were standard, but air conditioning was $350. The car used its own 425-cubic-inch engine.

A beautiful car was the Electra 225 Convertible, Model 4867. At $4,365 and 4,297 pounds, it was Buick's most expensive and heaviest car. All Electras used four decorative ventiports and had wide ribbed chrome gravel guards between the rear wheel and rear bumper. This model has the optional sport interior, consisting of four bucket seats in natural leather and vinyl, a central console with extra storage locker, and an extra speaker between the rear seats.

The Electra 225 Hardtop Sport Coupe, Model 4847, was the lightest Electra this year, weighing 4,153 pounds. It cost $4,062. All Electras used the 126-inch wheelbase chassis and were 221.7 inches long overall. Optional in this and the convertible were bucket seats in leather and vinyl.

The Electra 225 4-door Sedan, Model 4819, continued to use a vastly different roofline than did the hardtop model. It had fairly large rear quarter windows, full chrome door frames, a hidden centerpost, and rather narrow rear roof posts. At $4,051 it was the lowest priced Electra in the line. It weighed 4,241 pounds. The car was also available as the 6-window Pillarless Sedan, Model 4829, which cost $4,254 and weighed 4,284 pounds. This model was identical to the 4-door sedan, except that no centerpost was used, and the door windows had no external frames. The Pillarless Sedan used the large rear quarter windows.

The Electra 225 Hardtop Sedan, Model 4839, was built in 4-window form, and lacked the large rear quarter windows found in both the 4-door sedan and the pillarless sedan. It cost $4,186 and weighed 4,272 pounds. Upholstery was in Belfast cloth and leather-grain vinyl.

The SR 200 Skylark was an interesting one-off show car that in reality was only a slightly modified Skylark Convertible. It used a red and white vinyl interior, and was finished in red with a white racing stripe across the hood, rear deck, and the custom fiberglas top boot. Air scoops on the rear lower quarter panels were to direct cooling air to the rear brake drums.

Buick came out with two Silver Arrow Riviera show cars this year, both quite similar, but with the original version having a few more show-type frills than this second version. Both were painted in metallic silver, used their own special grilles, and had their headlights hidden behind large plastic pods on the leading edges of the fenders.

The Wildcat this year became its own series, consisting of three models. They were a 2-door hardtop, a convertible, and this 4-door Hardtop, Model 4639. It cost $3,871 and weighed 4,222 pounds. Wildcats were quickly identified by their own unique side trim.

A sprightly and sporty car was the new Wildcat Hardtop Sport Coupe, Model 4647, which cost $3,849 and weighed 4,123 pounds. In addition to having distinctive side trim, the Wildcats had their own exclusive grille. The vinyl top and bucket seats shown here were extra.

The most expensive car in the new Wildcat Series was the Convertible, Model 4667, which cost $3,961 and weighed 4,228 pounds. The Wildcats shared their bodies and 123-inch wheelbase chassis with the LeSabre and Invicta Series, but the exterior trim was exclusively Wildcat.

The Invicta Series became a one-model line this year, consisting only of this Estate Wagon, Model 4635, available in 2-seat form only. It cost $3,969 and weighed 4,397 pounds. It differed on the exterior from the LeSabre wagons in that it used a full-length chrome side bar and large signal-turn lights on the front fenders, just above the bumper side panels. It was powered by the 325 horsepower version of the 401-cubic-inch engine.

New for the LeSabre Series were two Estate Wagons, both identical on the outside and differing only in interior fittings. Shown here is the 3-seat version, Model 4445, which cost $3,526 and weighed 4,320 pounds. As before, the third seat faced rearward. The rear gate glass cranked down into the tailgate, and had to be lowered before the tailgate could be swung down. The interior was in all-vinyl, with chrome headliner ribs. The roof rack was an accessory.

The LeSabre Series continued to be Buick's low-price line of full-size cars. This is the LeSabre 4-door Sedan, Model 4469 which cost $3,004 and weighed 3,970 pounds. This year, all LeSabres, Invictas, and Wildcats used the same bodies, of 215.7 inches overall length.

New for the year was the LeSabre Convertible, Model 4467. In standard form, with an all-vinyl interior and 280 horsepower engine, it cost $3,339 and weighed 4,052 pounds. This model has been fitted with the optional bucket seats and central console.

The LeSabre Hardtop Sport Coupe, Model 4447, continued to use its interesting roof design, with the convertible-type rib lines pressed into the metal. The 3,924-pound car cost $3,070.

The LeSabre 4-door Hardtop, Model 4439, continued to use a roof line different from that used on the 4-door sedan. It cost $3,146 and weighed 4,007 pounds. The LeSabre signature appeared on the trailing edges of the rear fenders. All Buicks except the Electras used three decorative ventiports on the front fenders. This model is shown with the optional all-vinyl interior.

The only full-size Buick with a base price under $3,000 was the LeSabre 2-door Sedan, Model 4411, which cost $2,869. The car weighed 3,905 pounds. All LeSabres used the 280 horsepower engine.

One of Buick's show vehicles this year was this split-apart LeSabre 4-door Hardtop. Mounted on a motorized platform, the two halves of the car would separate, so that viewers on both sides of the platform could see the exposed cut-away parts.

Surprisingly, the Special Convertible, Model 4067, was found only in the standard sub-series, and not in the deluxe line. It weighed 2,768 pounds and cost $2,591, with the V-6 engine being standard, and the Fireball of Skylark Aluminun V-8 being optional at extra cost. Interiors were all-vinyl, with bucket seats and console available at extra cost.

The Special Deluxe sub-series was cut back to just two models, a 2-seat wagon, and this 4-door Sedan, 4119, which cost $2,521 with the V-6 or $2,592 with the V-8. On the exterior, it differed from the standard model only in that the deluxe version used a chrome trim bar running from the headlight area to the rear bumper. The standard version, designated the Model 4019, cost $2,363 with the V-6. Both weighed about 2,690 pounds. All Specials were 192 inches overall and used a 112-inch wheelbase chassis.

Buick's lowest priced car continued to be the Special 2-door Coupe, Model 4027, which cost $2,309. The 2,661-pound car was the only Special to use a centerpost and door frames. The Special models lacked the side chrome trim found on the Special Deluxe sub-series.

The Special Series continued to offer three wagon models, two being in the standard sub-series and one in the deluxe line. In the standard line was the 3-seat version, Model 4045, shown here with its rear-facing seat. It cost $2,740 and weighed 2,903 pounds. The standard 2-seat version, Model 4135, cost $2,659 and weighed 2,866 pounds. The deluxe version, available in 2-seat form only, was designated the Model 4135. It weighed 2,858 pounds and cost $2,818 with the V-6, or $2,888 with the V-8. All Special wagons continued to use the one-piece hatch-back rear gate.

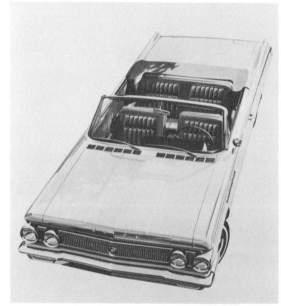

The only Special with a base price over $3,000 was the Special Skylark Convertible, Model 4367, which cost $3,011 and weighed 2,810 pounds. It is shown here with the optional bucket seats, but an all-vinyl interior was standard.

The only hardtop in the Special Series was the Special Skylark Hardtop Coupe, Model 4347, which weighed 2,757 and cost $2,857 with the Skylark Aluminum V-8 of 220 horsepower being standard. The car used different side chrome than did the Deluxe Specials, and a white or black vinyl top was optional at added cost. All-vinyl interiors and/or bucket seats were also optional.

Buick once again started to compete for municipal business, and offered the Special Police Special. The car was the Special Standard 4-door Sedan fitted with the Skylark aluminum V-8 of 200 horsepower and 11:1 compression ratio.

The Premier Landau Hearse still was the prestige funeral car in the Flxible line. It used an extended Electra chassis, and continued to use its large blank rear quarters, vinyl top and decorative landau irons. The Buick shield emblem appeared on the rear door post.

The Flxette Combination Car was produced by the Flxible Co. for those interested in economy. The car used the standard Electra chassis, and could be converted into a hearse or an ambulance in relatively short time. A wide range of interior fittings was available.

A rather pretty little vehicle, that would make an attractive panel truck, was the Flxette Funeral Service Car. It was built on the standard Electra 225 chassis. The vehicle was designed primarily for transporting equipment, caskets, and non-funeral transportation of bodies, but could be used as a hearse when necessary.

 The Flxible Co. of Loudonville, Ohio, continued to produce its range of ambulance and hearse bodies on Buick chassis, used the Electra 225 as the base for all styles. This is the large Flxible ambulance, using an extended chassis verison of the Electra.

This was a growth year for Buick, with all models except the year-old Riviera increasing in size. It was also the year that the slowly diminishing Invicta Series disappeared completely, and one in which further expansion was made to the highly popular Special line, including the Skylark, which now had a complete complement of models plus two individualized sport wagons.

In the world of production numbers, it was a year of slight growth also. Calendar year production was 482,685, which kept Buick safely in seventh place. Model year production was 511,666, which broken down by series ran: Special, 185,688; LeSabre, 135,163; Wildcat, 84,245; Electra, 68,912; and Riviera, 37,658.

The Special models reflected the most change, with the cars now having a new 115-inch wheelbase, as compared with the 112-inch wheelbase chassis used in the previous years. The car models were now 203.5 inches overall, as were the Special wagons. The Skylark car models followed the same dimensions of the Specials, but the new Skylark wagons used their own exclusive 120-inch wheelbase chassis and were 208.3 inches overall. In addition, better styling, safety, and handling were achieved through the use of 14-inch wheels rather than the previous 13-inch rims.

Not only did the Special's bodies and chassis receive a thorough going over, but two new engines were developed for the series. These were a new V-6 available in all models except the Skylark wagons, and a new V-8, available in all models including the Special Standard Series.

The new V-6 was a 225-cubic-inch block that developed 155 horsepower at 4400 RPM. It used a bore and stroke of 3.75 x 3.4 inches and a compression ratio of 9:1. The new V-8 was a 333-cubic-inch mill developing 210 horsepower at 4600 RPM. It used the same bore, stroke, and compression as did the V-6. In this chapter, all prices and weights listed are for the V-8, which cost $70 more and was sixteen pounds heavier than the V-6.

In the big car world, the LeSabre retained its 123-inch wheelbase chassis, but the car models grew to 218.9 inches overall, while the wagon models were now 216.7 inches. The standard engine in the LeSabre cars was the new 300-cubic-inch block that developed 325 horsepower at 4400 RPM.

The Wildcat Series, which shared its bodies and running gear with the LeSabre, increased by one model through the inclusion of a 4-door sedan in addition to the 4-door hardtop. This series also used the 401-cubic-inch engine of 325 horsepower, as did the Electra Series. The least overall change was found in the Electra Series, which continued to use its 126-inch wheelbase chassis, its old engine, and grew only slightly to 222.8 inches.

As could be expected, the brand new Riviera changed very little, but it did receive a major change under the hood. This was a new V-8 of 425 cubic inches that developed 340 horsepower at 4400 RPM. It had a bore and stroke of 4.312 x 3.64 and a compression ratio of both Buicks for $50 extra, or $190 extra when fitted with two 4-barrel carburetors. As before, power steering and brakes were standard on Electras and Rivieras, cost $150 more on Wildcats, and $140 more on LeSabres and Specials. Air conditioning still cost $430 additional on Buicks and $35 more on the Specials.

Buick's most expensive, most unusual, and most attractive car was the year-old Riviera, Model 4747. It cost $4,385 and weighed 3,951 pounds. It is shown here in front of the Coronado Hotel in Del Coronade, Cal. Virtually unchanged from the 1963 models, the Rivieras continued to use their own exclusive 117-inch wheelbase chassis and were 208 inches overall. They used as standard power the 425-cubic-inch engine of 340 horsepower. This engine was optional in all other full-size Buicks.

The rear of the Riviera continued to be as attractive as the front end, and overall, the car was about as distinctive a vehicle as could be found. The simulated scoops before the rear wheel openings were strictly decorative.

The new length of the Electra 225 models was accented by the long rear overhang, most noticeable in the Sport Coupe and Convertible models. This is the Sport Coupe, Model 4847, which cost $4,070 and weighed 4,149 pounds. All Electras were identified by the four ventiports on the front fender, plus the return to the attractive standard rear fender skirts.

The Electra 225 6-window Hardtop, Model 4829, used the same roof styling and rear quarter windows as the 4-door sedan, but lacked the centerpost between the doors and the fixed window frames. It cost $4,261 and weighed 4,238 pounds. All Buicks used both a ridged hood and ridged trunk deck.

All large Buicks used the same dashboard, with trim varying between models. All instruments were now grouped in the two dial faces directly in front of the driver, but only the speedometer and gas guage were of the indicator type. Oil, generator, and heat conditions were signaled by warning lights. Heater controls were located above the radio. This is the Electra 225 version.

The Electra 225 4-window Hardtop, Model 4839, used its own distinctive roof line with blanked quarter panels. It cost $4,194 and weighed 4,229 pounds. The grilles were similar to those of the Wildcats, but not interchangeable. The chromed cross bars were die-cast. All Electras were built on a 126-inch wheelbase chassis and were 222.8 inches overall.

By far the most beautiful of the entire Electra 225 Series (if one likes ragtops) was the Convertible, Model 4867. Standard equipment included upholstery of natural leather and vinyl and electric windows. The rear seat speaker shown here was optional at extra cost. In base form, it cost $4,374 and weighed 4,280 pounds.

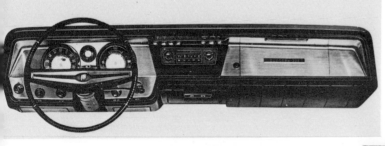

The Electra 225 Series still offered three 4-door models, the lowest priced of which was the 4-door Sedan, Model 4819. It cost $4,059 and weighed 4,212 pounds. All Electras came equipped with the Super Turbine transmission, and power brakes and steering.

The Wildcat Convertible, Model 4667, continued to be one of the best looking cars in Buick's total line. It sold for $3,455 and weighed 4,076 in basic form. This attractive model used the optional 340 horsepower engine of 425 cubic inches. It wears the accessory factory Formula Five chromed steel wheels. Its owner, William W. Cushing of Goshen, Ind., rebuilt the car from a junker. Currently in daily use, the car now registers 104.000 miles, with neither engine nor transmission ever having an overhaul.

A sporty hardtop was the Wildcat Sport Coupe, Model 4647, which cost $3,267 and weighed 4,003 pounds. This model sports the optional vinyl top and bucket seats with console. All Wildcats used carpeting throughout, and the coupe and convertibles used all-vinyl interiors.

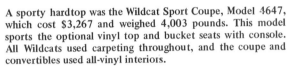

An interesting option, used fairly frequently on the Wildcat models, were these mag-type chromed steel wheels, seen here on the 4-door Hardtop, Model 4639. Standard power in the Wildcats was the 325 horsepower Wildcat 445 engine with a manual 3-speed transmission.

The Wildcats used the same basic bodies as did the LeSabres, but were quickly identified by the ribbed full-length chrome molding just above the rocker panels and the three vertical decorative ventiports on the trailing part of the front fender. The 4-door Sedan, Model 4669, cost $3,164 and weighed 4,021 pounds. The wheel discs were accessories.

Both the LeSabre 2-door Hardtop and the Convertible used a full-length piece of side chrome running from the leading edge of the front fenders to the taillights and incorporating the ventiports within the spear. The hardtop, or Sport Coupe, Model 4447, cost $3,061 and weighed 3,629 pounds. Its roof was still stamped with the decorative rib lines.

The LeSabre Convertible, Model 4467, was an attractive car, made even better looking with the accessory wire-type wheel covers and front fender signal-turning lights. It cost $3,314 and weighed 3,787 pounds. The LeSabre signature appeared on the trailing edge of the rear fender. Also available in the LeSabre Series were Buick's only full-size wagons, the Estate Wagon, in the 3-seat Model 4645, and the 2-seat Model 4635. Both were 216.7 inches in overall length. The 3-seat version cost $3,635 and weighed 4,362 pounds, while the 2-seat model cost $3,554 and weighed 4,352 pounds.

The only full-size Buick with a base price under $3,000 was the LeSabre 4-door Sedan, Model 4469, which cost $2,980 and weighed 3,693 pounds. LeSabres shared their bodies with the Wildcat Series. All models except the wagons were 218.9 inches overall.

Both LeSabre 4-door models used a short piece of side chrome extending from mid-point on the rear door to the taillights. The three ventiports were free floating on the front fenders. This is the LeSabre 4-door Hardtop, Model 4439, which cost $3,122 and weighed 3,730 pounds. Standard power in all LeSabres was the 210 horsepower V-8 with standard 3-speed transmissions.

The Special standard and deluxe models could be quickly identified by the chrome side trim running from headlight to taillight below the three ventiports. The deluxe models had it; the standard ones did not. This is the Special Deluxe 4-door Sedan, Model 4169, which cost $2,561 and weighed 3,034 pounds. In standard form it was the Model 4069, cost $2,468, weighed 3,016 pounds. The wheel covers shown here were accessories. An innovation on this year's Specials was the curved glass side windows. Upholstery was Brigade cloth in striped pattern.

New for the Special Deluxe sub-series was the 2-door Coupe, Model 4127, which cost $2,529 and weighed 3,014 pounds. It was simply a dolled-up version of the standard 2-door Coupe, Model 4069, which cost $2,414 and weighed 2,999 pounds. Standard power in all Specials was the 155 horse-power V-6 with 3-speed synchromesh transmission.

Although technically the Special Convertible, Model 4067 was listed in the standard sub-series, the car featured the chrome side trim found only in the deluxe sub-series. It cost $2,676 and weighed 3,115 pounds. All Special models, including wagons, and all Skylark car models were 203.5 inches overall and used the same totally new chassis of 115 inches wheelbase. All were available with either the V-6 or the V-8, though the prices and weights shown here are for the V-8 engine.

The Special Series offered just two wagons this year, one in deluxe sub-series, and the one shown here in the standard sub-series. Both were 6-passenger models, with the third seat not being available. The standard model was designated Model 4035, cost $2,760, and weighed 3,274 pounds. The deluxe version was the Model 4135, cost $2,858 and weighed 3,293 pounds.

The new Skylark Series was an expanded line of the former Special Skylark sub-series. The cars shared their bodies and chassis with the Special Series, but were quickly identified by a broad chrome bar running the length of the car, into which were set the three decorative ventiports. This is the new Skylark 4-door Sedan, Model 4369, which cost $2,740 and weighed 3,078 pounds.

The new Skylark Sport Coupe was a very pretty little car, especially when fitted with the interesting accessory vinyl top with chrome side trim. Designated the Model 4337, it weighed 3,065 pounds and cost $2,751 in basic form. A leather-grained vinyl interior was standard in this model, optional in the sedans. Bucket seats were available in the coupe.

The Skylark Convertible, Model 4367, had its appearance greatly improved by the new 115-inch wheelbase chassis and the 11-inch overall increase in length. It cost $2,905 and weighed 3,185 pounds. In standard form, it used an all-vinyl interior with bench seats.

Totally new was the Skylark Sportwagon, which used its own 120-inch wheelbase chassis and had its own body which was 208.3 inches in overall length. It featured a vista-dome roof and an all-vinyl interior. It was available in two standard versions and two Custom versions. The standard styles were the Model 4255 2-seat style which cost $2,989 and weighed 3,557 pounds, and the Model 4265 3-seat style which cost $3,124 and weighed 3,689 pounds. The Custom versions were the Model 4355 2-seat style, costing $3,161 and weighing 3,595 pounds and the Model 4365 3-seat style, costing $3,286 and weighing 3,727 pounds.

The interiors of the new Skylark Sport Wagons were tastefully done in all-vinyl, and the Custom models used the deep-pile carpeting throughout as standard equipment. The vista-dome windshield was in tinted glass, but really was more of a novelty than a practical window.

The Specials and Skylarks used a very similar dash, with a bar-type speedometer flanked on the left by fuel gauge and on the right by the optional clock. Heater controls lived in a vertical panel between the speedometer and the radio. This is the Skylark version.

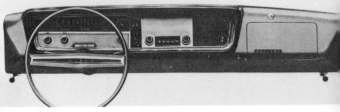

Returning with the new Opels was the Kadett 5-passenger Wagon, Model 34. It cost $1,793 and weighed 1,521 pounds, but the roof rack shown here was an option. The wagon used the same 91.5-inch wheelbase chassis as did the cars, but its body was 157 inches overall.

After more than a year of absence, the Opels returned, now in Kadett form and in three body styles. The boxiest of these was the 2-door Sedan, Model 31, which cost $1,655, and weighed 1,411 pounds. The sun-roof shown here was an optional accessory.

The new Opel Kadett Sport Coupe, Model 32, used the same basic body as did the 2-door sedan, but was blessed with a much more attractive roof line. It cost $1,818 and weighed 1,422 pounds. The tiny 2-door Opels used a 91.5-inch wheelbase chassis and were only 154.4 inches overall.

The Flxible Premier Landau hearse remained the company's prestige funeral vehicle, but this year it was more obvious that the car shared the same basic body with the ambulance. The rear quarter was still blank, but this was now accomplished by fitting a vinyl panel over the rear quarter windows. This panel was removable in the event a 6-window limousine style hearse was desired or if the vehicle was to be used as a combination ambulance-hearse.

Soon to disappear from the scene were the beautiful ambulances and hearses built by the Flxible Co. of Loudonville, Ohio. The company would phase itself out of this business during 1965. This is the Flxible ambulance, built on an extended Electra 225 chassis. It was built for the West End Fire Co. #3 of New Jersey.

And here we go — Buick did exactly what every other auto manufacturer was trying to do, and came out with a host of new model variations and a wide assortment of series and sub-series designed to cover the market's economic range with as wide a blanket as possible. Cover they did, but the result was as confusing an array of cars, models and prices as could be imagined.

Where once just Wildcats lived, there were now Wildcats, DeLuxe Wildcats, and Wildcat Customs. Electra sub-divided into Electras and Electra Customs, and LeSabre did the same thing in its own backyard. Only the Special lines, already expanded almost to capacity and the one-model Riviera Series remained untouched. However, the Special Standard designation was dropped, and that car became known simply as the Special.

Buick's most expensive car was the new Riviera Gran Sport, which cost $4,775. This was the basic Riviera fitted with the 425-cubic-inch engine and 4-barrel carburetor, a floor-four transmission, positraction rear end, and a host of other performance and trim items. Gran Sport Rivieras were identified by a small signature block just after the front wheel opening.

All of this had some effect on sales. Calendar year production was an excellent 653,838, which moved Buick up to fifth place, passing both Oldsmobile and Dodge. Model-year production was 600,787; which broken down by series ran: Special, 234,969; LeSabre, 144,996; Wildcat, 98,787; Electra, 86,810; and Riviera, 34,586.

No major changes took place in the Special line. The cars continued to use their year-old 115-inch wheelbase chassis, but were shortened slightly to a new length of 203.4 inches for the cars and 203.2 inches for the Special wagons. The Skylark Sport wagons retained their exclusive 120-inch wheelbase chassis, but they too were shortened slightly to a new length of 208.2 inches.

Power units in the Special range remained unchanged, with both the V-6 and the V-8 available in all Specials except the Skylark Sportwagons, which used the V-8 as standard power. In this chapter, all prices and weights are for the cars equipped with the V-8, which cost approximately $70 more and weighed 100 pounds more than the V-6.

The new LeSabre and LeSabre Custom models continued to use a 123-inch wheelbase chassis. Little changed, the cars were still 216.8 inches overall, and used for standard power the 300-cubic-inch V-8 that was used in the Specials.

In a surprise move, the new Wildcat family dropped its 123-inch wheelbase chassis and adopted the Electra's 126-inch wheelbase version. However, the sheet metal was not shared. The Electras grew to a new length of 224 inches overall, while the Wildcats had to be content with a growth to 219.8 inches.

The Riviera received a noticeable change in the grille

The beautiful Riviera, Model 49447, grew one inch, to a new overall length of 209 inches. The growth was caused primarily by a totally new rear end design, with the taillights now an integral part of the rear bumper. The decorative scoops in front of the rear wheel well were now gone, resulting in a much smoother appearance overall. The Riviera cost $4,318 and weighed 4,036 pounds.

The most noticeable change in this year's Riviera was the new grille, which used concealed headlights located in the very attractive ribbed chrome fender pods. The ribbed chrome theme was carried over to the wide rocker panel covers, which extended onto the lower edges of the doors. The mag-type chromed steel wheels were an added cost option.

work, with a full-width grille and hidden headlights gracing the front end. In addition, the car grew one more inch to a new length of 209 inches overall, though its wheelbase remained 117 inches.

All Wildcats, Electras, and Rivieras shared the same 401-cubic-inch engine of 325 horsepower with the year-old 425-cubic-inch mill being an option at $185 in the Riviera and $214 extra in all other models. As before, power steering and brakes were standard in the Electras and Rivieras, but cost $137 more on the Specials and LeSabres and $147 more on the Wildcats. Air conditioning cost $343 on the Specials and $421 extra on all other models. New for the year was a Gran Sport package that could be added for another $450.

In July, Edward T. Rollert, who is credited with conceiving and producing the highly successful Skylark, moved on to bigger things at General Motors, and Robert L. Kessler took over as Buick's general manager.

Buick seemed to go series wild this year, with all series except the Skylark dividing into two or more sub-series. Leading the run was the Electra Series, which divided into the Electra 225 and the Electra 225 Custom sub-series. This is the Electra 225 4-door Sedan, Model 48269, which cost $3,989 and weighed 4,261 pounds. In the custom sub-series it was designated the Model 48469, priced at $4,168, and weighed 4,292 pounds.

Available only in the Electra 225 Custom sub-series was the Convertible, Model 48467. It cost $4,350 and weighed 4,325. The Electras continued to use the four decorative ventiports on the front fenders, a tradition going back to the 1949 Roadmasters. The turn lights were standard.

ELECTRA 225...

Style-leader of the Electra 225 line was the Sport Coupe, Model 48237, whose new length was accentuated by the wide and very attractive ribbed side molding that extended from the front wheel well through the rear fender skirts and ended at the rear bumper. The high style wheel covers were standard. The car cost $3,999 and weighed 4,208 pounds. It was also available in the custom sub-series as the Model 48437, which cost $4,179 and weighed 4,228 pounds.

The Wildcat Hardtop Sport Coupe could be ordered with a wide variety of options, including the chrome steel wheels on this model and a vinyl top, not shown. It was available in all three sub-series. Shown here is the plain Wildcat, Model 46237, which was the least expensive model, costing $3,219 and weighing 3,988 pounds. In this form, it was the only Wildcat with a basic weight under 2-tons. In the Wildcat Deluxe sub-series it was the Model 46437, which cost $3,272 and weighed 4,014 pounds. In the Wildcat Custom sub-series, fitted with standard bucket seats and console, it was the Model 46637, cost $3,493, and weighed 4,047 pounds.

The Electra 225 4-door Hardtop, Model 48239, used a roof line with far sharper angles than that found on the sedan. It cost $4,121 and weighed 4,284 pounds. It was also available in the custom sub-series as the Model 48439, where it cost $4,300 and weighed 4,344 pounds. All Electras grew to 224 inches overall, but continued to use the 126-inch wheelbase chassis.

The Wildcat Convertible was available only in the Deluxe and Custom sub-series, with the main difference being that the Custom version, shown here, was fitted with bucket seats, central console, and rear seat speaker. In this form, it was designated the Model 46667, weighed 4,087 pounds, and at $3,651 was the most expensive Wildcat. In the deluxe sub-series, it was the Model 46467. There it cost $3,431 and weighed 4,069 pounds.

1965

The Wildcat 4-door Hardtop was available in all three sub-series. It is shown here in Custom form, where it was designated the Model 46639, and was fitted with standard bucket seats and central console. It cost $3,552 and weighed 4,160 pounds. In the Wildcat Deluxe sub-series it was the Model 46439, with a price of $3,338 and a weight of 4,075 pounds. The least expensive version was the standard Wildcat, Model 46239, which cost $3,278 and weighed 4,089 pounds.

The LeSabre Custom sub-series used a slightly wider center bar in the grille than did the standard LeSabres, and the cars were fitted with side signal-turn lights above the front bumpers. This is the custom Sport Coupe, Model 45437, which cost $3,037 and weighed 3,724 pounds. The vinyl top was extra. The style was also available in the standard LeSabre series as the Model 45237, where it cost $2,968 and weighed 3,753 pounds.

Both the Electra and LeSabre Series divided into two sub-series each, but the Wildcat Series went this one better, and divided into three sub-series. Available in only two of these sub-series was the 4-door Sedan, shown here in standard form. In this version it was designated the Model 46269, cost $3,117, and weighed 4,058 pounds. In the Wildcat Deluxe sub-series it was designated the Model 46469, cost $3,218, and weighed 4,046 pounds. All Wildcats this year used the Electra's chassis of 126-inch wheelbase, but were fitted with their own bodies of 219.8 inches overall length. The series continued to use fender side chrome instead of ventiports.

Available only in the LeSabre Custom sub-series was the Convertible, Model 45467, which cost $3,257 and weighed 3,812 pounds. However, a switch apparently was made after many 1965 Buick catalogs were distributed, as early brochures list the convertible in the standard LeSabre sub-series, and show the car with the standard LeSabre grille and lacking the side signal-turn lights on the front fenders.

LeSABRE...

The LeSabre 4-door Hardtop, Model 45239, cost $3,027 and weighed 3,809 pounds. It was also available as the LeSabre Custom, Model 45439. In this version it cost $2,101, weighed 3,811 pounds. The roof styling had a much sharper rear door corner than did the sedan models.

The lowest priced full-size Buick was the LeSabre 4-door Sedan, Model 45269, which cost $2,888 and weighed 3,788 pounds. It was also available in the LeSabre Custom sub-series as the Model 45469, where it cost $2,962 and weighed 3,777 pounds. The LeSabres this year did not share their bodies with any other series, but instead had their own 123-inch wheelbase chassis and were all 216.8 inches in overall length. They were quickly identified by the three ventiports on the fenders.

The Skylark Thin Pillar Coupe, Model 44427, differed from the Sport Coupe only in the use of a center pillar and fixed chrome window frames. The interesting top chrome was an extra cost option, and could be installed with or without a vinyl top insert. The Thin Pillar model cost $2,552 and weighed 3,146 pounds. All Specials and Skylarks shared the same basic bodies, used the same 115-inch wheelbase chassis, and were 203.4 inches in overall length.

The Skylark Sport Coupe, Model 44437, was simply a hardtop version of the Thin Pillar Coupe. It cost $2,692 and weighed 3,198 pounds. The chrome roof trim and vinyl top insert were extra cost options, as were the wheel covers with decorative hub spinners.

The Skylark Convertible was offered in two versions, the standard and the Gran Sport. The standard version, Model 44467, cost $2,842 and weighed 3,294 pounds. The Gran Sport model cost $3,299 and used as standard power the 400-cubic-inch engine of 325 horsepower.

The Skylark 4-door Sedan, Model 44469, used the same side chrome as did the Special Deluxe model, but was quickly identified by its ribbed chrome rocker panel and signature on the quarter panel. It cost $2,681 and weighed 3,194 pounds.

Introduced at mid-year was the Skylark Gran Sport, priced at $3,149. This was a deluxe version of the Sport Coupe, fitted with the 400-cubic-inch 325 horsepower engine instead of the standard 300-cubic-inch engine of 210 horsepower. Options included the vinyl top shown here, mag-type chromed steel wheels, transmission, bucket seats, console, tachometer, limited slip differential, and a host of other options, including super turbine transmission and power steering and brakes.

The lowest priced car in the entire Buick line was the Special Standard Coupe, Model 43427, which cost $2,362 and weighed 3,080 pounds. Buick referred to this model as "the thin pillar coupe" to distinguish it from hardtop models. The coupe did not appear in the deluxe sub-series.

The Skylark Sport Wagons continued to be offered in four variations, all with basically the same exterior, and all using the rather novel Skyroof design. This is the Custom Sport Wagon, which in 6-passenger form was the Model 44455, cost $3,092, and weighed 3,690 pounds; and in 9-passenger form was the Model 44465, cost $3,214 and weighed 3,802 pounds. Also available were two standard versions, the 6-passenger Model 44255, which cost $2,925 and weighed 3,642 pounds, and the 9-passenger Model 44265, which cost $3,056 and weighed 3,750 pounds.

The Special Wagon was offered in both the standard and the deluxe sub-series. This is the deluxe version, Model 43635, which cost $2,796 and weighed 3,369 pounds. The standard version was the Model 43435, which cost $2,699 and weighed 3,365 pounds. Both were 6-passenger models.

Surprisingly, the Special Convertible, Model 43467, appeared only in the standard sub-series, where in basic form it was devoid of any side chrome whatever except for the ventiports and the rear fender signature. It cost $2,618 and weighed 3,197 pounds. The wheel covers on this and the coupe were accessories.

With the coupe no longer in the Special Deluxe line, this sub-series was reduced to just two models, a wagon and the 4-door Sedan, Model 43669. In the deluxe sub-series, the sedan cost $2,506 and weighed 3,143 pounds. With the exception of the chrome side bar, the car was virtually identical to the standard version, Model 43469, which cost $2,415 and weighed 3,117 pounds. Even in the deluxe sub-series the wheel covers shown here were accessories.

Look who came to dinner — the new Opel Kadett 2-door Sedan, Model 31. The little car, down in price to $1,618, weighed only 1,411 pounds and was only 154.4 inches overall. The car was unchanged from the 1964 models. A sun roof was optional but not popular.

The Opel Kadett Wagon, Model 34, used the same 91.5-inch wheelbase chassis as did the other Opel models, but it was 157.3 inches overall. It cost $1,753 and weighed 1,521 pounds. The roof-type luggage rack, covering almost the entire roof, was an extra cost item. The car used roll-up windows in the doors, sliding central windows, and fixed rear quarter windows.

The Skylarks and Specials had a new dashboard, similar to but far more attractive than the 1964 version. This is the Skylark model, wearing more chrome trim than the Special style. The Skylarks used carpeting throughout, even running it up the kick panels.

The Opel Kadett Sport Coupe, Model 32, continued to be a much more attractive car than the rather sedate 2-door sedan. However, both used the same lower body, and varied only in roof design. The Sport Coupe cost $1,778 and weighed 1,442 pounds. All models used a 60.6-cubic-inch engine.

Appearing for the last time this year were the hearses and ambulances built on Buick chassis by the Flxible Co. of Loudonville, Ohio. Following this year's model run, Flxible left the professional car business to concentrate on other vehicular activities, primarily the manufacture of fine buses. One of the last models turned out by the company was this combination ambulance-hearse, which used a very high roof line and overall lines far inferior to previous Flxible designs. As usual, it was built on an Electra 225 chassis, but the chassis was not extended.

Except for the usual sheet metal changes, the addition of some very attractive grilles along traditional themes, and the shuffling of some series, there was not too much change in the Buick line this year.

A new series was created. This was the Skylark Gran Sport, which basically was the Skylark with last year's optional Gran Sport equipment added as standard fare. In addition, the Sport wagon became a series unto its own, having four major variations of one basic body. Gone from the ranks was the Wildcat DeLuxe Series, which really had only been an interim trim package between the Wildcat and the Wildcat Custom sub-series.

Calendar year production was 580,421, which was a slip that caused a tumble from fifth to sixth place. The drop allowed Oldsmobile to move back into fifth place. Total model year production was down 2,000 cars, dropping to 558,870. Broken down by series, it reads: Special, 209,314, down about 23,000 units; LeSabre, 147,399, up about 3,000; Wildcat, 68,584, down about 30,000; Electra, 88,225, up about 2,000; and Riviera, a record 45,348, up about 10,000 cars.

In the Special line, the cars continued to use the 115-inch wheelbase, but again grew slightly, with all models now being 204 inches overall. The standard power was still the 225-cubic-inch V-6 or the 300-cubic-inch V-8 of 210 horsepower. However, the V-6 was now rated at 160 horsepower at 4200 RPM. The V-6 was available in all

Special Models except the Sportwagon and the new Skylark Gran Sport.

The Sportwagon retained its 120-inch wheelbase chassis, but it, too, grew slightly to a new length of 209 inches. Its power was by a new 340-cubic-inch engine that developed 220 horsepower at 4000 RPM. It used a bore and stroke of 3.75 x 3.85 inches and a compression ratio of 9:1. An optional speed package with 4-barrel carburetor was available for $265. This package would raise the horsepower to 260.

The new Skylark Gran Sport models used the basic Special bodies, but under the hood it was a different story. There lived a new engine of 400 cubic inches that developed 325 horsepower at 4400 RPM. It had a bore and stroke of 4.18 x 3.64 and a compression ratio of 10.25:1.

Front or rear, the new Riviera was a completely different animal than it had been in 1965. In addition to the obvious exterior changes, the car was fitted with a new Circulaire ventilation system and a new exhaust system. It also sported a new series of exterior colors, with seven exclusively for use on Rivieras only. Standard interior equipment included notchback bench seats, but the high-back Strato Bucket seats were available at extra cost.

For the first time since its introduction, the Riviera was given a totally new body, both in size and design. Designated the Model 49487, it cost $4,378 and weighed 4,298 pounds. The car was now 211.2 inches overall and used a new chassis with a wheelbase of 119 inches. Its parking lights were hidden behind plastic panels on either side of the grille. The grille contained two movable panels which swung out of the way to expose the headlights when these were turned on. Standard power was the 425-cubic-inch engine of 340 horsepower.

The new Riviera grille contained hidden parking lights and concealed headlights. The parking lights lived behind the plastic panels on either side of the grille. When the headlights were turned off, they lived above the grille, under the hood overhang. When turned on, they automatically swung down into position as the grille panels swung out of the way.

Available on the Rivieras was the GS package, which included the large GS signature on the front fenders. This package included positraction rear axle, cast aluminum rocker arm covers, chrome air cleaner, and whitewall tires, and trim goodies not standard on the plain Riviera.

The LeSabres took advantage of the Sportwagon's new engine, and used that as standard equipment — or vice-versa. However, with this exception, there was little change in the series, except for a six inch increase in length to a new overall length of 217 inches.

The Wildcats and Electras continued to use the old faithful 401-cubic-inch block, though the 425-cubic-inch model of 340 horsepower was available for $255 extra. Both series retained the standard 126-inch wheelbase chassis, but the Wildcats grew slightly to a new length of 220 inches while the Electras shrunk slightly to a length of 223.5 inches.

Receiving a major going over was the Riviera, which still maintained its basic theme, but with some quality engineering added. The car now sported a brand new 119-inch wheelbase chassis and was 211.2 inches overall. Its finely sculptured grille and front end still used concealed beam headlights set back from the leading edges of the front fenders. Under the hood as standard power, again was the 425-cubic-inch V-8 or 340 horsepower. This engine, which had been standard in 1964, optional in 1965, and again standard this year, developed 340 horsepower at 4400 RPM, with a compression ratio of 10.25:1. Also available on request was the 401-cubic-inch engine of 325 horsepower, at a reduction in price of $175.

As usual, power steering and brakes were standard on Electras and Rivieras, and cost $145 extra on Wildcats and $135 extra on all other models. Air conditioning was now $343 extra on Specials, $420 extra on all other cars.

Appearing only in the custom sub-series was the Electra 225 Convertible, Model 48467, which cost $4,378 and weighed 4,298 pounds. It is shown here with the optional bucket seats, central console, and rear seat speaker. Regular equipment included bench seats.

All Electras this year sported a new grille, new front end styling and new rear end treatment. The cars were quickly identified by the four traditional ventiports, now cast into one single block on the front fender. This is the Sport Coupe, which in standard form was the Model 48237 which cost $4,032 and weighed 4,176 pounds. In custom trim it was the Model 48437, costing $4,211 and weighing 4,230 pounds. Rear fender skirts were standard trim on all Electras.

The Electra 225 4-door Hardtop is seen here in standard form, with a plain top, but more often than not this car was fitted with the optional vinyl roof. The standard version was the Model 48239, which cost $4,332 and weighed 4,323 pounds. Standard power was the 401-cubic-inch engine of 325 horsepower, but the 425-cubic-inch block of 340 horsepower was a popular option. All Electras used the Super Turbine automatic transmission and power steering and brakes as standard equipment.

All Electra 225 models except the convertible were available in either the standard or the custom sub-series. This is the 4-door Sedan, Model 48269 in the standard version, which cost $4,022 and weighed 4,225 pounds. It is seen here at the Chicago Auto Show wearing the popular optional vinyl top. In the custom sub-series it was the Model 48469, which cost $4,201 and weighed 4,292 pounds. All Electras were 223.5 inches overall and used a 126-inch wheelbase chassis.

The Wildcat Sport Coupe appeared in both the standard and custom sub-series, and was available with the Gran Sport package, as shown here. This package consisted of the 340 horsepower 425-cubic-inch engine with 4-barrel carburetor, dual exhaust, heavy duty exhaust, heavy duty suspension, positraction rear axle, whitewalls, cast aluminum rocker arm covers, and a chrome air cleaner. The GS plaques appeared on grille, rear quarter panel, rear end panel and dashboard. In standard form, the car was the Model 46437, which cost $3,326 and weighed 4,003 pounds. In custom form it was the Model 46637, cost $3,547, and weighed 4,018 pounds. The mag-type wheels were optional.

The Wildcat 4-door Sedan, Model 46469, was available only in plain form, and did not appear in the custom sub-series. It cost $3,233 and weighed 4,070 pounds. Wildcats used the Electra's chassis of 126-inch wheelbase, but had their own bodies, which were 217 inches in overall length. All Wildcats used three ventiports stacked in a vertical pattern. Standard power was the 401-cubic-inch block of 325 horsepower with a manual transmission.

Appearing in both Wildcat and Wildcat Custom sub-series, and being eligible for the Gran Sport package was the Convertible. In standard form, it was the Model 46467, which cost $3,480 and weighed 4,065 pounds. In the custom range it was the Model 46667. This version had a base price of $3,701 and weighed 4,079 pounds.

The Wildcat 4-door Hardtop appeared in both the standard and custom sub-series, but not with Gran Sport trim. In standard form, as shown here, it was the Model 46439, which cost $3,391 and weighed 4,108 pounds. The Custom version, Model 46639, cost $3,606 and weighed 4,176 pounds. All Wildcats had new front sheet metal, grilles, and rear end treatment.

The engine compartments of all cars had become pretty crowded, and the new Wildcat GS models were no exception, especially when fitted with power steering and brakes, as in this model. This car used the cast aluminum rocker arm covers, but is fitted with the standard painted air cleaner instead of the GS chrome-plated unit.

Appearing only in the LeSabre Custom sub-series was the Convertible, Model 45467, which cost $3,326 and weighed 3,833 pounds. It could be ordered with the standard bench seats, an optional notch-back rear seat with speaker, as shown here, or with the optional Strato-Bucket seats.

1966

As did all other LeSabre solid-top models, the 2-door Hardtop appeared in both the standard and custom sub-series. In standard form, as shown here, it was the Model 45237, which cost $3,022 and weighed 3,751 pounds. The custom style was the Model 45437, costing $3,109 and weighing 3,746 pounds. All LeSabres were identified by the three side ventiports in a solid fender bar.

The LeSabre 4-door Hardtop was available in both standard form, as shown here, or in the Custom sub-series. In the standard sub-series it was the Model 45239, which cost $3,081 and weighed 3,828 pounds. The custom version was the Model 45439, costing $3,174 and weighing 3,824 pounds. Standard power was the 340-cubic-inch V-8 of 220 horsepower and a 3-speed manual transmission, but the 260 horsepower engine and Super-Turbine automatic were popular options.

The only full-size Buick with a base price under $3,000 was the LeSabre 4-door Sedan, Model 45269, which cost $2,942. It weighed 3,796 pounds. The car was also available in custom version, where it was the Model 45469, which cost $3,035 and weighed 3,788 pounds. All LeSabres offered new grilles, new front sheet metal styling, new rear end treatment, and new bumpers, trim and ornamentation. All were 217 inches in overall length and used their own 123-inch wheelbase chassis.

Appearing in both the Skylark Gran Sport and the plain Skylark sub-series was the Convertible, shown here in GS version. The GS models used their own distinctive grille with GS plaque, had simulated hood ventiports, special rear trim panel, and used notchback front seats as standard equipment. The GS Convertible was designated the Model 44667, cost $3,167, and weighed 3,532 pounds. In standard form it was the Model 44467, cost $2,904, and weighed 3,259 pounds.

New for the year was the Skylark 4-door Hardtop, Model 44439, which replaced the 4-door sedan in that series. The 4-door sedan was dropped completely from the Skylark Series, although the new hardtop used the sedan's basic lower body but with a new roofline. It cost $2,916 and weighed 3,285 pounds. It was not available in Gran Sport version. Unlike the Specials, which continued to use the traditional ventiport fender decoration, the Skylarks now used three decorative ventiports in a vertical stack behind the wheel well.

Buick's prestige wagon continued to be the Sport Wagon, now considered a series of its own. It was available in Custom or standard versions and in 6- or 9-passenger style. This is the 6-passenger Custom Sport Wagon, Model 44455, which cost $3,155 and weighed 3,720 pounds, with the roof-rack and mag-type wheels being accessories. It differed from the standard models in that it used full length chrome trim, outlining the wheel wells and had a chrome gravel shield between the rear well and the rear bumper. In 9-passenger form it was the Model 44465, which cost $3,293 and weighed 3,844 pounds. In standard version, the 6-passenger version was the Model 44265, which weighed 3,881 pounds and cost $3,173. All Sport Wagons used their own 120-inch wheelbase chassis, and were 209 inches in overall length.

The Skylark Sport Coupe was available in both Gran Sport and standard versions. This is the GS style, Model 44617, which cost $3,019 and weighed 3,428 pounds. It offered the 325 horsepower Wildcat 445 V-8, heavy duty suspension, and mag-type chromed steel wheels as standard equipment. In standard Skylark form, the car was the Model 44417, which cost $2,757 and weighed 3,152 pounds. The new tapered back Strato-Bucket seats were optional in both versions.

The Specials and Skylarks this year had a completely new body with a wider and lower profile, new roofline, new grille and headlight design, and new rear end and taillight treatment. This is the Special Deluxe 4-door Sedan, Model 43669, which cost $2,555 and weighed 3,156 pounds. It was also available in the Standard sub-series as the Model 43469, costing $2,471, weighing 3,148 pounds.

Appearing only in the Special Deluxe sub-series was the Sport Coupe, Model 43617, which was simply a hardtop version of the Thin Pillar Coupes found in both Special sub-series. In hardtop form it cost $2,574 and weighed 3,130 pounds. All three coupe models used the same basic body and all three used the attractive tunneled rear window design.

Buick's lowest priced car continued to be the Special Coupe, this year known as the Thin Pillar Coupe, Model 43407. It cost $2,418 and weighed 3,091 pounds. It was also available in Special Deluxe style, where it was the Model 43067, which cost $2,502 and weighed 3,223 pounds. Standard engines in the Special Series were the 225-cubic-inch V-6 or the 300-cubic-inch V-8.

The Skylark Thin Pillar Coupe appeared in both the standard and the Gran Sport sub-series. The body was identical to that appearing in the two Special sub-series, but with distinctive trim differences. In the standard Skylark sub-series, it was the Model 44407, which cost $2,694 and weighed 3,145 pounds. In the Skylark GS sub-series, it was designated the Model 44607, which cost $2,956 and weighed 3,479 pounds. A 3-speed manual transmission was standard.

Buick's little workhorse wagons continued to live in the Special Series, where they were divided into standard and deluxe models. Although the exteriors of the two sub-series were almost identical, quick identification could be made by the signature position. On the standard models, it appeared at the trailing edge of the rear fender, while on the deluxe versions it appeared on the trailing edge of the rear doors, or just behind the doors on the Sport Coupe. This is the Special Wagon, Model 43435, which cost $2,764 and weighed 3,399 pounds. In deluxe version it was the Model 43635, cost $2,853 and weighed 3,427 pounds. Both were 6-passenger cars.

Again the Special Convertible appeared only in the standard sub-series, and not in the deluxe line. It was designated the Model 43467, cost $2,671, and weighed 3,223 pounds. All Specials and Skylarks used the same 115-inch wheelbase chassis and shared the same bodies with the overall lengths being 294 inches. Optional in the Specials was the 340-cubic-inch V-8 of 365 horsepower.

1966

Large Buicks were no longer being assembled in Australia, but were still being imported on special order. The cars were then converted to right hand drive, as is mandatory in Australia. This Electra 225 4-door Hardtop is a former government car, and even today, large Buicks are very popular with top Australian government officials.

The new Opel Kadett 2-door Sedan, Model 31, was available in both standard and deluxe versions this year. In standard form it cost $1,657 while in deluxe version appeared this year only, and was not imported in 1967. All 2-door Opels used the same basic lower body, and were 161.6 inches in overall length. All used the same chassis of 96.1-inch wheelbase.

New for the year was the Opel Kadett Fastback Sport Coupe, Model 32, which cost $1,816 and weighed 1,442 pounds. It used the same basic lower body as did the 2-door sedan, but was fitted with a fast-back styling that gave it a sort of humpback appearance. This year, the Opels were the lowest priced cars in the entire GM line.

The interior of the new Opel Sport Coupe, was in rather attractive trim, considering the low price of the car. All instruments were set in the three dial faces directly in front of the driver. The short-stick sport shift shown here was standard on the sport coupe, optional at extra cost on the 2 and 4-door sedans. Standard equipment was a column mounted shift lever.

Imported this year only was the Opel Kadet 4-door Sedan, Model 30, which in plain form cost $1,780 and in deluxe trim cost $1,868. Opels continued to grow in popularity, and this year were sold and serviced by more than 600 Buick dealers. The sedans used a completely different body than did the 2-door models, were 164.6 inches in overall length, and weighed 1,620 pounds.

The new Opel Kadett Wagon, Model 34, was the highest priced car in the line, costing $1,898. It weighed 1,654 pounds. Opels were available with a 54 horsepower engine as standard equipment, or with the optional 59 horsepower 4-cylinder block. Top speed, with the large engine, was about 83 MPH. The rooftop luggage rack on this model was an extra cost accessory.

There were many visual changes in the cars this year, and several mechanical changes also, yet overall the changes were all in the realm of progressive design, and no really radical innovations appeared.

Calendar year production was 573,866, which was below that of 1966. However, Oldsmobile's production slipped even more, and thus the two companies switched places in the ranking list, with Buick becoming fifth in rank and Oldsmobile taking sixth place. Model year production was 562,507, up about 4,000 cars. Of this, the breakdown by series reads: Special, 193,333, down about 16,000 cars; LeSabre, 155,190, up about 8,000; Wildcat, 70,881, up about 2,000; Electra, 100,304, up about 12,000; and Riviera, 42,799, down 3,000.

The Specials and Skylarks, though sharing identical bodies and running components, this year had distinctive

grilles and other trim items to differentiate one series from the other. The bodies grew one inch to a new length of 205 inches overall. The 225-cubic-inch V-6 was still standard in the line, but was not available in as many models, such as the convertibles and wagons. The standard V-8 continued to be the 333-cubic-inch engine of 200 horsepower that also was used in the LeSabre Series. The Sportwagon Series was reduced by two models via the discontinuing of the Sportwagon Custom sub-series. Now, only the six- and nine-passenger Sportwagons were available.

A new sub-series, the G.S. 400, replaced the Gran Sport Series, It used as basic power a newly designed 400-cubic-inch block that developed 340 horsepower at 5000 RPM. It had a bore and stroke of 4.04 x 3.9 inches and used a 10.25:1 compression ratio. A one-model sub-series called the G.S. 340 used the 340-cubic-inch engine and the G.S. 400's hardtop body.

In the big Buick line, the big news was a brand new 430-cubic-inch engine that was standard in all Wildcat, Electra, and Riviera models. This engine developed 360 horsepower at 5000 RPM, used a bore and stroke of 4.18 x 3.9 inches, and had a compression ratio of 10.25:1.

On the accessory side, Buick came in with a whole carload, including power disc brakes, which cost $150 extra on the Specials, $80 on the Riviera, and $120 on other models. Also available were 300-and 340-cubic-inch engines for the Specials, a 400-cubic-inch high performance package for the LeSabre, and a Gran Sport package for the Riviera at $140 extra. Power steering and brakes cost $150 extra on the Wildcats, $140 more on other models, but were standard on Electras and Rivieras. Air conditioning was $343 extra on the Specials, $420 more on all other models.

The Riviera with the Gran Sport optional package was priced at $4,607 in base form, with such extras as the chromed steel wheels and the vinyl top being extra. The GS package included a dual inlet air cleaner, heavy duty suspension, positraction differential, a 34.2:1 rear axle ratio, whitewall tires, and the GS ornamentation adjacent to the Riviera signatures. This example is owned by Jim Campbell of Perry, Mich.

The Riviera chassis used the X-frame design, with no outer rails, but a very heavy central section enclosing the open drive shaft. Dual exhaust was standard equipment, with two mufflers and two resonators being used. The 2-piece drive shaft was linked by double universal joints.

Except for a new grille, restyled rocker panel moldings, and new taillight treatment, the exterior of the Riviera remained virtually unchanged. Designated the Model 49487, it was Buick's most expensive car, with a base price of $4,469. It weighed 4,189 pounds, used its own 119-inch wheelbase chassis and was 211.3 inches overall. The chromed steel wheels were accessories.

Only a small insignia on the rear quarter panel differentiated the Electra 225 Custom models from the standard versions on the exterior, with the primary differences being found in interior fittings and upholstery. This is the Electra 225 Custom 2-door Hardtop, Model 48457, which cost $4,245 and weighed 4,242 pounds. Its lines were greatly accented by the new roof design, especially when the top was fitted with the optional vinyl covering. In the standard version, it was the Model 48257 which cost $4,075 and weighed 4,197 pounds.

The Electra 225 4-door Sedan was available in both the standard and custom sub-series, and also could be ordered with the new Limited trim package, which included luxurious interior fittings and a vinyl top. It is seen here in the custom version, but wearing an optional vinyl top. In this form it was designated the Model 48469, and had a base price of $4,270 and weighed 4,312 pounds. In standard form, as the Model 48269, it was the least expensive Electra, costing $4,054 and weighing 4,246 pounds. All Electras were 223.9 inches in overall length.

The Electra 225 4-door Hardtop was available in both the standard and custom sub-series and also could be equipped with the Limited interior and vinyl top. In the custom sub-series it was designated the Model 48439, which cost $4,363 and weighed 4,336 pounds. The standard version was the Model 48239, costing $4,184 and weighing 4,293 pounds. This unusual vehicle is the Custom Limited version, and is believed to be the only Custom Limited turned out without the factory-installed vinyl top. It was ordered by an Ohio customer who wanted the Limited interior trim package but did not like vinyl tops. The Limited signature appears on the rear quarter panels. The car is currently owned by Dale Perkins of Cincinnati.

The Electra 225 Custom Convertible, Model 48467, was the most expensive car in the Electra Series, costing $4,421. The 4,304-pound car was not available in the standard sub-series. All Electras featured the new sweepline styling and were identified by the four ventiports which followed the curve of the body sculpture. All Electras used small rear wheel skirts.

In addition to its rather ugly standard hubcaps, Buick this year offered these three attractive optional wheel covers, plus the mandatory wheels on the far right, which were used when the car was equipped with power disc brakes on the front. The chrome plated wheels, second from the left, were not shell coverings, but were the actual steel rims in mag-wheel design. They used no hub caps.

The Wildcat Sport Coupe used the new sweepline styling which included this attractive rear window and deck treatment. Shown is the Wildcat Custom Sport Coupe, Model 46687, wearing the optional vinyl top. In basic form, it cost $3,652 and weighed 4,119 pounds. In the standard sub-series it was the Model 46487, with a base price of $3,382 and the weight of 4,021 pounds. The wheel discs shown here were standard, as were the rear fender skirts. Optional this year was the console with floor selector and built-in tachometer. Also available was the Wildcat Gran Sport package for both the Wildcat Sport Coupe and Convertible models. This package included the usual performance kit, plus a different grille and mag-type chromed steel wheels.

The Wildcat 4-door hardtop was available in both the standard and custom sub-series. It is shown here in custom trim, where it was designated the Model 46639. In this form, it cost $3,652 and weighed 4,119 pounds. The standard version, Model 46439, cost $3,437 and weighed 4,069 pounds. All Wildcats used the same 126-inch wheelbase chassis as the Electras, but were 220.5 inches long overall. Wildcats used as basic power the 430-cubic-inch block of 360 horsepower.

The Wildcat Custom Convertible, Model 46667, was the most expensive car in that series, costing $3,757 and weighing 4,046 pounds. The car also appeared in the standard sub-series for the last time this year, where it was designated the Model 46467. In this form, it cost $3,536 and weighed 4,064 pounds. Wildcat Custom models used full-length chrome side trim, curving downward from above the front wheel openings. The standards did not use this trim.

The Wildcat 4-door Sedan, Model 46469, was available in the standard sub-series only, and did not appear in the custom sub-series. It cost $3,227 and weighed 4,008 pounds. All Wildcats used the new ventiport design, with the ports incorporated into the rocker panel molding.

The new Trinity Coach Co. of Duncanville, Tex., began building a full line of hearses and ambulances this year, utilizing Buick chassis exclusively. Actually, the company continued where the Flxible Co. of Loudenville, Ohio, left off, after the Ohio firm decided to leave the professional car market once and for all. Trinity built on stretched Electra chassis. standard wheelbase Electra chassis and standard Wildcat chassis. This Trinity-Buick ambulance, called the Triune, used the standard 126-inch Electra wheelbase chassis, but had an overall length of 219 inches. The ambulance sold for $8,100. Also available in this series was a combination ambulance and hearse for $8,015; a landau equipped hearse for $8,115; a limousine funeral car or hearse for $7,950; a limousine combination ambulance and hearse for $7,850, and a service car, which resembled a glorified panel truck, for $8,050. The top of the company's line was the stretched Electra version called the Royal Landau, which sold for $9,415. The stretched versions were 243 inches in overall length.

The new LeSabre Sport Coupe used a long sweeping rear window, in keeping with the overall sweepline styling of the car. This produced unusually narrow and pointed rear quarter windows. In the standard version, the coupe was the Model 45287, which cost $3,084 and weighed 3,819 pounds. The custom version was the Model 45487, costing $3,172 and weighing 3,853 pounds.

The LeSabre 4-door Sedan continued to appear in both the standard and the custom sub-series. In standard form, as shown here, it was the Model 45269, which cost $3,002 and weighed 3,847 pounds. The custom, Model 45469, cost $3,096 and weighed 3,855 pounds. All LeSabres featured new sweepline body styling and were 217.5 inches in overall length on a 123-inch wheelbase chassis.

The Sportwagon, now spelled as one word, used the Skylark grille, but was still considered a series of its own. However, rather than being divided into standard and deluxe sub-series, all models were now classed as standard, with a "custom" trim package available. It continued to use its own exclusive chassis of 120-inch wheelbase and was 214.3 inches overall. As the 6-passenger Model 44455, it cost $3,202 and weighed 3,722 pounds. As the 9-passenger style, it was the Model 44465, costing $3,340 and weighing 3,876 pounds. This model wears three very popular and very attractive accessories — the roof-top chrome luggage rack, the new wood-grain side applique, and the chromed wire-spoke wheel covers. The cars used the same fender ventiports as did the Special Series. It still used the interesting roof panel windows that were stylish but of no real practical use.

The LeSabre 4-door Hardtop used a sweepline roof almost identical to that used on the 4-door sedans, but of course, lacked the sedan's centerpost and full door window frames. It was available as the standard, Model 45239, which cost $3,142 and weighed 3,878, or the custom, Model 45439, which cost $3,236 and weighed 3,873. There was no appreciable exterior difference between the standard and custom sub-series. LeSabres used a new die cast grille and new headlight and taillight pods.

Appearing only in the LeSabre Custom sub-series was the Convertible, Model 45467, which cost $3,388 and weighed 3,890 pounds. With this year's overall price increases, Buick no longer had a full-size model with a base price under $3,000. All LeSabres used as standard power the 340-cubic-inch block of 220 horsepower, but the high performance 400-cubic-inch block was available at an extra $263.

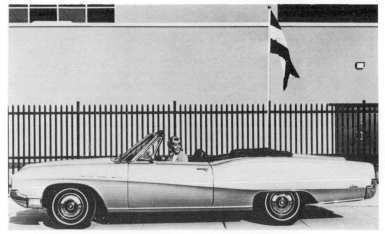

The Skylark GS 400 models used the same bodies as other Skylarks, and the chassis dimensions were the same, but the chassis itself was a much heavier piece of machinery than was used on the conventional models. Both the side rails and bracing were much stronger, and the suspension was of a heavy duty type. The car used a complete dual exhaust system.

The Skylark Convertible was available in both plain form and as the GS 400 model, shown here. In plain form, it was the Model 44467, which cost $2,945 and weighed 3,335 pounds. In the GS 400 sub-series, it was designated the Model 44455, which had a base price of $3,167 and weighed 3,505 pounds. As the GS 400, it had its own cast grille, simulated hood scoops, 340 horsepower 400-cubic-inch engine with 4-barrel carburetor, dual exhausts, and heavy duty suspension.

The new Skylark GS 340 Coupe offered sporty appearance and high performance at a relatively low cost of $2,845. Designated the Model 34017, it weighed 3,220 pounds. It was the only Model available in the GS 340 sub-series, and was a hit of the youth-set at the Chicago Auto Show, where it was first unveiled. The car used the same mechanical components and body as the GS 400 hardtop, but cost was kept down through the use of less interior trim. It used broad racing stripes on the sides, and the simulated hood scoops matched the color of the stripes.

The Skylark 2-door Coupe continued to be a pillared version of the hardtop model. This year it was available both in plain version or in the new GS 400 sub-series, as shown here. This was the only year that this style would be available in GS form. In plain trim, it was the Model 44607, which cost $2,956 and weighed 3,439 pounds. In plain form, it used the 340-cubic-inch, 220 horsepower engine.

The Skylark 4-door Hardtop, Model 44439, used the same basic lower body as did the Skylark and Special 4-door sedans, but this style was not available in the Special Series. It cost $2,950 and weighed 3,373 pounds. The vinyl top and wheel covers were added cost accessories. All Skylarks used the same 115-inch wheelbase chassis as used by the Special Series.

The GS 400 Sport Coupe, Model 44617, differed from the GS 340 primarily in trim options. It used the same body as the Skylark Sport Coupe, but was fitted with the 400-cubic-inch engine with 4-barrel carburetor. GS models used different side trim from the Skylarks, and were not fitted with the rear fender skirts. This model wears the optional vinyl top, and has been fitted with the new power disc brakes on the front, as indicated by the special wheels, hubcaps and wheel rings that were used with the disc brakes. The simulated hood scoops were standard.

The Skylark Sport Coupe, Model 44417, was an attractive and sporty looking car, especially when wearing the optional vinyl roof and optional side trim with rear fender skirts. The top still used a tunneled rear window, but the tunnel wasn't as deep as it had been in previous models. In standard form, the car cost $2,798 and weighed 3,199 pounds.

The Skylark Series was Buick's only full series that was not divided into standard and deluxe sub-series. However, all 2-door models were available in Gran Sport form. Thus, the brand new Skylark 4-door Sedan, Model 44469, appeared in one form only, where it cost $2,767 and weighed 3,324 pounds. It used the same body as the Special 4-door sedan, but Skylarks used their own distinctive grille, low chevron-type ventiports, and attractive rear fender skirts.

Although the Special 2-door Coupe, Model 43407, was not officially listed in the deluxe sub-series, it apparently could be ordered in deluxe trim as this example shows. The car wears the full-length side chrome and front fender signature of the deluxe sub-series, but still is the 2-door coupe, with centerposts, listed only in the standard sub-series. In regular form, it weighed 3,137 pounds and at $2,481 was Buick's lowest priced car.

The Special series was still divided into standard and deluxe sub-series, but this is the last year that the standard sub-series would appear. This is the Special 4-door Sedan, Model 43469, which cost $2,532 and weighed 3,196 pounds. The car was devoid of any side trim whatever, but this model does use a small optional bar on the rocker panels. The Special standard models wore their signature on the trailing edge of the rear fenders.

The Special Deluxe 4-door Sedan, Model 43669, was quickly distinguished from the standard version by its full-length chrome side strip, which began at the three decorative ventiports and ended at the trailing edge of the fender. Deluxe models wore their signatures on the leading edge of the front fender. The sedan cost $2,615 and weighed 3,205 pounds. All Specials used the same distinctive grille, and all car models were 205 inches in overall length.

Appearing only in the special Deluxe sub-series was the hardtop Sport Coupe, Model 43617, which cost $2,636 and weighed 3,202 pounds. All Specials used a new sculptured hood and hood molding, and were fitted with rather massive wrap-around bumpers both front and rear.

The Special Wagon used a longer body than did the car models, being 209.3 inches overall. It was available in both the standard and the deluxe sub-series. In standard form it was the Model 43425, which cost $2,812 and weighed 3,425 pounds, while the deluxe version was the Model 43635, costing $2,901 and weighing 3,317 pounds.

With the Opel Kadett 4-door sedan no longer being imported, the Kadett 2-door Sedan, Model 31, became the line's family-type economy car. It cost $1,695 and weighed 1,548 pounds. All Opels used a 95.1-inch wheelbase chassis, but the overall lengths varied with each body style. The 2-door Sedan was the shortest, with an overall length of only 161 inches.

Equipped with the new sun roof option was this Opel Kadett Sport Coupe. The "pneumonia hole" had only limited popularity. With an overall length of 164.6 inches, the coupe was the largest Opel produced this year.

The Opel Kadett Wagon, Model 39, surprisingly was a bit shorter than the sport coupe, being just 164.4 inches in overall length. It cost $1,980 and weighed 1,658 pounds. The large and very practical roof-top luggage rack was an accessory.

New for the year was the Opel Rallye Kadett Coupe, which was really the sport coupe with some special equipment such as road lights, a blockout hood, and racing stripe on the side. It was not equipped with hubcaps.

A German freighter spawns an invasion of Opels. In the forefront is the Kadett Sport Coupe, Model 32, which this year could be ordered with an optional sun roof. In plain form, as shown here, it cost $1,905 and weighed 1,592 pounds. The Coupe was 164.6 inches long overall.

The interior of the new Opel Rallye Kadett Coupe was fitted with a variety of functional gauges, including tachometer, ammeter, and oil pressure gauge, in addition to the warning lights for oil pressure and generator output. The car used a 4-speed transmission with floor shift.

Calendar year production took a big jump up to 652,049, but other companies jumped also, and as a result, Buick had to be content to retain its fifth place rank in the industry. Model year production rose to 651,823, an increase of almost 90,000 cars over 1967. Of this, production by series was: Special, 227,470, up over 4,000 cars; LeSabre, 179,748, up over 24,000 cars; Wildcat, 69,969, down about 1,000; Electra, 125,362, up over 25,000 cars; and Riviera, 49,284, up almost 7,000.

In the small car ranks, the Special Series was dropped, but a new Skylark Custom Series was invented, which held all cars in the previous Skylark range except for the coupe, which was not produced this year.

In a complicating move, Special DeLuxe and Skylark models now shared two different chassis. All 2-door models, including the station wagons, were built on a 116-inch wheelbase chassis; while all 4-door models, including the station wagons, were built on a 112-inch wheelbase chassis. The 2-door models were now 200 inches overall, while the 4-door cars were 204.7 inches overall and the wagons were 209 inches overall.

The Sportwagon also continued to have its own chassis, but it was now of 121-inch wheelbase and the wagon was 214 inches overall. The Gran Sport models continued to use the chassis and basic bodies of the 2-door Skylark models.

The V-6 engine was given an increase in displacement, going up to 250 cubic inches, but its horsepower was dropped back to 155 at 4200 RPM through the reduction in compression from 9:1 to 8.5:1.

In the small Eights, Specials, Skylarks and the GS 350 now used a brand new 350-cubic-inch engine with a bore and stroke of 3.8 x 3.85 inches which developed 230 horsepower at 4400 RPM in the standard models and 280 horsepower at 4600 RPM in the GS model. The GS 400 continued to use the unchanged 400-cubic-inch engine that developed 340 horsepower at 5000 RPM.

The LeSabre line was virtually unchanged, still being built on its 123-inch wheelbase chassis being 217.5 inches overall. However, under the hood lived the new 340-cubic-inch V-8 that was powering the popular Special line.

Likewise, there was little mechanical or dimensional change in the Wildcat and Electra lines. Both series continued to share the 126-inch wheelbase chassis, and the Wildcats retained their overall length of 220.5 inches, while the Electras grew one inch to a new overall length of 244.9 inches.

The Rivieras retained their 119-inch wheelbase chassis, but grew to a new overall length of 215 inches. Wildcats, Electras, and Rivieras continued to use the year-old 430-cubic-inch engine that was rated at 360 horsepower at 5000 RPM.

Of note is that the 215-cubic-inch Buick engine, no longer in production for Buick cars, was picked up and modified by the renowned Rover Company of England. Coupled to a Borg-Warner automatic transmission, this engine was used in Rover luxury sedans for the next couple of years. Another version of this engine began to appear in both the Rover 4 x 4 in 1970, and in the Morgan Plus-8s.

Buick's 14-millionth car rolled off the line on April 19, 1968. It was this Electra 225 4-door Sedan, Model 48269, which cost $4,200 and weighed 4,253 pounds. It was fitted with a vinyl top. The sedan was also available in the custom sub-series as the Model 48469, costing $4,415 and weighing 4,304 pounds.

The new Riviera had a restyled grille and hood, new bumpers, and restyled wheel openings. The concealed headlights lived in pods above the grille, and dropped into position as the grille doors opened when the units were turned on. The parking lights were moved inward and were more prominent in the bumper. Designated the Model 49487, the Riviera had a base price of $4,615, and thus was Buick's most expensive model. The 4,222-pound car used the 430-cubic-inch engine with 4-barrel carburetor and the Super Turbine automatic transmission. It was 215.2 inches long and stood on a 119-inch wheelbase chassis. A vinyl top was an extra-cost option.

Showing off its power and positraction differential is the new Riviera GS. This package also included heavy duty suspension 3.42:1 rear axle ratio, whitewall tires, and chrome air cleaner. The vinyl top and chromed steel wheels were accessory items. GS models were identified by the small signature plaque on the rear roof quarter. The GS package cost $132 extra.

The new Electra 225 cars used an attractive die cast grille in egg crate style, and were quickly identified by the four ventiports in a single bar that followed the curve of the side sculpture. This is the Electra 225 Custom 4-door Hardtop, Model 48439, identified by the small crest on the rear quarter panel. It cost $4,509, with the vinyl top being extra, and weighed 4,314 pounds. It was available in the standard Electra 225 sub-series as the Model 48239, which cost $4,330 and weighed 4,270 pounds. Both Electra 4-doors could be ordered with the Limited trim package, which included a vinyl top and luxurious interior fittings.

The Electra 225 Sport Coupe was also available in the Custom sub-series was the Convertible, Model 48467, cost $4,400 and weighed 4,223 pounds. The vinyl top was an added-cost item. In standard form it was the Model 48257, which cost $4,221 and weighed 4,180 pounds. All Electras used two very long bar-type taillights which covered almost the entire width of the rear bumper. The cars were 224.8 inches long, had a 126-inch wheelbase chassis.

Appearing only in the Electra 225 Custom sub-series was the Convertible, Model 48467, which cost $4,541 and weighed 4,285 pounds. All Buicks this year used concealed windshield wipers. The standard power unit in Electras was the 430-cubic-inch block with 4-barrel carburetor and 10.25:1 compression ratio. Automatic transmission, power steering and brakes were standard on all Electras, and the convertible had power windows and 2-way power seat as standard equipment.

The Wildcat 4-door Hardtop was available in both the standard and the custom sub-series, but there was no exterior difference between the two models. In plain form, it was the Model 46439, which cost $3,576 and weighed 4,133 pounds. In custom trim, Model 46639, it cost $3,791 and weighed 4,162 pounds. The vinyl top and chromed wheels on this model were extra cost options.

All Wildcats used their own distinctive grille, die cast into three hollow rectangles. This is the Wildcat Sport Coupe, which in standard trim was the Model 46487, costing $3,521 and weighing 4,065 pounds. In the custom version, it was the Model 46687, which had a base price of $3,742 and weighed 4,082 pounds. Optional side trim on these models consisted of a full-length thin chrome piece running the entire length of the sculptured ridge.

Available only in the Wildcat Custom sub-series was the Convertible, Model 46667, which cost $3,873 and weighed 4,118 pounds. It used a glass rear window, hidden windshield wipers, and was powered by the Wildcat 430-cubic-inch engine with 4-barrel carburetor. The small rear fender skirts were standard on all Wildcats, but the chromed steel wheels were an accessory.

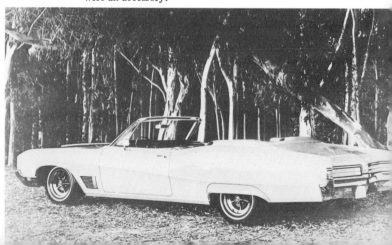

Appearing only in the standard Wildcat sub-series was the 4-door Sedan, Model 46469, which cost $3,416 and weighed 4,076. Wildcats continued to use the same 126-inch wheel-base chassis as used on the Electras, but their overall length was 220.5 inches. They used their own ventiport design, in a block just behind the front wheel opening.

The lowest priced full-size Buick continued to be the LeSabre Sedan, Model 45269, which cost $3,141 and weighed 3,946 pounds. It was also available in the LeSabre Custom sub-series as the Model 45469, which had a base price of $3,235 and weighed 3,950.

Continuing high on the popularity list was the LeSabre 4-door Hardtop, Model 45239, which cost $3,281 and weighed 3,980 pounds. The car was also available as the LeSabre Custom, Model 45439, which was priced at $3,375 and weighed 4,007 pounds. There was no noticeable exterior difference between the standard and custom sub-series in the LeSabre Series. LeSabres continued to use their exclusive 123-inch wheelbase chassis and were 217.4 inches in overall length.

The standard Wildcat 430 engine, used in both Wildcats and Electras, continued to be a rugged and long-lived power unit. It was fitted with a standard 4-barrel carburetor, and in basic form would develop 360 horsepower. It used cast aluminum alloy pistons and a nodular iron crankshaft. The block and heads were cast iron. In standard form, it used a compression ratio of 10.25:1.

The new Wildcat 350 engine offered big performance in a light-weight package, even when equipped wtih the standard 2-barrel carburetor as shown here. The engine used a bore and stroke of almost square 3.8 x 3.85 and developed 230 horsepower in its most basic form or 280 with the GS 350 performance package and 10.25 compression ratio. Standard compression was 9:1.

One of the most attractive cars in the LeSabre Series was the 2-door Hardtop, Model 45287, which cost $3,223 and weighed 3,923 pounds. In the custom sub-series, it was designated the Model 45487, which cost $3,311 and weighed 3,932 pounds. All LeSabres used the three ventiports in a solid bar across the front fender, following the sculpture line of the fender.

Available only in the LeSabre Custom sub-series was the Convertible, Model 45467. It cost $3,504 and weighed 3,966 pounds. All LeSabres used the Wildcat 350 V-8 with 2-barrel carburetor and 3-speed column shift. Automatic transmission and larger engines were available at extra cost.

The Sportwagon continued to be a series of its own, with its two models using the same body. They were the 6-passenger, Model 44455, which cost $3,341 and weighed 3,975, and the 9-passenger Model 44465, costing $3,499 and weighing 4,118 pounds. The Sportwagons used their own chassis of 121-inch wheelbase and were 214.1 inches in overall length.

An attractive option on the sportwagons was the wood trim applique which followed the new curve of the side trim line. The Sportwagons used the ventiport bar of the Special Deluxe Series, and were not fitted with rear wheel skirts. The wood paneling was also used on the tailgate.

The Gran Sport 400 line now was considered a series of its own, even though it used the same bodies as used on the Skylarks. It was powered by the 400-cubic-inch V-8 developing 340 horsepower. This is the Sport Coupe. Designated the Model 44637, it cost $3,127 and weighed 3,514 pounds.

New for the year was the Gran Sport 350, now considered a one-model Series. It used the same body as used by the Skylark sport coupe, and was fitted with the 350-cubic-inch V-8, though horsepower was increased to 280 through the use of a 4-barrel carburetor and 10.25:1 compression ratio. Designated the Model 43437, it cost $2,926 and weighed 3,375 pounds. The racing stripe, air scoop on the hood, and small ventiports on the front fender were standard, but the vinyl top was extra.

A rather attractive small car was the California GS. This car, which was really the GS 350 package installed in the Special Sport Coupe, was introduced only on the West Coast in 1967, but was brought out on a national basis this year. Standard equipment included the vinyl top and chromed steel wheels. Special side trim was used, fender skirts were omitted.

The top priced car in the small Buick line was the Gran Sport 400 Convertible, Model 44667, which cost $3,271. It weighed 3,547 pounds. Standard equipment included a floor shift, heavy duty 3-speed transmission with Hurst linkage, 4-barrel carburetor with chromed dual induction air cleaner, and functional hood scoop. Options included heavy duty suspension front and rear, 4-speed floor shift with tachometer, and the chromed steel wheels. No skirts were used on GS models.

1968

The 4-door Hardtop, Model 44439, appeared only in the Skylark Custom sub-series, and was not available in the standard Skylark line. It cost $3,108 and weighed 3,481 pounds. All 4-door Skylarks used a 116-inch wheelbase chassis and were 204.7 inches long overall. The vinyl top and wheel covers shown on this model were extra cost options.

Although a 2-door coupe, with pillars, appeared in the Special Deluxe line, the Skylark line did not use such a model, offering instead two versions of the hardtop Sport Coupe, This is the Skylark custom version, Model 44437, which cost $2,956 and weighed 3,344 pounds. The custom models used the 350-cubic-inch V-8, while the two standard models used the V-6 as standard equipment, with the V-8 being optional. All custom models used small rear wheel fender skirts as standard equipment.

The Skylark Series was now divided into two sub-series, the standard and custom. However, only two models appeared in the standard line. One was the 4-door sedan, shown here in custom trim. In this form it was designated the Model 44469, cost $2,924, and weighed 3,374 pounds. Skylarks used the three long ventiports in a straight bar curving down with the front fender line.

In an unusual move, each Special Deluxe model was a different length. The longest of the lot was the Station Wagon, Model 3435, which was available only with the V-8 engine. It cost $3,001, marking the first time that a Special ever had a base price in excess of $3,000. It used the Skylark's 116-inch wheelbase chassis, weighed 3,670 pounds.

Appearing only in the Skylark Custom sub-series was the convertible, Mode 44467, which cost $3,098 and weighed 3,394 pounds. All 2-door Skylarks used a 112-inch wheelbase chassis and were 200.7 inches long. For the first time, Buick used concealed windshield wipers on all models, and a glass rear window on its convertibles. The convertible interior was all-vinyl.

The Special sub-series was now gone, and what had been the Special and Special Deluxe sub-series now was simply the Special Deluxe Series, consisting of three models. All used the same bodies and chassis as used in the Skylark line. This is the Special Deluxe 4-door Sedan, Model 43469, which weighed 3,336 pounds and cost $2,669. It had a 116-inch wheelbase chassis and was 204.7 inches overall. Its grille was the same as used on the Skylarks.

The totally new Special Deluxe 2-door Coupe, Model 43427 could be fitted with either the V-6 of 250-cubic inches and 155 horsepower or the V-8 of 350 cubic inches and 230 horsepower. A 3-speed column mounted shift was standard. The car cost $2,618 and was the lowest priced vehicle in the Buick fold. It weighed 3,244 pounds, used a 112-inch wheelbase chassis and was 200.6 inches long. The vinyl top and wheel covers on this model were accessories.

The most expensive car in the Opel Kadett line was the Rallye Kadett, Model 92-R, which cost $2,314. It used the same body as the sport coupe, but was fitted with chrome wheels without hubcaps, running lights, blackout hood, and racing stripes. Under the hood lived the 80 horsepower engine, with the 102 horsepower model being available. Inside there lived a console gear shift, adjustable seat backs, and an improved flow-through ventilation system.

The Opel Kadett Station Wagon continued to be built in 2-door 5-passenger form only. Designated the Model 39, it cost $2,070, weighed 1,781 pounds, and was 164.4 inches in overall length. The large and practical roof-top luggage carrier was an accessory.

The lowest priced car offered by Buick dealers was the Opel Kadett 2-door Sedan, Model 31, which this year had a base price of $1,785. The little German built car weighed 1,693 pounds and was only 161 inches long overall. All Opels used a 95.1-inch wheelbase chassis.

The Opel Sport Coupe was no longer available in plain form, but appeared as the Rallye Kadett, the LS Kadett, or as this Deluxe Sport Coupe, Model 95. In this form it was the lowest priced of the coupes, costing $2,041. The 1,715-pound car was also the longest Opel, being 164.6 inches overall. Standard power was the 55 horsepower 4-cylinder block with an 8.2:1 compression ratio, but the 80 and 102 horsepower engines were available at extra cost. When fitted with the larger engines, the car became the LS Kadett, Model 99, with a price of $2,163 for the 80 horsepower version.

New for the year was the Opel Kadette Sport Sedan, Model 91. It used the same lower body as the 2-door sedan models, but its rear roof treatment was given a rather interesting sweep, somewhat like that used on the sport coupes. It cost $1,944, weighed 1,715 pounds, and was 161 inches in overall length. It carried the script "Kadett L" for Luxus or deluxe.

Calendar year production really soared this year. Buick produced 713,832 vehicles and shot up to fourth place as Plymouth slipped badly and dropped behind Buick and Oldsmobile. Model year production was 665,422, which was about 14,000 more cars than produced in 1968. However, the Special lines dropped severely, going down to 188,613 cars, which was a reduction of almost 39,000 units. The Wildcat line also dropped, going down to 17,453, a reduction of over 2,000 cars. On the other hand, production of both the LeSabre and Electra models went up substantially. LeSabre climbed to 197,866, an increase of over 18,000 cars, while the Electra lines went up to 159,618, an increase of over 33,000 cars. The Riviera also went up, increasing by over 3,000 cars for a total production of 52,872.

The Specials and Skylarks received new grilles and taillights, but no sheetmetal or dimensional changes. A new 3-speed automatic was available as an option. This differed in both size and design from the transmission used on the larger cars. Under the hood there was little change, except for a new air cleaner on the V-8 models.

The V-6 cars still used the 250-cubic-inch block of 155 horsepower, while the other models used the unchanged 350-cubic-inch V-8. The GS 400 continued to use its 400-cubic-inch block which developed 340 horsepower at 5000 RPM. The GS and California models could be equipped with optional air scoops that fed cool air directly into the air cleaner via twin snorkels extending through the hood.

This year's popularity leader, the LeSabre Series, was completely redesigned inside and out. This included new bumpers, grilles, lamps, hood, and interior trim. The 123-inch wheelbase was retained, but the new sheetmetal resulted in the car growing one inch to a new overall length of 218 inches. Under the hood, everything remained the same except that a newly designed air cleaner was added. The basic engine remained the 350-cubic-inch model used in the Special V-8 series.

A surprise move occurred in the Wildcat Series, where the cars became smaller in both size and weight. The completely redesigned Wildcats, with longer noses and shorter tails, now used the LeSabre's 123-inch wheelbase chassis rather than sharing the 126-inch wheelbase chassis with the Electras. They also shared the LeSabre's basic bodies, resulting in an overall length of 218 inches. However, they retained the 430-cubic-inch engine used in the Electras and the Rivieras, and thus in a sense they became LeSabres with Electra engines — the concept of the old Century Series, which was to stuff the largest engine into the smallest body that would hold it and thus come up with a relatively hot performing car. Included in the redesign of the Wildcat were new suspension, new transmission, and new power steering.

Also completely redesigned was the Electra Series. This year the cars kept their old 126-inch wheelbase chassis and 224.8-inch overall length, but new refinements of the sweepline styling made the cars look longer and lower. On all Buicks this year, a notable change, and one which many

people disliked, was the removal of front vent windows.

Few styling innovations were made on this year's Riviera, with styling remaining basically the classic fast-back design introduced in 1963. A new grille and marker lamps graced the front, but little else was changed. The car remained 215 inches overall and continued to use its own exclusive 119-inch wheelbase chassis. On the engineering side, the Riviera received new front suspension and an exclusive electric fuel pump, and a redesigned central console.

In the management ranks, on April 7, Lee N. Mays, Buick's current general manager, succeeded Robert L. Kessler, who had been general manager since 1965.

As could be expected, Buick's most expensive car continued to be the Riviera, Model 49487, which had a base price of $4,701. It weighed 4,309 pounds, used its own exclusive chassis of 119-inch wheelbase, and was 215.2 inches overall. The car this year used fairly wide chromed gravel shields on the bottoms of both front and rear fenders, on the rocker panels and into the doors. The headlights were still concealed behind slide-away grille panels.

The Riviera Gran Sport was quickly distinguished from the regular Riviera this year by its use of rather narrow rocker panel covers, no gravel deflectors, and a thin bar of side trim. The cars had a somewhat strange appearance from this angle due to the fact that the lower bumper line ended at a point above the front axle line. The Riviera Gran Sport package added $132 to the Riviera's base price. All Rivieras used the standard 360 horsepower 430-cubic-inch V-8.

The Electra 225 Custom Sport Coupe, Model 48457, was an outstandingly attractive car with a base price of $4,502. It was also available in the plain Electra 225 sub-series as the Model 48257, which had a base price of $4,323. The cars weighed about 4,220 pounds. All Electras used their own exclusive chassis of 126.2-inch wheelbase and were 224.8 inches long overall. The vinyl tops were an extra-cost item added to virtually all Electras.

The lowest priced car in the Electra 225 Series was the 4-door Sedan, Model 48269, which had a base price of $4,302, with the vinyl top being extra. It weighed 4,238 pounds. The car was also available as the Electra 225 Custom, Model 48469, which cost $4,517 and weighed 4,281 pounds. It could also be ordered with the Limited trim package which included the vinyl top. Power steering and brakes and Turbo-Hydramatic transmission were standard equipment on all Electras.

The Electra Custom 225 4-door Hardtop, Model 48439, is shown here with the Limited trim package, which included a vinyl top in one of several matched or choice colors. The package carried the Limited signature on the rear roof quarter panel. In plain form, the custom version cost $4,611 and weighed 4,328 pounds. All Electras were fitted with chromed rocker panels and rear fender gravel guard, and stainless steel wheel cut-out moldings. All used the four horizontal ventports on the front fenders, and wore skirts over the rear wheels.

A definite asset to anyone's driveway was the Wildcat Custom Sport Coupe, Model 46637. It cost $3,817 and weighed 4,134 pounds, with the chromed steel wheels and vinyl top being extra. It was also available in standard form, as the Model 46437, which cost $3,596 and weighed 3,926 pounds. All Wildcats were identified by the six vertical ventports behind the front wheel.

Appearing only in the Electra Custom 225 sub-series was the Convertible, Model 48467, which cost $4,643 and weighed 4,390 pounds. The Electras continued to use the very wide taillights, set in twin bars almost the full width of the rear end. The lights this year were covered by an attractive chrome grid. Back-up lights lived on either side of the license plate bracket.

Appearing only in the Wildcat Custom sub-series was the Convertible, Model 46667, which cost $3,948 and weighed 4,152 pounds. All Wildcats were powered by the standard 430-cubic-inch engine of 360 horsepower. A 3-speed manual transmission was standard equipment.

1969

Appearing for the last time was the standard Wildcat sub-series, which consisted of three models, including its exclusive 4-door sedan. The sedan, Model 46469, was not available in the Wildcat Custom sub-series, and would be phased from production at the end of the season. It cost $3,491 and weighed 4,102 pounds.

The Wildcat 4-door Hardtop was available in both the standard and custom sub-series. It is seen here in custom trim, as the Model 46639, which featured an all-vinyl interior and chrome rocker panels. It cost $3,866 and weighed 4,220 pounds. In plain form, it was the Model 46439, costing $3,450 and weighing 4,204 pounds. All Wildcats and Le-Sabres shared the same basic bodies and chassis this year, and all were 218.2 inches in overall length.

Gracing one of San Diego's many yacht harbors is this LeSabre Custom Convertible, Model 45467. It cost $3,579 and weighed 3,958 pounds. It was not available in the standard sub-series. All LeSabres used a 3-speed maunal transmission as standard equipment, but the automatic transmission was installed in most cars for an additional cost of $360.

The LeSabre 4-door Hardtop was available in both the regular or the custom sub-series. This is the custom version, Model 45439, which cost $3,450, weighed 4,073, and offered as standard equipment an all-vinyl interior and chrome wheel cutout trim, rocker panel covers, and rear fender gravel shield. In plain form, it was the Model 45239, which cost $3,356 and weighed 3,983 pounds. The turn lights on the front fenders were optional, as were the wheel covers shown here.

Buick's lowest priced full-size car continued to be the LeSabre 4-door Sedan, Model 45269, shown here, but the base price was now up to $3,216. It weighed 3,966 pounds. The car was also available as the LeSabre Custom 4-door Sedan, Model 45469. In this form it cost $3,310 and weighed 3,941 pounds. All LeSabres used the Wildcat 350 engine with 2-barrel carburetor.

The LeSabre Sport Coupe was available both in custom trim, as shown here, or in standard form. In the custom sub-series it was the Model 45437, which cost $3,386 and weighed 4,018 pounds. The standard version, Model 45237, cost $3,298 and weighed 3,936 pounds. In an unusual move, the LeSabres now shared their 123.2-inch wheelbase chassis with the Wildcats, and both series used the same basic bodies of 218.2 inches overall length.

The Sportwagon continued to be a two-model series of its own, with both styles using the same basic body with the Skyroof still in vogue. In 6-passenger form, as shown here, it was the Model 44456, which cost $3,465 and weighed 4,106 pounds. The 9-passenger version, Model 44466, cost $3,621 and weighed 4,231 pounds. The wagons continued to use their own exclusive chassis of 121-inch wheelbase and were 214.1 inches overall.

The wood-trim option for the Sportwagon this year was placed above the body sculpture instead of below it as it was in 1968. The trim applique was completely surrounded by a stainless steel border, and enveloped the three fender ventiports. It was now available as the LeSabre Custom 4-door Sedan, Model 45469. In this form it cost $3,310 and weighed 3,941 pounds. All LeSabres used the Wildcat 350 engine with 2-barrel carburetor.

California GS

An off-shoot of the GS 350 was the California GS, Model 43327. This car used the same GS 350 engine as did the plain model, but standard equipment included the Turbo Hydra-matic 350 transmission with floor selector, and a vinyl top. It was identified by the California signature which appeared on the rear fenders and on the bubble side of the functional hood scoop.

The GS 400 Convertible, Model 44667, cost $3,325 and weighed 3,594 pounds. All GS 400 cars used as standard equipment the Wildcat 400-cubic-inch engine with 4-barrel carburetor and 10.25:1 compression ratio. A 3-speed manual transmission was standard, but automatic or floor-four could be ordered. The GS models had their own grilles and were identified by the "400 signature on the rear fender and side of the hood air scoop.

The Gran Sport 400 Series included the coupe and a convertible. The GS 400 Coupe was the Model 44637, shown here with optional vinyl top, wire spoke wheel covers, and side trim. In base form it cost $3,181 and weighed 3,549 pounds. All GS models used their own distinctive grille of very large egg crate design.

The Gran Sport 350 continued to be a one-model series which was an economy version of the GS 400 cars. Designated the Model 43437, it cost $2,980 and weighed 3,406 pounds. Standard power was the Wildcat 350 engine with 4-barrel carburetor and 10.25 compression ratio, compared with the 9:1 ratio used on Skylarks. Identity marks included a functional hood scoop and the GS 350 plate on the rear fenders. This model has been fitted with a vinyl top and power disc brakes, both extra-cost options.

1969

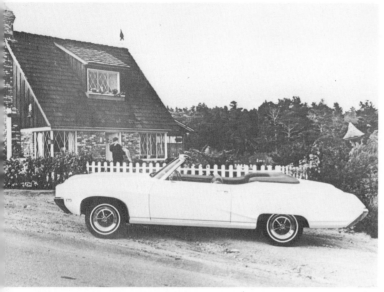

Available only in the Skylark Custom sub-series was the Convertible, Model 44467, which cost $3,152 and weighed 3,398 pounds. All Skylarks and Specials shared the same bodies and chassis, but not all models were available in all sub-series. The standard engine for Skylarks was the 350-cubic-inch V-8, with the 250-cubic-inch Six being available only in the plain Skylark sub-series.

Available only in the Skylark Custom sub-series was the 4-door Hardtop, Model 44439, which cost $3,151 and weighed 3,477 pounds. This version wears the chrome rocker panel covers and wheel cutout trim which was optional when the sweep-spear side molding was not ordered. All 4-door Skylarks were built on the 116-inch wheelbase chassis and were 204.7 inches overall.

The GS cars used their own dash with several options available. The padded steering wheel shown here was standard on the GS 400, and California GS, optional on the GS 350. Bucket seats were optional in both series, as was a non-shifting floor console, or the consolette with floor mounted shift selector for manual transmissions or a full-length console for automatic transmissions.

The Skylark 4-door Sedan was built in both standard and custom forms. It is shown here in plain form as the Model 43569, which cost $2,826 and weighed 3,328 pounds. The regular Skylark used no side trim, while the custom versions could be fitted with a sweep-spear chrome molding running from the headlights to the leading edge of the rear wheel opening, and from the trailing edge of that opening to the rear bumper. The custom version was the Model 44469, which cost $2,978 and weighed 3,397 pounds. Skylarks were quickly identified by the three ventiports near the front wheel.

Appearing in both the Skylark and Skylark Custom sub-series was the Sport Coupe. It is shown here in custom form, where it was the Model 44437, which cost $3,009 and weighed 3,341 pounds. The standard version, Model 43537, cost $2,847 and weighed 3,298 pounds. Buyers of custom models had a choice of sweep-spear side molding or chromed rocker panel covers with wheel cutout trim.

Buick came up with an extremely radical show car this year. Called the Century Cruiser, the pancake shaped machine was first shown at the New York Auto Show. Except for the Buick signature on the trailing edge of the body, below the rear fins, there was no relation between this car and anything currently being built by Buick.

1969

New for the year was the Special Deluxe Police Special, Model 43369. This was the Special Sedan, fitted with either the Six or the V-8, and available with either manual or Super Turbine transmissions and 2- or 4-barrel carburetors. Factory installed optional special equipment included a 60 ampere alternator, police-cruiser speedometer, flasher lights, etc.

Despite the fact that the Special Deluxe Series was destined to disappear at the end of the model run, the series received two new cars this year. They were two variations of the Station Wagon. Both were available only with the V-8 and in 6-passenger form, and the differences were mainly in interior trim. The lower priced wagon was the Model 43435, which cost $3,092 and weighed 3,736 pounds. The fancier version was the Model 34346, which had a base price of $3,124 and weighed 3,783 pounds. The wagons were 209.1 inches in overall length, 54.5 inches high, and used the long chassis of 116-inch wheelbase.

Aimed at municipal fleets was the LeSabre Police Cruiser, Model 46469. This rather modified car used the standard LeSabre body, but the engine was the 430-cubic-inch Wildcat model with 4-barrel carburetor and 10.25:1 compression ratio. It could be ordered with the standard LeSabre interior, or with the all-vinyl interior of the LeSabre Custom sub-series, at extra cost. Such items as flasher light-siren bar, shown here, were optional.

Appearing for the last time this year was the Special Deluxe Series. The line would be dropped at the end of this production year, and the cars would be moved to the Skylark Series, which in effect they were since the only difference between the cars was in the exterior trim and interior fittings. This is the Special Deluxe 4-door Sedan, Model 43469, which cost $2,724 and weighed 3,301 pounds. Specials continued to use the three fender ventiports, a design mark going back to the first real postwar models produced in 1950.

Buick's lowest priced car was the Special Deluxe 2-door Coupe, Model 43427, which had a base price of $2,673. It weighed 3,245 pounds. The car was 200.7 inches long and 53.4 inches high, and was built on the short chassis of 112-inch wheelbase.

The Skylarks and Specials continued to use the same chassis, built in two sizes. Convertibles and 2-door coupes used the 112-inch wheelbase version, while 4-door models and station wagons used the 116-inch wheelbase version. This unit is fitted with the standard 350-cubic-inch V-8 with 2-barrel carburetor, but power steering has been added.

The Opel Kadett Super Deluxe Sport Coupe, Model 95, used the same body as the Rallye Sport, but was of much more dignified taste. It weighed 1,664 pounds and cost $2,090, with the vinyl top being extra. All Opels except the Rallye Sport and the new GT were available in a wide variety of colors and inside trim.

The Opel Kadett Station Wagon, Model 39, no longer had its own exclusive length, but joined all the other Opels except the 2-door Sedan in being 164.6 inches overall. It weighed 1,742 pounds and cost $2,110, with the large roof-top luggage rack being extra.

The Opel Kadett Rallye Sport Coupe, Model 92, was equipped with a 67 horsepower 4-cylinder engine. Standard equipment included a floor-four in a console, radial-ply tires, silver-painted rims with chrome lug nuts, tachometer, power disc brakes on the front, a console-mounted oil pressure gauge and ammeter, and running lights on the front bumper. It was available only in red, gold, yellow, or green, with black striping and black hood panels being standard. It cost $2,318 and weighed 1,717 pounds. Optional equipment included a more powerful engine and automatic transmission.

New for the year was the totally different Opel GT, a sporty 2-passenger mini-coupe based on the standard Opel chassis of 95.1-inch wheelbase. It cost $3,348 and weighed 1,815 pounds. It used rather radical aerodynamic styling of the Gran Turismo school and measured just slightly over four feet in height.

The Opel Kadett Sport Sedan, Model 91, did not use the lower body of the 2-door sedan, as would be expected, but instead used the lower body of the Coupe. It was fitted with a more formal roof and less rear slope than the coupes. It cost $1,993, weighed 1,664 pounds.

The lowest priced car in a Buick showroom this year was the little Opel Kadett 2-door Sedan, Model 31, which had a base price of $1,825. It weighed 1,625 pounds. It was also the shortest Opel, being the only one with an overall length of only 161.6 inches.

Due to heavy 1970 model year production during late 1969, and relatively light 1971 model year production during late 1970, Buick's 1970 calendar year production was down substantially. The figure rested at 459,931, down almost 250,000 units from the 1969 figure. Still, this same phenomena was experienced by other car makers, too, and therefore Buick still kept its fourth place rank.

Conversely, 1970 model year production stood at a very healthy 666,501, which was 1,000 more cars than the 1969 run. Of this amount, the Skylark Series, which had been the former Special Series, accounted for 226,421, which was 38,000 more cars than produced in 1969. Production of the LeSabre reached 200,622, up almost 3,000 cars, and the new Estate Wagon Series accounted for 28,306 vehicles. On the negative side, Wildcat production dropped to 23,615, which was about 44,000 less Wildcats than were turned loose in 1969. Electra production dipped

The new Riviera, Model 49487, had a longer hood, and a completely new grille made up of vertical bars set into a very heavy upper frame, and bending under the lower front end in the same curve pattern as the front bumper. The headlights, once again exposed, no longer were an integral part of the grille. Also new was the distinctive side trim. The Riviera in basic form weighed 4,216 pounds and cost $4,854, with the Gran Sport package being $132 more. It was built on a new chassis of 119-inch wheelbase length, and was 215.5 inches overall.

The Rivieras still continued to use their exclusive chassis of very heavy Cruciform design. The car used finned aluminum front drum brakes, but more often than not was fitted with power disc front brakes.

to 150,201, a drop of more than 8,000 cars, and even the steadily climbing Riviera took its first bad nosedive, with production dropping to 37,336, a loss of over 15,000 vehicles.

The Specials were technically gone, their place being taken by the expanded Skylark line, which included Skylarks, Skylark 350s, and Skylark Customs, plus the two GS lines and the Sport wagon line. All 2-door models used the well-proven 112-inch wheelbase chassis, but new body styling gave them an added two inches of length, with these cars now being 202 inches overall. The 4-door models continued to use the 116-inch wheelbase chassis and were now 206 inches overall in their new bodies.

The completely redesigned Sportwagons now shared the 116-inch chassis of the Skylarks, having given up their exclusive 121-inch wheelbase chassis. Also, Sportwagon bodies were now two inches shorter than they had been, now measuring 212.6 inches overall. Power options continued to be the well-proven V-6 of 250 cubic inches and 155 horsepower, and the equally well-proven 350-cubic-inch V-8, now rated at 260 horsepower at 4600 RPM with a 9:1 compression ratio or 315 horsepower at 4800 RPM with a 10.25:1 ratio.

The new GS 455 was equipped with a brand new 455-cubic-inch block with a 4.3 x 3.9 inch bore and stroke. Running a compression ratio of 10:1, the engine was rated at 350 horsepower at 4600 RPM. This same block, but rated at 370 horsepower at 4600 RPM, also appeared as the standard power plant in this year's new Estate Wagon Series, the LeSabre Custom 455, the Wildcat Custom, Electra 225, Electra 225 Custom, and Riviera Series.

The freshly designed LeSabre line also grew, going to a new 124-inch wheelbase chassis and being 220 inches overall. The series was also expanded, with the LeSabre Custom 455 sub-series being introduced as a line in which to install the big new engine. The standard LeSabre sub-series and the LeSabre Custom sub-series continued to use the 350-cubic-inch block found in the Skylarks.

Totally new for the year was the Estate Wagon Series, a two-model line based on the same common body. The models were a six- and nine-passenger version. The wagons used the LeSabre chassis with 124-inch wheelbase, but were 223.3 inches overall. Also using both the LeSabre chassis and basic bodies was the Wildcat Series, now reduced to just the Wildcat Custom line, since the standard Wildcat sub-series was dropped.

Also vastly redesigned was the Electra Series, still sub-divided into the Electra 225 and the Electra 225 Custom. The cars, as did other Buicks, grew slightly, now having a 127-inch wheelbase chassis and an overall length of 225.8 inches which was almost one inch longer than this year's Cadillac DeVille.

As could be expected, the only car that didn't change in many ways was the Riviera. However, big plans were underway for this car, and in 1971 the Riviera would be one of the most startling and most attractive cars to roll out onto the American highways.

1970

Buick's prestige sedan was the Electra 225 Custom 4-door Hardtop, Model 48439, with the optional Limited luxury decor package. In base form, it cost $4,771 and weighed 4,385 pounds. The Limited package was identifiable by the Limited signatures appearing on the lower portion of the rear roof quarter. The car was also available in the Electra 225 sub-series as the Model 48239 which cost $4,592 and weighed 4,296 pounds. All Electras used a new chassis of 127-inch wheelbase length, and all were 225.8 inches overall.

The Electra 225 Custom 4-door Sedan, Model 48469, is shown here with the optional Limited decor group, which included a luxury interior and vinyl top. In basic form, it cost $4,677 and weighed 4,283 pounds. It was also available in the standard Electra 225 sub-series as the Model 48269, which had a base price of $4,461 and weighed 4,274 pounds.

Sadly, Buick found that it had little market for its beautiful Electra 225 Custom Convertible, and so the car was phased out of production during the model year. Designated the Model 48467, it cost $4,802 and weighed 4,341 pounds.

The Electra Sport Coupe appeared in both the standard and custom sub-series. It is shown here in custom form, as the Model 48457, which cost $4,661 and weighed 4,297 pounds. In the standard version it was designated the Model 48257 and cost $4,482 and weighed 4,214 pounds.

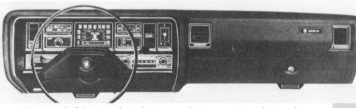

All large Buicks continued to use the same attractive and highly functional dash that was used in 1969. This is the Electra version, fitted for air conditioning, with ducts both within and below the dashboard.

The new Riviera dash followed the general theme of the dash on the large Buicks, but placed the radio controls outside of the driver's control panel. The dash was heavily padded and decorated with wood-grain applique in the recessed lower half.

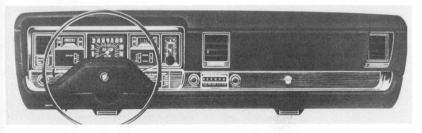

Appearing for the first time since 1964 was the new Estate Wagon, now considered a series of its own, although it used the LeSabre's new chassis of 124-inch wheelbase. The series consisted of one basic style of 223.3 inches overall length, divided into 6- and 9-passenger models, and being available with optional wood trim and vinyl tops. In 6-passenger form, the car was the Model 46036, which cost $3,923 and weighed 4,691 pounds. The 9-passenger style, with its rear-facing back seat, was the Model 46046, which cost $4,068 and weighed 4,779 pounds. Both versions used the same exteriors, were fitted with the three decorative ventiports of the LeSabre Series, and wore chrome rocker panel covers and front and rear fender gravel shields.

For the first time since its introduction, the Sportwagon did not use its Skyroof, with the raised roof deck and small windshield and side roof windows. In fact, with the Special wagon discontinued, the Sportwagon became Buick's economy wagon. It now used the Skylark's 116-inch wheelbase chassis, but was 212.6 inches long. It was available as the Model 43435, costing $3,210 and weighing 3,775 pounds, or the Model 43436, which cost $3,242 and weighed 3,898 pounds. Both were 6-passenger models. The chromed roof rack and chromed steel wheels on this version were accessories.

In a rather surprising move, the LeSabre Series this year divided into three sub-series. They were the LeSabre, the LeSabre Custom with its all-vinyl interiors, and the new LeSabre Custom 455, which appeared this year only and was really the LeSabre Custom fitted with the new 455-cubic-inch engine. Appearing in all three sub-series was the 4-door Sedan. In plain form it was the Model 45269, costing $3,337 and weighing 3,970 pounds. As the LeSabre Custom it was the Model 45469, costing $3,431 and weighing 3,950 pounds. With the big engine it was the Model 46469, which cost $3,599 and weighed 4,107 pounds. The exteriors were virtually identical.

The 5-millionth car to roll from Buick's plant at Doraville, Ga., was this LeSabre Custom 455 4-door Hardtop, Model 46439, which in basic form cost $3,739 and weighed 4,143 pounds. This version has been fitted with the optional vinyl top. The hardtop was also available as the LeSabre Custom Model 45439, which cost $3,571 and weighed 3,988 pounds, and the LeSabre Model 45239, which cost $3,477 and weighed 4,018 pounds.

Appearing in all three LeSabre Custom sub-series, and not available as a Custom 455, was the Convertible, Model 45467. It cost $3,700 and weighed 3,947 pounds. All LeSabres were built on a new 124-inch wheelbase chassis and were 220.2 inches overall. The cars, which featured totally new body styling, continued to use the three ventiports on the front fender.

After the Flxible Co. of Ohio left the ambulance and hearse business, it sold its dies to the Trinity Co. of Texas, and this firm ran off a linited number of such vehicles on Buick chassis for a couple of years. By 1968 that company also stopped using Buick chassis, and for two years no Buick professional cars were turned out. However, with the new Estate Wagon introduced this year, Automotive Conversions of Troy, Mich., started to produce these Model Amblewagon conversions. The cars used the new Estate Wagon bodies, and were fitted with 2-stretcher ambulance interiors. The main attraction of Amblewagons was the fact that they cost less than half of what a full-size ambulance cost, and that they could be converted back to station wagon form. The company built a wide variety of ambulance and hearse bodies on station wagons of several different makes, including Chevrolet, Mercury, Ford, and International.

Appearing in all three LeSabre sub-series was the Sport Coupe, seen here as the LeSabre Custom, Model 45437. In this form, it cost $3,507 and weighed 3,921 pounds. As the high power Custom 455, Model 46437, it had a base price of $3,675 and weighed 4,066 pounds; and as the economy LeSabre, Model 45237, it cost $3,419 and weighed 3,866 pounds. The vinyl top was extra.

Appearing for the last time was the Wildcat Custom Series, now reduced to three models all in one series and all using the same chassis and bodies of the LeSabre Series. This is the 4-door Hardtop, Model 46639, which cost $3,997 and weighed 4,187 pounds. There was no 4-door sedan in the Wildcat Custom Series.

The Wildcat Custom Sport Coupe, Model 46637, is shown here with added-cost vinyl top and chromed steel wheels. In basic form it cost $3,949 and weighed 4,009 pounds. Wildcats differed from the LeSabres only in grille, exterior trim and the fact that they used just two decorative ventiports on the lower front fender panel. All Wildcats used as standard power the new 455-cubic-inch V-8.

Destined to disappear with the rest of the Wildcats at the end of the model year was the Wildcat Custom Convertible, Model 46667. It cost $4,079 and weighed 4,214 pounds. All Wildcats used all-vinyl interiors, chrome rocker panels, and gravel shields on the front and rear fenders.

New for the year was the GS-X. This 4-wheel bomb used the standard GS 455 body and running gear, but was fitted with the Stage I performance package and sported a unique exterior, modified by the use of fiberglas spoilers both front and rear, a special black-out racing hood and full length racing stripes running from headlight to headlight completely around the car. It cost $4,171, and was available on special order only. Production was about 875.

The GS Sport Coupes all looked alike this year, with only small signature plaques identifying the various models. The coupes came in two basic sub-series, the Gran Sport 434, costing $3,098 and weighing 3,434 pounds, which used a 315 horsepower version of the 350-cubic-inch engine, and the Gran Sport 455, costing $3,283 and weighing 3,620 pounds, which used the 455-cubic-inch engine of 350 horsepower. Also available was the GS 455 Stage I, which used the 455-cubic-inch block with speed package including high-performance cam.

Appearing for the first and last time was the new Gran Sport 455 Convertible, Model 44667, which cost $3,469 and weighed 3,619 pounds. All GS models used the basic bodies and chassis of the Skylark models, and were 202.2 inches in overall length. Quick identification was made by the red striped rocker panel molding, and the twin air scoops on the hood, which fed outside air directly into the dual breathers on the air cleaner. All GS cars used 4-barrel carburetors, and were fitted with their own distinctive grilles. Chromed steel wheels were standard.

With the Special Series gone for good, the Skylark series divided into three sub-series, the Skylark, Skylark 350, and Skylark Custom. The only style to appear in all three sub-series was the 4-door Sedan. It is shown here in the Custom sub-series, as the Model 44469, which used stainless steel wheel opening moldings. In this form, it cost $3,101 and weighed 3,499 pounds. In the 350 sub-series it was the Model 43569, and weighed 3,418 pounds. The lowest priced version was the plain Skylark, Model 43369, which cost $2,847 and weighed 3,409 pounds.

Available only in the Skylark Custom sub-series was the 4-door Hardtop, Model 44439, which cost $3,220 and weighed 3,565 pounds. The vinly top and chromed steel wheels were accessories. All 4-door Skylarks used a 116-inch wheelbase chassis and were 206.2 inches in overall length.

Buick's lowest priced car was the Skylark 2-door Sedan, Model 43327, which cost $2,796. The 3,350-pound car was found only in the plain Skylark sub-series, and was not available in the 350 or custom lines. It used the same body as the sport coupes, but was fitted with a centerpost and full-frame doors.

The Skylark Custom Convertible, Model 44467, cost $3,275 and weighed 3,499 pounds. All 2-door Skylarks were built on the short chassis of 112-inch wheelbase and all were 202.2 inches overall. For the first time, the Skylark series did not use ventiport decoration on its sides.

The Skylark Custom Sport Coupe, Model 44437, had a base price of $3,132 and weighed 3,435 pounds. It was also available in the Skylark 350 sub-series, where it was designated the Model 43537. In that form, it cost $2,970 and weighed 3,375 pounds. Skylarks and Skylark 350 models were available with either the Six or V-8, but Skylark Customs had the 260 horse V-8 only.

The most expensive Opel continued to be the GT Coupe, Model 93, which cost $3,328. It used its own exclusive chassis of 95.7-inch wheelbase, compared to the 95.1-inch wheelbase chassis used by other Opels. It was 48.2 inches high, 161.6 inches long, and weighed 1,780 pounds. Its standard power was the 67 horsepower Four with a floor-four transmission, but a 102 horsepower engine and automatic transmission were options. Its pop-up headlights gave it a frog-like appearance at night.

One of Buick's show cars this year was the Opel Aero GT, which made its initial appearance at the New York Auto Show. It used a highly modified version of the standard GT body, and was equipped with a reverse-slant rear window and an integral roll bar similar to that used on the Corvettes. Weather protection was by removable roof panels.

The new Opel Kadett DeLuxe Sport Sedan, Model 91, offered fastback roof styling, a 63 horsepower engine, floor-four transmission, front bucket seats with head restraints and adjustable backs, and carpeting front and rear all for a base price of $2,043. It weighed 1,671. For the economy minded, there was the Opel Kedatt 2-door Sedan, Model 31, which cost $1,877 and weighed 1,640 pounds. The Model 31 had an overall length of 161.6 inches, all other Opels except the GT were 164.6 inches in overall length.

The Opel Deluxe Sport Coupe, Model 95, shared its body with the Rallye Coupe, but was a much more sedate looking car. It weighed 1,673 and cost $2,139, with the vinyl top being extra.

The Opel Kadett Rallye Sport Coupe, Model 92, continued to be the racy version of the Sport Coupe. It cost $2,378 and weighed 1,729 pounds. the popularity of the Opels could be attested to by the fact that the little German cars were now being sold and serviced by over 2,000 Buick dealers.

For the first time, the Opel Kadett Wagon, Model 39, was available in two forms, as a standard model or as the deluxe version, which included the wood-grain applique for the first time. It had a base price of $2,159 and weighed 1,762. The luggage rack, body moldings, and wheel covers were standard on the deluxe model. With the back seat folded, the rear compartment offered 55.6 inches of open floor space for cargo.

The 1971 Riviera rolled out into the public's gaze, and the reaction was spontaneous, if not mixed. A great many people thought it was the most beautiful car to appear in many a year. A great many others took the opposite stand. It seemed that few people with any automotive awareness had no feelings about the car. It was a design that was either liked immensely or disliked with the same fervor.

Both body and chassis of the Riviera were totally new, with the wheelbase being lengthened to 122 inches and the overall length stretched to 217.4 inches. The car had a symmetry of design seldom accomplished on late model cars, from its striking forward raked front end to its distinctive and beautiful boattail rear end. And, for a welcome change, not one single line of the new Riviera was shared by any other car in the General Motors stable.

Because of new emmissions standards this year, compression on all engines had to be reduced to 8.5:1. This meant that the large Buicks, with the 455-cubic-inch engines, needed some mighty fancy engine engineering just to keep up horsepower while satisfying government requirements. Still, the job was accomplished to an admirable degree, and as wide a variety of engines were available this year as were in the past.

As could be expected, the Riviera used the 455-cubic-inch block of either 315 or 345 horsepower. The LeSabre lines, the new Centurion (which replaced the Wildcat), the Estate Wagons, and the Electra 225 Series used either the 350-cubic-inch block of 230 or 260 horsepower or the 455-cubic-inch mill of 315 horsepower. The small Buicks used either the little 250-cubic-inch V-6, now rated at 145 horsepower, or the 350-cubic-inch V-8 with 230 or 260 horsepower, The GS models could be equipped with the 455-cubic-inch block of 315, 330 or 345 horsepower.

The small Buicks continued to use two separate chassis, one for coupes and one for 4-door models. These dimensions were unchanged, remaining again at 112-inch and 116-inch wheelbases respectively. Slightly different styling resulted in new overall lengths of 203 inches for the coupes, 207 inches for the 4-doors, and 212 inches for the Sportwagons.

Both the LeSabres and the new Centurions shared the same all-new 124-inch wheelbase chassis and 220-inch bodies. The all-new bodies featured very this windsheild pillars, flow-through ventilation, new and flowing line design, and completely new wrap-around instrument clusters.

Also using an all new chassis was the Electra Series.

The new Riviera, Model 49487, rolled out this year and reaction was as mixed as could be possible. Many people hated the design, while others, including the author, thought it was one of the most beautiful cars to come along in years. In any event, it caused quite a stir in the automotive circles. The 4,464-pound car cost $5,253 in base form.

Not only did the new Riviera have a totally new front, it had a totally new rear in boat-tail styling, unlike anything ever put on the road before. The car used its own 122-inch wheelbase chassis and was 217.4 inches overall. Power was by the 455-cubic-inch engine, with the Turbo Hydramatic 400 automatic transmission being standard.

The interior of the new Riviera was distinctively Buick and distinctively Riviera. Standard appointments included the wrap-around control panel, console with floor-mounted shift selector, and upholstery in leather and vinyl. Power steering and front disc brakes were standard, but power windows were $133 and air conditioning was $445 extra.

Adding performance to beauty, Buick continued with the GS option for the new Riviera. This option, signified by the small GS initials behind the front wheel cutouts and on the trunk deck, cost an extra $200. It included the modified high-performance 455-cubic-inch engine, chromed air cleaner, white stripe tires, heavy duty suspension, and a posi-traction rear axle. The vinyl roof option cost an additional $130.

1971

They were still on a 127-inch wheelbase chassis, but there was now an all-coil spring version for the cars and a rear leaf spring version for the Estate Wagons. The newly designed Electra body shell was shared by Cadillac Calais and DeVille models.

Model year production dropped to 551,188, primarily because of the recessed economy that hit hard at all auto companies early in the year, plus a monstrous strike that hit all General Motors companies very hard. The recession caused a drop of more than 115,000 Buicks this year. Of the production, all models but the new Centurion were down. Centurion production was 29,398, which was about 6,000 more cars that 1970's comparable Wildcat production.

Skylark production dipped to 184,075, down a horrendous 42,000 cars; LeSabre's production was even worse, going down to 153,835, a drop of 47,000 cars; the Estate Wagon production was 24,034, down over 4,000; Electra's production dipped to 126,036, down over 24,000,; and Riviera's production dropped to 33,810, down almost 4,000.

Wearing the optional Limited trim package is this Electra Custom 2-door Hardtop, Model 48437, which cost $4,980 and weighed 4,386 pounds. The plain Electra, Model 48237, cost $4,801 and weighed 4,447 pounds. All Electras used their own chassis of 127-inch wheelbase and were 226.2 inches overall. They continued to use the four decorative ventiports on the hood.

Appearing only in the LeSabre Custom sub-series was the Convertible, Model 45467, which cost $4,324 and weighed 4,122 pounds. Standard power in the LeSabres was the 350-cubic-inch block with 2-barrel carburetor, but a 4-barrel version or the 455-cubic-inch block was available. A manual 3-speed transmission was standard, with automatics being available at extra cost.

The Electra 225 Series was reduced to just two models, a 2-door and a 4-door hardtop, with these placed in two basic sub-series. This is the Electra 225 Custom 4-door Hardtop, Model 48237, cost $4,801 and weighed 4,447 pounds. All Electras used their own chassis of 127-inch wheelbase and were 226.2 inches overall. They continued to use the four decorative ventiports on the hood.

The LeSabre Sport Coupe was available in both the plain form, shown here, or in the Custom sub-series. In plain trim it was the Model 45257, which cost $4,061 and weighed 4,044 pounds. In the Custom range, the car was designated the Model 45457, which cost $4,149, and weighed 4,058 pounds. All LeSabres were built on a 124-inch wheelbase chassis, were 220.7 inches overall, and were 53.6 inches high.

The LeSabre Series continued to be divided into standard and custom sub-series, with most models being available in both ranges. This is the 4-door Sedan in plain form. In this range it was the Model 45269, which cost $3,992 and weighed 4,081 pounds. In the Custom version it was the Model 45469, costing $4,085 and weighing 4,093 pounds. In plain form, the sedan was the only full-size Buick with a base price under $4,000.

The LeSabre 4-door Hardtop appeared in both Custom and plain forms. The Custom version, shown here, was designated the Model 45439. It cost $4,213 and weighed 4,099 pounds. In the plain version, Model 45239, it cost $4,119 and weighed 4,087 pounds. All LeSabres continued to use the three decorative ventiports on the hood. The vinyl top shown here was an added cost item.

Still considered a series of its own was the Estate Wagon line, which consisted of a six- and nine-passenger model, both using the same basic body. The 6-passenger version was the Model 46035, which cost $4,640 and weighed 4,833 pounds. The 9-passenger version was the Model 46045. It had a base price of $4,786 and weighed 4,917 pounds.

The dashboards of the new LeSabres were both very attractive and very functional, with all controls in a wrap-around panel directly in front of the driver. This is the interior of the Custom Convertible, equipped with power windows, air conditioning, AM-FM radio, and speed control. This year Buick reverted to a concept used from 1928 to 1939. That was a combined ignition and steering column lock. However, the new lock, located on the steering column, was now also coupled to the starter switch, whereas the original steering column lock utilized a starter switch working in conjunction with the accelerator pedal.

Replacing the Wildcat Series was the new Centurion Series, which consisted of three models, including the 4-door Hardtop, Model 46639. It cost $4,307 and weighed 4,298 pounds. Centurions shared their 124-inch wheelbase chassis and 220.7-inch overall length bodies with LeSabres.

More often than not the Estate Wagon was ordered with its optional wood-grain trim package. This package consisted of the wood-grain applique on sides and tailgate, a stainless steel trim strip from the front fender to the taillights, and very wide chrome covers for the rocker panels, door bottoms, optional vinyl roof covering and the chrome luggage rack.

The pride of the new Centurion line was the very attractive Sport Coupe, Model 46647. It cost $4,678 and weighed 4,216 pounds, with the vinyl top being extra. All Centurions were powered by the 455-cubic-inch block with 4-barrel carburetor. The high-performance 455-cubic-inch engine with dual exhausts was optional.

One of the better looking convertibles on the road this year was the new Centurion, Model 46667. It cost $4,678 and weighed 4,271 pounds. Standard transmissions on Centurions were the 3-speed manual models, but automatics were optional at extra cost. Centurions did not use the renowned ventiports, and in fact, were virtually devoid of side trim.

The GS Series continued to feature its attractive convertible. Designated the Model 43467, the car in basic form cost $3,476 and weighed 3,761 pounds. It used the standard body and trim of the Skylark Custom Convertible, plus the GS vented hood. It was also available in Stage I or in 455 form.

The GS Stage I continued to appear as a high-performance version of the Skylark Sport Coupe, but was considered a series of its own. In basic form, it was designated the Model 43437, cost $3,285, and weighed 3,538 pounds. Standard equipment included the functional vents in the hood, Formula Five chromed wheels, and the 350-cubic-inch block with 4-barrel carburetor. A 3-speed manual transmission was standard, but floor-fours and automatics were available.

In addition to the GS Stage I and GS 455 models, the sport set was offered the new GS-X. This was an optional trim package for the Sport Coupe, and featured front and rear spoilers, a black-out hood with the twin vents and tachometer, special paint job, special grille, and deep-dished chrome wheels with wide track-type tires.

An even hotter version than the Stage I was the GS 455 Sport Coupe. This car featured all of the standard equipment of the Stage I, but was powered by the 455-cubic-inch block with a 4-barrel carburetor. Dual exhaust and posi-traction rear ends were standard on all GS cars.

The new Riviera was given show car treatment via a custom silver paint job, special side mirrors, custom side trim, and a silver-gray leather interior. It was called the Silver Arrow, a name taken from the former Riviera Silver Arrow show cars.

Buick produced a series of show cars this year, but none were what could be considered very radical. One of these was the Centurion, which was actually a slightly modified Centurion Convertible, trimmed in gold plate rather than in chrome and stainless steel. The car was finished in pearl white with a gold vinyl interior.

Both the rear door treatment and the wide centerposts distinguish the Skylark 4-door Sedan from the 4-door Hardtop. This is the Skylark Custom version of the sedan. Designated the Model 44469, it had a base price of $3,288 and weighed 3,565 pounds. It was also available in the Skylark sub-series where it had a base price of $2,897 in 6-cylinder form or $3,018 with the V-8.

One of the most popular cars in the Skylark Series was the Custom Sport Coupe, Model 44437, which was available only with the V-8. In base form, it cost $2,968 and weighed 3,431 pounds. This version, owned by B.J. Slattery of Glen Ellyn, Ill., wears the optional chrome side trim and vinyl top. The car was also available in the Skylark sub-series, in either 6- or 8-cylinder form. As a Six, it cost $2,847. During the year, Buick produced its 2-millionth Skylark, and the car was identical to this model, except that it was fitted with a white vinyl top.

The Skylark Custom Convertible, Model 44467, as could be expected, was the highest priced car in the Skylark Series, costing $3,462. It weighed 3,565 pounds. The 350 horse-power block with 2-barrel carburetor was standard, but a 4-barrel carburetor version was available.

Available only in the Skylark Custom sub-series was the 4-door Hardtop, Model 44439, which cost $3,397 and weighed 3,595 pounds. All Skylark 4-door models used a 116-inch wheelbase and were 207.2 inches overall. Standard drive was a 3-speed manual, with automatics being extra.

The Sport Wagon was now reduced to a one-model Series, consisting only of the Model 43436, a 6-passenger wagon costing $3,515 and weighing 3,990 pounds. It used the 116-inch wheelbase of the large Skylarks, but was 212.7 inches overall. Surprisingly, the car used the side trim (or lack of it) of the plain Skylark models. The roof rack was an option.

Appearing only in the Skylark sub-series was the 2-door Sedan, Model 83369, which was available either with the V-6 or the V-8 engine. Plain Skylarks used no side trim, while Skylark Custom models were fitted with three decorative ventiports just behind the front wheel cutout. The 2-door Sedan had a base price of $2,847 and weighed 3,228 pounds. It was Buick's lowest priced car, and in 8-cylinder form, was the only Buick with a base price under $3,000

Buick's only really radical show car this year was the Opel CD, a highly modified version of the Opel GT. The fiberglas body utilized a one-piece windshield and side windows, with the entire section swinging out of the way for entry or exit. Special cast magnesium wheels and wide racing tires were used.

Unlike the station wagon and the sedan models, the Opel Series 1900 Sport Coupe used dual headlights and a grille of black plastic. Designated the Model 57, it cost $2,326 and weighed 2,066 pounds. All Series 1900 models used rubber padded bumper guards as standard equipment.

Appearing virtually unchanged, but now regarded as part of the Series 1900 line was the Opel GT Coupe. It weighed 2,009 pounds and cost $3,334, thus being Opel's lightest yet most expensive car. Standard equipment included the bumper mounted running lights, retractable headlights, twin exhaust extensions, locking gas cap, and special wheels with chromed bolt-on hubcaps. It was available with floor-four or automatic transmissions.

The Opel GT Show Car was really the Opel GT fitted with a variety of racing accessories and wearing custom chromed magnesium wheels with knock-off hubs and Goodyear Rally tires. It was finished in a special silver mist paint.

The Opel Series 1900 Rallye Coupe used an interesting interior based on a modified version of the dashboard used in all models of that series. In addition to the regular gauges, the panel used dial type ammeter and oil pressure gauge, and was equipped with tachometer and clock. When installed, the radio controls fitted in the recessed space directly above the shift lever.

Using the same basic body of the Series 1900 Sport Coupe was the new Opel Rallye Coupe, Model 57R. It cost $2,485 and weighed 2,038. The cantilever type roof ended in a rather short rear deck. The Rallye used as standard equipment large running lights below the bumper, special chromed wheels with bolt-on hubcaps, and a special paint job with black-out hood. The vinyl roof was an extra cost option.

The Opel line was greatly expanded this year, through the inclusion of both the Kadett and the new 1900 Series, plus deluxe models in both versions. Lowest priced of all Opels was the Kadett 2-door Sedan, Model 31, which cost $1,823 and weighed 1,635 pounds in basic form. It used a 95.1-inch wheelbase chassis and was 161.6 inches in overall length and 55.4 inches high. It was also available as the Deluxe 2-door, Model 31D, for $1,989.

The new Opel Kadett 4-door Sedan was available as the standard Model 36, or as the DeLuxe Model 36D, shown here. This version cost $2,064 and weighed 1,684 pounds. The plain version cost $1,898. DeLuxe versions were fitted with chrome side trim and bright window frames, and were available with the larger engine option and automatic transmission.

The Opel Series 1900 4-door Sedan, Model 53, cost $2,311 and weighed 2,081 pounds. As did the wagon and the 2-door sedan, it used its own special grille of polished aluminum and had bright trim around the wheel cut-outs, rocker panels, and window moldings. Assist straps were fitted to the center-posts.

The Opel wagon line was expanded to two versions this year. This is the lower priced Kadett, Model 39, which cost $2,289 and weighed 1,762 pounds. Shown here in its native Germany, this version wears the optional deluxe wheel covers and side trim. The chromed roof rack was standard, as was the outside rearview mirror.

New in the Opel line was the sporty Series 1900 Station Wagon, Model 54, which cost $2,438 and weighed 2,128 pounds. The 1900 Series was quickly identified by its own special grille and its ventless door windows.

Much more dignified than the sport coupe was the Opel Series 1900 2-door Sedan, Model 51, which cost $2,221 and weighed 2,128 pounds. All of the Series 1900 models had as standard equipment the 1.9 liter engine, floor-four transmission, and power brakes with front discs. An automatic transmission was optional at added cost.

Despite a dismal economic outlook at the start of 1972's model year, Buick went ahead with an expansion program based primarily on the fact that even though it didn't do that well in 1971, Buicks still sold better percentage-wise than did most other American cars.

Buick's big car line again consisted of sixteen different models, including two wagons and two convertibles, divided into the LeSabre, LeSabre Custom, Centurion, Estate Wagons, Electra 225, Electra 225 Custom, and Electra 225 Custom Limited Series and sub-series.

The LeSabre line received its own 3-speed Turbo Hydramatic transmission for use with the 350-cubic-inch engine. LeSabres powered by the 455-cubic-inch engine continued to use the same transmission as was used in the Centurions, Electras and Rivieras.

In all of the large models, only minor trim changes were made, with the cars being basically the same as the 1971 models. This story carried over to the Riviera also, where some front end, grille, and taillight changes were added to differentiate one year from the other. All large Buick 2-door models and the Riviera could be equipped with a new power-operated sun roof option.

The Skylark Series received its usual cosmetics, but no real sheetmetal or engine or mechanical changes. Reinstated was the Skylark 350 sub-series, and a totally new design, the Sun Coupe was introduced into this series.

The Sun Coupe basically was a return to the slide-back roof that first appeared on the 1939 Buicks. This concept has enjoyed wide favor in Europe over the years, but was never too successful in the U.S., primarily because buyers wanted either a hardtop or a convertible, but not a combination of both. Still, with government safety standards becoming more and more severe each year, all auto makers agree that the day of the convertible is gone. Within a few years, possibly by 1974, there will be sort of a substitute to those people (such as the author) who still like to put the top down whenever weather permits.

The Riviera GS continued to be a high performance option installed on the basic Riviera for an additional $200. This included the 260 horsepower version of the 455-cubic-inch engine, posi-traction rear end, and special GS trim. An electrically powered sun roof was available on Rivieras for an additional $600, and air conditioning cost $520 extra.

Still maintaining its very beautiful and very unusual lines was the Riviera, Model 4Y87. The car this year had a base price of $5,149 and weighed 4,399 pounds. Its standard power was the 250 horsepower 455-cubic-inch engine. Rivieras used a 122-inch wheelbase chassis and were 218.3 inches overall. The car was also available with a vinyl roof for $130 extra.

The Electra Series continued to be divided into the Electra 225 and the Electra 225 Custom sub-series, with the prestige Limited trim package being available only in the Custom models. Both sub-series used the same exterior trim and engines, and varied only in interior trim. This is the Electra 225 Custom 2-door Hardtop, Model 4V37. In basic form, it cost $4,951 and weighed 4,411 pounds. In the plain Electra 225 sub-series, it was the Model 4U37, which cost $4,781 and weighed 4,380 pounds. It was also available with the Sun Coupe optional roof, which added another $575 to the basic prices. All Electras were built on a 127-inch wheelbase chassis, and were 227.9 inches overall, which was ½-inch longer than this year's Cadillacs.

Buick's prestige vehicle was the Electra 225 Custom Limited 4-door Hardtop. In basic form, the car was the Model 4V39, which weighed 4,495 pounds and cost $5,059. It was also available in the plain Electra 225 sub-series, in which it was the Model 4U39, costing $4,889 and weighing 4,484 pounds. This all-white version is owned by Lee Mays, Buick General Manager. The car is fitted with the little signal light reminders mounted on the front fenders.

The Estate Wagon was still a one-style series, consisting of two models using the same body. It was available as the Model 4R35, a 6-passenger version costing $4,589 and weighing 4,963 pounds, and as the 9-passenger Model 4R45, which cost $4,728 and weighed 5,032 pounds. It was available only with the 225 horsepower engine of 455 cubic inches.

The Sport Wagon continued to be a one-model Series, consisting only of the Model 4F36. The 6-passenger car cost $3,443 and weighed 3,936 pounds. It used the 116-inch wheelbase chassis of the 4-door Skylarks, but was 213.7 inches overall. All Skylarks, GS models and Sport Wagons were 76.5 inches wide. The Sport Wagon used as standard power the 150 horse 350-cubic-inch block.

The Centurion Series continued to be a high-powered relative of the LeSabre Series, with both lines using the same bodies, but having different grilles, hoods, and rear treatment. Centurions were powered by the 225 horsepower 455-cubic-inch block, with the 260 horsepower version of this engine being available for $100 extra. This is the Centurion 2-door Hardtop, Model 4P47, which weighed 4,331 pounds and cost $4,579 with the vinyl top being standard equipment. The car was also available with the Sun Coupe retractable roof panel for an extra $550. Also in the Centurion Series were the 4-door Hardtop, Model 4P39, which cost $4,508 and weighed 4,401 pounds, and the Convertible, Model 4P67, costing $4,616 and weighing 4,233 pounds.

The LeSabre Series continued to be divided into a plain and a Custom sub-series. This is the Custom 4-door Hardtop, Model 4N39, which cost $4,169 and weighed 4,238 pounds. The Custom models were identified by chrome rocker panel covers and rear fender stone guards and the Custom plaque below the LeSabre signature on the front fenders and trunk deck. In plain form, the car was the Model 4L39, which cost $4,079 and weighed 4,226 pounds.

Appearing only in the LeSabre Custom sub-series was the Convertible, Model 4N67, which cost $4,291 and weighed 4,233 pounds. All LeSabres were built on a 124-inch wheelbase chassis and were 221.9 inches overall. The cars used as standard power the 155 horsepower 350-cubic-inch engine, but the 180 horsepower version of this block was available for $50 extra. Turbo Hydramatic transmissions were now standard in all full-size Buicks.

The LeSabre Custom 4-door Sedan, Model 4N69, cost $4,047 and weighed 3,958 pounds. LeSabres continued to use the three decorative ventiports on the hood, a Buick style innovation dating back to the old Supers and Roadmasters of 1949.

As could be expected, the Flint Police Dept. has used Buicks for years. Appearing on the streets are these LeSabre 4-door Sedans, Model 4L69, modified for police use with the inclusion of the optional 180 horsepower 350-cubic-inch engine. In civilian form, the cars cost $3,958 and weighed 4,166 pounds. This model was the only full-size Buick to have a base price under $4,000.

Also available in both the LeSabre and LeSabre Custom sub-series was the 2-door Hardtop, shown here in Custom form. In this version, it was the Model 4N57, which cost $4,107 and weighed 4,149 pounds. The vinyl top was $126 extra. In standard trim, the car was the Model 4L57, which cost $4,024 and weighed 4,132 pounds. The chromed steel wheels were an accessory. The car was also available with the sun roof for an additional $600. Unlike the Skylark roof, this special order top consisted of an electrically operated solid panel in the roof which would retract similar to the roofs on the 1939 models.

The GS Series continued to be a highly refined and high-performance group of cars based on Skylark chassis and bodies but using a 190 horsepower version of the 350-cubic-inch block as standard power. The cars were also available as GS 455 models, in which form they were powered with the 225 horsepower engine of 455 cubic inches. This GS Sport Coupe, Model 4G37, is owned by Glen Cline of Flint, MIch. In base form, it cost $3,225 and weighed 3,475, with the vinyl top being extra.

As could be expected, the sun roof option was also available in the GS Series, but unlike the Skylarks where the sun roof was a standard item, it had to be special ordered on GS models. Also available in the GS Series was the Convertible, Model 4G67, which cost $3,406 and weighed 3,517 pounds. Because of federal safety standards, all companies were beginning to phase out true convertibles, replacing the styles with such things as sun roof models.

The GS engine room was crowded, to say the least, especially when fitted with air conditioning and power steering and brakes, such as worn by this model. This is the Stage 1 model, fitted with the 350-cubic-inch engine. The 455-cubic-inch engine cost an additional $165.

The Skylark Custom sub-series was quickly identified by its heavy chrome rocker panel covers and rear stone guard, special grille, and Custom plaques below the Skylark signatures. This is the Sport Coupe, Model 4H37, which cost $3,225 and weighed 3,423 pounds. All Skylarks, regardless of sub-series, were powered by the 150 horsepower V-8, with the 175 horsepower version being optional. Both engines were 350-cubic-inch displacement.

The Skylark Custom sub-series used a totally different grille than did the plain Skylarks. This is the Custom 4-door Hardtop, Model 4H39, shown here with its optional vinyl top which cost $105 extra. In base form, it cost $3,331 and weighed 3,546 pounds. All Skylarks were equipped with 3-speed manual transmissions, wtih automatic transmissions being $225 extra.

Appearing only in the Skylark Custom sub-series was the convertible, Model 4H67, which cost $3,393 and weighed 3,476 pounds. This model is shown with the optional chromed steel wheels. All 2-door Skylarks used the 112-inch wheelbase chassis and were 202.8 inches overall.

Available in all three Skylark sub-series was the Sport Coupe, shown here in the Skylark 350 version. In this sub-series it was designated the Model 4D37, cost $3,124, and weighed 3,403 pounds. In the plain Skylark version it was priced at $2,993 Actually, both Skylarks and Skylark 350 models were identical, with the 350 really being an optional trim package added to the base car for a price of about $135.

New for the year was the sun roof option, available only on Skylark Sport Coupes in the Custom sub-series or with the 350 trim package. The unit, which cost an additional $250 over the basic price of the car, is shown here on the Skylark 350 model. Unlike the sun roofs in the 1939 and 1940 Buicks, this version used a sliding vinyl soft top instead of a solid panel.

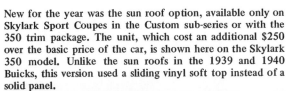

The Skylark Series again expanded into three sub-series, but this year only V-8 engines were offered, and the Six was gone for good. The lowest priced car in the line, and the only one available only in the plain Skylark sub-series was the 2-door Sedan, Model 4D27. The car, sometimes known as the 2-door Coupe, cost $2,925 and weighed 3,348 pounds. It is shown here with its optional vinyl top and wheel covers.

The Skylark 4-door Sedan also appeared in all versions. It is shown here in with the 350 trim package, in which form it had a base price of $3,104. As the plain Skylark, Model 4D69, it cost $2,973 and weighed 3,408 pounds. As the Skylark Custom, Model 4H69, it cost $3,228 and weighed 3,408 pounds. All 4-door Skylarks continued to use the 116-inch wheelbase chassis and were 207.3 inches overall.

The Opel line continued in its two major series, now strictly the plain Opels, divided into standard and deluxe models, and the much more popular Opel 1900 Series. This is the 1900 2-door Sedan, Model 51, which cost $2,434 and weighed 2,127 pounds. The 2-door Sedan style was also available as the Opel Model 31, which cost $2,175 and weighed 1,981, and the Opel Deluxe, Model 31D, which cost $2,307 and weighed 1,987 pounds.

The Opel GT continued to be a car apart from its brothers. Designated the Model 77, it cost $3,333 and weighed 2,121 pounds. The car used the same 95.7-inch wheelbase chassis as used by the Series 1900 models, but was 161.9 inches in overall length and 62.2 inches wide. Surprisingly, its engine was the same 75 horsepower block used on all Opels. A floor-four was standard on all Opels, but an automatic transmission was available for an additional $220.

A cute little car was Opel 1900 4-door Sedan, Model 53, which cost $2,523 and weighed 2,178 pounds. It was not available as the plain Opel line. All small Opels used a 95.1-inch wheelbase, while the Opel 1900 models used a 95.7 inch wheelbase. The small Opels were 161.6 inches overall and 61.9 inches wide, while the 1900 models were 164.6 inches overall and 64.3 inches wide. In addition to the cars shown here, there were two Opel station wagons, the plain Model 39, which cost $2,582 and weighed 2,082 pounds, and the Opel 1900, Model 54, which cost $2,657 and weighed 2,216 pounds.

The Opel 1900 Sport Coupe, Model 57, used the basic frontal styling of the Opel sedans and wagons, but its rear end treatment was similar to that used on the GT model. It cost $2,529 and weighed 2,160 pounds.

The Opel 1900 Rallye Coupe, Model 57R, was simply a sporty version of the Sport Coupe. It cost $2,706 and weighed 2,182 pounds. Standard trim included a black-out hood and plastic grille, quad lights and bumper-mounted running lights, special paint and striping, and aluminum wheels with chrome bolt-on hubcaps. It used the same 75 horsepower 4-cylinder engine of 115 cubic inches as used in all Opels.

Again Buick played the name game, with the result that some confusion resulted between the brand new Century Series and the existing Centurion Series. The new Century Series, bearing the proud name of the red hot Century models of years back, replaced the Skylark Series. The cars used the same 350-cubic-inch engines of 150 and 175 horsepower of the former Skylarks, but utilized totally new bodies, including the Colonnade Hardtops. The Series was divided into three sub-series, the Century, Century Luxus, and the one-model Regal. The cars used the same wheelbase dimensions of the former Skylarks, but the 112-inch and 116-inch wheelbase chassis were of totally new design.

In addition to this name switch, all Buicks except the Riviera showed a noticeable new appearance, including the deeply downturned hood-line, pioneered earlier on other GM products. The Riviera continued to use its beautiful styling with the boat-tail rear end, but was fitted with a new grille and headlamp treatment, and a coupe de ville style optional vinyl top.

The prestige Electra Series continued to be a two-model line, divided into Electra 225 and Electra 225 Custom sub-series, with limited trim available in the Custom models. Standard equipment on these cars included the 455-cubic-inch block of 225 horsepower, Turbo Hydramatic transmission, power brakes with front discs, and power steering. Air conditioning was a $500 accessory, and a powered sun roof was available as an option of the 2-door models for an extra $590. A manual sun roof cost $540.

The Estate Wagon continued to be a one-style series of its own, using the Electra's chassis of 127-inch wheelbase, and engine of 225 horsepower. It was still available in six- or nine-passenger form, and could be fitted with a vinyl roof for an additonal $140.

Both the Centurion and LeSabre Series used the same chassis of 124-inch wheelbase, and the same bodies of 224.2 inches overall length. However, the LeSabres used as standard power the 350-cubic-inch engine of 150 horsepower, or the 175 horsepower version for an additonal $45. The Centurions used as standard power the 175 horsepower engine, with the 455-cubic-inch block of 225 horsepower being an additional $125. Only the Riviera used the 455-cubic-inch block of 260 horsepower, or the 260 horespower optional version.

Both the Centurion and LeSabre Series now had the Turbo Hydramatic transmission, and power steering and brakes as standard equipment. In addition, the Centurion Series held Buick's only remaining convertible, a sad factor which makes one want to cram the new national safety standards down someone's throat.

Totally new for the year was the Century Regal Colonnade Hardtop, which was an interesting coupe design, but really not a hardtop in the former sense of the word. It was joined by the Century Colonnade Hardtop, which used a completely different top design, but again was of the pillared design, and not a hardtop in the true sense of the word. Again, the new safety standards had made their presence felt.

The former Sport Wagon was now part of the Century line, but was available once more in six-or nine-passenger versions. It used a one-piece tailgate, hinged at the top in hatch-back fashion. The wagons used power brakes with front discs as standard equipment, while these were a $45 accessory on other Century models.

All Century cars used a 3-speed manual transmission as standard equipment, with the automatic being available for $215 extra. A GS package was available on the Century Hardtop Coupe for an extra $175, while the 455-cubic-inch engine was available on this model only for another $235. An electric sun roof for these models cost $325, while the manually operated version cost $275.

The new Riviera offered a totally new front design, with the new grille and the parking and head lights all being located in one large package. In base form, the car cost $5,149, with the vinyl top being $125 extra. Also available was the sun roof option, which cost $540 when manually operated, or $590 when electrically powered in conjunction with power windows which cost an additional $130. The car used its own exclusive chassis of 122-inch wheelbase, and was 223.4 inches in overall length and 79.9 inches high.

Optional on the Riviera was the Gran Sport package, which cost an additional $140 above the price of the car. The package included the 260 horsepower Stage I option on the 455-cubic-inch engine, steel-belted radial ply tires, heavy duty springs and shock absorbers, front and rear stabilizer bars, heavy duty wheels and trim plaques.

The Electra Series, Buick's top of the line luxury class, continued to be divided into both the Electra 225 and Electra 225 Custom sub-series, with the Linited trim package available in the latter. Shown here is the Custom 4-door Hardtop with Limited trim. In base form the car cost $5,060, with the Limited package being an additional $179, plus an additional $140 for the vinyl top. In plain form, as the Electra 225, it cost $4,890. Also available was the 2-door Hardtop, which in the Electra 225 sub-series cost $4,782 and in the Custom version cost $4,952. All Electras were 229.8 inches overall and 79.3 inches wide.

The Estate Wagon continued to be Buick's prestige wagon. It was available in both 6- and 9-passenger form, with the 6-passenger model costing $4,589 and the 9-passenger version costing $4,728. The rear seat faced forward and the tailgate window was electrically operated. The luggage rack and vinyl top were accessories. The Estate Wagon used the 127-inch wheelbase chassis of the Electra series, but was 229.5 inches overall, and 79.6 inches wide.

The Centurion Series, with the exception of the convertible, used the same basic bodies as used in the LeSabre Series, and for all practical purposes were quite similar to the LeSabres in exterior appearance. However, in the Centurions, the standard engine was the 175 horsepower 350-cubic-inch block, while the optional engine was the 225 horsepower 455-cubic-inch block. This is the Centurion 4-door Hardtop, which cost $4,338 in base form. Also available was the Centurion 2-door Hardtop, which cost $4,286. Unlike the LeSabres, the Centurions did not use the ventiport trim on the hoods.

1973

The 350 trim package was also available on the Century models for an additional $96 on the 2-door styles and $86 on the 4-door models.

All Buicks used the new energy absorbing front and rear bumpers specified by the federal government, and had a new positive-lock jacking system which ended all guesswork about where on the bumper to place the jack. Also meeting federal standards was the Buick exhaust gas recirculation system that was used on all 1972 models shipped to California. This year, the system was used on all Buicks.

What effect these various federal standards will have on the auto industry remains to be seen. Emission controls, while possibly helping the atmosphere, are likewise cutting overall horsepower and total engine performance. Bumper and safety standards have created totally different front and rear designs, the eventual loss of all convertibles, and a new concept regarding hardtops. All makers are feeling the pressure, and the engineers and designers are going to have to wade through many cans of worms in order to meet the requirements. The cars of 1973 have already started some interesting and different trends - - it seems the future should be far from dull. But, when better, or different cars are built - - for sure, Buick will be building them!

Buick's only convertible this year was the Centurion, which cost $4,476. The highly attractive car was reported to be the last "rag top" from a company that once prided itself on being the home of the convertible. Because the convertible was included in the Centurion Series, the sun roof option was not available on the Centurion 2-door Hardtop.

1973

A very stylish car was the LeSabre 2-door Hardtop. It is shown here in plain form, which cost $4,024. In the Custom sub-series it cost $4,107. Unlike the samller Buicks, the large hardtop models were true hardtops, with cantilever roofs and no centerposts or side roof bracing. The vinyl tops on all LeSabre and Centurion models cost an additional $123, while a powered sun roof on the 2-door models cost $590 extra.

The LeSabre Series continued to be divided into the plain and Custom sub-series, but except for a small Custom plaque below the LeSabre signature, there was no exterior difference between the two. This is the LeSabre Custom 4-door Hardtop, which cost $4,168. In plain form, it cost $4,079. All LeSabres used a 124-inch wheelbase chassis, were 224.2 inches in overall length.

Buick's small prestige wagon was the Century Luxus Station Wagon, which cost $3,587 in 6-passenger form or $3,700 as a 3-seat model. It was quickly identified from the more plain Century version by the heavy chrome rocker panel covers and gravel shield on the trailing lower edge of the rear fender. All Century wagons used the 116-inch wheelbase chassis, but were 216.6 inches long.

The Century Luxus Colonnade Coupe used the same formal roof styling as used on the Regal Coupe, but its grille was that of the regular Century line. The car was a pseudo-hardtop, with small opera windows in the large rear quarter panels. In basic form, it cost $3,275, with the vinyl top being an additional $100. It could be equipped with an electric sun roof for $325, or with a manual sun roof for $275 extra. The chrome rocker panels quickly identified the Luxus models.

The LeSabre 4-door Sedan followed the styling of the hardtop, but used the centerpost between the doors. In Custom trim, as shown here, it cost $4,047. In plain form it cost $3,958 and was the only full-size Buick with a base price under $4,000. All LeSabres were 79.6 inches wide.

The prestige car of the small Buick line was the Century Regal a one-model sub-series consisting only of this Colon-nade Hardtop Coupe style. The car used the same formal roof as found on the Century Luxus Colonnade Coupe, but had its own distinctive grille and trimmings. The car, costing $3,412 in base form, used the 112-inch wheelbase chassis, but was 210.7 inches overall. This is the only Century model that had no counterpart in the previous Skylark Series.

The Century Colonnade Coupe was also available with the 350 trim package. When thus dressed, it was officially designated the Century 350. The option cost $95 extra, plus $275 for a manually operated sun roof if wanted. The car was also available with a Gran Sport package for an additional $175, or with the 455-cubic-inch engine for another $235.

The Century Colonnade Hardtop Coupe used a completely different roof line than did the Century Regal or Luxus versions of the car. Built on a 112-inch wheelbase chassis of totally new design, the car had an overall length of 208.4 inches. It cost $4,013 in base form.

The new Century Station Wagon used a hatch-back type of rear gate, hinged at the top, which in many ways made loading easier, but did away with the ability of using the tailgate for extra support of long loads. For the first time in years, the small wagon was available in both 6- and 9-passenger form, The 6-passenger wagon cost $3,424, while the 3-seat version cost $3,537.

The Century Colonnade 4-door Hardtop Sedan was no longer a hardtop in the true sense of the word, since it now used a center pillar between the doors. It cost $3,013, the same as its companion Colonnade 2-door Hardtop, The 4-door models used a 116-inch wheelbase chassis of totally new design, and were 212.4 inches overall. All Century models were 78 inches wide.

The Century 350 Colonnade Sedan was really a trim package added to the regular Century model. The package cost an additional $85 and included interior trim and other items. However, the vinyl top was still an additional $100.

The Century Luxus 4-door Colonnade Hardtop was simply a more trimmed version of the regular Century 4-door models. All Century cars were equipped with a standard transmission, with an automatic costing an additional $215.

Buick's offering to the sport set continued to be the Opel GT, which continued its Gran Turismo styling for still another year. It cost $3,346, was 161.9 inches in overall length, and 62.2 inches wide. It used the same chassis and power units of all other Opels. Standard equipment included the new sport wheels, vinyl interior, foam-padded adjustable bucket seats, full carpeting, a control-center panel of instruments, and a gearshift console.

The new Manta Series was actually a one-model series divided into three sub-series via a number of trim options. The luxury version of the line was the Manta Luxus, which cost $2,769. It was also available as the Manta for $2,579, or could be fitted with a sun roof for an additional $104. A vinyl top was standard on the Luxus, not available on the Manta.

Appearing exclusively in the Opel 1900 Series was the 4-door Sedan, which cost $2,537. The car retained much of the styling of 1972, and continued to use the 1.9-liter cam-in-head engine. A floor-four gearbox and power brakes were standard equipment on all Opels.

About the author

"A dream come true."

That's how George H. Dammann described the initial writing of 70 YEARS OF BUICK back in 1972. The realization of this dream was based on the fact that with Buick, for the first time in his life, George was able to sit down and attend to the compilation, photography, writing, and layout of a book on a full-time basis, with virtually no other concerns coming into the picture. Sadly, as it turned out, 70 YEARS OF BUICK was also the last book on which George could work undisturbed and on a full-time basis.

George began his automotive writing career in the early 1950s, but the luxury of being able to devote his talents to full-time automotive writing eluded him for the next 20 years. True, for 10 years he wrote a multitude of freelance automotive articles for several hot rod, auto racing and general circulation magazines. But, to support a growing family during these years, he also worked full-time as a reporter and staff writer on two upstate New York newspapers—first the *Orange County Post* and then the *Middletown Times-Herald Record*. The same situation held true while he was doing staff promotional writing for NASCAR and later for NHRA. Again these jobs were squeezed between full-time newspaper editorial jobs.

In 1962 George moved to the Chicago area, as assistant editor for the *National Underwriter*, the country's leading trade magazine for the insurance business. There he quickly established himself as an expert in all types of automotive, transportation, and cargo insurance, and for many years traveled the length and breadth of the U. S., Canada and Mexico seeking out and writing major articles regarding transportation and automotive insurance.

In 1968, he conceived the idea for what was to become the first Crestline automotive book. ILLUSTRATED HISTORY OF FORD was thus compiled on a part-time basis, and was subsequently updated and published by Crestline in 1970. Then followed 50 YEARS OF LINCOLN MERCURY in 1971 and 60 YEARS OF CHEVROLET in 1972. Both the Ford and Chevrolet Books became immediate success stories, while the Lincoln-Mercury book turned a smaller but still comfortable profit for Crestline. With the success of the Chevrolet book, it was decided that the Crestline Automotive Series would be continued ad infinitum, and that George would be the principal writer for the series. Thus, he left the National Underwriter, pulled up a chair at Crestline, and devoted his full-time energies to 70 YEARS OF BUICK.

The move came at a very opportune time. George had become totally disenchanted with the National Underwriter, due to (of all things) his rapid rise through the company ranks. In his own words:

"For years, by the Underwriter's own admission, I was the best road man that they ever had. I loved living out of a suitcase, travelling approximately 50% of my time to all parts of North America, and turning out scores of articles, the likes of which had never been seen. (George had acquired a multitude of awards from various press and insurance associations for his in-depth articles). However, as a reward for being an excellent road man and writer, I was promoted to associate editor, named to head the Chicago office, and was told to sit behind a desk and oversee what everyone else was doing. And I just wasn't about to sit behind a desk for 50 weeks a year, watching others do what I should have been doing in the first place."

George and the Underwriter parted cordially in the spring of 1972, and George took over as automotive director of Crestline. Through the remainder of that year he worked exclusively on the Buick book. Upon the completion of that book, he began to supervise the initial staff research of 70 YEARS OF CHRYSLER and oversee the total workings of AMERICAN FUNERAL CARS & AMBULANCES and THE DODGE STORY, both being compiled by Thomas McPherson, George did do all of the writing, photography and layout for the Chrysler book, but it appears that it will be many more years before another book comes out with the "Dammann" by-line, despite the fact that eight other books are currently in the works at Crestline. In George's words:

"Again, success has spoiled a good thing. With the series growing by leaps and bounds, someone was needed to oversee the total picture—someone who understood all phases of photography, writing and editing, layout, printing, binding, in other words, the whole ball of wax—and that someone turned out to be me!"

But, at least the current situation is different. Crestline's writers are scattered across the country, the major collections used for photographic research stretch from New York to California, and major antique auto meets occur in virtually every state. So, George still spends a good deal of his time on the road, not doing the actual writing, but still definitely well involved in the total picture.

At least George had a chance to do Buick in its entirety as Buick is a car for which he has held a warm spot for a good many years. At the time the book was written, Buicks in George's past included a 1940 Special 2-door; a

1946 Super convertible; a 1949 Super sedan; a 1951 Special sedan; a 1951 Super sedan, and a 1954 Century Riviera.

At the time the book was being published, George was in a real quandary. He was totally in love with both a 1971 Riviera and a 1970 Cadillac convertible. Both cars were white with black tops and interiors, and both were exactly what George wanted. But the budget would be strained by either car, and getting both at the same time was totally out of the question. So George, a dyed in the wool "convertible freak" went with the Caddy, though sadly eyeing the Riviera.

Since that time, a Riviera still has not found its way into the Dammann stable. However, two Buick related high points did occur. One happened at the 1973 national meet of the Buick Club of America. Here, George was allowed to take the famed 1910 Buick Bug on an extensive test drive at Buick's home office. In his words:

"The car is unbelievable in its response, rough as a buckboard ride, and virtually devoid of any sort of brakes. I've never in my life driven anything with which it could be compared. But it gave me a healthy respect for Burman and Chevrolet, who had the guts to take it out on rough dirt tracks and run it wide open—those men had to have nerves of steel!"

The other high point occurred just before 70 YEARS OF BUICK came up for revision. Although a Riviera never entered the barn, a new 1975 LeSabre Custom convertible has joined the Dammann fleet as the Number One car.

The Dammanns, George and Gloria, Carole and Eric, live in a semi-rural area near Glen Ellyn, where they oversee an ever-changing fleet of cars, trucks and motorcycles that often overflow their 10-car capacity barn and two-car garage. Among the current favorites are a 1920 Ford roadster, 1922 Ford centerdoor, 1936 International hot rod, 1934 Ford coupe, 1946 Lincoln Continental, 1957 Corvette, a pair of 1966 Thunderbirds, his and hers 1968 and 1970 Cadillac convertibles, a 1973 Concord Motor home, and the new 1975 LeSabre convertible, not to mention George's 1200 full-dress (overdressed) Harley Davidson, Eric's Kawasaki, Gloria's Bridgestone, and Carole's one-horsepower Arabian gelding. Also at this writing, other vehicles lurking around the Dammann car farm are a 1964 Thunderbird, 1965 modified Pontiac GTO, 1959 Edsel, 1968 Ford Fairlane, and 1969 Ford XL—all convertibles, of course. No one can say that the Dammanns, in total, are not automotive minded!